T0351497

Hard Time

HARD
TIME

Reforming the Penitentiary in Nineteenth-Century Canada

TED McCOY

AU PRESS

Copyright © 2012 Ted McCoy

Published by AU Press, Athabasca University
1200, 10011 – 109 Street, Edmonton, AB T5J 3S6

ISBN 978-1-926836-96-6 (print) 978-1-926836-97-3 (PDF)
978-1-926836-98-0 (epub)

Cover and interior design by Marvin Harder, marvinharder.com.
Printed and bound in Canada by Marquis Book Printers.

Library and Archives Canada Cataloguing in Publication

McCoy, Ted, 1978-

    Hard time : reforming the penitentiary in nineteenth-century
Canada / by Ted McCoy.

Includes bibliographical references and index.
Issued also in electronic formats.

ISBN 978-1-926836-96-6

    1. Prisons—Canada—History—19th century. 2. Prisoners—
Canada—Social conditions—History—19th century. 3. Prison
reformers—Canada—History—19th century. 4. Convict labor—
Canada—History—19th century. 5. Punishment—Canada—History—
19th century. 6. Criminals—Rehabilitation—Canada—History—
19th century. I. Title.

HV9960.C2M34 2012   365'.7097109034   C2012-901606-3

We acknowledge the financial support of the Government of Canada
through the Canada Book Fund (CBF) for our publishing activities.

Assistance provided by the Government of Alberta, Alberta Multimedia
Development Fund.

This publication is licensed under a Creative Commons License,
Attribution–Noncommercial–No Derivative Works 2.5 Canada: see
www.creativecommons.org. The text may be reproduced for noncommercial purposes, provided that credit is given to the original author.

To obtain permission for uses beyond those outlined in the Creative
Commons license, please contact AU Press, Athabasca University, at
aupress@athabascau.ca.

 Canadian Patrimoine   **Government**
Heritage   canadien   **of Alberta** ■

Contents

Tables

Acknowledgements

I owe my thanks to a broad community who, in a variety of ways, are responsible for the existence of this book. Trent University and the Frost Centre for Canadian and Indigenous Studies offered ongoing financial and intellectual support. I am grateful as well to the Social Sciences and Humanities Research Council of Canada for additional research funding. Many friends and colleagues were invaluable sources of encouragement along the way. These include Kevin Plummer, Gillian Balfour, Julia Harrison, Winnie Janzen, Cam Hayden, Cristine Bye, Fiona Coll, Michel Hogue, Betsy Jameson, Sarah Carter, Adrian Smith, Melissa White, Sherry Hergott, and Shayne Arnold. I owe a special debt of thanks to Meaghan Beaton for her camaraderie. The enthusiastic staff at Athabasca University Press made the final steps possible, particularly Pamela Holway, who was a generous and supportive editor. Copy editor Joyce Hildebrand made numerous thoughtful suggestions that improved the final text.

Joan Sangster encouraged my first efforts to think about legal and social history and has been a trusted mentor and friend. Bryan Palmer supervised the original dissertation and was unfailing in his support, good humour, and patience. I owe a tremendous debt to my parents for their boundless emotional and financial support. Finally, this book is dedicated with love to Marika Strobl.

Introduction

In 1849 a government commission of inquiry heard the details of a troubling incident at Kingston Penitentiary. It involved the warden, Henry Smith, and the punishment of a prisoner named Narcisse Beauché, whom the staff regarded as a troublesome inmate. Beauché was no stranger to punishment, having been disciplined on at least two dozen occasions since arriving at the prison. This time, Beauché had evidently awoken in a state of terror and was screaming and climbing the bars of his cell in desperation. Warden Smith arrived and ordered, "Open the doors! I will bring this scoundrel out." Guards removed the prisoner and attempted unsuccessfully to place a gag in his mouth. Beauché promised to be quiet, but, upon returning to his cell, he continued to scream about something under the bed. Again, the warden ordered him removed. The guards then held the prisoner to the floor while Smith beat him with a length of rope until he was bloodied and subdued. Beauché was twelve years old. This disciplinary encounter with the warden turned out to be his last. He did not leave his cell again until he was declared insane and transferred to the provincial lunatic asylum.[1]

The Beauché incident was part of the evidence presented before the 1849 Brown Commission in its investigation of Canada's first penitentiary, in Kingston. Other witnesses provided accounts of prisoners who were starving and the sexual abuse of female inmates by members of the staff. On the punishment of Narcisse Beauché, the commissioners concluded, "The thought of the Warden of a high penal institution, in the middle of the night and while evidently labouring under personal excitement, flogging a manic lad with his own hands is too horrible to dwell upon."[2] Nor was the Beauché incident an isolated outburst of violence. The investigation uncovered a disciplinary regime that had inflicted thousands of corporal punishments upon men, women, and children, often for the slightest of infractions. The commission, led by George Brown of Toronto, publisher of *The Globe*, investigated every area of the penitentiary, searching for evidence to support charges of cruelty and mismanagement.

What had gone wrong? In the 1820s, the emerging concept of the penitentiary was thought to belong to the vanguard of humanitarianism and enlightenment. The penitentiary was regarded as a progressive solution to crime, one that would force criminals to do penance for their crimes while also giving them the skills and moral training necessary for their successful return to society. In the early 1830s, Upper Canadian politicians embraced the institution as a humane alternative to public whippings or hangings, and in 1835 Kingston Penitentiary opened. Within a decade, however, the entire endeavour was mired in insolvency and corruption, and violence was rampant within its walls. The penitentiary had also failed in a more fundamental way. It had not reduced crime, as its promoters had promised. The dismayed Brown Commission concluded simply, "The moral reformation of convicts is unknown." The need for change was apparent. In view of the commission's findings, the Upper Canadian government might have retreated, abandoning the penitentiary as an ineffective response to criminal behaviour. But the commission of inquiry proposed solutions that evinced optimism about the future of the penitentiary in Canada.

Hard Time is a book about penal reform in Canada and the rise of the modern Canadian penitentiary. From one generation to the next, reformers condemned the failures of their predecessors, assigning blame and formulating solutions that promised to move the penitentiary in new directions. Previous interpretations of the nineteenth-century penitentiary have chronicled the "failure" of reform but have for the most part neglected the broader historical impact of reform movements on the evolution of the penitentiary.[3] At the heart of the penitentiary reform project lay a contradiction: while reform was flawed, it also moved the penitentiary in new directions that made it less miserable and debasing. It is indisputable that, as the nineteenth century progressed, fewer prisoners died of untreated illnesses, fewer were brutally whipped for breaking the rules, and more emphasis was placed on education, religious instruction, and industrial training in an attempt to reform and rehabilitate prisoners. The penitentiary reform movement contributed to such changes.

At the same time that conditions improved, however, the institution also expanded its practices of physical and moral surveillance and its exercise of control over the lives of prisoners. These developments were facilitated by the growing concern among reformers about the individual needs and moral condition of inmates. This ambiguity of outcome complicates our efforts to judge reform as a social movement. What should we use as a measure of success or failure? Seeing reform merely as a project of reinvention cannot speak to the larger and ongoing failure of the penitentiary to reduce crime, to transform individuals, and, in general, to reinforce faith in modern, enlightened solutions. Neither can such a view fully address how reform ideas themselves were often subverted in ways that sustained larger structures of domination and, in effect, made the institution itself one of the pillars of class control, racism, and gender inequality.

In *Discipline and Punish*, Michel Foucault was the first to suggest that reform was a continuous condition of the modern penitentiary rather than merely a response to its failures. I use this perspective on reform as my point of entry into the study of the penitentiary to suggest that the discourse of reform was a constant influence on the direction in which the prison developed. Canadian prison reform was influenced by internationally renowned figures such as England's John

Howard and Elizabeth Fry and American Louis Dwight, along with some of the towering figures of Canadian history like George Brown. It is important to recognize, however, that reform was also promoted and carried out by figures who remained relatively unknown. These included penitentiary wardens, chaplains, and inspectors, who reacted to the same sense of crisis and failure but from a more immediate perspective. In this sense, reform itself was both an idea and a practice: it unfolded not only because of overarching ideological shifts but also as a result of what happened within the walls of the penitentiary.

My focus in this book is more on the effects of nineteenth-century penal reform than on its intent. I am interested in the larger ideological climate in which reform developed, but I also seek to understand the penitentiary experience as it evolved in the wake of reform and its influences. This entails a study of penitentiary practices in the nineteenth century, but I also intend to understand something more about prison life itself, advancing on terrain established by historians like E. P. Thompson, Douglas Hay, and Peter Linebaugh, all of whom wrote about the law and punishment with a focus on experience and human agency.[4] Thompson in particular suggested that agency was at the core of class struggle. In *The Making of the English Working Class*, he wrote, "We cannot have love without lovers, nor deference without squires and labourers. And class happens when some men, as a result of common experiences (inherited or shared), feel and articulate the identity of their interests as between themselves, and as against other men whose interests are different from (and usually opposed to) theirs."[5] It may seem obvious, but we cannot have prison history without prisoners. Their interests were undoubtedly set against those of their keepers and, indeed, against those of reformers who sought to improve their lot (as well as their moral character). So much of prison history is the story of relationships among these disparate groups. There is much to learn from tracing the ways in which agency and experience played out in the operation and evolution of the penitentiary.

My study of punishment writes individuals back into the story by focusing on their place in the interplay of ideology, practice, and human experience. Inevitably, viewing the historical prison from this perspective leads to some sobering observations. Throughout the nineteenth century, despite its overt intentions, the reform movement generated a particular legacy of social harm and oppression, costs that were often exacted in terms of human suffering. This history can be read in the experiences of prisoners who lived through the growing pains of an uncertain and untested social practice. Many were victims of violent and inhumane penitentiary officials and staff who distorted and subverted the humanitarian goals of the reform movement. Prison history is also populated by those who experienced the penitentiary in ways that were more than merely punitive in the legal sense: the sick, the disabled, members of racial and ethnic minorities, and women and children. Even as the reform movement pushed the penitentiary to modernize and become more humane, these prisoners continued to experience discomfort, neglect, and abuse to a greater degree than others. Ultimately, as this book documents, it was the most vulnerable members of nineteenth-century Canadian society who paid the greatest price for the failures of criminal justice policy. With this lesson, we can use the penitentiary to paint a much more nuanced portrait of Canada in its formative modern era.

The reform movement focused on three key priorities that together shaped the penitentiary over the course of the nineteenth century. I take my direction from these priorities, using them as a springboard to the multiple dimensions and intricacies of penitentiary history. The first, and most central, was a concern with labour and with transforming inmates into productive workers. Second was the growing desire to effect the moral reformation, or rehabilitation, of individual prisoners.[6] The third priority was to make the penitentiary a more humane institution by eliminating violent methods of punishment in favour of approaches promoted by an emerging class of professional criminologists, such as the isolation of individuals deemed especially troublesome. In exploring these concerns, I also consider questions about criminality that touched on each. First and foremost, who were the men and women inside Canadian prisons? This is a question with which reformers grappled constantly in their efforts to address the three central priorities of the reform program.

The areas of concern to reformers also speak to questions confronting nineteenth-century Canadian society as a whole, questions about how to organize labour and how to respond to the pressures of the industrial revolution, and, more broadly, how to help individuals adapt to, and participate in, the new capitalist order. The history of the penitentiary is central to these questions. It allows us to see how one institutional response to change embodied the hopes and failures of Canadian modernism.

LABOUR

The modern penitentiary was an innovation of industrial capitalism. It constituted one reply to the question of how industrial society should organize its workforce. Arguing that this question is fundamental for any society, H. Clare Pentland points to the period between 1820 and 1850 as the critical moment in Canada's transition from a capitalist labour market to industrial capitalism.[7] During this period of transition, we find the rise of the penitentiary.

The penitentiary was one reaction to pressing issues raised by a rapidly changing society at the start of the industrial revolution. Among them was how an industrial capitalist society should respond to the poor and marginal elements of the population. Karl Marx reflected on this in a passage from the *1844 Manuscripts*:

> Political economy . . . does not recognize the unoccupied worker, the workingman, in so far as he happens to be outside this labor relationship. The cheat-thief, swindler, beggar, and unemployed; the starving, wretched and criminal workingman—these are *figures* who do not exist for *political economy* but only for other eyes, those of the doctor, the judge, the grave digger, and bumbailiff, etc.; such figures are specters outside its domain.[8]

While Marx never directly explored the function of the penitentiary within the broader political economy, subsequent generations of his students expanded on his invocation of "specters outside its domain."[9] They illustrated how the capitalist state gradually learned to accommodate people who stood at society's margins, while at the same time marginalizing them further by excluding them from the political economy. The penitentiary was a key institution in this process, as were hospitals, insane asylums, orphanages, and reformatories. The combined histories of these institutions help us to understand the emphasis on labour within the penitentiary. Recognizing the ideological underpinnings of prison labour makes clear the larger significance of the penitentiary to the political economy of this era.[10]

The penitentiary played an important role in the construction of class in nineteenth-century Canada. In *The Social Organization of Early Industrial Capitalism*, Michael Katz, Michael Doucet, and Mark Stern argue that capitalism gives rise to a particular class structure, one that provides "the basis of a system of inequality." As they go on to point out, "just as the essential attributes of capitalism [have] remained fixed, its structural inequality continues to define social and economic relations." Attention to class also reveals what these authors call "the structured inequality of social experience" (2). I advance a similar structural view of social experience, one that "reflects the belief that the dimensions of social and human experience are not random, the result of luck or genetic superiority. To the contrary, the relations between inequality, exploitation, bureaucracy, and the pain and contradictions of private life are neither accidental nor ephemeral" (41). Incorporating the notion of class into penitentiary history sheds light on the relationship between economic and social change and human experience. Attention to class is an essential ingredient in any attempt to attribute motivation to the penitentiary reform movement, which was, after all, merely the efforts of particular men and women who sought to change the course of social practice. Their efforts were made up of words and actions, and both are important. While ideological developments within the reform movement were often distinct from the practices that formed the experience of imprisonment, we cannot distance ourselves from the attempt to understand the meaning of reform. This requires striving to understand how individuals made sense of the ideas that reformers espoused. I argue that these ideas were not merely subjective discourses divorced from historical circumstance. Positioning the reform movement within a historical materialist framework helps us to grasp the relationships between social practices and the structures that sustain those practices and their accompanying discourses. This view also facilitates an understanding of the penitentiary both as the manifestation of a particular ideology and as an institution that was the product of social forces. We can identify both as sites of class struggle.

Much of Canadian prison history has focused on the new institution as a primarily legal innovation in the social response to crime.[11] It was this, but it was also part of the broader social upheaval ushered in by the advent of an industrial urban economy. As an institution, the penitentiary incorporated long-standing ideas about poverty, dependence, and idleness in new form. Clearly, labour was linked to imprisonment for centuries before the rise of the modern penitentiary. The first penitentiary promoters looked to older responses to idleness and poverty and found examples in the European workhouse and the English Bridewells of the sixteenth century. Labour stood at the core of these established institutions and offered a ready-made solution for the growing social disorder of the industrial age. In the nineteenth century, these institutional innovations were applied to another form of social disorder—crime.[12] While institutional confinement was an innovation in legal punishment, it was not an entirely new idea at its formative moment near the end of the eighteenth century.

The modern penitentiary developed in Upper Canada at the same time that the northeastern United States was undergoing a transition to industrial capitalism. In New York and Pennsylvania, the first American penitentiaries were constructed to mimic large-scale industrial factories. Canadian legislators were moved by the apparent modernity of what they witnessed in the United States and modelled the Canadian penitentiary on these new examples. Thus, from the earliest years of the nineteenth century, legal punishment in Canada, as in the United States, was tied to the model of industrial development. Not only did prisons share the design and discipline of the new factories; they shared their unending drive for profit. On these points, my interpretation borrows from the first political economy of punishment, Georg Rusche and Otto Kirchheimer's *Punishment and Social Structure,* which argued that the evolution of the penal system was directly linked to changes in the labour market and the relations of production.[13] In the case of Kingston Penitentiary, the relationship may have reflected aspirations for industrial development more than the actual speed of industrialization in Upper Canada. Ultimately, it proved impossible for Kingston Penitentiary or other federal institutions to compete in the capitalist marketplace, and this failure played an important role in how the Canadian penitentiary developed.

Prison labour was also inherently ideological. Not only was labour an economic imperative, but the actual practice of making prisoners work appealed deeply to the moral and religious culture of the nineteenth-century bourgeoisie, with its deep suspicion of idleness. Reformers increasingly viewed labour not only as a source of profit but also as a method of individual reform. The new focus allowed prison reformers and administrators to emphasize the ideological importance of the penitentiary labour project even after the original economic aspirations of prison industry proved unfeasible.

In spite of the importance of labour in shaping the penitentiary as a social institution, the multiple failures of the penitentiary served to reveal the limitations of the governing imperative of labour. The theory that hard labour produced moral reform rested on the assumption that prisoners were healthy enough to perform hard labour. As prison medical records confirm, not all prisoners met this standard. Some were too physically weak or ill or too mentally disabled to work. Even as medical care improved throughout the century, the chronically ill and the disabled continued to be held to the standards of moral reform imposed by the guiding imperative of labour. Thus the penitentiary doctor increased his power in two respects. As the century progressed, doctors became the exclusive experts on questions surrounding health and illness. Empowered to make distinctions between the healthy and the ill, between the sane and the insane, doctors also formed judgments about who among the penitentiary population could be considered "a worker." Those whom medical diagnosis deemed unfit for labour were inevitably marginalized and, as a result, experienced the penitentiary very differently from those who were able, and expected, to work. In spite of improving medical care, penitentiaries struggled and failed to adapt to these "unproductive prisoners."

The evolution of constructions of criminality stands as a counterpart to the ideological history of prison labour. Both within the penitentiary and in the broader society, prevailing discourses about class (and likewise about race) contributed to notions regarding the relative propensity for criminal behaviour. Gertrude Himmelfarb's study of poverty in this era underscores the important role played by discourse in the creation of dominant cultural ideas. Himmelfarb explores the construction of poverty as primarily a moral issue, arguing that discourse plays a part in constituting class struggle.[14] A similar approach, one that tracks changing discourses about class and morality, can contribute to an understanding of how society conceived of the criminal. In the simplest terms, the ways in which criminals were talked about, written about, and understood played a part in how penitentiary reform developed. Such discourses helped to determine how the penitentiary was structured and what was considered appropriate and necessary when dealing with the criminal. The discourse of criminality, especially as it related to penitentiary labour, sprang from many sources, but key among them were discourses that linked idleness, poverty, and criminality. I probe these discourses and connect them to the political economy of punishment as a way to better understand how reform developed in concert with the Canadian penitentiary.

VIOLENCE

After the shocking testimony before the Brown Commission, reformers advocated a more humane approach to corporal punishment in the penitentiary. But what would such an approach look like? In spite of reformers' efforts, wardens and other staff tasked with maintaining security in penitentiaries were loathe to give up corporal punishment. On questions of violence, there was a divide between reform ideas and penal practice. As a result, violence in Canadian penitentiaries exhibited a curious resilience in the face of reformers' efforts to extinguish it. However, the conditions under which violence persisted were also undoubtedly the product of the rise of reform. The persistence of violence is one of the best examples of the failure of reform and what that failure produced: an enduring state of imperfection and the accompanying moral consternation that kept the process in motion.

Penitentiary history in Canada has tended to underestimate the degree to which violent punishments persisted in spite of reformers' efforts. In part, this can be attributed to revisionist historians who viewed the penitentiary as a revolutionary departure from the violent methods of punishment that dominated the eighteenth century. Michel Foucault and Michael Ignatieff both argue that the penitentiary was a new mode of punishment that swept away the violent methods of the past.[15] Many Canadian historians have employed the same model, charting a reformist progression from a legal system that mandated public whipping, the pillory and stocks, and execution to one that relied on an institutional form of punishment.[16] A number of scholars detail responses to the Brown Commission after 1849, but few consider the ongoing use of violence in Canadian penitentiaries beyond this era.[17] What sustained these practices? How did they persist in the face of a vigorous reform opposition?

In part, we can look to the successful dissemination of reform discourses throughout the penitentiary system to understand how corporal punishment survived in new forms in the latter half of the century. Reformers promoted the virtues of rationality and humanitarianism in penal administration. While prison wardens seldom shared the view that corporal punishment should be eliminated, they were more than willing to adopt the language of reform to describe and rationalize such practices. They spoke of their duty, their detachment and impartiality, and, above all, their intense regret over the continued use of corporal punishment. Such language often obscured the degree to which corporal punishment operated as it always had—in a punitive, emotional, and retributive fashion. The fact that corporal punishment was not eliminated ensured that the penitentiary continued to be an oppressive and domineering institution. The ever-present threat of physical violence produced an atmosphere of unease and mistrust, and even of antagonism, within the modern prison.

The adoption of reformist discourse was only one side of an important dichotomy that sustained corporal punishment. In order for administrators and staff to pose as rational and detached bureaucrats, they required a foil. This they found in the portrayal of certain criminals as irrational and incorrigible. The notion of incorrigibility played upon the most inflammatory constructions of criminality, and it allowed the use of violence to be blamed on a class of prisoners who were so unmanageable, so dangerous, and so inherently violent that only violence itself could compel them to good behaviour. Prisoners from racial or ethnic minority groups were far more likely to be deemed incorrigible and therefore more likely to be subjected to corporal punishments—one illustration of the power of particular constructions of criminality to influence penal practice. Such constructions also obscured some of the reality of how and why corporal punishment was employed. In fact, the use of violence was a rather more routine matter than official discourses suggested.

Still, it is indisputable that the reform movement succeeded in reducing the incidence of corporal punishment. What took its place? Toward the end of the nineteenth century, the penitentiary moved toward practices that involved segregating individuals labelled as incorrigible, brutish, and dangerous. This entailed the construction of new "isolation wings" in which to house such offenders. The same constructions of criminality that had been used to justify corporal punishment played a role in determining how these new practices were deployed, especially as penal discipline became increasingly individualized toward the end of the century. This development mirrored the bourgeoning concern in the reform movement with assessing the criminal character of the individual offender as a precursor to his or her rehabilitation. The trend was linked to the rise of claims to criminological expertise on the part of penitentiary authorities who sought to increase their powers of professional discretion over what happened to penitentiary inmates. The move toward the individual criminological assessment of each prisoner was a harbinger of criminological and legal developments that would characterize the penitentiary of the twentieth century. It laid the groundwork for additional penal innovations such as the remission of sentences, indeterminate sentencing, and, eventually, parole.

Methods of classification of prisoners were, however, in their infancy in the late nineteenth century. In Canada, they were further hindered by the rudimentary and often halting nature of prison development across a vast geography. At the same time, the problem of violence, to which reformers continually pointed, brought issues of criminality to the forefront of penal practice and encouraged penitentiaries to define individuals in terms of their degree of incorrigibility. Another manifestation of the new focus on classification was the growing concern with the reformation, or rehabilitation, of inmates.

REFORMATION AND CRIMINALITY

Penal reform in the nineteenth century suggested that criminal justice should not only punish criminals but also transform them. Indeed, the idea of reformation was paramount in the evolution of the Canadian penitentiary during the second half of the nineteenth century. The penal reform movement in Canada took direction from international developments in this area—from innovators like Alexander Maconochie and Sir Walter Crofton. Both were penal reformers who suggested a new progressive system of punishment in which prisoners would work in their own interests, moving from one stage of personal development to another until they were prepared to join society again. Managing this process required specific knowledge of each offender. Reformers advocated learning about the criminal's personal history to better understand the influences of immorality, intemperance, or childhood trauma These ideas about reformation were wedded to the evangelical spirit of the early Victorian era. The reform movement emphasized the positive

potential of education and religion in the process of reformation, bringing penitentiaries and reformatories closer together by introducing to
the prison system a new concern for the offender's soul. However, much
as in the case of corporal punishment, there was a clear divide between
reform views and what prison staff were willing to implement as penal
practice. Some wardens protested that education and religion were
distractions that took prisoners away from their work, thereby disrupt-
ing the economy of the penitentiary. Some questioned the "softening" of
penitentiary sentences through such programs. In the context of debates
about "coddled" prisoners, it was commonly argued that programs
stressing education and moral reformation diminished what should have
been an altogether unpleasant and punitive experience.

Hopes about rehabilitation ran up against an additional barrier.
In order for these efforts to succeed, each prisoner would need to be
considered as an individual. As David Garland argues in *Punishment
and Welfare*, the Victorian penitentiary was ill-equipped for this
project; the modern penitentiary was designed to treat every prisoner
the same. Thus, for much of the nineteenth century, even if prisoners
managed to internalize the lessons of education or religion, they continued to experience the penitentiary in much the same way as every
other inmate. Garland suggests that the penitentiary recognized individuals but not *individuality*.[18] This is a critical distinction, one that
raises particular questions about the idea of criminality. In *Discipline
and Punish* and subsequent writings on subjectivity, Michel Foucault
demonstrates how the exercise of professional power served to divide
individuals both from others and within themselves.[19] He explores the
ways in which specific penal methods and professional discourses central to the penitentiary project constituted "dividing practices," serving
to define and classify individuals—separating them, for example, into
"the mad and the sane, the sick and the healthy, the criminals and
the 'good boys.'"[20] Foucault suggested that, by providing medical and
scientific rationales for such categories, the exercise of professional
power made these divisions more concrete.

In the nineteenth-century penitentiary, the construction
of criminality and, indeed, the experience of imprisonment were

influenced by a number of structural and subjective forces, central among them class and race. In this book, I explore the constructions of criminality associated with the working class and the unemployed and the ways in which these constructions circumscribed the experience of certain prisoners. Attention to assumptions about race and ethnicity helps to explain why incarceration was an especially isolating and oppressive experience for minorities. Black and Chinese prisoners, in particular, were targets of specific constructions of criminality that substantively altered their experience of the penitentiary: both groups were regarded as inherently depraved or incapable of moral reform. Similarly, I probe the experience of First Nations prisoners in western Canada with an eye to the specific constructions of criminality (and prison experience) that accompanied the colonial agenda. Gender divisions were also important, and I attempt to uncover some of the obscured history of women's experience within the penitentiary. Recent scholarship illustrates that the study of gender also has much to tell us about men in prison. The intensely homosocial nature of the institution suggests that masculinity is an important category of analysis.[21] It is also essential to acknowledge that structural and subjective forces defined and constrained prisoners and keepers alike. Just as particular constructions and subjectivities defined prisoners, keepers were immersed in an environment that was intensely regulated, and their experience was often oppressive.

How were prisoners understood in this era? Throughout the latter half of the century, penitentiary officials and a great number of reformers continued to adhere to broad notions of criminality that made the goals of individual rehabilitation unlikely to succeed. Ideas about criminality were drawn from pessimistic views of the working class and the supposed propensity of working-class individuals for crime. Racial minorities and women were the targets of similarly negative associations. Such negative stereotypes had the effect of ensuring that prisoners were seldom regarded as individuals in the ways promoted by reform ideology. Instead, prisoners were typecast as "criminals" in broad stereotypical categories. The distinction between a prisoner and a criminal may seem trivial, but prevailing social perceptions of "criminals" and criminality carried with them broad moral implications that ultimately subverted the goal of individual reformation. The fact that "criminals" could be subjectified in a wholly negative fashion had striking implications for the types of treatment and punishment that became permissible within penitentiaries. As with corporal punishment, efforts at rehabilitation often fell prey to such constructions. This contributed to the subversion of the reform program, which often produced unintended outcomes.

The way in which reformers thought about prisoners and the potential for rehabilitation is part of the cultural history of the penitentiary. Ideas matter a great deal in prison history, even when we cannot draw a direct line from ideology to practice. In many cases, the failure of reform ideas shaped the penitentiary in essential ways that can be understood only by tracking the course of the deviation—the process whereby the idea was subverted. The history of reformation as a goal of reform is one of the clearest examples of the process of subversion. The attempt to create an institution that would influence the minds and behaviour of criminals failed as unequivocally as had the earliest ideas about the prison as a profitable capitalist venture.

How did prisoners live? This question turns our attention to some of the key problems faced by the reform movement. In particular, the answers speak to why the notion of reformation remained largely a theoretical construct. In one sense, prisoners lived in the world that reform created. This included the intensely regulated life of a penitentiary inmate, who was constrained by a system of overbearing rules and regulations that governed how prisoners slept, ate, worshipped, and communicated with each other. But this is only a small part of the total picture of how prisoners actually lived within these regulations.

A particular dynamic of power played out at the centre of every rule and regulation in the penitentiary. Drawing on the work of Foucault, I refer to the concept of power not as an entity but as the basis of the human interactions at the heart of these rules and regulations. Fundamental to Foucault's studies on power was a new concept of social relationships that included the notion of "power relations."

The power relations within the prison could be found in the strategies and tactics that characterized the social relationships found in the institution. Many aspects of penitentiary life were considered and directed by the reform movement, but much that was beyond reformers' control took place haphazardly within prison walls. I look at how these elements of penitentiary life played out, attempting, as Foucault did, "to get a grip on the actual mechanisms of the exercise of power" in the specific context of penal institutions.[22]

Attending to the particularities of these social relationships brings to the fore prisoners' efforts to resist domination. Resistance included everything from the smallest transgressions to outright rebellion. This part of prison history exposes the multiple ways in which reform failed or was subverted and recognizes prisoners' agency in this process of subversion. I draw on the work of several historians who have chronicled the impact of resistance and transgression on the ideological structures of law and authority. Peter Linebaugh's history of London executions reveals the deleterious effect of popular ridicule upon long-standing symbols of British legal authority.[23] Similar resistance in the penitentiary helps us to understand that authority was often mediated and negotiated by those under its domination. The history of active resistance and rebellion also reveals a more complete picture of how prisoners lived. James C. Scott's *Weapons of the Weak* explores how the "hidden transcript" of resistance emerges in the face of seemingly insurmountable domination in peasant societies.[24] A similar "transcript" can be tracked through Canadian prison history. In *Cultures of Darkness*, Bryan Palmer argues that the lived experience of the marginalized is most clearly expressed, and hence most accessible, through their acts of transgression against those who would oppress them. This is a valuable lesson when we consider prisoners, who were among the most marginalized populations in Canadian history. Their transgressions and resistance give us a glimpse into what it meant to be subject to the oppressive regimes of penitentiary life. Finally, it is important to recognize that keepers and guards also resisted and transgressed against the penitentiary order in their own particular ways. Sometimes this took the form of complicity in prisoner resistance, but it could also involve various forms of corruption and abuse that undercut the goals of penitentiary reform.

I consider five penitentiaries from different parts of Canada. Kingston Penitentiary, which opened in 1835, was the first institution of its kind in Upper Canada (later Ontario). When plans for its closure were announced in April 2012, it had operated continuously for 177 years. It is the central focus of this book for two main reasons. First, because it operated for most of the nineteenth century, it best illustrates the historical evolution of penal practices. After 1867 it formed the backbone of the country's new federal prison system. Key issues of penitentiary governance and penal reform often played out within Kingston's walls in ways that are more apparent than in other institutions, some of which only operated for a short period of time. Second, the historical sources related to Kingston Penitentiary are more abundant and consistent than those connected to other institutions. Four other federal institutions are, however, woven into the story. St. Vincent de Paul was the first penitentiary in Québec, opening in 1873 at the site of an old provincial reformatory. Manitoba Penitentiary, founded in 1872, was originally located at Lower Fort Garry and moved to a newly constructed building at Stony Mountain in 1877, where it came to be known as Stony Mountain Penitentiary. British Columbia Penitentiary was erected at New Westminster in 1878. Finally, Dorchester Penitentiary was established in New Brunswick in 1880, taking the place of smaller institutions in Halifax and Saint John. Together, these five institutions constituted the federal penitentiary system in its final form between 1880 and 1900.

Labour

The idea that a prisoner must work is extraordinarily powerful. Prison labour, which formed the foundation of the modern penitentiary, had vast economic and ideological importance. Economically, an organized and industrial program of prison labour differentiated penitentiaries of the nineteenth century from their predecessors. Prison design after 1800 was based on industrial factories, and penitentiary discipline and routine were influenced by the industrial working day. Moreover, the products of prison labour were expected to defray the cost of the institution, if not turn a profit. These practicalities of prison labour developed alongside an influential ideology about the redemptive power of work: prison labour was intended to redeem criminals, who had transgressed against society's moral codes. It was to make idle and unemployed workers whole again, ready to rejoin society as productive citizens.

This chapter explores how labour shaped the modern penitentiary. I begin with the ideological and historical connections between labour and imprisonment from ancient times to early modern Europe. I then move into the Canadian penitentiary itself, delving into the world created by penitentiary labour under the administration of

Kingston Penitentiary's first warden, Henry Smith. Smith's regime in the 1830s and 1840s was troubled, violent, and fraught with scandal. I argue that these troubles were connected to the inherent difficulty of implementing industrial programs in the new institution. When the ideological and economic demands of the labour regime could not be met, the resulting penal regime became oppressive and violent. The degeneration of the original ideals of penitentiary labour influenced institution and penal reform in Canada throughout the nineteenth century. I gleaned much of the information about this period from the evidence uncovered by the commission of inquiry under George Brown that investigated Kingston Penitentiary in 1849. Thus, the chapter draws a portrait of the first years of the penitentiary through the eyes of its participants and contemporaries. This portrait distills the essential administrative and economic difficulties that plagued the early institution. By 1849 the idea that the demands of industrial labour could shape the penitentiary crumbled. Prison reformers rallied against the discipline that the industrial system required and looked for new solutions that stressed evangelicalism and moral reform.

THE ORIGINS OF LABOUR UNDER CONFINEMENT

In the ancient world, the connections between labour and practices of confinement were minimal. However, a brief look at punishment in ancient times illustrates the significance of the departures that occurred in the medieval and early modern periods. Early Roman society had no formal systems for imprisonment. Public prisons were little more than pits into which were lowered the condemned, who were subject to prolonged torture and had no real hope of reprieve. Although some Roman prisoners were forced to work on large public projects, these were in essence capital sentences in which prisoners were worked to death as slaves.[1] The first "prison reform" occurred under Constantine in the early fourth century, when the emperor decreed that prisoners held in custody must be kept in good health with access to food and daylight. Constantine's *Theodosian Code* also stipulated that judges should inspect the prisons to prevent corruption and excessive brutality to prisoners awaiting trial.[2] After the fall of the Roman Empire, legal regulation under Germanic rule became much less complex. Capital and corporal punishment were both preferred over any type of imprisonment.[3]

Imprisonment under early Christian canon law assumed the first elements of "correction." Christian notions of penitence and salvation were wedded to the physical segregation of offenders. Canon law, as it was applied to monks, secular clergy, and laypeople, was the earliest Christian articulation of an institutionalized disciplinary system. Monastic discipline connected labour to confinement as a complete system of correction. The idea of isolation as a spiritual punishment stretched back to the rule of St. Benedict of Nursia in the sixth century, when serious offenders were isolated and made to labour in cells called *ergastula*. In the twelfth century, this idea became more institutionalized in monasteries that contained rudimentary prisons. Monastic imprisonment was used in combination with restricted diet and often included elements of ritualized corporal punishment. This practice was significant because it combined isolation, labour, and imprisonment for a specific period of time as a means of finding spiritual salvation: in effect, these were the first prison "sentences." Under Pope Innocent III (1198–1216), the increasing use of inquisitorial justice exposed laypeople to these methods of punishment by confinement.[4]

In jurisdictions such as England that were not subject to canon or Roman law, the common law still provided for some forms of imprisonment. Following the Norman Conquest in 1066, William I constructed the Tower of London to hold royal prisoners and the king's enemies. In 1166 Henry II ordered that all sheriffs build gaols in each county to hold criminals awaiting trial, but like the early Roman prisons, these gaols did not serve the purpose of pure punishment. It was not until widespread changes occurred in European attitudes toward poverty and pauperism that institutional confinement was expanded to include labour. As a result of this ideological shift, institutional confinement, responding to poverty and increasing urbanization, began to incorporate labour.

In early modern Europe, imprisonment emerged as a *noncriminal* sanction against poverty and idleness. After 1500, European authorities increasingly questioned the "worthiness" of society's poor and began to consider poverty a social threat. Prior to this shift, European society was prone to see "the poor of Christ" in all kinds of marginal populations, including the impoverished, the sick, the lepers, and abandoned children. In the sixteenth century, reformers began to view some segments of the poor as "undeserving." Among these were beggars and vagrants, who would subsequently be pressed into "earning" their redemption from poverty. Members of this group were subjected to one of two forms of bondage. The first was as "volunteers" on galley ships; the second, which became increasingly common, was as inmates of workhouses.[5]

In the sixteenth century, societal condemnation of idleness and poverty in England found widespread expression in institutional form. In 1553 Bishop Nicolas Ridley persuaded the king to donate Bridewell Palace in London as the first house of correction. Inmates of Bridewell were subject to a strict regime aimed at correcting idleness. The early version of the institution included workshops for spinning and carpentry as well as a flour mill and a bakery. Inmates were paid wages for their work, from which room and board were deducted. In 1576 Elizabeth I ordered that houses of correction (which were often simply called Bridewells) should be constructed in every county in England. Vagrants were collected and put to work in these institutions.[6] Bridewells provided the moral model on which penitentiaries would eventually be based. As important as their practical function was their symbolic deterrence: Bridewells made incarceration the least desirable option for the poor.

At the end of the seventeenth century, the system of Bridewells lost much of its desired effect. Not only was it underfunded and poorly administered, but, more importantly, the Bridewell system, according to Max Grünhut, was a poor fit with seventeenth-century English law, which demanded more serious degradations upon criminals, often in the form of executions, mutilations, or corporal punishments.[7] Thus, for forms of idleness and vagrancy that bordered on criminal offences, judges were prone to consider harsher sentences than the Bridewell. Still, the idea of an institutional response to social disorder that centred on labour became deeply entrenched through the first century of English Bridewells. In the following century, a growing condemnation of capital punishment and torture led reformers to embrace the idea more completely as a form of legal punishment. The idea of a house of correction as a replacement for simple charity also gained widespread appeal with the English ruling class. In 1753 magistrate and novelist Henry Fielding proposed creating enormous workhouses for up to five thousand inmates, where the poorest and most hopeless cases—those who had little hope of ever buying their freedom—would face a life of hard labour.[8] In proposing a new type of institution, Fielding was one of the few to suggest that crime control and poor relief had not kept pace with urban growth in London.[9] His proposal contained the kernel of an idea that would explode into popular consciousness with the efforts of John Howard a generation later.

THE RISE OF THE PENITENTIARY

In the 1770s, a growing crisis of legitimacy surrounding legal punishment met with an emerging prison reform movement led by John Howard. This convergence gradually encompassed institutional forms of labour that had previously been reserved as a response to poverty. The legal crisis stemmed from growing uncertainty about the efficiency and legitimacy of the death penalty. Capital statutes throughout Europe had expanded steadily and rapidly through the eighteenth century. In England, the number of offences carrying the death penalty hovered around two hundred by the end of the 1700s. Paradoxically, and much to the frustration of legal authorities, ritual corporal punishment and public execution gradually lost much of their legitimacy and capacity to terrorize.[10] Judges and juries increasingly resorted to imprisonment or transportation, which involved deporting convicted criminals to a penal colony. After the American Revolution,

transportation was removed as an option, spurring a crisis of imprisonment in England as the prison population rose dramatically.[11]
These developments coincided with the early years of the Industrial
Revolution, when large-scale social and demographic changes
accompanied the rise of industrial capitalism. During this period,
dispossessed peasants flooded urban centres, London in particular,
and the number of poor people claiming assistance grew accordingly.
Reports of fever and epidemic in overcrowded local gaols alarmed
English authorities and provided the impetus for new thinking about
state punishment.

John Howard stepped into this void to propose a solution. A
wealthy country squire who had purchased his way out of indenture
due to his father's entrepreneurial success, Howard was an atypical landlord, avoiding the trappings of wealth and ruling his small
Bedfordshire estate through a combination of philanthropy and rigorous moral surveillance of his tenants. Michael Ignatieff argues that it
was Howard's Calvinist nonconformist beliefs that provided his sense
of moral authority.[12] This ascetic bent led Howard on an intense search
for a meaningful vocation, which he found in the cause of prison
reform. After his selection as a county sheriff, Howard discovered
widespread irregularity and abuse in local prisons. His disgust at the
chaos he witnessed motivated him to tour every prison in England and
Wales, an investigation that he chronicled meticulously in *The State of
the Prisons,* published in 1777. He condemned the failure to post rules,
the indiscriminate mixing of prisoners, and the unregulated exchange
between the prison and the community.

More significant than his revelations about the chaos of English
prisons were the solutions Howard proposed. His reform program was
based not on existing models of legal punishment but on European
responses to poverty. In his European travels, Howard had toured
workhouses in Amsterdam and Rotterdam, and he considered the
Rasp House to be the perfect institution. The Rasp House, essentially a highly regulated and disciplined workhouse moulded around
the industry of wood rasping, originated in the sixteenth century
and resembled modern penitentiaries in several respects. The routine

was highly regimented, inmates slept in cells and performed labour together, the diet was superior to that of English Bridewell residents, and hygiene was rigorously enforced by a staff physician. Howard was attracted to the intensely Protestant character of the institution and modelled his proposals for reform on what he had witnessed in Holland. The Rasp House suggested the possibility of an institution that would accommodate criminals, and its regime aligned with Howard's ascetic condemnation of idleness and disorder.[13]

Howard's proposals galvanized a broad reform constituency that included Whig reformers, Jacobin radicals, and evangelical Quakers. This group joined with parliamentary reformers and city magistrates to echo Howard's condemnation of the English prison system. The new reform movement was enshrined in the English *Penitentiary Act* of 1779, a piece of legislation that was a triumph for Howard's reform ideas and that set English prisons on a more modern and rational course. It provided for the construction of two new penitentiaries in London built to Howard's specifications. Providing accommodations for six hundred men and three hundred women, the prison's organization closely resembled that of the Dutch Rasp House. Prisoners were to be confined in separate cells during the night and would labour in association during the day. The labour would be "of the hardest and most servile kind in which drudgery is chiefly required and where the work is little liable to be spoiled by Ignorance, Neglect or Obstinacy."[14] The prison was originally called the Hard Labour House, but Howard settled on *penitentiary* as a more fitting name for the institution he had designed. After initial enthusiasm, however, the movement to build this new prison lost much of its force in the 1780s, and by 1785 the project was abandoned. Still, as Randal McGowen argues, because other forms of legal punishment fell out of favour at the same time, Howard's reform program entrenched the prison as the natural centre of legal punishment in England.[15] Additionally, England's *Penitentiary Act* served as a blueprint for the reform of existing institutions throughout the country. Dozens of prisons were reformed to more closely reflect Howard's program. Thus, the *idea* of a new system of discipline spread quickly, and over time, the reform movement initiated by Howard colonized the consciousness of local legal authorities throughout England, causing them to bend the shape of legal punishment to the principles he championed.

Prison reform in post-Revolution America mirrored what was happening in England with some key differences. American prison reform was linked to a broader movement of legal reform, which was greatly influenced by post-Revolution cultural transformations. In the aftermath of independence, Americans readily adopted the Beccarian notion that bad laws cause social disorder.[16] Eager to cast off the most oppressive English legal traditions, Republicans targeted the death penalty as the initial focus of reform. In the years after 1776, legal codes were amended to eliminate capital punishment for all but the most serious crimes. However, much like the end of transportation in England, the amendment of legal codes required a transformation in the infrastructure of American punishment. Thus, the next twenty years witnessed a flurry of prison construction throughout the American Northeast, beginning in Pennsylvania, where the Philadelphia gaol at Walnut Street was turned into a state penitentiary. Other states followed suit, and by 1833 the Auburn system, described below, was in operation in at least twelve states, including New York, New Hampshire, Missouri, Ohio, and Louisiana.[17]

The American preoccupation with reforming legal codes produced a certain confusion about what the new penitentiaries were intended to accomplish. David Rothman suggests that these early years were characterized by a widespread lack of consensus about the goals of the American prison system, particularly with regard to correction versus reformation. As he points out, "the confinement of a prisoner to a cell was convenient. Wardens did not intend for it to reform or elevate the criminal, or to have general applicability among all convicts."[18] Furthermore, much like English prisons prior to Howard's reforms, the American penitentiaries were chaotic. Disorder was rampant, and, much to the disillusionment of legal authorities, the prisons appeared to foster criminal subcultures and conspiracies that merely propagated crime—whereas, following Beccaria, the assmption had been that legal reform would reduce crime. In almost every respect, the American prisons lagged behind the English penitentiaries by the span of a generation. This pattern was finally disrupted in the first decades of the nineteenth century by the advent of new ideas about penitentiary design and the importance of the relationship between imprisonment and labour.

Reforms in New York State ushered in a new mode of legal punishment: contractual penal servitude.[19] Searching for new solutions to the ineffective early penitentiary system, New York experimented simultaneously with two new types of prison management in the newly constructed Auburn state prison. The so-called separate system involved the absolute isolation of prisoners in individual cells, where they slept, ate, and worked. The congregate system, later known as the Auburn system, was based on prisoners working together during the day and sleeping in individual cells. The solitary scheme was an abject failure: the isolated inmates quickly became sick, died, or became hopelessly mentally ill. In contrast, the congregate system was judged a success and thereafter formed the bedrock of the organization of prisoners in New York State.[20] The irony of this experiment carried out at Auburn is that the disagreement between isolation and congregate prisons became the dominant issue in prison reform debates for the next twenty years. Separate system institutions were constructed in multiple states. For two decades, prison reformers sniped at each other and charged the opposing system with failures, abuses, and distortions of the "pure" ideal of the penitentiary. Ultimately, however, the Auburn system became dominant throughout the American Northeast in the nineteenth century. The basis of its success was largely economic.

The Auburn system was based on practices that elevated discipline and production above all else. The radical program at Auburn was made possible by three legal reforms that permitted a more punitive and productive penitential system than the old one. First, new statutes introduced in 1819 repealed Republican laws banning the use of stocks, flogging, and irons in state prisons. This gave penal authorities the ability to punish prisoners in ways that would presumably improve productivity. Second, the law included provisions for making the penitentiary self-sufficient through the sale of inmate labour on the open market. To accomplish this, prison inspectors were instructed to locate the new institution near a marble quarry. Third, the law explicitly stated that the labour of New York prisoners could be sold to private contractors. This was perhaps the most revolutionary departure of all as lawmakers moved to integrate the penitentiary with capital markets in New York.[21]

In both disciplinary and economic terms, Auburn was an initial success. The discipline was of a magnitude never before practiced in American penitentiaries. The "silent system" demanded the absolute suppression of all communication. This regime was made possible by the 1819 repeal of restrictions on corporal punishment, and the law was eventually altered to such an extent that all prison officers could inflict summary punishment on any prisoners who broke the rules. This new disciplinary regime was essentially military in character and was carried out by prison authorities who had honed their severe approach as American officers in the War of 1812. Under this regime, the contract labour system quickly took root. A handful of private manufacturers brought machinery and tools into the institution and paid a fixed daily rate for the labour of the prisoners, providing a new revenue stream for Auburn and placing the institution in much better economic standing than had been the case before contracts with private enterprise. Although the state did not make a profit from these arrangements, the contracts provided valuable revenue to offset operating costs.[22]

While it reflected older forms of confinement such as the work-house or the Bridewell, the model created at Auburn was uniquely suited to the early period of industrialization in the American Northeast. Through the maturing of the Auburn system in New York and its expansion to other states, the penitentiary was increasingly drawn into the economic and social needs of capitalist development. As Rosalind Petchesky argues, the productivity of contractual penal servitude was inseparable from its ideological function of enforcing industrial discipline and the industrial work ethic.[23] Contractual penal servitude more fully integrated the prison with the capitalist system of production, even as this integration produced wide rifts of opposition and dissent. The new institutions were perfectly aligned with the emergence of industrial capitalism requiring a disciplined industrial workforce. This development could only have happened at this particular point of capitalist development: as Petchesky notes, it was a period of rapid accumulation, extreme competition, and very weak labour organization.[24] Thus, the use of prison labour was merely one manifestation of attempts to reduce wages as much as possible, a project that was aided and legitimated within the penitentiary by the stigma of criminality and imprisonment.

THE PENITENTIARY AT KINGSTON

Could contractual penal servitude be adopted in Upper Canada? In 1831 H. C. Thomson reported to the Upper Canadian House of Assembly on the question of whether to erect a penitentiary. His select committee report began by stating its primary question as a matter of truth: "The necessity of a penitentiary in this country must be obvious to anyone who has ever attended a court of justice in this province."[25] Given the trajectory of legal reform in both England and America, Thomson was merely confirming the inevitable conclusion that Canada too must embrace imprisonment in the reform of its legal codes. Introduced into Québec after 1763 and into Upper Canada thirty years later, the English Criminal Code was under strenuous attack by the turn of the nineteenth century. As in England, the death penalty in Upper Canada had lost much of its deterrent value as judges and juries had recoiled from the idea of enforcing brutal sentences for minor offences. Corporal punishment had lost its effect in a similar manner, and by the nineteenth century, the threat of banishment had also ceased to function as an effective deterrent. All of this spurred a crisis of legitimacy that mobilized the push for legal reform and, more specifically, new approaches to punishment.

Imprisonment existed in limited forms in Upper Canada prior to the push for a penitentiary. As indicated by a 1792 statute ordering each district to erect a gaol and a courthouse, provincial authorities considered the gaol an important part of the new provincial criminal justice system,[26] although making these institutions a local responsibility produced a striking inconsistency from one district to the next. Gaols were used primarily to hold offenders awaiting trial, and the early structures were suited to little else.[27] However, as the provincial population grew and social instability became more apparent, authorities looked to the gaol to address a growing sense of social crisis. In 1810 the legislature passed an act declaring that, until "houses of correction" could be built in the province, the existing "common gaols" could serve this purpose. As Peter Oliver notes, this act was the first vagrancy statute, as is clear from its direction that "all and every idle and disorderly person, or rogues and vagabonds, and incorrigible rogues, or any other person or persons who may by law be subject to be committed to a House of Correction, shall be committed to the said common gaols."[28] The impulse to incarcerate the poor and the idle was clear. Less certain was how the institutional response to such individuals would unfold. The local gaols proved ill-prepared for this project. There was no provision in most facilities for an industrial labour program; in some instances, the prisons were crude log structures. This incongruity between the institution and the statute was one more factor in the search for a new form of social response. The American example of an institution based upon industrial production proved extremely alluring to provincial legal authorities and reformers alike.

The reform movement combined two distinct constituencies with a particular stake in maintaining social order in Upper Canada: the Family Compact, represented by Chief Justice John Beverly Robertson, and an emerging bourgeoisie embodied by H. C. Thomson, sitting member for Frontenac and publisher of the *Upper Canada Herald* in Kingston. These distinct class interests converged over anxiety about the threat of crime and an increasing sense of demographic instability in Upper Canada.[29] While homegrown anxieties played a key role, it would be difficult to overestimate the American influence over the emerging Upper Canadian views about the penitentiary. Although English reform ideas under John Howard and Elizabeth Fry (the latter discussed in chapter 2) came first, it was the innovations of contractual penal servitude under the Auburn system that ignited the interest of the Canadian authorities. Thomson's report hints at early Tory attitudes about the penitentiary as a new form of punishment. He intended that it should be as harsh as possible in order to serve as a deterrent. He wrote that the penitentiary should be a "place which by every means not cruel and not affecting the health of the offender shall be rendered so irksome and so terrible that during his afterlife he may dread nothing so much as a repetition of the punishment, and if possible, that he should prefer death to such a contingency. This can all be done by hard labor and privations and not only without expense to the province, but possibly bringing it a revenue."[30]

A year after the first select committee report, H. C. Thomson and Thomas Macaulay were appointed commissioners by the House of Assembly to investigate different styles of penitentiary and to propose a plan. Unsurprisingly, their tour took them straight to Auburn in New York, where they inspected the penitentiary in great detail. In their pilgrimage to Auburn, the commissioners could count themselves among the ranks of other prominent foreign visitors who were drawn to tour the revolutionary institution. France dispatched Alexis de Tocqueville and Gustave de Beaumont to tour American institutions, England sent William Crawford, and Prussia's Nicholas Julius also visited.[31] After seeing Auburn, Thomson and Macaulay visited several other Auburn-style institutions, including Sing Sing and Blackwell Island near Hartford. The tour was intended to take the commissioners to isolation-style penitentiaries in Philadelphia and Boston, but they were turned back due to a cholera outbreak in the region. Thus, their report described the Philadelphia system based on annual reports, but their description of Auburn, drawn from their firsthand inspection, was far more vivid and persuasive. They regarded the separate system as an experiment that had not proved its value. Auburn was therefore put forward as the best choice for a Canadian penitentiary. Above all else, the commissioners were impressed by the discipline of the system and the image of the inmates labouring together in silence. Not only did the quiet represent safety; it also suggested possibilities of industrial productivity that proved an irresistible lure to Canadian officials.

While at Auburn, the commissioners met deputy keeper William Powers. After returning to Upper Canada, they carried out a correspondence with Powers to finalize plans for the construction of a Canadian penitentiary. Canadian authorities moved swiftly on the recommendations of the select committee. In early February 1833, the Bill for the Erection of a Provincial Penitentiary received royal assent. Thomson and Macauley selected a site for the penitentiary on a hundred-acre lot two kilometres west of Kingston. Mirroring Auburn's early development, the site was chosen for its proximity to vast limestone quarries in the area. The property sat between the highway and Hatter's Bay, a village on Lake Ontario. The first commissioners' report boasted, "Nothing indeed can surpass the convenience and beauty of this site."[32] Certainly, Thomson was also attuned to the potential advantages for his constituents that the new public institution would provide.[33] With the site of the new penitentiary chosen, the commissioners returned to New York State, where they convinced William Powers to leave Auburn and serve as building superintendent for the construction of the new institution. Since it was Powers who had provided the detailed plans for the governance of the Auburn system, the commissioners considered him indispensible in constructing the penitentiary to the correct specifications. The commissioners opted to have the penitentiary constructed by day labourers under Powers's direction rather than securing a contract. They judged that this would be less expensive and that once the penitentiary had reached a level of construction that would allow the arrival of inmates, the remainder of the institution could be completed by inexpensive convict labour. This decision would dramatically affect the profitability and governance of the institution. Construction delays dragged the completion of Kingston Penitentiary into the 1850s.

Although H. C. Thomson was the clear choice for the first warden, his death in 1834 prompted a search. Kingston physician James Sampson (who would later be appointed the penitentiary surgeon) put forward Henry Smith as a possibility. Smith was a Kingston magistrate and businessman, and was already connected to the penitentiary through his role as the district building commissioner. He was appointed warden at the first meeting of the new board of inspectors in 1835. Powers stayed at Kingston as deputy warden and continued to superintend the ongoing construction of the institution. By April 1835, the penitentiary was ready to accept its first prisoners, and in September of that year, fifty-five men and two women arrived at Kingston from the Home District to be admitted as the first Canadian penitentiary inmates.

NINETEENTH-CENTURY LABOUR IDEOLOGY

Although labour under confinement had long been regarded as an effective response to poverty and idleness, only in the late eighteenth century was it applied more regularly as a means of legal punishment. Why did the architects of the new methods of imprisonment settle on labour as the basis of the new system? The labour ideology that underpinned modern penitentiaries was rooted in two separate conceptions of the importance and utility of labour in the nineteenth century. The first was a deep-seated moral condemnation of idleness and a belief in the reformative value of work. This view, rooted in Christian theology, gradually gave way to ideas about labour that stressed punishment and deterrence. The second ideology had a more direct economic meaning: it positioned the penitentiary as a means of social and class control, and, increasingly, as a method of industrial discipline. The transition from the first meaning to the second shaped the evolution of the modern penitentiary in the early nineteenth century.

A wide spectrum of Americans were interested in prison reform issues at the end of the eighteenth century, but it was Quaker humanitarians who led the charge for new approaches to criminal justice, with New York and Pennsylvania at the centre of their efforts. In New York, the Quaker influence was best represented by merchant Thomas Eddy. Active in anti-poverty philanthropy, Eddy was also a leading legal reformer who helped draft legislation to abolish capital statutes in favour of lengthy prison sentences. He was made the first warden of Newgate Prison in New York City, an institution that he built on the foundations of his Quaker beliefs, which dictated a disciplined and ordered life based on self-denial, reflection through isolation, and, above all else, the unceasing routine of daily labour. Thoroughly familiar with the English reforms inspired by John Howard, Eddy pushed the new focus on cleanliness and routine in a direction that stressed individual reformation as the end result.

For some reformers, including Eddy, the idea of reformation was at the core of the new focus on labour. Adhering to an emerging Protestant ethic, Eddy believed that idleness was at the root of deviance. He promoted the idea that even the most depraved criminal could access moral salvation through disciplined labour. The newly constructed Newgate Prison was essentially a modification of early prison regimes that Eddy had witnessed in Pennsylvania. At the Walnut Street Prison in Philadelphia, for example, Quaker reformers had constructed early versions of the isolation system. In almost every way, Walnut Street was an institution devoted purely to the idea of reformation, its organization of criminals related directly to Calvinist notions of depravation and denial. The contribution of the New York reformers like Eddy was to marry these theological ideas about individual reformation to a mercantilist system of accumulation. At their root, however, both ideas positioned labour as a central agency of individual reform.[34]

Quaker religious doctrines were uniquely suited to the new forms of imprisonment.[35] Among the most important was a belief in the piety of capital accumulation as a complement to a life of personal self-denial. This new blend of Calvinism and capitalism saved entrepreneurs like Thomas Eddy from the guilt that arose from the pursuit of material self-interest by recasting it as a spiritual quest. In this light, accumulation was positioned as the opposite of poverty, idleness, and moral degradation.[36] It is significant that this was ultimately adopted more widely as a bourgeois ideology. It was appropriated by emerging humanitarian interests and imposed as a project of moral governance upon the poor. Under Eddy's stewardship, Newgate operated as a reformatory institution turned to capitalist pursuits.

American reformers in this period were in constant contact with their European counterparts and incorporated John Howard's practical reforms along with the heritage of the European workhouse. Eddy's humanitarianism pervaded this early prison experiment, and Newgate featured purely moral compulsions and a notable absence of corporal punishment. The regime did not last. After a series of riots, escape attempts, and uprisings, Eddy was ousted as warden and a stricter disciplinary regime was implemented at Newgate.[37] Although one lasting effect of the experiment under Thomas Eddy was the entrenchment of the connection between labour and reformation in the minds of penal reformers, in New York and, later, Upper Canada, the idea of reformation largely receded and became dormant as labour ideology swung toward industrial discipline under the system of contractual penal servitude. What remained was the expectation of profit and productivity, laying waste to old notions about hard labour or the treadmill that promoted work for the sake of work. The Quaker influence essentially transformed penitentiary labour into an institution geared toward the needs of capitalist accumulation.

The second strain of labour ideology emerged as humanitarian and philanthropic interests lost control of the early penitentiary agenda. After Thomas Eddy's failure to impose a primarily moral regime at Newgate, New York State moved in a newly punitive direction, abandoning the notion that prison labour rehabilitates criminals and instead focusing on the goal of disciplining and punishing crime through hard labour. Rather than moral governance, the penitentiary remained as a method of pure compulsion, deterrence, and punishment. According to New York Governor Dewitt Clinton, the penitentiary would serve to "crush" the spirit of "dangerous offenders."[38] Thus, in the minds of those governing the institutions born of Quaker evangelical impulses, the new direction replaced reformation with oppression. Elam Lynds, one of Auburn's earliest wardens, exhibited positive scorn for any hint of philosophical reflection in penitentiary administration. Lynds ruled with the whip and found that he was generally supported by his political masters.[39] Labour was still at the heart of this approach, though it now served primarily as a tool of discipline and a means to profit

In Canada, the Tory appetite for new methods of social control over an unstable demographic was perfectly aligned with the conception of the penitentiary emerging in New York State. Viewing the penitentiary as a potentially powerful method of industrial discipline, the Tory ruling class recognized the compatibility between the new institution and its views of a stratified society. In this sense, new ideas about penitentiary labour still served bourgeois interests, but by the time Kingston Penitentiary was built, this was an ideology stripped of its evangelical origins. In the decades after Kingston opened, however, it would become obvious (as it had in New York) that the labour ideology behind the institution was built on unstable foundations. Opposition to penitentiary labour in the 1830s would also reveal the first cracks in a long-standing Tory hegemony.

PENITENTIARY LABOUR AND ITS OPPONENTS

In both New York and Upper Canada, the penitentiary drew the ire of nascent workingmen's movements opposed to competition with convict labour. Opposition from the American movement directly followed Auburn and Sing Sing's entry onto the open markets with the products of contractual penal servitude. There were numerous dimensions to the growing opposition to convict labour. McLennan argues that while the labour question was spurred by the threat of unfair competition, the issue acted as a conductor for larger anxieties about economic transformation in the industrializing economy of New York State. As a number of crafts and trades industrialized, journeymen and apprentices faced a troubling transition to a system of waged labour. When the traditional protections of their crafts were threatened and then gradually fell away, mechanics opposed competition with the prison workforce not only on economic grounds but also because they regarded it as an affront to their dignity and respectability.[40]

The New York mechanics took action. In the early 1830s, the state legislature was besieged by letters and petitions demanding an end to the prison industrial system. Workingmen represented over 100,000 constituents, and New York legislators responded quickly. Public hearings in 1835 resulted in rules that contracts in the prisons could only supply goods that were not produced within the state. Furthermore, to avoid producing new workers within prison walls who might one day compete with free labour, legislators determined that only convicts with prior industrial training could be put to work in prison trades.[41] Throughout the 1830s, however, prison contract holders devised innumerable ways to circumvent these regulations. It was not until the 1840s that new legislation actually restricted the scope of prison industry in the state. Numerous prison contracts were voided due to past violations, and prison industry was transformed to focus on unskilled labour in the production of railroad materials and the fur-cutting industry. Even more significant, in the 1840s New York embarked on the construction of a new prison near Dannemora that would be entirely devoted to iron-smelting, an industry with no prior foothold in the state.[42]

Upper Canadian mechanics were less effective in opposing the rise of penitentiary labour. While Kingston Penitentiary was in the earliest stages of construction, Kingston mechanics marshalled their numbers to condemn the prospect of competition with convict labour. This opposition, spurred by concerns similar to those of the New York mechanics, was shaped and directed by Reform Party interests expressing some of the first substantial opposition to the Tory hegemony in Kingston. In 1833 a group of tradesmen and workingmen drafted a series of resolutions condemning convict labour in Upper Canada. A petition was presented to the House of Assembly informing legislators of the threat that the institution posed to honest workingmen in the province.[43] The mechanics' opposition tended to rise and fall with the prospect of electoral victory for the Reform Party. When Reform candidate William O'Grady was soundly defeated in the election of 1834, for example, the opposition movement retreated. Unable to mount a significant political challenge, the mechanics were easily placated by Tory authorities.

Kingston newspapers reiterated the government position on prison labour. Both the *Chronicle* and the *Gazette* assured the public that the products of prison labour would not be sold below market prices and that the goods would be dispersed throughout the province.[44]

Representing the riding of Kingston in the House of Assembly, Christopher Hagerman personified the duplicity of the Tory position on the labour question. When the opposition movement rose again in 1835 after the opening of the penitentiary, Hagerman assured Kingston mechanics that they would not be in competition with prison labour and that the convicts would be engaged in breaking stone for road construction. This position directly contradicted the grounds on which Tory authorities were proceeding in the pursuit of a penitentiary. When Macaulay and Thomson visited Auburn in the early 1830s, they accepted the Auburn system on Powers's assurances that the penitentiary could support itself (and indeed, turn a profit) through the strength of its prison industries and their advantageous competitive position with free labour. Within a year of opening, the Kingston mechanics were vexed to realize that Hagerman had lied and that the penitentiary was indeed engaged in contract labour on the open market.[45]

The opposition of free labour to contractual penal servitude exposed one of the central, yet unacknowledged, fallacies of nineteenth-century penal ideology: that industrial training provided the opportunity for convicts to re-enter the productive working class once they were released from the penitentiary. However, although penitentiary discipline could compel convicts to behave as workers while incarcerated, this provided no guarantee of continued productivity after release. Chief among the barriers to such a transformation was the working class itself, which viewed the penitentiary project with a combination of suspicion and disgust. This position illustrated early class struggle in the Kingston area. Members of the producing classes opposed what they saw as the degradation of their honour through the competition (and implied association) with penitentiary labour. This opposition also spoke to the effect the penitentiary had over class differentiation. The argument of the Kingston mechanics was largely based in protection of their specific skills, which were threatened by a new mode of production represented by the penitentiary, limited as its reach may have been. Furthermore, to the producing classes, a penitentiary constructed on industrial principles represented not only an economic threat but also a psychological one.

The labour ideology advanced in the penitentiary was rooted in industrial discipline of a class of workers who were well suited to the emerging industrial order, which demanded disciplined, often unskilled wage labourers to fulfill the demand of industrial production. In the opposition of the Kingston mechanics, this ideology came up against a producer ideology that associated the wealth of the nation with the skilled labour of master craftsmen and mechanics, and their alliance with manufacturers.[46] Wage labour seriously threatened this producer ideology, and penitentiary labour appeared as a particularly sinister manifestation of this threat. It is this ideological weight attributed to labour in the penitentiary that explains the scope of the opposition to contractual penal servitude. Though its economic reach in Canada was limited, the threat was taken seriously, all the more because of what it symbolized. The challenge mounted by mechanics of New York and Upper Canada was advanced on economic, political, and ideological grounds. By 1840 New York mechanics had successfully opposed the widespread adoption of contractual penal servitude. In Canada, it was the financial mismanagement of Kingston Penitentiary that produced the soundest defeat of the Auburn system, in the institution's first decade.

THE LIMITS OF PENITENTIARY LABOUR

The high hopes expressed at the initial adoption of the Auburn system in Canada were almost immediately dashed. By 1835 only the most basic elements of the plans provided by Powers were completed. The prison opened in a state that barely resembled the institutions in New York that had inspired it. Kingston contained no separate accommodation for women, no hospital facilities, and, most distressingly, no permanent workshops. The shops that were in operation by 1838 included a stone shed, a carpentry shop, and blacksmithing and shoemaker shops, but these were constructed in a "slight, temporary manner" and the inspectors reported that they would soon go to decay. Even the inner boundary wall was a flimsy wooden construction, presenting a pressing security concern.[47] In 1838 the inspectors reported that the penitentiary was still far from complete and made pessimistic projections for the completion date of various ongoing projects. Much of the available convict labour was consumed by the lagging construction of the north wing, which still had no permanent roof. The east wing of the building would take at least two years to finish, and the inspectors projected a similar delay for the boundary wall. There was even less hope for the workshops. An annual report stated that it would take the labour of two hundred convicts to build the shops as they were originally designed.[48] Christopher Adamson suggests that much of this delay was due to the scarcity of skilled labour in the Kingston region between 1833 and 1836.[49] However, even if skilled workers could have been found to assist with the construction, it was unlikely that the administration possessed the financial resources to hire such a workforce. Within two years of opening, penitentiary administrators were requesting more money from the provincial government than legislators were prepared to grant, but their pleas fell on deaf ears. Still expecting the penitentiary to draw funds from the products of private industrial contracts, the province slashed penitentiary budgets between 1838 and 1840 by 20 to 30 percent. By 1840 the administration was in debt by two thousand pounds and was forced to dramatically reduce spending, which included laying off newly hired guards and attempting to move forward on what the warden called "a reduced scale."[50]

Throughout these early years, the penitentiary held contracts for shoemaking, blacksmithing, some limited carpentry, and stonecutting connected to the limestone quarries. Still, the amount of labour performed on a contract basis was extremely limited. For example, in 1838 the blacksmiths, stonecutters, carpenters, and shoemakers performed 1,767 days of contractual labour, resulting in revenue of £214 17s. In comparison, construction and maintenance of the institution in 1838 consumed 41,053 days of labour. The bulk of the profitable production came from a small gang of twelve shoemakers producing Coburg boots for sale on the open market. In an irony that will be explored more fully in chapter 5, the shoemaker gang was composed of convicts who were elderly, infirm, or physically disabled and unfit for any other form of labour.[51]

The only glimmer of success occurred in 1840 with the construction of a rope factory. The ropewalk was constructed at great expense, and the penitentiary signed a contract with a private manufacturer to manage the operation. In the first year, the ropewalk contributed £769 8s to the penitentiary, an advantage gained on the basis of a daily rate of labour that was nearly twice that paid to the shoemakers. With an eye to the workingman's opposition movement, which had been dormant for five years, the inspectors noted that the ropewalk was an attractive industry as it would not interfere with the pursuits of the "honest mechanic."[52] But the financial advantage was short lived. In its second year, the price of rope depreciated by 25 percent and initial plans to expand the ropewalk to produce different gauges were abandoned. By 1844 the contract had lapsed and the ropewalk subsequently fell into disrepair. Finally, the warden determined that the machinery and equipment occupied ground required for the penitentiary garden, and the ropewalk was disassembled.[53]

The productivity of the penitentiary as a capital enterprise declined rapidly from the earliest years as the convict population increased. Labour performed on contract peaked in 1840 when 7,705 days were charged to private industry out of a total of 44,885 days for the entire institution. After that, productivity fell every year until the post-Confederation era. In 1847 only 1,387 days of labour were charged to private industry while the total labour performed had expanded to 130,206 days. The latter number reflects the rapidly increasing convict population, resulting in part from the transfer of Lower Canadian prisoners after the *Act of Union* in 1840.[54] As the penitentiary accepted more and more prisoners, they were simply folded into the seemingly never-ending construction project. In 1847 the inspectors reported that the workshops, outer walls, and roofs of the various buildings were nearing completion and that convict labour would soon turn to construction of the penitentiary hospital and women's prison. However, it was not until 1857 that the penitentiary was finally completed to the specifications provided by Powers in the early 1830s.

When Macaulay and Thomson visited the Auburn penitentiary in 1831, they were astonished by its resemblance to the most
advanced industrial factories in the American North. However, much
of the promise that sold the Auburn system all over North America
was merely an illusion. The institution was far from the orderly and
penitent haven that visitors witnessed. Untenable even in its original form in New York, the ideology and practice of contractual penal
servitude imported to Upper Canada was unsustainable under the
crushing inefficiency and ineptitude of the administration at Kingston
Penitentiary. Along with the abandonment and failure of labour
as a profitable venture, the promised order and "correction" that was
intended to accompany the Auburn system was also revealed to
be illusory.

ENFORCING PENAL SERVITUDE

Bryan Palmer notes that in the mid-1830s, the Kingston mechanics were perhaps the first to suggest that the penitentiary regime
at Kingston was characterized by pervasive brutality and ongoing
abuse.[55] The truth of these claims came to light a decade later under
the investigation of the Brown Commission. Along with the Auburn
approach to contractual penal servitude, Kingston imported Auburn's
legacy of violence. Visitors and dignitaries who toured the Auburn
penitentiary (and to a lesser degree, Sing Sing) saw the order and
silence of the institution but not the methods of compulsion that
enforced the discipline. The resort to violence was not in the design
of the earliest reformers. Rather, the disciplinary regime was improvised by personnel who were given charge of the institutions. It was
Captain Elam Lynds, taking command of Auburn in 1825, who insti-
gated much of the harshest physical punishment in the disciplinary
regime. Lynds prohibited all conversation, grimacing, signalling, smil-
ing, and eye contact between prisoners and with guards. He also set
the institution to a military rhythm, instituting the lockstep march
and militaristic uniforms.

Much of the new disciplinary regime, particularly the absolute curtailment of communication, was an effort to break down the old inmate subcultures of traditional penitentiaries. With these privileges fell the last lingering ideas of prisoners as bearers of "customary rights," ideas that had characterized prisons in the eighteenth century.[56] W. David Lewis notes that these rights died hard under a new legal spirit determined to crush the criminal offender under the might of the state. For example, convicts and their supporters mounted a legal challenge against the new practice of summary whippings instituted under Lynds in 1825. They were defeated when a local judge ruled that summary whipping, despite the existence of a statute to the contrary, was "the common law right" of the master.[57] With the blessing of legal authorities, penitentiary officials everywhere gradually implemented more punitive disciplinary regimes.

Soon after the 1825 legal challenge in New York, reports of unrestrained brutality at Auburn came to light. In 1826 a pregnant inmate died as the result of a whipping. The situation at Sing Sing was worse. There the discipline became completely arbitrary and subject to no administrative control. The keepers were instructed to strike the convicts with whatever weapon came to hand for the slightest infractions of the rule of silence. By 1828 there were rampant reports of the increasing violence practiced on Sing Sing inmates, with some accounts charging that the prisoners were being whipped on particularly sensitive parts of the body including the genitals. Mark Colvin notes that the severity of discipline at Sing Sing was due in part to the impression that urban convicts from New York City were inherently more dangerous and depraved than their upstate counterparts.[58] As Rothman argues, this deviation can be explained by remembering that in the 1820s, the penitentiary was still regarded as a social experiment, and this granted administrators a large degree of leeway. The notion that prisoners might yet overpower their keepers was still a palpable concern in the penitentiary's first decade, and this created the conditions for grievous abuses. When questions were raised, penitentiary authorities vigorously defended their use of violence. An official at Auburn argued to the state legislature in 1834 that convicts "must be made to know that *here,* they must submit to every regulation, and obey every command of their keepers." The same year, the chaplain at Auburn opined, "It would be most unfortunate . . . if the public were to settle down into repugnance to the use of such coercive means."[59]

Wherever the Auburn system was implemented, harsh disciplinary regimes followed. Penitentiaries throughout the Northeast gradually came to rely almost exclusively on corporal punishment (but not exclusively on the whip in every institution). McLennan argues that it was, in part, the necessities of the contract labour system that motivated much of the demand for this order enforced by violence. When discipline was at its strictest, profit for the contract system was maximized. Thus, the discipline of the Auburn penitentiary was calculated to create docile subjects in order to wring out of them the maximum productivity.[60]

Given the American experience with the Auburn system, it is unsurprising that the same violent regime was replicated at Kingston Penitentiary. The potential for abuse was heightened by Warden Henry Smith's ongoing quest to consolidate his power and authority over the penitentiary administration. In the first years after opening, Smith feuded with Deputy Warden William Powers, who had accepted a reduced salary from his previous position as building superintendent. The relationship between Smith and Powers deteriorated rapidly in the first years after Kingston opened. On two separate occasions, Smith brought a series of superficial charges against Powers, which the penitentiary board eventually dismissed. Smith had deep Tory roots in the Kingston area that Powers lacked, and this explains the support Smith enjoyed from the first penitentiary board.[61] The tension reached a breaking point in 1840, and Powers departed, a decision that split the penitentiary board on whether Powers or Smith was to blame for the administrative strife. The board came down on the side of Smith, partly because Powers was an American and they regarded it as unusual that he should hold a public posting in Upper Canada.[62]

Powers's departure did not end the climate of conflict at Kingston. The deputy warden position was changed to the rank of assistant warden to clarify that Smith possessed the highest authority in the institution. The new position was filled by Edward Utting, who became the chief disciplinary officer at Kingston. Utting was not the submissive figure Smith had hoped for. A former warden of Westminster Bridewell, Utting assumed the role of strict disciplinarian over both convicts and keepers in his new position at Kingston. Not only did he implement a new spirit of discipline over the prisoners; he laid charge after charge against the penitentiary staff, reporting each instance of incompetence and laxity that he discovered. Warden Smith worked to undermine and ultimately disgrace Utting.[63]

In 1846 Smith and his son, sitting Tory member Henry Smith Jr. drafted new penitentiary legislation, which was tabled in the House of Assembly without being reviewed by the penitentiary board. Using his son to directly influence the new legislation, Warden Smith manoeuvered past the board to increase further his power and authority. The 1846 act gave him the authority to hire and fire penitentiary officials without the board's approval. It also increased the salary of the warden and decreased the salaries of other senior penitentiary officials. As the act was written, it gave Smith a voting seat on the board of inspectors and the power to determine sentencing for Kingston prisoners. Although these measures were eliminated from the final version, Smith still assumed sweeping new powers. With his newfound authority, he removed Assistant Warden Utting from his post and appointed a new deputy. He also appointed his second son, Francis (Frank) Smith, as the new kitchen keeper. Disgusted at Smith's bald pursuit of power and their own marginalization, the penitentiary board members resigned in 1846. Although Warden Smith's power at Kingston was at its zenith in that year, he would soon be overtaken by the growing public awareness that the penitentiary was rife with corruption and abuse.

The attack on Smith's regime came from two directions. First, after largely ignoring the penitentiary for a decade, Canada West newspapers focused their attention squarely on the affairs of the institution. Articles appeared in the *Hamilton Spectator* and the Toronto-based *Globe* proclaiming an all-out crusade to rescue the inmates of Kingston Penitentiary. This mission was spearheaded by the *Globe*'s editor, George Brown, who charged that the penitentiary had become a "den of brutality" and informed his readers of the rampant and unrestrained corporal punishment practised at the penitentiary. In an 1846 editorial, Brown thundered:

> A hundred and fifty lashes must be given in this den of brutality every day the sun rises. Who can calculate the amount of pain and of agony that must be imposed in this pandemonium? Who can tell the amount of evil passions, of revenge, and of malice, that must be engendered by such treatment? A penitentiary is a place where the prisoner should reflect on the past, and be placed under such a system of moral training as may fit him for becoming a better member of society. Will the lash do that?[64]

The second attack came from within the administration. Penitentiary surgeon James Sampson laid formal charges against Frank Smith, the warden's son. The charges of misconduct against Smith included shooting arrows at convicts, improper conduct with female prisoners, abusing the convicts for his own pleasure, and a host of financial corruptions in his position as kitchen keeper. Frank Smith was acquitted of all charges before the penitentiary board, but this did little to calm the furor brewing in the press. Although the warden, Henry Smith, enjoyed the support of the penitentiary board even in the face of these challenges, changes in the political landscape of Canada West in 1848 ended his good fortune. When Reform swept the Tories from power in early 1848, the first act of the Baldwin-Lafontaine government was to create a commission for the investigation of the management of Kingston Penitentiary. The commission was intensely partisan, containing five Reform supporters and falling under the leadership of George Brown, who served as secretary.[65] The commission would soon expose the litany of abuse and irregularities that had developed under contractual penal servitude at Kingston Penitentiary.

The Brown Commission investigated eleven main charges against the Smith regime. These fell under three broad categories—peculation, cruelty, and mismanagement. The investigation of corporal punishment elicited the most disgust. The official charge against the Smith administration was "pursuing a system of punishment, in the management of the discipline—cruel, indiscriminate, and ineffective" (Brown Commission, 182). In the course of their investigation of this charge, the commission uncovered evidence of a horrific disciplinary regime. The sheer volume of punishment at Kingston, hinted at in the press but revealed in full by the investigation, made a damning case against the warden and his staff. Proper records had not been kept between 1835 and 1842, but the penitentiary registers for 1843 showed 770 corporal punishments. By 1845 this had risen to 2,102, and by 1846, to 6,063 punishments for 262 prisoners (189). The Brown Commission report estimated that by 1846 the penitentiary was inflicting seven corporal punishments per day, and that the total represented four to five punishments per year for every man, woman, and child in the institution (189). The severity of these punishments was found grossly disproportionate to the nature of offences, and punishment was wildly inconsistent, in part because five different officials in the penitentiary were authorized to order punishment. Thus, for minor transgressions, prisoners sometimes suffered only bread and water or the dark cell, but for the same infractions, perhaps talking at dinner, the most severe punishments, including flogging, could be inflicted.

Between 1835 and 1842, the only punishments at Kingston were corporal. These included the cat-o'-nine tails and a rawhide whip. The cat-o'-nine tails—or "the cats," as it was commonly known—was traditionally an instrument of military discipline. It was made of lengths of rope with three knots on each thong. Before being flogged, prisoners were stripped to the waist and bound to the "triangle," which spread the arms and legs outwards, leaving the bare back exposed.[66] After 1842 the penitentiary added punishments of isolation and restraint, including shackling or ironing of the arms and legs, solitary confinement, and, after 1847, "the box." The box was a restraining punishment: prisoners were locked in a coffin-like enclosure designed to keep the body in an immobilized standing position, sometimes for as many as eight or nine hours at a time. The Brown Commission heard testimony from Maurice Phelan on his experience with the box. Punished for quarrelling, Phelan was confined this way for nine hours. He described how he fainted repeatedly and when he got out was "completely benumbed" (Brown Commission, 45).

The commission also uncovered evidence of the indiscriminate and brutal use of corporal punishment. Flogging with the cats was administered for the slightest infractions, including talking, laughing, and making eye contact with keepers and guards. Furthermore, prisoners were frequently flogged on successive days, which did not allow for proper healing of the wounds from previous whippings. The commission cited evidence about prisoner Donovan, who suffered floggings on seven successive days in May 1845 and was flogged four times within a week the following month (185). Witnesses testified that prisoners with severely lacerated backs, "positively black, from previous punishment," were flogged with the cats. A former assistant warden, Edward Utting, testified that prisoners had begged him not to whip them "when their backs were much bruised from former punishment" (184). This testimony was underlined by evidence of the bodily damage inflicted by corporal punishment, and particularly by the cats. Witness John H. Freeland testified, "The cat lacerates the back and breasts, the blood flows, and the skin becomes black." James Kearns added, "The cats were laid on the bare back; it made the whole back raw; brought blood at almost every stroke" (183).

The scandal deepened when investigators uncovered evidence of the unrestrained punishment of women, children, and the mentally ill. The commissioners discovered that at least five prisoners exhibiting signs of mental illness had been brutally flogged. In December 1847, penitentiary surgeon James Sampson reported that prisoner James Brown was insane. Punishment registers examined by the Brown Commission showed that the prisoner was flogged with the cats at least thirty-six times, receiving a total of 1,002 lashes (198).

The surgeon would not testify that Brown was insane at the time of these punishments, but other penitentiary officials and keepers did: Chaplain R. V. Rogers testified that he had always considered Brown to be insane and that Brown was often punished for acts committed under the influence of insanity. At least ten other witnesses, all penitentiary staff members, declared that they considered Brown to be mentally ill (197). In his own defence, an unrepentant Warden Smith stated that Brown "was not mad, but a violent, bad character, who deserved all the punishment he got, and was the better for it" (196).

The Brown Commission report had less to say about the flogging of women at Kingston except to condemn the practice. The evidence stated that female prisoners as young as twelve had received corporal punishment. The report noted that twelve-year-old Elizabeth Breen had been whipped on six separate occasions with the rawhide. The commission concluded, "We are of the opinion that the practice of flogging women is utterly indefensible" (190). When the penitentiary statute was rewritten in 1851, the government passed an amendment banning corporal punishment for women.

Although the corporal punishment of women elicited disgust, it aroused nowhere near the controversy of floggings inflicted on young children throughout Smith's regime. The Brown Commission's condemnation of the flogging of child prisoners was absolute. The report stated, "It is horrifying to think of a child of 11 to 14 years of age, being lacerated with the lash before 500 grown men; to say nothing of the cruelty, the effect of such a scene, so often repeated, must have been to the last degree brutalizing" (192). The evidence presented before the commission was difficult to dispute. Eleven-year-old Alexis Lafleur was flogged thirty-eight times with the rawhide and six times with the cats. Peter Charboneau, age ten, was flogged sixty-two times with the rawhide and was also subjected to the box at least thirteen times. Eight-year-old Antoine Beauché (brother of Narcisse) received forty-seven corporal punishments in the eight months after his committal to the penitentiary. All four children mentioned in the report were punished for trifling and childish behaviour such as talking, staring, making faces, or winking, and all were French Canadians (190–95).

In each of the four cases, Warden Smith and other penitentiary staff argued that the punishment was necessary due to the troublesome, difficult, or incorrigible character of the children in question. The warden insisted that Lafleur was a "wild character" and that his punishments were all necessary (191). When cross-examined by the warden, Thomas Costen stated that "Peter Charboneau is a very bad, troublesome little boy; idle and talkative . . . he was never punished without a cause" (193). Edward Utting, however, testified in Charboneau's defence: "He was a mere child. He should have had a kind word, rather than punishment" (198). Yet among the penitentiary officers who were involved in the punishment of children, they often offered the same defence in each case. In one reply, keeper Thomas Hooper protested that Beauché was "continually breaking the rules while here. . . . It was absolutely necessary to punish him to keep him in proper order" (194). These obtuse references to necessity and order received the commission's highest condemnation. The report concluded that such punishments represented "another case of revolting inhumanity" (194). Interestingly, the Brown Commission made no specific comment on the appropriateness or inhumanity of imprisonment itself as a punishment for children. In this early era, it was accepted that children (like women) should be subject to the same punishments as male adults. In many respects, this was a class issue. Several historians of childhood point out that working-class children worked alongside adults as a matter of basic familial economic survival.[67] Moreover, in the early part of the nineteenth century, there was little notion of "separate" institutions designed to foster children from youth to adulthood, particularly in working-class life.[68]

While the corporal punishment regime demonstrated barbaric practices, much of the inhumanity of the Smith regime seemed to be embodied in the actions of Henry Smith's son, Frank Smith, the kitchen keeper. The third of the eleven charges against the warden accused him of culpability in reference to his son, by "permitting the said F. W. Smith for nearly two years, to set every feeling of humanity and rule of good order at defiance" (Brown Commission, ii). It was a broad charge, but the commission was in possession of overwhelming evidence that much of the chaos of the penitentiary could be directly attributed to Frank Smith. This evidence was supported by testimony given two years earlier in the penitentiary board investigation of Dr. Sampson's charges against the kitchen keeper. It painted a picture of Frank Smith as a terror to convicts and keepers alike. The warden's son had been regarded with much suspicion when he was given the position of kitchen keeper in 1846. At thirty years of age, he had been the deputy sheriff of the Midland District and regarded as a "damned rascal" (126). He was relieved of his position as sheriff due to financial irregularities. When Warden Smith proposed his son to replace Edward Utting as his deputy warden, the board balked at this suggestion and gave Frank Smith the position of kitchen keeper instead. Although subordinate to the deputy warden, the kitchen keeper had a high degree of financial responsibility since he was in charge of thousands of pounds worth of property throughout the penitentiary. It had not taken Frank Smith long to turn this to his financial advantage. Witness after witness testified to Smith's ongoing exploitation of his position and the vigorous trafficking of penitentiary goods to the guards and outside interests. He had received groceries and produce on peniten- tiary accounts for his own use, and there was no piece of penitentiary equipment Smith would not dispose of for financial gain.

More troubling than the financial corruption was Frank Smith's treatment of the prisoners. He would knock convicts' heads together when seated at dinner, strike them in the elbows and knees with his key ring as they passed, or stand at the door of the cellblock and throw potatoes and stones at the convicts in their cells. Frank Smith found all of this hilarious. On repeated occasions, he had used the peni- tentiary fire engine (a rudimentary pump on wheels) to drench the prisoners as they worked outdoors (303). He would compel prisoners to open their mouths on the pretense of searching for chewing tobacco and then throw salt or snow into them, or spit tobacco juice into them (305). Other keepers in the penitentiary also suffered. On one occa- sion, Smith surprised keeper Little by throwing flour into his eyes When former guard Thomas Fitzgerald was asked by investigators why the convicts and guards had not complained about this abuse, he simply stated that all of them were afraid of Frank Smith: the guards because of his connection to the warden, and the prisoners because of the threat of future retribution (302). His authority unquestioned, Smith had used the penitentiary and its inmates as his personal source of entertainment. Sometimes prisoners who were favoured were enlisted in his pursuits. Fitzgerald testified that Frank Smith would stand by in the washhouse laughing as a group of convicts held a fellow inmate's head underwater in a basin (302).

The hospital keeper testified that on several occasions he had witnessed convicts with "blackened faces" who would perform routines for Smith's amusement. In blackface, the performers would wrestle each other or dance and gesticulate wildly (301). There was also veiled suggestion in the testimony that Frank Smith took sexual liberties with the female convicts. A former matron, Julia Cox, testified that Smith had been seen "putting women in the blackhole," and that he very rarely visited this part of the prison in the regular course of his duties (303). All of this created a portrait of an institution that was ruled under a veil of silence and discipline, yet was punctuated by incidents of utter bedlam. Through it all, Warden Henry Smith presided and failed to intervene.

Frank Smith's most troubling transgressions involved incidents of cruel and sadistic torture of the prisoners under his care. He seemed unable to resist the opportunity to inflict suffering and misery on prisoners in a vulnerable state. This impulse was frequently satisfied upon prisoners trapped in the box, immobilized and utterly helpless. Discharged convict Henry Wilson testified that Smith had stuck pins into his arms and legs. Another former prisoner testified that Smith had thrown water on him while he was confined in the box. A former hospital keeper told the commission that Frank Smith once shook and rolled the box onto the ground with prisoner Richard McCanna inside. When the trapped man cried out and asked for a drink of water, Smith taunted him and said, "No, let him die." McCanna had been badly injured and blistered from rolling in the box and spent two days in the hospital as a result (301–2). Finally, Frank Smith was investigated for shooting arrows at the convicts for sport. Several prisoners told the commission that they had almost been wounded by Smith in this way. An Aboriginal man named Abraham had been struck in the eye by an arrow and eventually lost his sight (303–6). Some claimed that Abraham had been wounded by a flying splinter in the shed where he worked, but Dr. Sampson testified that the damage was inflicted by Smith's arrow.

It is worth noting that for most of these charges, convicts and keepers invariably came forward to deny Frank Smith's culpability, claiming that none of it had happened. Such was the polarizing effect of the kitchen keeper as a divisive and destructive force in the penitentiary. Smith had cultivated favourites among the penitentiary guards and within the convict population, a chosen few who participated in his antics or benefited from his corruption. In other cases, prisoners were clearly intimidated by the prospect of retribution that might stem from testifying against the warden's son. Prisoners knew better than to speak out against abuses. Thus, when charges came to light, a second prisoner or guard was always willing to contradict damning testimony. But contradictory testimony did not dissuade the Brown Commission from recognizing the kernel of truth in the troubles caused by Frank Smith. On the charges against him, the commission concluded, "All the evils which could possibly arise from such an appointment have arisen out of this one: peculation, cruelty, favouritism, and every species of irregularity, all clouded from observation, if not openly encouraged, because the chief agent was the warden's son" (126).

The eighth charge against Warden Smith investigated the starvation of prisoners by the penitentiary staff. This charge arose in part from questions about why construction projects at Kingston had proceeded so slowly. In the preliminary investigation, ex-keeper William Coverdale reported that he had frequently seen convicts sitting during work hours. When he had questioned the attending keepers, he had been told that these prisoners were too weak to work from a lack of food. Ex-keeper Gleeson testified to similar conditions, noting that on many occasions he had excused the convicts under his direction from their work and allowed them to sit beneath a shed because they were so exhausted. Ex-keeper McCarthy reported that he hadn't the conscience to keep the men at hard work due to their depleted condition and that their appearance convinced him that their complaints about the food were valid (169). Ex-keeper William Smith (no relation to the warden) added that the starvation of the convicts not only was inhumane but greatly affected the productivity of the institution. He believed that there was a great waste of labour and couldn't say how the buildings had ever been completed given the health of the convicts. Much of the starvation may have been due to the disciplinary regime, particularly after the arrival of Frank Smith. William Smith noted that the keepers put the greatest part of the blame on Frank Smith due to his tendency to patrol the shops, report the men for disciplinary infractions, and reduce them frequently to bread-and-water diets (170). Even when prisoners were not on short rations, the quality of the food provided was often abysmal.

Table 1 details the legislated diet for penitentiary inmates in a typical year during this period. As meagre as the rations appear compared to contemporary appetites, the Brown Commission revealed that corners were cut everywhere. Much of the meat was provided on contract, but even the contractors testified that the quality was poor. Contractor Samuel Breden noted that the meat was delivered in the afternoon or evening, only after the day's business at the markets was finished. He testified, "They usually sent what remained over the day's sales" (174). What remained was of the worst quality. "Poor, skinny meat" is how several witnesses described the cuts delivered to the penitentiary. Guard Kearns described meat so rotten that he could not stand over it, and William Smith described the meat as "black and disagreeable, and smelling strongly" (174).

Again, the investigation centred on Frank Smith. Gatekeeper Cooper testified that on one occasion guard Watt had inspected the meat upon arrival and ordered it sent back to the butcher as unfit. Frank Smith had intercepted the cart on its way from the penitentiary and ordered the meat to be returned to the kitchen for the evening meal (177). Similar evidence was heard regarding sour and mouldy bread infested with worms or rat feces (180).

TABLE 1   Convicts' Daily Diet at Kingston Penitentiary, 1838

SUNDAY RATION	WEDNESDAY RATION	MONDAY, TUESDAY, THURSDAY, FRIDAY AND SATURDAY
BREAKFAST	*BREAKFAST*	*BREAKFAST*
Brown Bread ...... 1/2 lb.	Brown Bread ...... 1/2 lb.	Brown Bread ...... 1/2 lb.
Fresh Beef .... 3/8 lb.	Salt Pork .... 3/8 lb.	Fresh Beef .... 3/8 lb.
Potatoes....... 1/44 bush.	Potatoes....... 1/44 bush.	Potatoes....... 1/44 bush.
Salt .... 3/88 lb.	Salt .... 3/88 lb.	Salt .... 3/88 lb.
Pepper .... 1/44 oz.	Pepper .... 1/44 oz.	Pepper .... 1/44 oz.
Vinegar .... 1/44 pint.	Vinegar .... 1/44 pint.	Vinegar .... 1/44 pint.
Molasses ...... 1/16 pint.	Molasses ...... 1/16 pint.	Molasses ...... 1/16 pint.
Pease, for	Pease, for	Pease, for
Coffee[a] ..... 1/66 quart.	Coffee ...... 1/66 quart.	Coffee ...... 1/66 quart.
DINNER	*DINNER*	*DINNER*
Brown Bread ...... 1/2 lb.	Brown Bread ...... 1/2 lb.	Brown Bread ...... 1/2 lb.
Fresh Beef .... 3/8 lb.	Salt Pork .... 3/8 lb.	Fresh Beef .... 3/8 lb.
Potatoes....... 1/44 bush.	Potatoes....... 1/44 bush.	Potatoes....... 1/44 bush.
Salt .... 3/88 lb.	Salt .... 3/88 lb.	Salt .... 3/88 lb.
Pepper .... 1/44 oz.	Pepper .... 1/44 oz.	Pepper .... 1/44 oz.
Vinegar .... 1/44 pint.	Vinegar .... 1/44 pint.	Vinegar .... 1/44 pint.
Pease for	Pease for	Pease for
Soup .... 2/66 quart.	Soup .... 2/66 quart.	Soup .... 2/66 quart.
Flour .... 1/15 lb.	Flour .... 1/15 lb.	Flour .... 1/15 lb.
Soup .... 1 quart.	Soup .... 1 quart.	Soup .... 1 quart.
SUPPER	*SUPPER*	*SUPPER*
Brown Bread ...... 3/8 lb.	Indian Meal.... 1/88 bush.	Indian Meal.... 1/88 bush.
Molasses ...... 1/16 pint.	Molasses ...... 1/16 pint.	Molasses ...... 1/16 pint.

[a] As a cost-cutting measure, dried peas were ground and mixed into coffee.
SOURCE: "Report of the Board of Inspectors of the Provincial Penitentiary for 1838," *Appendix to the Journal of the House of Assembly of Upper Canada*, 1839, 209.

Prisoners at Kingston had little recourse against the deficient diet. As a matter of defence, several penitentiary officers testified to the commission that the prisoners had not complained about the quality of the food. Given the potential for swift retribution, the lack of vocal complaint is unsurprising. However, other evidence pointed to the degree of suffering caused by the diet and the measures taken by prisoners to survive. Gleeson testified that he had known convicts to take salt from the dinner table in their handkerchiefs. During the day, the convicts ate salt to stimulate their thirst so they could drink enough water "to fill up their guts" (169) Other convicts found unconventional sources of food throughout the penitentiary. Keely reported that he had seen convicts with cold mush in their hands that they had stolen from the hog pens. Ex-keeper McCarthy confirmed Keely's testimony: a convict named Bernard would go "twenty times to the hog-pen, and bring in offal, such as potatoes, from the hogs, and divide it among the Convicts" (169). Other prisoners had been seen eating out of slop buckets as they delivered them to the hogs.

The weight of the Brown Commission came down upon Warden Smith and ended his tenure at Kingston Penitentiary. The commissioners concluded simply, "We consider it a good and valid reason for the removal of the Warden or any other Officer of a Penitentiary, that he has not come up to the full standard of efficiency. Sins of omission as well as sins of commission, we hold, should be summarily visited with dismissal" (290). The litany of abuses, mismanagement, and corruption all pointed to the penitentiary's fundamental failure to effect the reformation of criminals. The penitentiary chaplain, R. V. Rogers, distilled the argument that prevailed with the commission: "The objects of such a prison have been totally misunderstood by the authorities; the Warden and Inspectors appeared to view the prison merely as a place of security. . . . The fact is, that nothing can be worse than the present condition of the Penitentiary as a moral school" (120). Other witnesses advanced similar accusations. William Smith disparaged the warden for his failure to provide religious instruction, library books, or time with the chaplains. This charge, however, represented no small measure of short-term revisionism by the Brown Commission. At no time in the first fifteen years of the penitentiary were the designers, administrators, or inspectors at Kingston explicitly interested in or charged with convict reformation. Still, the commission emphasized this failure, foreshadowing the direction of penitentiary reform in the aftermath of the Smith regime. Kingston

Penitentiary had been constructed on the Auburn plan with the expectation of absolute disciplinary control and industrial profitability. On these foundations, reformers would attempt to add considerations of individual moral reformation.

LABOUR IN THE CONFEDERATION ERA

The first contracts with outside manufacturers were secured in 1849, providing prisoner labour for shoemaking and cabinetmaking. A tailoring shop was added the following year. Tradesmen in the first two industries again protested on the grounds of both unfair competition and the disrespect that teaching their trades to convicts brought upon their craft.[69] Contract labour, however, continually failed to fulfill its economic potential. By the mid-1850s, out of five contract operations at Kingston, only two were employing their full complement of workers: because contractors could not make profits under the contract terms, they reduced the rate of work. In 1857 they requested a reduction in the price of daily labour as well as a 50 percent reduction in the number of convicts employed. While contractors struggled to make profits under the terms of agreements signed with the penitentiary, wardens and inspectors made constant concessions to the contractors. But by the 1850s, the contract labour system, even at the reduced rates, was defraying a significant portion of the penitentiary's maintenance costs.[70] Still, while the board of inspectors heartily supported the contract system, officials at Kingston Penitentiary often lamented the negative effect that outside contractors had on discipline. Not only did they bring prisoners into contact with outside influences through private managers and foremen, but the continued concession to the needs of contract labour undermined the authority of penitentiary officials.[71]

After Confederation, contract holders operating from Kingston Penitentiary struggled to find profitable outlets for the products of prison labour. By 1875 an economic crisis in Ontario and Québec had dealt a serious blow to industries at Kingston as the contracts for locksmithing, shoemaking, cabinetmaking, and carpentry all lapsed or were cancelled.[72] The 1870s and 1880s also saw more vigorous opposition to penal contractual labour, first from the Canadian Labour Union and then from the Canadian Trades and Labour Congress, which protested teaching trades to convicts.[73] H. Clare Pentland argues that Canadian organized labour in the 1870s was relatively ineffective in its opposition to penitentiary labour and, at the same time, was not unduly harmed since the economic reach of penitentiary industries was very limited.[74] The penitentiary labour project was dramatically hobbled by the low skill level of the prisoner workforce. Even when productive labour was available, some wardens claimed that it was impossible to find skilled prisoners to undertake such industries. Warden John Foster at Dorchester noted in 1888 that the number of skilled mechanics was extremely small and the majority of prisoners were "a class difficult to train in the use of tools."[75]

In 1897 Douglas Stewart, the penitentiary inspector, reported the same troubling phenomenon throughout the entire penitentiary system: "A striking feature of the returns . . . is the undue proportion of those who have not had the advantage of a training in any trade or profession, and who consequently have been seriously handicapped in the race for existence."[76] In the absence of skilled labour, officials turned to non-productive tasks such as stone breaking and oakum picking.[77] These forms of labour contributed little economically and, more problematically, carried the negative associations of "hard labour," which was considered a form of punishment and granted little in the way of the expected moral reformation.

In spite of the fact that prison labour was not economically viable, reformers in the post-Confederation era continued to promote its importance to the larger penitentiary project. The discourse surrounding labour was distinctly moral, positioning labour as the primary agent in the reformation of criminal individuals. According to Inspector Moylan, the personal qualities bestowed by participation in penitentiary labour included the "formation of habits of industry, self-control, and the feeling of self-respect created by a sense of independence."[78] The potential for developing such qualities was frequently cited as the primary reason for keeping the prisoners working, although proponents of prison labour saw other benefits as well. In 1876 Moylan stated, "The object to be obtained by the employment of prisoners at labour is threefold: Firstly, to create a deterrent effect on the convict himself, and on the criminal class; secondly, to produce a reformatory effect on the prisoner; and thirdly to recoup as far as possible, the cost of his maintenance."[79]

Although Moylan constructed penitentiary labour as one of the primary agencies of moral reformation, specific discussion about how such reform actually took place seldom occurred. Moylan distinguished labour from other reformatory influences offered by the penitentiary. "While education and religion are quickly forgotten," he wrote, "the lessons of industrial labour stay with the prisoner long after his sentence ends."[80] He also suggested that it was not imprisonment itself but the act of working that transformed the criminal. Such discourse demonstrates the ideological weight given to labour, but it also points to the prevailing construction of all penitentiary inmates as workers. In 1880 Moylan wrote, "We should not lose sight of the fact that, the prisoner must have been, or at any rate, ought to have been a worker before he was committed to prison. The crime or offence for which he is now undergoing punishment by enforced labour and detention, has not cancelled his existence; it has only made his retirement to a certain extent from the labour market compulsory."[81]

The penitentiary provided the compulsion for convicts to return to the productive world in the practical as well as the moral sense. In reformers' eyes, labour would make men whole again. In 1886 Moylan wrote, "The convict should be taught to respect labour and to follow it as one of the best means of attaining self-respect, of manhood, and the way to supporting himself, upon his liberation, through the fruits of his own energy and industry."[82] Moylan's faith in the reformatory potential of labour was curiously disconnected from the reality of prison populations in the nineteenth century. For a number of reasons, he could not see the differentiation between the producing classes "outside" and the criminal classes "inside." In addition to the threat of competition, organized labour opposed the penitentiary on the grounds that criminals could never attain their respectability or their skill. This distinction, as we will see below, would be increasingly marked by a variety of medical classifications of who could and could not be considered a worker in the penitentiary.

Reform

The 1850s were a turning point for the Canadian penitentiary. The Brown Commission initiated a new spirit of penal reform that dramatically changed penitentiary administration in Canada and set the stage for the federal penitentiary system of the post-Confederation era. On the one hand, much about the penitentiary was resistant to change. Kingston continued to be based on the Auburn system of industrial discipline, and the "bricks and mortar" of the institution, still in the final stages of completion by the 1850s, created a rigid institutional organization that was difficult to transform. On the other hand, the ideology of the penitentiary underwent dramatic changes, quickly transforming from a Lockean perspective that stressed punishment, retribution, and deterrence to a far more liberal concept based on individual transformation and moral persuasion. This transformation was influenced by the rise of a new reform movement that set new priorities for the modern penitentiary.

This chapter tracks the parallels between Canadian penal reform and international reform movements. I begin with a discussion of the most influential reform thinkers and promoters in the years after 1850 in both America and England. I then connect this international movement to developments in the Canadian penitentiary as it moved forward from the 1849 Brown Commission. These developments provide a critical context for understanding the federal penitentiary system that was established in the decades following Confederation.

GEORGE BROWN'S REFORM PRESCRIPTION

A second Brown Commission report was filed ten months after the first, in April 1849. It was concerned with finding solutions to the ruinous direction taken by Kingston Penitentiary in its first fifteen years. Significantly, the need for a penitentiary was never explicitly questioned. Instead, Brown turned his attention to other prison regimes that might provide some direction. The solutions offered in the second report hint at a new direction of prison reform in the aftermath of Smith's regime. Brown proposed that the penitentiary be reformed along moral principles: indeed, the language of moral reformation permeated the second report. The commissioners enjoined "Christian people" to ensure that "prisons shall not become the moral tomb of those who enter them, but rather schools where the ignorant are enlightened and the repentant strengthened—in which . . . the permanent moral reform of the convict is the chief aim" (Brown Commission, 281). The idea of moral reform was not wholly new. When Thomson and Macaulay surveyed American penitentiaries in the 1830s, they had found that both the Auburn and Philadelphia systems placed heavy emphasis on reformation. Although the Upper Canadian leaders had been impressed by this priority (though not as moved as with the potential for profit), subsequent reformers would recognize that promises of moral reform were vastly exaggerated.

Although many American penitentiaries were suffering similar setbacks to those that plagued Kingston, the Brown Commission looked south for solutions. In late 1848, Brown and fellow commissioner William Bristow travelled to seven states to inspect penitentiary systems on which they could base their recommendations for Kingston Penitentiary. Whereas previous Canadian delegations had been swayed by the Auburn system, Brown and Bristow were not impressed with the three New York State penitentiaries—Auburn, Sing Sing, and Clinton. In part, this stemmed from the depth of their penitentiary experience accrued during the Kingston investigation: they asked different questions than had previous delegations, and they inspected these institutions with a more critical eye. They were troubled that American penitentiary administrations had become completely partisan and were swept from office with every political change in the state legislature. Although they noted that the prisons provided several tips for the management of a contract labour system, the commissioners were disappointed to observe that moral reform played no part in the New York prison regime.

Even though Auburn had had a critical influence over the establishment of Kingston Penitentiary, by 1848 it seemed to offer nothing more to the reform of the Canadian system. Brown and Bristow were also unconvinced by the separate-system institutions they inspected at Philadelphia and Boston, despite the advantages they observed. They found the discipline and regularity of the separate system impressive and were genuinely moved by the depth of feeling invested by the Prison Discipline Society in the principles of reform. They considered Cherry Hill a surprisingly dignified and enlightened institution with humane discipline and an impressive concern with moral reformation. The commissioners found the prisoners well fed and their demeanour "respectful and subdued; no bitterness or feeling was manifested, no rudeness, and very little sullenness" (286). The fundamental drawback of the separate system, however, was the prevalence of mental illness associated with constant solitary confinement. There was much debate about the mental illness statistics and few conclusions about their meaning, but incidents of mental illness were too high for Brown and Bristow to ignore. Officials at the Cherry Hill penitentiary defended their institution against charges of higher-than-normal incidents of mental illness. They stated to Brown and Bristow that the silent system exhibited as much insanity as the separate system but that insanity was more frequently identified under conditions of solitary confinement. The commissioners were not furnished with statistics that could confirm such claims or allow comparison of one institution to another. Still, one return from Cherry Hill indicated that the institution had recorded 119 cases of insanity from 1837 to 1846, and this number appeared excessive on its own terms. By contrast, the commissioners reported that the Charlestown penitentiary in Massachusetts, organized on the congregate Auburn system, recorded only nine cases of insanity in the same period (286).

Brown and Bristow were particularly moved by what they witnessed at Charlestown, where the liberal views of the warden, Frederick Robinson, struck a chord with them. Robinson's first annual report stressed his commitment to kindness and moral reform above all other principles. This created a very different prison regime than that proposed by previous advocates of the Auburn system. The rule of silence was considerably relaxed among the prisoners. They received letters and visits from friends and family, were dressed in better quality clothing, and enjoyed choir practice and a debating society. The commissioners noted, "The great aim of the system is to raise the self-esteem of the Convict, to rouse his ambition, and to prove to him the beneficial results of morality and industry" (282).

The Massachusetts penitentiary was also unique in that it considered imprisonment itself as punishment and offered no other sanctions or punishments after the arrival of prisoners. "The system does not contemplate deterring the evil-doer outside, or deterring the discharged Convict by a knowledge of the hardships of the penalty from a return to evil courses," reported the commission. "Everything is done to make the prisoner comfortable and happy and remove from his mind all feeling of degradation" (282). The commissioners were also impressed that the Massachusetts penitentiary was financially solvent to a degree unparalleled at other prisons. For twenty-seven years, convict labour had defrayed the entire cost of food, salaries, and transportation for the prisoners (283). The commission was careful to note that the success of the "ultra-humane" system at Massachusetts was made possible only by the fact that convicts would be released into an enlightened New England society where "active benevolence" was at work to help the former prisoner in a way that strengthened the resolve of the reformed man. The suggestion was that less-enlightened societies could not abandon the deterrent principle of punishment so easily (283).

After detailing what worked and what did not in contemporary American penitentiaries, the second Brown Commission report made suggestions for reforming Kingston Penitentiary. The commissioners sketched a vision of an institution purely devoted to the moral refor- mation of its inmates through education: "As of first importance, we earnestly recommend that the means of moral, religious and secular instruction, shall occupy much greater prominence than they at pres- ent do in our own or any of the American Penitentiaries" (292). The recommendations stressed that the pecuniary interest of the peniten- tiary must never stand in the way of the reformation of the criminals. The commission quoted John Howard, a name seldom invoked by the previous Kingston Penitentiary administration, in his argument for a more moral penitentiary. Howard had stated that the true prin- ciples of the prison system ought to be "to seclude the prisoners from their former associates; to separate those of whom hopes might be entertained from those who are desperate; to teach them useful trades; to give them religious instruction; and to provide them with a recommendation to the world and the means of obtaining an honest livelihood after the expiration of their term of punishment" (297).

Although the commissioners championed a return to reform principles, their report was short on detailed recommendations for specific reforms at Kingston Penitentiary. They proposed a combina- tion of the two dominant prison systems, congregate and separate. This was to be implemented as a multi-staged disciplinary process in which the newly arrived convict would be isolated at the discre- tion of the warden and chaplain. Once the prospect of reformation had been assessed by these officials, the convict could be placed into the congregate system to labour with the other prisoners. A system of classification would place similar prisoners in work gangs that were isolated from the rest of the prison population in order to prevent "the worst evil" of the congregate system in which the convict became known to too many prisoners (288).

The report also stressed the importance of ecclesiastical and secular education as the foundation of moral reformation. In the Smith era, religious observance in the penitentiary had been erratic. While there had been a resident Protestant chaplain, a Catholic priest had visited very infrequently and services for both denominations had been irregular. Brown was an evangelical Catholic and this lack of spiritual guidance in the penitentiary greatly troubled him. The commissioners recommended full-time and salaried chaplains of both denominations. They suggested that regular divine services be held and that all convicts attend Sabbath school. Much like the provisions for religion, education in the early penitentiary had been haphazard. Convicts had taught each other in a short thirty-minute period after dinner, but there had been no regular program of instruction. Some convicts who could read would do so, but others were unlikely to improve their abilities during incarceration. The Brown Commission stressed education as a primary component of moral reformation: "Holding, as we do, that ignorance is the most fruitful parent of crime, we would recommend the cultivation of the intellectual as well as the moral faculties of the convicts" (294). Thus, the report suggested a shift in the direction of an adult reformatory rather than a penitentiary. This was a dramatic departure.

The Brown Commission proposed to reorganize penitentiary governance. The suggestions for organizing the administration of Kingston Penitentiary were subsequently enshrined in the 1851 *Act for the Better Management of the Penitentiary* (hereafter *Penitentiary Act*). These changes would provide the administrative structure to carry forward the reform agenda. First, to avoid the power struggles that had plagued Smith's regime, it was suggested that the warden have absolute authority within the penitentiary. The warden would be no mere functionary of statute or regulation. Instead, the commissioners stressed that "a higher, a holier purpose must guide his every action. . . . His position, and so he must feel it, is that of a high minister of justice appointed to fulfill the benevolent object of the Penitentiary—the reformation of the unfortunate men committed to his care" (290). The *Penitentiary Act* required the warden "to have in charge the health, conduct and safe keeping of the Prisoners; to examine into and seek the success of the religious, moral and industrial appliances used for the reformation of the convicts; and to exercise over the whole establishment a close supervision and personal direction."[1] The intent of such an expansive mandate was clear—it provided for a single seat of authority and responsibility for all matters in the penitentiary. Henry Smith had claimed ignorance of many aspects of the institution under his control; the new warden would be responsible for every aspect of the penitentiary.

Balancing the authority of the warden would be a newly empowered inspectorate. The report suggested that two paid inspectors, appointed by the government, should replace the previous system of local worthies who had volunteered their time and possessed little expertise about penal matters. The new inspectors would provide a check on the authority and administration of the warden. This would be undertaken through constant inspection of Kingston Penitentiary and its financial affairs, essentially making the penitentiary administration directly responsible to the provincial government. More importantly in terms of the new concern with reform, Brown suggested that these inspectors would serve as the conduit to the larger world of prison reform through communication with various philanthropic associations and individuals engaged in reform work throughout the Western world (291).

The new position was intended to be far more administrative than inspectorial. The inspectors were made responsible for the "system of discipline and management pursued in the Penitentiary, and for its success and practical efficiency."[2] In spite of this, the office of inspector held no executive power and was restricted to giving instructions and policy to the warden. Acting as the eyes of the government, the inspectors were expected to make monthly visits to the penitentiary during which every cell was to be visited, every department observed, and each financial and duty register scrutinized. All of this was to be communicated to the government in a system that was intended to rationalize penitentiary administration and open it to the principles of responsible government (290).

Two other reforms characterized the 1851 *Penitentiary Act.* The first was a more specific declaration of the principles of reform that were central to Brown's criticisms of the early institution. This stipulated detailed instructions on the material conditions of imprisonment at the institution, including an expanded role for the penitentiary surgeon and a more rational program of medical inspection. These material changes were intended to make imprisonment more humane through better diet, clothing, cells, and standards of hygiene. The second reform concerned the new spirit of individual reformation. The central figure in this reform was the penitentiary chaplain. The *Penitentiary Act* stipulated that the Protestant and Catholic chaplains be "diligent in seeing and conversing with the convicts at all reasonable times in the cells, or in his private room, or in the Hospital, and in administering to them such instruction and exhortations as may be calculated to promote their spiritual welfare, moral reformation and due subordination."[3] As part of this moral project, the chaplain was expected to be one part confidant and one part criminologist. He was responsible for keeping a register tracking the personal history of each convict under his care, including personal details about education, habits of temperance, the crime committed, and admissions of guilt or innocence. In addition, the chaplain was to report on his conversations with each convict in order to track his progress, both "morally and intellectually." Much like the administrative duties of the warden, the moral responsibility of the chaplain was a heavy burden: the 1851 *Penitentiary Act* essentially made the chaplain the primary facilitator of moral reformation for every convict in the penitentiary. The chaplain was aided by a new full-time school instructor, who would provide basic secular instruction to each inmate.

These points of education, religion, and reformation generated much tension in the decade after the new statute. Through his recommendations and their encapsulation in the new *Penitentiary Act,* Brown emerged not just as a critic of the former administration but as the leading advocate for prison reform in Canada. He envisioned an evangelical and philanthropically oriented system of punishment that would finally succeed in the aim of reforming criminal offenders. However, after the close of the commission of inquiry, Brown was no longer connected to the administration of Kingston Penitentiary. In his place, the dual inspectorate and new warden assumed the task of carrying forward the reforms enshrined in the 1851 *Penitentiary Act*. The tensions that developed between these two administrative poles characterized the evolution of penitentiary reform and practice in the 1850s.

REFORM IN ACTION? THE PENITENTIARY IN THE 1850S

The 1851 *Penitentiary Act* legislated that the dual inspectorate should be the promoter of contemporary reform thought in the Canadian penal system. The first inspectors appointed by the governor general in Council were Andrew Dickson and Wolfred Nelson. Dickson, a former sheriff of the United Counties of Lanark and Renfrew, had connections to the new Reform government; this secured him the appointment. His counterpart, Wolfred Nelson, brought a more dynamic wealth of experience to the position. The son of an English schoolmaster, Nelson grew up at Sorel in the British military stockade. He apprenticed as a surgeon with the British army and served as a medical officer in the War of 1812. After ten years of medical practice in Lower Canada, Nelson experienced a political reawakening as a Reformer, casting off his Tory background. His experience among the French-Canadian people certainly motivated the transformation. Entering politics in 1827, he narrowly defeated the Tory incumbent in the riding of William-Henry, which encompassed his home town of Sorel.

After serving seven years in the House of Assembly, Nelson travelled to England, where his political leanings became more radical. He despised the abuses of the ruling class and, upon returning to Canada in 1837, aligned himself with the Patriote party. Joining forces with Louis-Joseph Papineau, Nelson was thrust into the Lower Canada Rebellion, serving as a determined military leader of the tiny Patriote forces. His initial victory at Saint-Denis cast him as a hero, but within a month, the British had captured him and he was imprisoned in the Montreal gaol. Nelson never came to trial for his role in the Rebellion; instead, along with six other Patriotes, he was banished to Bermuda by Lord Durham in 1838. But his banishment was revoked, and he returned to New York State. When his friend Louis-Hippolyte La Fontaine became attorney general in the Baldwin-Lafontaine government, Nelson was allowed to return to Montreal, where he established a new medical practice. He won election to the House again in 1844 and continued his fight for French-Canadian rights. In 1851 at the age of sixty, Nelson was appointed penitentiary inspector, along with Dickson. Given his turbulent and radical past, this represented a remarkable transformation in the shape of penitentiary governance compared to the Tory-dominated administrations of Kingston's first two decades.[4] Nelson considered himself uniquely suited to the position. On his appointment, he wrote, "My sojourn for seven months in the Montreal Jail gave me such a practical knowledge of prison affairs, the accursed abuses that prevailed there . . . and the uncalled for miseries that were inflicted on the prisoners induced me to accept."[5]

In 1852 Nelson presented a report to the government titled "A General Review of Prison Economics." In effect, this was his distillation of the penal reform ideas he had gathered in his first year as inspector. His views tended mainly toward practical remedies for the miseries of the prison experience. Drawing on his medical expertise, Nelson outlined new regulations for clothing, diet, and hygiene. While these details appear obvious to today's reader, they were stated emphatically by Nelson as a rebuke of an era of penal management during which such concerns were overshadowed by security and economy. The second primary concern Nelson addressed was related to the ideas of classification and isolation as defined by the Brown Commission recommendations. Nelson's statements on the necessity of identifying different levels of criminality show a penal system at odds with its basic disciplinary structure, which aimed to treat all prisoners exactly alike.

Nelson proposed identifying prisoners by their convicted crimes, a policy that was curiously punitive of the worst offenders. "Some mark should be put upon the worst class of prisoners, that their very dress may indicate the crimes of which they have been guilty." This was necessary, he explained, so that "a younger and lesser offender may know, that he is not so degraded as some others, and that this feeling may lead him to repentance and reformation."[6] Nelson suggested the harshest forms of classification for convicted murderers: they should be made to wear black with a scarlet "M" adorning their back and chest so that they could be identified and "shunned as if they were a walking pestilence, loathsome lepers whose very appearance would contaminate and defile." And finally, the murderers should be kept "forever apart" in a shed, visited only by the chaplain in a place inscribed with the words "The Murderer's Den: No Hope Here From Man."[7] Nelson's harsh approach may be attributable to the assassination of his friend Louis Marcoux during the 1834 election: the accused murderer had been acquitted, and this perceived injustice had enraged Nelson.[8]

Finally, Nelson's statement on the role of reformation was curiously vague, with few specifics about how a prisoner's transformation might actually occur. He simply suggested that more humane conditions and attention to prisoners' needs would result in their reformation: "In the vast majority of cases, reformation will assuredly follow a judicious and benign treatment, whereby the reckless will be subdued, the old offender reflect, and all will soon understand that they alone are to blame for the misfortunes to which they have been exposed." In even vaguer terms, the inspector suggested that long dormant feelings, smothered by bad association and habit, would be kindled into a bright flame. Much as Brown had argued, Nelson pointed to religious instruction as the spark that would ignite such feelings. His views on the religious duties of the chaplain also mirrored Brown's. Though he stressed that the chaplains should be fairly paid for their labour, Nelson echoed the high standards for the prison chaplains set in the 1851 *Penitentiary Act*. "It would be the fault of the clergyman," he wrote, "if he were not very soon beloved and revered, and if his visits were not anticipated with the utmost anxiety."[9]

Nelson's feelings about the reformation of prisoners were more ambivalent than those of Brown. His doubts may have stemmed in part from the ongoing debate throughout this period about whether the penitentiary should be punitive or reformative. Many Canadian authorities continued to subscribe to the idea that retributive punishment was more important. Although the idea of reformation had a toehold in the Canadian administration, it was still outweighed by the idea of punishment and deterrence. Nelson's positions on the penitentiary were particularly influenced by Sir Joshua Jebb, the British surveyor general of prisons. Jebb expressed his views on the purposes of imprisonment in 1856: "In carrying out a sentence of imprisonment, penal and reformatory objects should be equally kept in view, the penal element of discipline being first, not so much in importance as in order. Paley, however, says 'the end of punishment is twofold, amendment and example' thus placing the reformatory element first. Great caution, therefore, is necessary in maintaining the two elements in their due proportion, and judiciously introducing them according to circumstances."[10] Jebb, and British penal authorities in general, tended toward the more punitive side of the debate compared with their American counterparts. The Prison Discipline Society in Boston was most representative of the softer American reform position. Under the leadership of Rev. Louis Dwight, the society assumed an evangelical approach to prison discipline, stressing reformation, humanity, and the power of prayer in penitentiary administration. While ideas along these lines were introduced in Canada by Nelson and Brown, they ran headlong into the pragmatism of Canadian wardens, who tended toward the punishment perspective. This was particularly true of Henry Smith's replacement, D. A. Macdonell.

Macdonell was a former British military officer and commander in the Canadian militia. After serving as a justice of the peace, he was elected to the House of Assembly as a Reformer in 1834. Although he won re-election in 1836, he was defeated in three successive elections before being appointed Crown lands agent and sheriff of the Eastern District in 1848. When Henry Smith was suspended during the Brown inquiry that year, Macdonell became his temporary replacement. The appointment was made permanent in 1851.[11] Although the new warden was familiar with reform ideas advanced by Brown and the dual inspectorate, he never truly adopted these positions in his administration of Kingston Penitentiary. Certainly less violent and punitive than his predecessor, Macdonell poured his energies into practical concerns, especially the security of the institution and the potential threat of uprising and riot. As Peter Oliver argues, Macdonell became increasingly convinced throughout the 1850s that many of the convicts were vicious and dangerous. (The development of this idea is explored in the next chapter.) Throughout the decade, he developed a resoundingly bleak view of human nature. It followed that only unbending strength in his role as warden would keep the penitentiary from boiling over into violence and chaos.[12]

Macdonell's resistance to placing reformation at the centre of the penitentiary project was coupled with the failure of the chaplaincy to play a transformative role in how the penitentiary operated. Brown and Nelson had counted on the chaplains to drive forward the "moral machinery" of the institution. However, both chaplains, Catholic Angus MacDonell (no relation to the warden) and Protestant Hannibal Mulkins, were largely indifferent to the high expectations placed upon their office. In the early 1850s, MacDonell was unhappy that his suggestions and criticisms were ignored by the administration, and in the aftermath of being reprimanded for offering these critiques, he largely withdrew from taking an active role in the daily affairs of the penitentiary. Mulkins was just as indifferent and often failed to perform his daily spiritual duties.[13]

Among the more striking examples of resistance to the reform program was the penitentiary staff members' attitude toward the education of inmates. Officials balked at the idea that an hour of every workday should be devoted to education. The most vocal opponent of prison education was chaplain MacDonell, who complained, "The condition of the convicts . . . is better, and the means of acquiring knowledge greater, than that of the majority of children and honest and industrious farmers in many parts of the country."[14] This was a common sentiment among penitentiary officials who were generally reluctant to provide more education than was strictly necessary. The following year the Inspector's report stated: "Too often it occurs, when a youth has had 'some smattering of learning,' above what was required for the ordinary wants of life, he must aim, to be sure, at some higher position! He must become a professional gentleman! Or a merchant—too frequently merely to encumber avocations already overstocked. The education that should be given in all charitable institutions should be such . . . [that] undue aspirations will not be entertained nor will ambition lead astray."[15] This position essentially echoed that of Joshua Jebb, who believed that prisoner instruction was generally wasteful: "I am decidedly of opinion there is more school instruction and far less labour than is useful or necessary. . . . There is no use instructing criminal children unless they are in some way provided for on discharge."[16] On this issue, Andrew Dickson distinguished himself from his co-Inspector Wolfred Nelson. He signed a "dissenting report" that refuted these attitudes, calling them unenlightened and insisting on the benefits that followed from basic education. He stressed that the education at Kingston was not comparable to a classical or even common-school education: "The institution is by no means 'a real academy of arts and sciences,' as on the contrary it only affords the convicts . . . the means of obtaining what society ought long since to have secured them—the elements merely of a useful education."[17]

As much as they argued for the importance of education in the penitentiary, both inspectors evidently realized the limitations of their position. They could recommend an education program and even stipulate the conditions under which it should proceed, but they were powerless to secure the commitment of penitentiary administrators and staff at Kingston. Thus, while some key reform ideas permeated the inspectors' office in the 1850s, the adoption of these ideas at Kingston Penitentiary was extremely slow. The resistance and indifference of authorities in the penitentiary often cancelled much of the reformatory intent of the 1851 *Penitentiary Act*. But little attention was called to this failure by the inspectors or penitentiary administrators. Because Macdonell's regime was more financially stable and the prison more secure than under Henry Smith, official reports toward the end of the 1850s merely praised the penitentiary for its efficiency.

At the end of the 1850s, a new penal philosophy developed on the periphery of the British penal system. While Joshua Jebb maintained his grip on Pentonville and his influence over British penal policy, prison authorities in more far-flung locations experimented with new ideas about penitentiary organization and practice. The most revolutionary of these was Alexander Maconochie, a Royal Navy officer with a keen interest in the colonial enterprise. In 1836 Maconochie joined Sir John Franklin as his private secretary on a voyage to Van Diemen's Land, a British penal colony near Australia. In 1837 the Society for the Improvement of Prison Discipline asked him to report on the treatment of convicts that he had observed there. His report, tabled in the British House of Commons in 1837, was so damning that Franklin dismissed him. In 1840 Maconochie was given a chance to put his ideas about penal reform into practice when he was appointed superintendent of the British penal colony on Norfolk Island.[18]

Sitting 930 miles northeast of eastern Australia, Norfolk Island was among the most remote prison colonies in the British Empire and probably featured the worst conditions of any penal regime under British or American control at that time. Violence and fear ruled the island, which housed "doubly convicted" criminals—Australian convicts who had committed crimes while serving their original penal sentence. Riots and uprisings rocked the penal colony in the years before 1840, and as many as thirteen prisoners were executed for murders committed within the colony. After assuming command, Maconochie moved swiftly to implement a new regime. He instituted a "mark system" based on a prison currency to be earned through labour and good behaviour. Prisoners were grouped into teams and charged with earning enough marks to "repay" their debt to the government. To relieve overcrowding, Maconochie allowed prisoners to build their own dwellings with personal garden plots attached. He built Protestant and Catholic churches and a school, and organized an orchestra and a choir. He also allowed the prisoners to form their own police force under the command of prison officials, and he settled disputes with public trials in which the convicts participated. As symbolic gestures, he allowed the prisoners to dress in civilian clothing and permitted crosses and tombstones on the graves of deceased prisoners.

During Maconochie's tenure, the colony on Norfolk Island became safe and free of violence. However, these progressive reforms incited a firestorm of indignation and anger in both Australia and England when the news reached his superiors. The biggest controversy was caused by reports that Maconochie had allowed the prisoners to participate in a celebration of Queen Victoria's birthday in May 1840. He had served drams of severely diluted rum to the convicts and organized a pageant with singing and theatrics in honour of the Queen.[19] He was recalled from his position in 1844 and did not work again in prison administration until 1849, when he was appointed governor of the new prison in Birmingham. This appointment lasted only two years.[20]

While Maconochie did not enjoy a distinguished career as a prison administrator, he found a receptive audience for his ideas in the English prison reform community. He authored several works on prison reform, the most influential being *Australiana* (1837), his condemnation of the Van Diemen's Land colony, and *Crime and Punishment* (1846). At a time when British penitentiaries under Colonel Jebb were becoming more punitive and oppressive, Maconochie proposed taking penal reform in the opposite direction. Maconochie's *Crime and Punishment* laid out a series of reforms that, if implemented, would dramatically reorder the priorities of legal punishment. Placing moral reformation above punishment, Maconochie argued that British prisons had utterly failed in the mission of reforming criminals: "Our prisons and penal establishments are held to deteriorate, not improve: they receive men bad, and discharge them for the worse."[21] *Crime and Punishment* placed reformation at the centre of the penal question, asking, "Is moral evil incurable?—or have we not yet discovered the cure?" He argued that the old system contained no element of persuasion beyond physical degradation, which was combined with a "mystical" attachment to religion that falsely attempted to reconcile the infliction of violence.[22] Maconochie proposed providing prisoners with a clear choice to follow the path toward reformation and abstain from what was forbidden. He argued in 1847 that such a course was in stark contrast to prevailing penitentiary practice:

> Instead of working on the fears of those subjected to it, it seeks to call out their manly exertion and emulation. Instead of unnecessarily depressing, it seeks to raise them. Instead of subjecting them to a minute discipline which leaves them nothing to think of but to obey, it desires to give them a sphere of free agency, even while in prison, which shall exercise their powers of thought and self-command against the hour of their discharge. It is thus not content with making them good prisoners (though this is also among its objects), but it desires still more to train them to be good free men.[23]

Replacing compulsion through violence with rational appeals to self interest, Maconochie's mark system was revolutionary in that it completely reversed the role played by labour. Instead of sentencing men to a certain amount of time as a punishment, it sentenced them to a certain amount of labour. This meant that convicts could work toward their release. Maconochie argued that while their incarceration would still be punitive, their motivation for labour would be entirely different: "By substituting a powerful internal stimulus to exertion for that physical coercion which must be at best an imperfect and external one, while all necessary bondage and suffering as the consequences of crime would be retained, direct 'slavery' would be banished from among our secondary punishments."[24] The idea of voluntary labour as an inducement to reform may have had more resonance in Britain than in America, perhaps because contractual penal servitude was not practiced in British prisons. Also, British penitentiaries were far more likely to resort to brutalizing and unproductive labour such as the treadmill and the crank than were American prisons. Yet Maconochie's proposals were still a reversal of the basic relations of punishment in which physical compulsion was replaced with moral persuasion. Thus, *Crime and Punishment* proposed a progressive system of punishment that would assist the prisoner in advancing through the stages of his own reformation via the persuasion of labour.

The idea of a penal system built on progressive stages of labour was further developed and promoted in the Irish penal system under the direction of Sir Walter Crofton. Like most of the leading officials in the Victorian penal system, Crofton came from a military background. He retired from the Royal Artillery as a captain in 1845. While subsequently working as a magistrate, he became interested in prisons and reformatories, and in 1853 he was appointed as commissioner of inquiry into Irish prisons. The following year, he became director of Irish convict prisons and held this position until 1862.[25] Crofton's penal philosophy was based on the same principles advocated by Captain Maconochie at Norfolk Island. He proposed a system built around progressive stages that appealed to a prisoner's self interest as he or she progressed toward eventual release. Certainly influenced by Maconochie's writing from the 1840s, Crofton introduced a marks system to Irish prisons in 1855.[26] He also innovated the use of separate facilities for different categories of prisoners so that convicts would be housed in "intermediate" prisons that provided more freedoms before their release to society. The reform movement in 1850s Britain—organized around two societies, the Social Science Association and the National Reformatory Union—rallied around Crofton's ideas as the best chance for reforming the intellectually moribund British system. Its prominent members included Lord Brougham, Matthew Davenport Hill, Thomas Barwick Lloyd-Barker, and Mary Carpenter.

Just as Auburn and Pennsylvania had constituted two opposing camps in American reform debates, a divide opened between the Irish and the British systems in the late 1850s. The British system and its primary proponent, Sir Joshua Jebb, were regarded as more punitive and deterrence-oriented—the outgrowth of early American philosophy that had given birth to the separate system, which was replicated at Pentonville penitentiary. The Irish system was regarded as more progressive and enlightened, and as altogether scientific. The relative value of these systems was vigorously contested and debated by British authorities, but penal reformers in Britain and North American were taken with what appeared to be more advanced penal methods unfolding in the Irish system. Ultimately, the divide was manifested between penal reformers and penal administrators: reformers assumed the Irish position in their recommendations and administrators adhered to tested principles that stressed security.

At the end of the 1850s, penitentiary governance in Canada was reorganized again. In 1857 Inspector Nelson lobbied the Cartier-Macdonald government for the creation of a penitentiary board of directors that would extend the traditional powers of the inspectorship. The board would assume supervision of penal institutions (both the penitentiary and gaols), as well as public, charitable, and sanitary institutions. In effect, the new board would become a social welfare agency, overseeing a number of different institutions. The new statute, enacted in 1859, created a five-man board that consisted of Wolfred Nelson, as the chair; Dr. J. C. Taché, a Tory politician; Kingston Warden D. A. Macdonell; provincial auditor John Langton; and E. A. Meredith, former president of McGill College and one of the province's most senior civil servants. In one respect, the new board was a big step forward for penitentiary reform, and, indeed, for government involvement in social welfare institutions in Canada. The five-man board was stacked with political heavyweights. At least two of the members, Nelson and Meredith, were keenly interested in the cause of penal reform in Canada. Still, both Peter Oliver and Richard Splane note that the political structure in the provincial Department of Justice kept the board from having real influence over future legislation or decision making at the ministerial level.[27] Although the board became aware of these constraints in the early 1860s, the 1859 statute had given its members sufficient authority and independence to engage in direct criticism of the government and to push actively for new reforms in both penal and social welfare administration.

As a whole, the new board was an ambitious group, anxious to move the penitentiary further toward the goal of a reformatory institution along the lines of the Crofton system. Some board members were more enthusiastic than others. While Warden Macdonell did not revise his views on the necessity of punishment, E. A. Meredith took a leading role in pushing penitentiary governance closer to the reform position staked out by Crofton. Meredith expressed his view of reform in a biting critique of the Auburn-style discipline at Kingston Penitentiary. In a far-reaching analysis published in 1861, he likened the doors of Kingston Penitentiary to Dante's gates of hell—"Who enters here leaves hope behind." While he admitted that the penitentiary under Macdonell had perfected the Auburn style of discipline, he argued that this offered only a hopeless cycle of "rigid repression" and "uncompromising coercion."[28] All of this utterly failed to encourage reformation, self-reliance, self-respect, or self-control in penitentiary inmates. In the place of the Auburn system, Meredith endorsed the principles of "reformatory prison discipline," thus firmly aligning himself with reform movements in Britain and America.[29] In 1862 he summarized the basic elements of the reformatory prison discipline that he hoped to implement at Kingston:

1. A scheme of conduct classification of the convicts, accompanied by distinctive badges and money gratitudes [sic]

2. Every convict should be able to earn . . . the remission of a certain fixed portion of his sentence

3. Convicts who by their steady good conduct have risen to the highest class in the Penitentiary, should enjoy certain advantages in the institution . . . the main object of this phase of their convict life being to prepare them for their return to social life.[30]

Where the Auburn system endeavoured to treat every inmate exactly alike, the Crofton system recognized each prisoner as an individual who controlled the destiny of his or her eventual release. This was a significant departure that, in the view of reformers, would at last place individual reformation above the dictates of punishment and deterrence.

The Canadian penitentiary board adopted Crofton's reforms at the same time that American reformers were beginning to consider a similar position. The American prison reform movement was reinvigorated in the mid-1860s through the efforts of the New York

Prison Association. The association sponsored a comprehensive tour of penitentiaries and gaols throughout the United States and Canada, including Kingston Penitentiary. In their report of this tour, E. C. Wines and Theodore Dwight thoroughly condemned the state of the prisons they visited.[31] The authors endorsed the Crofton system as the most enlightened method of prison discipline. These ideas were affirmed in 1870 at an International Prison Congress in Cincinnati, where delegates set out forty-two principles governing the new direction in prison reform. The principles included several points that Canadian reformers, particularly Meredith, had made in the 1860s about the centrality of personal reformation to the prison reform project. For example, Principle 13 stated, "There must be serious conviction in the minds of prison officers that the imprisoned criminals are capable of being reformed." This idea was complemented by Principle 6: "The prisoner's destiny during his incarceration should be put in his own hands."[32] The influence of the leading British reformers on the new American direction was obvious, and although Canadian reformers were already convinced of the superiority of the Crofton system, the Cincinnati congress gave them what appeared to be a modern and rationalized model for penal reform.

The reform movement in Canada, represented largely by the penitentiary board created in 1859, rallied around the notion of reformatory prison discipline as the enlightened path forward for Canada's gaols and penitentiaries. In their 1866 annual report, the penitentiary board restated the principles of the reform program they intended to implement at Kingston, attempting to bring the Canadian system into greater harmony with the Crofton system. First, every inmate would go through an initial period of isolation. Second, each inmate would be classified according to his or her conduct by means of a "mark system." Finally, it would be in each convict's power to earn remission of a portion of his or her sentence.[33] However, the board's new optimism ran headlong into vigorous resistance from Warden Macdonell and Department of Justice officials. For example, in 1864 Macdonell reported that his views on penitentiary discipline were "quite decisive and fixed." As a caution against any relaxation of penitentiary discipline, he cited the "fearlessness and daring" of convicts and listed various "diabolical acts" committed by prisoners, including stabbings, escapes, and attempted murders of guards. He concluded, "I think it essential to express my decided opinion that any relaxation in its stringency would be dangerous to the peace and regularity which should be continually maintained. Moreover, I consider that the discipline in every particular, as now in force here, has been humanely carried out."[34] In view of his privileged position as both warden and penitentiary board member, Macdonell's opinions on discipline carried the day throughout the 1860s. However, Meredith continued to exercise considerable influence over the Department of Justice in the years immediately prior to Confederation and was responsible for drafting the first post-Confederation *Penitentiary Act* in 1868, the result of which was to dramatically increase the power of the penitentiary board in the governance of the new federal penitentiary system.

After Confederation, the federal government was pressed to create a national penitentiary system, and the new Department of Justice quickly established a presence for federal penitentiaries in all regions of the country by designating former colonial penitentiaries in the Maritimes as federal institutions. In 1868 the government assumed responsibility for the Saint John Penitentiary and the Halifax Penitentiary, both of which were fairly old but serviceable. Jonathan Swainger argues that the change to federal control of these institutions was more a symbol of nationhood than actual justice policy: "In effect, the image of a *national* system of penitentiaries was an early demonstration of the freshly minted and broadly conceived relationship between the public and federal government."[35] Five years later, the government created a federal penitentiary in Québec by transforming the St. Vincent de Paul youth reformatory outside of Montreal into a federal penitentiary. In 1872 the federal government designated Manitoba's Lower Fort Garry as a federal penitentiary and began construction of a new institution at Stony Mountain, outside of Winnipeg.[36] Newly constructed prisons opened in Manitoba and British Columbia in 1877 and 1878. By 1880 Canada had forged a more coherent network of penitentiaries. In that year, Halifax and Saint

John were closed and all federal prisoners transferred to the newly constructed Dorchester Penitentiary in New Brunswick.[37] This was the final configuration of the federal penitentiary system until the first decade of the twentieth century.

Drafting the new *Penitentiary Act* was Meredith's opportunity to truly implement the principles of the Crofton system in Canadian penitentiaries. The 1868 act contained several elements of that system. For example, it provided for gratuities paid to prisoners for overtime labour and drafted a system of rewards to balance the effect of punishments for bad behaviour. Because Meredith had identified Macdonell as a major impediment to reform, the act attempted to diminish the warden's executive power. Meredith designed an administrative structure that centralized all power in the penitentiary board and removed the warden as a voting member. Macdonell complained to Prime Minister (and Justice Minister) John A. Macdonald that he was being squeezed from the meaningful administration of the penitentiary.[38] When the warden finally retired in 1868, board member J. M. Ferres was appointed warden. However, the opportunity for the board to implement any of its reform platform at Kingston evaporated when Ferres died less than two years after his appointment. Almost as quickly as the reformers had seized the moment for significant change, it had passed. After Confederation, Meredith was removed from the penitentiary board and appointed under-secretary of state for the provinces.[39] Replacing Ferres as warden was John Creighton, an outsider to the small prison reform community. The new warden was a pragmatist, and his immediate concerns were practical issues, particularly overcrowding and the threat it posed to discipline, cleanliness, and order.

Following Meredith's departure from the penitentiary board, the Canadian reform movement utterly stalled. Without Meredith driving an agenda for change, the remaining penitentiary board directors— T. J. O'Neill, James King and F. X. Prieur—reverted to expressing praise for Kingston that was curiously disconnected from reality. In 1871 the board reported its satisfaction with the "moral advances" being made at Kingston under the new warden, John Creighton: "Experience proves almost daily that humane treatment, accompanied by some tangible tokens of recognition of good conduct, is the truly efficacious way of influencing the convict."[40] The praise for the new system was accompanied by a dose of nationalistic pride, one of the few times such a sentiment would appear in connection with Canadian penitentiaries. This pride was based on a comparison to American prisons. In 1872 the directors toured a number of penitentiaries in the United States and reported on the shocking discipline they witnessed:

> In passing through the work-shops, and seeing the prisoners at their allotted labours, they could not divest themselves of the feeling that they were looking at machines rather than human beings, so steady and regular, so involuntary and automatic did their motions appear. This rigid discipline and strict precision in the observance of the rules of the prisoners afford proof that the most rigorous and inexorable treatment is practiced to bring about such results. But the man of heart, the philanthropist, who regards the reformation and not the debasement and punishment of the criminal as the primary object to be attained in penal institutions, cannot approve of a system so repressive, so devoid of all sympathy, and so replete with severity.[41]

The directors suggested that there was no comparison to the contented prison population at Kingston. Their 1873 annual report quoted Creighton as saying that "in none of them are the convicts so healthy, and if I may use the expression, so happy looking as with us." Creighton even invoked the moral authority of reformer Mary Carpenter, who had visited Kingston in 1872 and had reportedly declared, "In the whole course of a life-long experience, in the old world and the new, [I have] never seen so large a number of convicts who exhibited fewer traces of crime or depravity in their aspect of being."[42] This peaceful state of affairs continued for another year, when Warden Creighton reiterated, "I still maintain that in few prisons, anywhere, will a more healthy, happy looking body of convicts be found than those detained in this penitentiary."[43] The positive tone of the penitentiary board reflected its success in attaining power in Canadian penitentiary administration. However, without an agitating force at its core, the board ceased to function as an agent of change and instead assumed the position of defending the status quo.

WOMEN'S PENAL REFORM

The women's penal reform movement developed on a parallel course with the larger cause of reform. In England, Elizabeth Fry initiated the cause of women's penal reform a generation after John Howard. Fry was a Quaker minister and an active anti-slavery campaigner. In 1813 she turned her attention to London's Newgate Prison. Much like Howard's original investigations, Fry found the conditions of women's imprisonment in a deplorable state. Although motivated by the mission of religious conversion, she realized that the amelioration of the physical suffering of woman prisoners was paramount. By 1816 she had initiated a group dedicated to improving conditions for women in prison. The Ladies Association for the Improvement of the Female Prisoners at Newgate organized Bible classes and workshops, and, most importantly, provided funds to hire a matron to oversee the care of female inmates. A decade later, Fry published *Observations in Visiting, Superintendence and Government of Female Prisoners,* which was based on the efforts she had poured into Newgate.[44]

Fry's volunteerism and writing advanced ideas that would finally come to dominate the women's prison reform movement in the 1850s. She stressed women's responsibilities to their "fallen sisters" and argued that women must take the lead in reforming their own sex. Building on this basic premise, penal reformers countered the popular notion that women could not be reformed, instead advocating for the conditions by which this moral project could succeed.[45] *New-York Tribune* editor Margaret Fuller devoted herself to these ideals in the 1840s, countering the notion that fallen women were lost to society. In an address to the female inmates of Sing Sing in 1844, Fuller told them, "The conduct of some now here was such that the world said: —'Women once lost are far worse than abandoned men, and cannot be restored.' But, no! It is not so! I know my sex better!" Fuller advanced environmental explanations for female crime, a perspective rarely employed in this era. As she told her audience at Sing Sing, "Born of unfortunate marriages, inheriting dangerous inclinations, neglected in childhood, with bad habits and bad associates, as certainly must be the case with some of you, how terrible will be the struggle when you leave this shelter!"[46]

The key issue in the women's reform movement was advocacy for separate institutions for female convicts. It was assumed that this first step would end the neglect and segregation of the early prison regimes. The proposals for female prisons were based on purely middle-class ideas about femininity, domesticity, and morality. Women's reformers advocated institutions that would stress domestic and feminine models in homes for "fallen women." The harsh discipline of penitentiaries and convict prisons would be replaced by "maternal guidance" of trained matrons. This impulse was also expressed in charitable institutions providing "aftercare" for discharged female convicts. In 1845, the female wing of the New York Prison Association opened a home for discharged prisoners—essentially a halfway house for women to gain their bearings and avoid arrest subsequent to release. After a short residency, discharged convicts were placed into domestic service.[47]

The women's penal reform movement in Canada closely paralleled the movement in England. Lucia Zedner notes that in the United Kingdom, there was no sustained women's movement that reflected the American interest in the plight of women prisoners. Zedner argues that by mid-century even the leading proponents of the movement in England, such as Fry, were uncertain of the direction that reform should take. The slow development in Canada not only reflected this morass but also illustrated the larger issue of Canadian authorities being slow to take up more comprehensive reform ideas from either England or the United States.

Zedner further argues that notions of individualization were more important for reformers concerned with women offenders than for those involved with men. Victorian prisons routinized men's punishment to the detriment of individual reformation. Zedner suggests that, in contrast, the women's penal reform movement stressed the importance of the rehabilitation of each individual.[48] There is little evidence, however, that such an attitude was ever replicated in Canada. Canadian authorities certainly accepted that "separate" accommodations and punishments were necessary, but this was often the extent of the consideration for the unique needs of female prisoners. Canadian penal authorities conceded that the women at Kingston should be housed in better and separate accommodations. Mostly as a result of the urging of the Brown Commission, Kingston Penitentiary began construction of a separate institution for women in 1852 and completed the structure the following year. It was entirely self contained and surrounded by a high wall, and it featured workspace and hospital facilities dedicated for female prisoners. Nonetheless, by the mid-1850s, the new women's quarters were already overcrowded and some inmates were forced to sleep in workrooms or corridors.[49] Much like solutions proposed in this era for juvenile offenders, reformers increasingly advocated for the use of non-penal institutions operated by churches and private charities. In 1859 Wolfred Nelson praised female asylums in Lower Canada run by the Sisters of Mercy religious order. Magdalen Asylums—or Bon Pasteurs, as they were called in Montreal—were essentially workhouses for poor and destitute women. Penitentiary authorities looked to such institutions to assume the work of female reformation that had been all but abdicated by penitentiary officials. Attitudes about feminine criminality were slowly thawing in this era. Prior to the 1850s, there was little discussion about the reformation of female inmates. In 1859 Nelson praised the Magdalen Asylum in Montreal for carrying out the work of reformation:

> The whole economy of this refuge is perfect and admirable; the
> kind and sisterly treatment soon subdues the most hardened,
> leads to serious reflection, and ere long to repentance and reformation and as soon as their bodily and mental health is restored they

are permitted to leave this benign and hospitable retreat and are generally received in the bosom of some respectable family as assistants or domestics, and this at a great distance from their former haunts and associates as can be obtained, for the good sisters are always on the look out to procure for them respectable and comfortable situations.[50]

Despite Kingston Penitentiary making no marked changes in how it administered female convicts in the post-Confederation era, some of the issues of overcrowding were relieved by the opening of the Mercer Reformatory in Toronto in 1874, which gave magistrates another option for the imprisonment of female offenders.

JAMES MOYLAN AND CANADIAN PENAL REFORM

Though politically neutralized, the Canadian reform movement was given new life with the appointment of penitentiary board member James G. Moylan, whose appointment to the penitentiary administration was an exercise in Tory patronage. An Irish Catholic newspaper writer and editor, Moylan arrived in the United States from Ireland in 1851 and until 1856 wrote for the *New-York Daily Times* as a Washington correspondent. He moved to Upper Canada in 1856 and worked as a professor of classics and literature in the Jesuit college at Guelph until 1858. He purchased the *Catholic Citizen of Toronto* newspaper in 1859 and renamed it the *Canadian Freeman*. Through the *Freeman*, Moylan turned his focus to the defence of Irish Catholic rights in Canada. The paper was fiercely partisan, aiming its vitriol against Clear Grits and voicing consistent support for John A. Macdonald's nationalist cause. Moylan's *Freeman* was instrumental in securing Irish Catholic support for Macdonald during the first federal election campaign of 1867, and the new prime minister was appropriately grateful.

Anticipating a reward for his services to the Conservative Party, Moylan set his sights on the wardenship of Kingston Penitentiary. When John Creighton was selected to replace D. A. Macdonell, Moylan was shuffled into the foreign service as emigration agent of Canada in Ireland. However, in 1872 Macdonald appointed him to the penitentiary board of directors.[51] By 1875 the only significant changes to the penitentiary system concerned centralization under the Department of Justice, which occurred at the expense of the reform agenda of the penitentiary board. When John A. Macdonald's Tories were defeated in 1875, the new Liberal government under Alexander Mackenzie drafted revised penitentiary legislation that significantly weakened the power of the penitentiary board. Authority and control was returned to the Department of Justice. The penitentiary board was disbanded and James Moylan appointed as the lone penitentiary inspector for the entire dominion. As the inheritor of the reform legacy of Brown, Nelson, and Meredith, Moylan faced tremendous challenges due to the inertia within the penitentiary system and the Department of Justice after 1875. But he also focused his efforts on taking prison reform in a new and increasingly insular direction with an emphasis on issues of individual criminality and reformation. In contrast to the sunny portrait drawn by his predecessors, Moylan often saw a much darker side of Canadian penitentiary inmates.

Moylan's first step as penitentiary inspector was to reconnect with the international prison reform movement. This proved difficult. He sent recent Canadian annual reports to wardens and governors of state prisons in the United States and contacted the Directors of Penal Prisons in Great Britain and Ireland. He was interested in studying how other prisons were organized and administered, but his overtures received almost no response. Moreover, the inspector's attempt to come to grips with contemporary penology came to little because Department of Justice officials were interested primarily in information related to criminal statistics and financial viability.[52]

In 1875 Moylan asked the minister of Justice to allow a tour of penitentiaries in the United States so he, or the warden of Kingston, could witness new methods of penal practice in action. The new minister saw no reason for such a tour. Moylan's repeated requests for travel were ignored or denied for years on end. Thus, to his great dismay, almost as soon as he became penitentiary inspector, Moylan found himself sidelined from meaningful contact with the international penal reform movement. He felt this most bitterly in Canada's (and his) exclusion from the three international prison congress meetings that occurred in the 1870s. Canada sent no representative to the first meeting in Cincinnati in 1870, nor to the immediate follow-up in London in 1872. Pleading for a chance to attend the Stockholm meeting in 1877, Moylan informed the minister that E. C. Wines had contacted him to express his disappointment and regret that Canada was not represented at the first two congress meetings and to express "a strong hope that so great a mistake would not again occur."[53] The opportunity to send a delegate to Stockholm passed, however, leaving Moylan to forge ahead as a one-man reform movement within the Canadian penitentiary administration.

Moylan maintained an unwavering faith that the penitentiary possessed the potential to reform criminals. He called reformation "the supreme end to be kept in view" and identified "hope, as the great regenerative force."[54] Although his faith in the principles of reformatory prison discipline was unshakable, Moylan was vexed by the limitations the Canadian system imposed on its realization. The Crofton system was designed around the progressive classification and segregation of inmates as they moved toward their release. In the Irish system, this included segregation into separate penal institutions. However, the Canadian penitentiary system as it stood in 1880 could not accommodate any type of progressive classification of inmates. Moylan viewed the inability to enact some sort of system of classification as the central impediment to prison reform in Canada. He saw prisoners as belonging to two simple categories: those who could be reformed and those who could not. For him, successful prison reform depended on finding a way to recognize the difference between these two groups. Efforts to realize this would shape much of the reform of the late nineteenth century.

Substantive change came very slowly to Canadian penitentiaries. The shape of penal practice over the course of Moylan's twenty years as penitentiary inspector assumed only hints of his reform agenda. It is significant that the changes he managed to implement dovetailed with security interests, which often made the prison more oppressive for the most marginal members of the penitentiary population. This created a unique prison system in which penal practice incorporated the old and the new, creating a climate in which reform existed in constant tension with more domineering and punitive practices. The fact that these developments were motivated by reform did not make their oppression any less grinding.

At the end of his career, Inspector James Moylan was a frustrated man. He had spent nearly thirty years in the bureaucratic wing of the Canadian penitentiary system, the last twenty as inspector. For two decades, he had advocated for reforms in the penitentiary system that would move it in the direction of penological advances in Europe and the United States: namely, a less punitive and more reformatory style of penitentiary practice. As if finally sensing that his efforts had come to nothing, Moylan used his final report to list the mundane problems that plagued each penitentiary.[55] The guards were paid too little. The insane asylum at Kingston was an international disgrace. Labour programs were ineffective and unprofitable. Moylan detailed all of this in seething tones, concluding with a description of the cesspool at Kingston Penitentiary. Water from the bay of Lake Ontario next to the penitentiary was leaking into the newly constructed pool. On his final inspection, Moylan observed fourteen or fifteen prisoners trying to empty the pool with a small hand pump. He reported, "The quantity got rid of during the day was more than replenished from the time the day's work closed until it began the next morning." The prisoners continued like this for weeks at a time, attempting, as one official joked, to "drain Lake Ontario."[56] Moylan's disgust over this futile exercise summed up his resignation about penitentiaries in Canada. Above all of these problems, the larger failure remained the penitentiary's inability to reform criminals. The few reformatory principles that the penitentiary retained were ineffective, and Moylan found himself powerless to implement new principles of prison reform. His ultimate frustration stemmed from the unrelenting stream of recidivists, incorrigibles, and habitual offenders who populated each penitentiary. Crime did not recede. Prisoners were not reformed.

|||

Criminality

In the early 1850s, Susanna Moodie visited Kingston Penitentiary
to see the notorious convicted murderer Grace Marks. She described
the visit in her 1853 book, *Life in the Clearings Versus the Bush*. In the
course of her inspection, she observed the male prisoners eating
breakfast together in the dining hall:

> The convicts are mostly of a dull grey complexion, large eyed,
> stolid looking men with very black hair, and heavy black brows. . . .
> . . . There were many stolid, heavy-looking men in that
> prison—many with black, jealous, fiery-looking eyes, in whose
> gloomy depths suspicion and revenge seemed to lurk. Even to look
> at these men as they passed on, seemed to arouse their vindictive
> feelings, and they scowled disdainfully upon us as they walked on
> to their respective places.[1]

Nearly twenty years later, penal reformer Mary Carpenter undertook
a similar tour. Penitentiary Inspector James Moylan recounted the
famous reformer's visit with obvious pride:

The good lady stood near the door and closely scrutinized each one as he filed past her. When all had taken their places, she walked between the rows still scanning every individual keenly, her examination resulting in her declaring subsequently that in all her experience in Great Britain and Ireland, on the Continent, in Australia, New Zealand, or the United States, she had not seen so large a number of men who bore less the impression of crime on the countenance. Intelligent visitors have oft and again endorsed this opinion.[2]

Moodie's description played on common middle-class anxieties about criminals. She emphasized their deformed physical nature, describing a racialized and menacing category of men, rightly kept apart from respectable society by the walls of the penitentiary. In contrast, Carpenter saw hope; she came away with the impression that the faces of the men at Kingston bore no traces of the criminality that she had observed elsewhere. Both descriptions were based on the notion that criminality and criminal tendencies could be identified, evaluated, and judged by a critical observer. The contrasting views help to illustrate that the ways in which criminality was conceived, identified, and evaluated was often at the heart of the penitentiary reform project. This chapter explores how the prevailing construction of criminality played an important role in the evolution of the reform movement and corresponding prison practices in the nineteenth century.

How did those involved with penitentiaries understand and classify individuals? How did they conceive of prisoners as a population? In many ways, Michel Foucault overstates the importance of the impulse to understand individual offenders in modern penitentiaries. The desire to "know the criminal" was seldom expressed in the nineteenth century, even after the transition to a more reformatory style of institution in the post-1850 era. Certainly, penitentiary officials would not have stated their concerns about criminality in such terms. While officials identified and classified criminality in particular ways, such classification often served larger concerns about discipline and institutional security, and ignored questions of individual reform. However, it is undeniable that by the 1850s, penal reformers had influenced a shift in thinking about criminality. The transformation was very slow (particularly within penitentiaries) and was often expressed in discursive forms that had little real effect on practice. This speaks to the fact that in the Canadian experience, penal practice often took years or decades to catch up with changes in reform thinking. Thus, Canadian penitentiary officials often classified criminality in ways that were only minimally linked to the reform project. Their constructions of criminality incorporated elements from several different influences. This chapter explores how criminality was constructed by influential penal reformers in the post-1850 era, and how penitentiary officials understood and contributed to these constructions.

Three key constructions of criminality played a role in Canadian penitentiaries. First, reformers promoted the idea of moral reformation based on an essentially optimistic and liberal view of criminal individuals. This optimistic view was offset by a more negative and pessimistic construction of criminality that was connected to "incorrigibles" and hardened offenders, those individuals who could not be reformed or reclaimed, only contained. The third, broader construction connected criminals to apprehensions about class, poverty, race, and gender. The latter two constructions often existed in tension with the reform view of liberal individualism. In the larger sense, though, the three constructions often coexisted, with different views of criminality deployed by different actors connected to the penitentiary. I argue that these prevailing discourses shaped penitentiary policy and the experience of imprisonment. Never static, each construction both complemented and subverted the effect of the others. After exploring the reform view of criminality, I examine the negative associations more specific to the Canadian experience. Finally, I look in more detail at constructions of criminality connected to structural and subjective categories including class, gender, and race.

During the Enlightenment, purely religious perspectives on deviance gave way to rationalist arguments about criminality that characterized the classical era of jurisprudence.[3] This era positioned the criminal as an individual who had made a rational decision to engage in crime. The reformed legal codes and rationalized methods of punishment (penitentiaries rather than torture and execution) were intended to show the criminal the direct and unwavering consequence of these transgressions. In the early decades of the nineteenth century, a new conception of criminality and deviance rose in tandem with the penitentiary reform movement. The classical formation of deviance as a rational choice to be punished was eclipsed by an increasing concern with moral disorder in the community and the family, a disorder that was manifested in the individual. Society in North America and Britain transformed rapidly in the years after 1800. The increasing pace of industrialization and urbanization weakened the bonds of colonial society and created the impression that moral disorder produced crime and deviance. Legal and penal reformers looked to the weakening moral influence of family and church and identified a new source of crime and deviance.[4] This gave rise to a neoclassical "positivist" criminology: that is, a view of criminality based on measuring and quantifying criminal behaviour objectively and scientifically. This new perspective was intimately linked with new forms of punishment.[5]

An important distinction must be made between the emergence of criminological science in the nineteenth century and what was manifested in practice in Western penal systems, particularly in the Canadian example. In one sense, the classical school of criminology was extremely influential on prison reform in the earliest decades of the nineteenth century. Becarria was read by late eighteenth-century legislators who moved toward penal confinement as the most rational response to crime and deviance. However, it also became clear very quickly that the classical notions of deviance were deficient in structuring actual penal practice. As Ian Taylor, Paul Walton, and Jock Young argue, "It was impossible in practice to ignore the determinants of human action and to proceed as if punishment and incarceration could easily be measured on some kind of universal calculus: ... classicism appeared to contradict widely-held commonsensical notions of human nature and motivation."[6] This "commonsensical" approach motivated positivist conclusions of the neoclassical school, which desired to better understand the particular criminality of each offender. Moreover, while it could be said that penal reformers or administrators in England and North America adopted such practicality, their positivist inclinations had more in common with evangelical social investigation than with emerging European criminology in the second half of the nineteenth century. There is little evidence of direct communication or influence between early criminologists and penal reformers. This remained true even as new theories shifted to biological positivist explanations for crime. For example, the work of the Italian positivists Enrico Ferri and Caesare Lombroso was largely unknown or was dismissed by penal reformers and administrators in England and the United States. Paul Rock argues that the science that underlay nineteenth-century British penal systems was rooted in an "abstracted empiricism" that owed nothing to the theories of criminological science.[7] The constructions of criminality that developed in Canadian penitentiaries in the post-Confederation era were the product of an inherently practical understanding of deviance influenced by the lessons of previous generations of penal reformers.

A two-pronged method of addressing criminality characterized such practical notions of deviance. First, the cause of criminality in each individual would be investigated and discovered. Already convinced that environment and childhood played a determinative role, penal reformers searched for clues to the moral deficiency in the criminal's past. Second, the penitentiary would provide the moral guidance required to address the causes of criminality in convicted individuals. This involved a campaign of moralization to address the identified deficiencies, with the influences of religion and education providing the moral building blocks toward the reformation of the criminal.

A contradictory impulse was at work in the solutions to the new concepts of criminality. Although the new approaches to criminality were highly individualized, mid-nineteenth-century penal regimes were almost universally designed to treat every offender exactly alike. In the early Victorian era, prisoners were subjected to an unyielding routine, so alhough prisons may have included elements intended to moralize the offender, these were ultimately impersonal and highly regimented.[8] David Garland characterizes this uniformity as the defining feature of Victorian penal responses to criminality. He argues that the discipline of British prisons made no direct reference to criminal type or individual character: "The differentiations that did exist were mainly administrative and segregational, carrying little importance in terms of treatment or conditions. The main classification system categorized a prisoner as one more individual to be subjected to a uniform and universal regime."[9]

Garland's argument draws on Max Grünhut's descriptions of nineteenth-century methods of isolation. Grünhut writes that the separate system "resulted in a complete extinction of all personal traits which could act as reminders of the prisoner's individuality, and this made the whole scheme even more commendable to those who wished criminal law and prison discipline to be based on a system of strict retribution."[10] On the basis of these conclusions, Garland describes a Victorian system that was based purely on the tenets of classical criminology. In the Canadian example, the impulses of both classical and neoclassical approaches to criminology were present but were largely manifested in the simplest attempts to understand criminality on a practical level. In many cases, it was the tension between the classical approach and more positivist interpretations of the cause of crime that played the largest role in how penitentiaries responded to the idea of criminality.

The penitentiary chaplains were often the most vigorous promoters of a positivist view of criminality and the potential for reformation. David Rothman describes how Auburn penitentiary officials collected detailed biographical details of each prisoner, but the search for the cause of crime was not intended to affect how each convict was punished; rather, the collected information would be passed along to philanthropic or Christian societies interested in the amelioration of crime. As Rothman argues, the early penal reformers were quite convinced that a failure of upbringing—specifically, the collapse of the family's moral control—caused criminality.[11] This idea gained strength in both American and Upper Canadian society in the 1820s and 1830s. The same year that Kingston Penitentiary opened, the *Kingston Chronicle and Gazette* published a list of the "prevalent causes of crime":

1. Deficient education, early loss of parents, and consequent neglect.

2. Few convicts have ever learned a regular trade; and if they were bound to any apprenticeship, they have abandoned it before their time lawfully expired.

3. School education is, with most convicts, very deficient, or entirely wanting.

4. Intemperance, very often the consequences of loose education, is a most appalling source of crime.

5. By preventing intemperance and by promoting education, we are authorized to believe that we shall prevent crime in a considerable degree.[12]

Although Kingston followed the Auburn model to every possible detail and collected biographies of discharged prisoners, no element of the penitentiary administration subscribed to the above environmental theories of crime. Prior to the Brown Commission in 1849, there was no real reform movement or philanthropic organization in Upper Canada interested in this type of investigation. After 1850 penitentiary chaplains began to display some rudimentary interest in the causes of crime and the background of the convicted men and women at Kingston. Much like the early criminological endeavours at Auburn, this background search concentrated on the childhood and moral upbringing of the criminal offender. Hannibal Mulkins, the

Protestant chaplain at Kingston, expressed his sympathy with this approach in 1852:

> How often are the inmates of this Prison viewed by Society with feelings of terror and abhorrence only, as the pests of society, deserving only hatred from their species and suffering for their crimes. But when we see . . . how many were left Orphans in their early childhood; how many were never taught, even the moral law; how many even totally or partially unable to read; what numbers were brought up in irreligion, surrounded with vicious examples; what numbers were led to crime, by intemperance and ignorance; how many had little education, but a training in vice, partly of their parents and partly of themselves; —when we see these facts, should not indignation in the bosom of society, give place to pity? Should not the chief question be, not how shall we punish, but how shall we convert the sinner from the error of his way?[13]

After 1852 Mulkins tracked statistics for "early social condition" and "moral condition" for the convict population. The results, published in annual reports, were intended to provide a portrait of the social origins of crime. The 1852 report of "early social condition" showed that out of a total of 255 newly admitted inmates, "33 were Orphans; 60 were deprived of one of their parents; 122 left home when young; 90 had no means of support; only 77 had a trade; 16 were born in slavery." The statistics for moral condition are more revealing in terms of the categories created by the penitentiary chaplaincy, which led the reader to obvious conclusions about the causes of crime: "20 were ignorant of the Ten Commandments; 174 used profane language; 34 had immoral parents; 56 had parents who habitually used profane language; 27 had parents who were very unkind and severe; 93 were gamblers; 164 used Tobacco; 180 kept not the Sabbath Day holy; 117 neglected to read the Bible; 104 never attended a Sunday school; and 146 had a rash and violent temper."[14]

In examining an offender's childhood for clues about criminality, commentators and penitentiary officials often identified intemperance as a primary reason, either directly or indirectly, for children's corruption. In 1860 the penitentiary inspectors reported on the youth reformatory at Penetanguishene: "A large portion of the parents of these unfortunate lads were drunkards. More than half the boys had themselves been addicted to drinking, and kept bad company."[15] The stress on temperance also crossed over from childhood influence to the direct moral ruin of convicted criminals. A statistical table published in an 1855 annual report noted that of 179 newly admitted convicts, only one totally abstained from alcohol and not one was a member of a temperance society.[16] In another example, an 1844 edition of the *Canadian Temperance Advocate* discussed the link between intemperance and criminality: "Where would be the harm of reminding these victims of alcohol of the evil they had done themselves, their families, and the community in consequence of using these liquors and persuading them to their entire disuse after they are again restored to liberty? In reaching the climax of modern drinking, which has qualified them for a prison, who can compute the amount of contamination which their example has shed around them!"[17] This idea proved remarkably resilient through the second half of the nineteenth century due to the growing strength of temperance movements. Penitentiary chaplains resorted to the same explanations from one decade to the next. In 1887 Robert Jamieson, a Protestant chaplain in British Columbia, noted, "Nearly all, if not all the prisoners owe their degradation and imprisonment directly or indirectly, to our country's greatest curse, namely intoxicating liquors."[18]

Moral concerns about childhood influences and criminality reflected the growing apprehension in the Victorian age with impulse control and moral governance. As Martin Weiner argues of Victorian England, "Crime was a central metaphor of disorder and loss of control in all spheres of life. Criminal and penal policy articulated the effort to counter this perception by fostering disciplined behaviour and a broad ethos of respectability."[19] In the Canadian context, this ethos was likewise often expressed in terms of "respectability," especially by penitentiary chaplains. The real effect of the statistics concerning moral character that prison chaplains collected, however, was minimal. For the most part, the dissemination of such information merely helped to justify reformers' instincts that a more rigorous moral agenda was needed in the penitentiary. If moral deficiencies were understood to be the cause of criminality, it followed naturally that a program stressing religion and education was the solution. Chaplain Hannibal Mulkins stated this moral mission forcefully in 1860:

> The criminals in a Christian country, are the few remaining barbarians and savages in its borders, whom its laws have not restrained, nor its civilization reclaimed, nor its religion purified. Every criminal reformed is a victory gained over ignorance and barbarism, and one citizen saved to the State. The law magnifies itself in arresting and bringing these out-laws, these savages, these criminals, under its power, and incarcerating them in a Penitentiary, whose beneficent and holy mission then commences, where, in their mental, moral, and religious renovation, its beneficent and sacred mission is consummated.[20]

The changing construction of criminality as a social disorder ran parallel to the new conception of the penitentiary as a moral institution. The focus on morality, however, also obscured some important social statistics that penitentiary authorities and administrators were less comfortable exploring.

With the adoption of environmental explanations of criminality, constructions of criminality in the 1850s and 1860s remained largely individualized; discussion of the relationships among class, poverty, and crime was avoided. This spoke to the continuing view of poverty (and by extension, criminality) as an individual moral failure rather than a structural category. Penitentiary populations were overwhelmingly drawn from the working class and the unemployed, but only on rare occasions was this acknowledged by reformers or penitentiary officials. At the end of the century, Douglas Stewart, a penitentiary inspector, noted, "Common labourers constitute about four per cent of the population, but embrace thirty-six per cent of our convict population. Farmers and skilled mechanics constitute a very small percentage."[21] In fact, Stewart was grossly underestimating the class homogeneity of penitentiary inmates in the second half of the nineteenth century. In 1858, the first year that trades of committed convicts were reported, out of 305 received prisoners at Kingston, 184 were listed as labourers (60 percent). This too may have been misleading since there was no recorded category for the unemployed.[22] If trades with low levels of apprenticed skills are combined with the unemployed and unskilled, 66 per cent of the incoming convicts in 1858 were working class and located in the lower echelons of a proletarian hierarchy.[23] In the first year after Confederation, unemployed, unskilled, and low-skilled workers made up 68 percent of the incoming convicts at Kingston. This number rose to 72 percent in 1878. In part, this peak reflects the economic crisis in Ontario and Québec through the middle of the 1870s, but the proportion of working-class prisoners remained high until 1900: in 1898 65 percent of new convicts were clearly working class, drawn from those of "low status" in this broad labouring contingent.[24] Underscoring these statistics is the fact that in each sample year above, the majority of convictions involved property and financial crimes, not serious felony or violent offence, and were punished with short sentences of two to four years. While such statistics pointed to relatively obvious social trends connecting poverty and criminality, the class conclusions reached by reformers focused on very different explanations for working-class criminality. In addition to the moral categories noted above, penitentiary officials and reformers associated working-class criminality with a growing fear and suspicion rooted in social constructions of poverty revolving around the "dangerous classes," sometimes referred to as the "residuum."

INCORRIGIBLES

Not all prisoners were regarded equally when officials and reformers considered criminality. In the earliest years of Kingston Penitentiary, officials were greatly dismayed to discover that some individuals were committed to the penitentiary repeatedly for the same crimes. In 1839 Warden Smith noted that, of 148 convicts, fifteen were serving a second sentence in the penitentiary, and two were serving a third.[25] Between 1837 and 1857, the recidivism rate at Kingston generally hovered between 8 and 15 percent of the total convict population.[26] In these early years, officials explained recidivism by suggesting that prison sentences were too short to allow for the complete reformation of prisoners. Referring to recent American legislation, Smith argued that individuals convicted a second time should be committed to the penitentiary for life.[27] As W. David Lewis notes, however, recidivism was notoriously difficult to track. Some prisoners may have used assumed names upon conviction or may simply have been incarcerated in different gaols or jurisdictions.[28] Eventually, explanations for recidivism that blamed inadequate measures of reformation fell away, and officials located the reasons in the recidivists themselves. This gave rise to a parallel construction of criminality focused on recidivists and life-term prisoners, a construction that existed outside the realm of discourses promoting individual reformation and was instead broadly pessimistic and fearful.

The "habitual criminal" or "incorrigible offender" thus came to be seen as a class apart from the prisoners perceived to be more normal. Throughout the second half of the nineteenth century, the Victorian impulse to classify prisoners according to the degree of criminality helped to explain this stratum. Inspector Stewart included this description of three main types of convicts in his 1897 annual report:

1. Those who in their normal condition are law-abiding and industrious, but who are suffering the penalty of some overt act committed during a temporary lapse of self-control.

2. Those who are thriftless and devoid of moral principle, and have adopted crime as an easy means of livelihood.

3. Those who delight in crime and who spend their days and nights in planning future exploits in it.[29]

The third category vexed penitentiary officials to no end. In the 1860s, England enacted legislation to address the problem of the incorrigible and habitual offender. Weiner notes that calls for the control of this class of criminal came from across the political spectrum, uniting radicals and liberals. Sir Walter Crofton appeared before Parliament with other members of the Social Science Association to demand harsher penal regimes for repeat offenders.[30] While this position seems inimical to the spirit of Crofton's reformatory prison discipline, his calls for harsher punishment for this class of criminals illustrates the degree to which reformers disavowed themselves of responsibility for individuals they considered beyond the pale of reform efforts. M. D. Hill stated in 1866 that habitual criminals should be consigned to prisons that were "harsher by many degrees" than standard convict prisons.[31] Reformers and legislators in England found consensus on this issue, and legislation in 1864 and 1865 made penal regimes much more restrictive and punitive. Not only was early release for repeat offenders repealed, but the new regulations provided a higher minimum sentence of penal servitude for repeat offenders. These measures were extended by passage of the *Habitual Criminals Act* in 1869. The act made sentences for repeat offenders even heavier and included provisions for the police supervision of all released prisoners to combat repeat offences. The new legislation also gave magistrates sweeping powers to summarily imprison former offenders on suspicion of crime.

Canadian criminal codes were not amended to keep pace with English developments. As a result, the issue of incorrigibles and repeat offenders became the exclusive concern of penitentiary officials after conviction occurred. Inspector Moylan's disgust for recidivism was obvious in an 1877 annual report, in which he wrote, "The recommitted convicts are the bane of our Penitentiaries. They are, for the most part, hardened and confirmed criminals. They require to be dealt with firmly and severely."[32] In the years after Confederation, the issue of incorrigibility became one of overwhelming concern to penitentiary officials. Chapter 6 explores the penal practices enacted to control, contain, and repress this class of criminal, measures that included both violent punishments and increasing measures of physical segregation from the general penitentiary population. Perhaps the most significant aspect of incorrigibles relative to constructions of criminality was how penitentiary officials identified these individuals and perceived their threat. The incorrigibles occupied a place of particular scorn in the eyes of penitentiary officials even though few could agree on what specific behaviour or qualities defined them.

Who were the incorrigible offenders? Paradoxically, incorrigibles were often identified by both the worst and best behaviour. A clear indicator of incorrigibility was violent disruptive or resistant behaviour, which served as a useful justification for the harshest disciplinary measures. Conversely, penitentiary officials also mistrusted the overly compliant behaviour of experienced prisoners who followed rules for the wrong reasons, as illustrated in Inspector Moylan's 1890 report:

> A large proportion of the convicts are well-behaved from purely self-interested motives. They are unwilling to prolong their stay within prison walls by the forfeiture of remission time, or to lose any privilege through misconduct. None are so careful in avoiding these penalties as the habitual criminal. His experience has taught him that, the easiest and most comfortable way of serving out his sentence is not to run counter to rule or authority. . . . He puts in his time, without change of heart, without any purpose of amendment, and, as a consequence, upon release, drifts again, at once, into his old habits.[33]

The irony of this argument seems to have been lost on Moylan, who had tirelessly argued in favour of the Crofton system, which was based entirely on self-interested compliance with penitentiary regulations leading to a swift release. For Moylan and other reformers, the issue was still avowedly moral. One of the biggest moral concerns with incorrigibles was not the depravity of habitual offenders but their influence upon other impressionable members of the penitentiary population.

The notion that the worst prisoners should be kept separate from the prison population was present throughout the century, but it gained momentum in the years after Confederation and began to influence penal policy. Fears about incorrigibles led to major transformations in penal practice and construction in the 1890s as penitentiaries created isolation-style maximum-security wings. In the decades before this change, officials frequently blamed incorrigibles for the failure of reformation in the rest of the penitentiary population. John Foster, warden of Dorchester, noted that only two or three "bad prisoners had an extraordinary influence, destroying all the reformatory influences."[34] The penitentiary board complained in its 1870 annual report that the incorrigible offenders were turning penitentiaries into "nurseries of crime."[35] This was an often-repeated claim. Inspector Moylan explained in 1879 that the incorrigibles' "pernicious influence" caused young and impressionable inmates "to have a morbid fascination for their more guilty associates, and to entertain the desire to rival if not excel their vicious exploits."[36] The fear that incorrigibles would transmit criminal dispositions to merely misguided youths was pervasive in the discourse of this era. In 1888 Inspector Moylan described how the incorrigible's "most congenial occupation" was to corrupt the innocent by the recital of his "wicked deeds." The inspector concluded,

> In this way, young men undergoing imprisonment for a first offence, committed, perhaps, under the influence of liquor or some other excitement, who are not naturally vicious and who could be reclaimed if removed from evil influences, lose their self respect, become corrupted, sink to the level of the incarnate fiend who accomplished their moral ruin, and on their release, are ready to emulate and even excel their tutor in a life of vice and crime. Thus, it is that hundreds are led into a career of wickedness and infamy, through contact with the confirmed and callous evil-doer. This is no fancy sketch.[37]

The concern with incorrigibles appears remarkable when we consider that penitentiary authorities attributed the failure of the entire reformatory project to this handful of offenders. It is particularly interesting given that incorrigibility remained a fairly flexible and undefined construction. Sometimes attributed to recidivists or life convicts, in many cases it was also applied more broadly to groups that penitentiary officials and staff considered more dangerous, morally irredeemable, or marginalized than "normal" penitentiary inmates. In many cases, such constructions were not individual at all, instead conforming to broader constructions based upon race, gender, and class differentiations.

THE DANGEROUS CLASSES

Perhaps the greatest blow to the individualist aspirations of the reform era was the continuing tendency to view criminality in relationship to negative constructions of poverty and the working class. The liberal individual was an idealized construction that facilitated the reform desire for reformation and rehabilitation. However, penitentiary officials tended to subscribe to widely held ideas about the convict population that were connected to constructions of the social residuum and the "perishing and dangerous classes," constructions of fear and loathing that associated the poor and working class with an emerging criminal class. This construction was broad and subject to change throughout the nineteenth century, but it had three primary iterations.

The notion of "classes dangereuses" was first popularized in French literature describing the depredations of urban poverty, decay, and crime. Such descriptions in the works of Hugo, Sue, and Balzac contrasted the social conditions of the urban landscape with bourgeois anxieties about the threat to social order from outsiders and the poor, a population on the margins of urban life. Louis Chevalier quotes Hugo's *Les Misérables,* which describes the spreading contamination of crime and poverty: "that indigent class which begins with the last small tradesman in difficulties and sinks from wretchedness to wretchedness down into the lowest depths of society, to those two beings to whom all the material things of civilization descend, the scavenger who sweeps the mud and the ragpicker who collects the rags."[38] Hugo describes a demographic menace, the lowest and most marginal members of society who threatened to drag the respectable into their shameful ranks. More than just a condemnation of poverty, this literature forged a powerful connection between poverty and crime in the French imagination. Chevalier argues that, particularly in the works of Balzac and Hugo, crime and poverty become synonymous; through descriptions such as that quoted above, the labouring classes were associated with the dangerous classes. Demographically, crime moved from a social condition on the margins of society to all urban spaces, invading and infecting the entire city.[39] This perception that crime was rampant was due in part to the fact that the contemporary bourgeoisie were often unable or unwilling to discern the difference between the labouring and dangerous classes.[40] Chevalier elaborates on how the perceived connection between these two classes spread to the general population in France:

> Most of the characteristics of the bourgeois population's attitude to the laboring classes were thus borrowed from an older attitude to a population which had been regarded as not belonging to the city, as suspect of all the crimes, of all the evils, all the epidemics and all the violence, not merely because of its own characteristics, but on account of its origins outside the city and of immigration which had incontinently been put down to a proliferation of the beggars of old.[41]

In contrast to the French constructions of the dangerous classes, many English reformers staked their moral agenda on the ability to identify the difference between the working class and the dangerous classes. The English had similar anxieties to those of the French about the poor and working classes, associating both with a compromised morality. The 1834 Poor Law helped separate the deserving from the undeserving poor, identifying what Bentham had called the dependent poor's defective "moral sanity."[42] Gertrude Himmelfarb argues that the idea of morality played a critical role in these constructions. Morality helped build consensus about the identification of social problems and the search for policy solutions.[43] With clear lines drawn between what was moral and immoral, social reformers in England distinguished the dangerous classes from the labouring classes. Mary Carpenter drew a distinction between the dangerous and labouring classes: "There is, and will long be, a very strongly defined line of separation between them, which must and ought to separate them, and which requires perfectly distinct machinery and modes of operation in dealing with them."[44]

The machinery Carpenter referenced was the growing list of institutional solutions for attending to the moral shortcomings of the dangerous classes. Through the 1850s, this included not only the penitentiary and other prisons but also new institutional solutions geared to the most vulnerable members of the dangerous classes, particularly women and children. Carpenter's *Reformatory Schools* (1851) focused on the children of the dangerous classes and the search for institutional solutions that would save them from slipping into a life of crime and destitution. With the correct moral intervention, children could be prevented from association with the dangerous classes, whom Carpenter defined as "those who have already received the prison brand, or, if the mark has not yet visibly set upon them, are notoriously living by plunder, . . . whose hand is against every man, for they know not that any man is their brother."[45] Henry Mayhew, a reformer and social commentator, had the same tendency to classify and identify the dangerous classes. In *London Labour and the London Poor,* published in serial form throughout the 1840s, Mayhew classified different strata of London society, identifying most stridently the social outcasts, who, he argued, were a "national disgrace to us all."[46] These characterizations by reformers such as Carpenter and Mayhew helped promote social projects that Gareth Stedman Jones characterizes as the "remoralization of the poor."[47] By identifying both poverty and criminality with moral failure, reformers positioned themselves as privileged purveyors of solutions to the day's most pressing social problems. But more importantly, these attitudes aligned mid-nineteenth-century conceptions of crime with the liberalism and individualism of the age: solutions to social problems would be found through the transformation of individual morality. In this sense, the detailed classifications demarcating the poor from the criminal were important because they identified marginal groups who could be saved from moral ruin and separated them from those beyond reclamation.

In North American constructions of the dangerous classes, the categories and distinctions of the English reformers became much less clear. One primary difference was that North American commentators discussing the dangerous classes of Europe tended toward descriptions that invoked a greater revulsion for what the class represented. An 1848 edition of the *Canadian Temperance Advocate*, for example, exposed the "disgusting" lifestyle of ragpickers in an exposé of Paris's dangerous classes.[48] Similarly, an 1865 *New York Times* editorial described London's dangerous classes with revulsion: "In London, you find them in street after street and lane upon lane, thousands by thousands, hungry, filthy, ignorant, imbruted and cunning; vagrants, thieves, beggars, 'tramps,' burglars, outcasts, and all the nameless crowds of people living daily from hand to mouth. Here they burrow and live and breed."[49] These descriptions exploited poverty for its sensationalism, but by the 1860s, the distinction between European and American poverty had become blurred as US cities began to exhibit the same conditions of poverty and dislocation after the pace of industrialization quickened.

By the late 1850s, Americans had "discovered" the dangerous classes in their midst, and, as in England, these classes became the target of progressive social reformers. However, because the American construction was accompanied by greater apprehension and mistrust, reformers in the United States took a more alarmist position than their English counterparts. Among the most vocal commentators on the dangerous classes was Charles Loring Brace, a prominent reformer and the founder of the New York Children's Aid Society. Brace investigated poverty in New York City, emphasizing the presence of the dangerous classes, who, he argued, were "not so numerous as in London, but more dangerous."[50] The solutions he proposed in *Dangerous Classes of New York* (1872) included changing the material circumstances of New York's poorest populations, a mission that would "draw them under the influence of the moral and fortunate classes, that they shall grow up as useful producers and members of society, able and included to aid in its process."[51] This reflected the belief that the poor could be saved, but only if they could be protected from contamination by more dangerous and morally irredeemable elements.

Brace was not subtle about emphasizing the criminality and moral ruin of the dangerous classes. In 1872 he wrote that New York's dangerous class "might leave the city in ashes and blood."[52] Such sentiment reflected a growing turmoil over hardening class distinctions in the American Northeast and the fear of impending class war. Jeffrey Adler argues that cities were regarded as a powder keg of violent possibility and the dangerous classes could be the spark that would ignite widespread violence. Such fears were confirmed by several incidents of social and industrial violence, the most devastating among them the New York City Draft Riots of 1863.[53] Three days of rioting and as many as 120 deaths convinced the New York City bourgeoisie of the terrible potential of the dangerous classes.[54] Thus, concerns about the dangerous classes, particularly in the American context, revolved around a specific apprehension over their threat to the political and industrial order. In the 1860s, this was expressed in the position that those belonging to the residuum could not be given the vote lest they simply sell their allegiance to the highest bidder. At other times, such as during the Draft Riots, the dangerous classes represented the threat of armed resistance. This unknown element was mistrusted by allies of both the ruling and working classes. Marx and Engels warned that the dangerous classes, whom they referred to as the "lumpenproletariat," were just as likely to become the reactionary tool of the bourgeoisie as allies of the proletariat.[55]

In the late Victorian era, anxiety about the dangerous classes was recast through the renewed investigations of "social explorers" like Charles Booth, who pioneered new methods in social research through a detailed analysis of the material conditions of poverty. All the same, moral associations between poverty and criminality persisted in

Booth's work. He lumped together "occasional labourers, street-sellers, loafers, criminals, and semi-criminals," adding to them the "homeless outcasts," whom he described as consisting "mostly of casual labourers of low character," along with those "who pick up a living without labour of any kind." Although fundamentally sympathetic, Booth despaired of this most miserable of classes. "Their life is the life of savages," he wrote, adding that "they degrade whatever they touch and as individuals are incapable of improvement."[56] The renewed anxiety with "contamination" was tied to parallel concerns in the growing social hygiene movement, which stressed the moral danger inherent in poor living conditions, disease, and extreme urban poverty. Still, the underlying danger was regarded as the contamination of the poorest members of society by a criminal class. As Booth noted, the lowliest classes "help to foul the record of the unemployed."[57] Much as with concerns about incorrigible offenders, the threat was that those of "low character" would drag others down to their degraded level.

Although the classification of the dangerous classes was associated with constructions of criminality, it was also a fairly elastic designation that was applied to multiple marginal groups who elicited apprehension. As the notion of dangerous classes was popularized in the mid-nineteenth century and adopted in North America, the construction often broadened beyond the urban poor to include other threatening elements in society. For example, an inspecting physician of the lazaretto in Tracadie, New Brunswick, stated in his 1885 annual report that "lepers belong to the dangerous classes of the community which require perpetual confinement."[58] The intemperate were also a popular target, charged with swelling the ranks of the dangerous classes and producing "debased and degraded offspring."[59] The Knights of Labor in Nanaimo invoked the construction to campaign against Chinese immigration to Canada, arguing that "all who have ever come into close contact with them are satisfied that they are not only a most undesirable but a positively dangerous class to any country having free popular institutions."[60] In 1882 the North West Mounted Police labelled starving First Nations bands in the North-West as a dangerous class requiring "power, as well as care, in handling."[61] All of these groups represented some degree of threat, a common element they shared with prisoners, who had already demonstrated their capacity to transgress against social order.

WOMEN

In the Victorian rush to classify, understand, and correct criminality, gender became a key explanatory category, with female offenders occupying a distinct category of criminality in this era. Just as incorrigibles and children engendered unique penal policy, feminine criminality separated the female offender from her male counterpart in the penitentiary. The root of differential responses to women in Canadian prisons can be found in broader gendered constructions that contributed to the notion of a separate and unique feminine criminality. This gendered criminality was intimately linked to two key stereotypes of Victorian femininity: the idealized wife and mother, and the fallen woman. These stereotypes were constructed on notions of middle-class feminine respectability, relegating women to the domestic sphere and holding them to a higher moral standard than men. The idealized woman was innocent, pure, self-sacrificing, patient, sensible, gentle, modest, and altruistic.[62] This stereotype was aimed at middle- and upper-class women, who were expected to reign over the domestic sphere and see to the care of their families. In her work on feminine criminality, Lucia Zedner illustrates how this powerful idea also ensnared working-class women, subjecting them to the same imposed, often unreachable standards and serving to articulate and enforce social and sexual norms.[63]

The counterpart to idealized femininity was the "fallen woman," an equally powerful stereotype in the construction of criminality. Zedner argues that the fallen woman was judged not merely on the basis of the crimes she committed but by her contravention of the norms of femininity. Thus, whereas male convicts were judged to have committed rational (albeit antisocial) acts in aid of their own pleasure or gain, feminine crime hinted at a much more threatening moral turpitude. This was due in part to a list of crimes, primarily attributed to women, that were defined by their very threat to idealized feminine respectability, including sexual crimes, prostitution, drunkenness, and vagrancy. In 1860 the Canadian penitentiary board reported on the "moral leprosy" that was infecting Canada's urban centres, noting that nearly all of the 3,500 women in Ontario gaols were prostitutes for which the prisons "serve as boarding houses and places of shelter. . . . When they have reached the lowest depths of degradation, they wander, during the summer months, in the fields in the immediate neighborhood of our larger towns, and in winter find shelter in the gaol."[64] Victorian writing about such crimes stoked a moral panic that was tied to the concerns noted above about the dangerous classes, "low" cultures, and urban poor. Mayhew's bombast on the issue of female crime was typical: "In them one sees the most hideous pictures of all human weakness and depravity—a picture the more striking because exhibiting the coarsest and rudest moral features in connection with a being whom we are apt to regard as the most graceful and gentle form of humanity."[65]

Due in part to the powerful dichotomy between idealized and fallen woman, female convicts were often subject to particularly harsh condemnation. The fallen woman was irredeemable. Victorian writers denigrated female criminals as the lowest members of society in condemnatory tones that were seldom applied to male convicts. In *Our Convicts* (1864), Mary Carpenter wrote, "The very susceptibility and tenderness of woman's nature render her more completely diseased in her whole nature when this is perverted to evil; and when a woman has thrown aside the restraints of society, and is enlisted on the side of evil, she is more dangerous to society than the other sex."[66] A few years later, Carpenter expanded on the degradation that differentiated the criminal woman:

> The women of this degraded portion of society will be generally found to differ in many respects from those belonging to a higher sphere. Their intellectual powers are low, and from having been left uncultivated, are in a state of torpidity from which it is very dif-

ficult to raise them. This peculiarly low intellectual condition in females of the lowest social grade is accompanied by a very strong development of the passions and of the lower nature. Extreme excitability, violent and even frantic outbursts of passion, a duplicity and disregard of truth hardly conceivable in the better classes of society render all attempts to improve them peculiarly difficult.[67]

Such discourses suggested that female criminals could not be saved. This created a problem for penal administrators and reformers, who were nonetheless charged with their care. In the case of Canadian penitentiaries before and after Confederation, gendered differentiation of criminality resulted in widely divergent and marginal experiences for female convicts.

Attitudes about female criminality were often manifested in penal practice. In the early years of Kingston Penitentiary, this was illustrated by the ongoing marginalization and abuse of female prisoners. At first, female convicts were given no specific accommodations, but they were nonetheless isolated as much as possible from the male population. In the earliest years of the penitentiary, the small number of female convicts made this manageable. As the female population increased in the 1840s, isolation became more difficult and efforts to separate women resulted in their physical neglect. In the Brown Commission investigation, commissioners were horrified by reports of the poor hygienic conditions allowed to prevail in the female quarters. For example, in 1846 the women's cells were overrun with an insect infestation since he wooden cells housing most of the female convicts had been constructed hastily to provide relief from overcrowding. A former matron, Mrs. Coulter, testified that the insects were so numerous that the women constantly swept them from their cells with brooms. When she appealed to the warden for relief and asked him to allow the women to sleep in another part of the prison, Smith refused. Coulter recalled, "The women suffered very much; their bodies were blistered with the bugs; and they often tore themselves with scratching." On one occasion, she disobeyed her orders and let the women out of the cells. "The torture the poor women endured was horrible," she said, "and [I] could not resist their entreaties to let them out." Finally the women convicts struck and refused to work until the warden addressed the insect problem, after which Smith ordered the cells to be scrubbed with lime.[68]

In addition to physical neglect, female convicts sometimes endured the sexual misconduct of guards charged with their care. In 1852 it was discovered that convict Ann Irvine had been impregnated by a guard, who was subsequently dismissed. Although the inspectors determined that the guard had acted "very negligently, if not criminally," no charges were brought against him.[69] Several other incidents of pregnancy in this era were attributed to sexual assaults committed in local gaols or by sheriffs en route to the penitentiary with female convicts.[70] The sexual abuse that penitentiary staff and officials inflicted on women in the penitentiary reflected the prevailing belief that female convicts were already morally disgraced and unworthy of the protection that would be afforded by social norms of the era. Echoing a common discourse, the Catholic chaplain, Angus MacDonell, described the female convicts in his 1852 annual report: "Unfortunately the majority of them are common prostitutes, diseased of body, and debased in mind from a long continuance in a career of crime; lost to all shame, and bent upon nothing but the gratification of their beastly passions."[71] Cast in such tones, women at Kingston were clearly vulnerable to sexual abuse, for which they were customarily blamed.

The crimes for which female convicts were imprisoned seldom corresponded to common discourses about feminine criminality. Of the 164 women committed to Kingston Penitentiary between 1835 and 1850, all but six were convicted of some form of larceny or theft. Two women were convicted of assault in 1846, and one of arson in 1847. Only three women were imprisoned for serious crimes. Ann Little was convicted of manslaughter in late 1849 and served a seven-year sentence. Mary Douglas, convicted of murder in May 1841, had her death sentence commuted to ten years at Kingston. The third woman was Grace Marks, a sixteen-year-old domestic servant who was convicted of murder in November 1844.[72]

Marks is perhaps the most well-known prisoner in all of Kingston Penitentiary's long history. She and James McDermott, a stable hand, were convicted of murdering their employer, Thomas Kinnear, and were suspected in the death of Kinnear's housekeeper, Nancy Montgomery. Both were sentenced to death. McDermott hanged for the crime, but Marks's sentence was commuted to life. Some accounts of the case portrayed Marks as an unwitting accessory to murder, while others played on the image of Marks as an evil seductress who corrupted McDermott and incited him to commit murder. The Marks case reflected the prevailing cultural ambivalence about women, notably in its association of unbridled female sexuality with moral depravity and crime. Susanna Moodie's detailed contemporary account of the murder, *Life in the Clearings Versus the Bush,* distilled this ambivalence in the author's evident desire both to condemn and exonerate. Moodie portrayed Marks as a pretty and intelligent girl but with a "silent, sullen temper."[73] She described how Marks pushed a reluctant McDermott to commit the murders, only to be overtaken by waves of regret in the aftermath of the crime. Moodie, who described herself as "very anxious to behold this unhappy victim of remorse," encountered Marks during a tour of Kingston Penitentiary. Observing Marks in captivity, Moodie emphasized her "air of hopeless melancholy" but added that it was balanced by facial characteristics that gave her a cunning and cruel expression. Noting that, following her visit, Marks became mentally ill and was transferred to the Toronto Asylum, Moodie concluded, "Let us hope that all her previous guilt may be attributed to the incipient workings of this frightful malady."[74]

Amidst the growing women's penal reform movement, the most remarkable change in the mid-nineteenth century was the noticeable softening of discourse about female criminality in the penitentiary. Unlike earlier references to female inmates that cast them as the worst in the institution, late nineteenth-century descriptions assumed a more sympathetic tone. When official reports mentioned female prisoners (and they did so infrequently), they were regarded as "frail ones" and "poor creatures."[75] As in the earlier era, women continued to be convicted primarily for non-serious crimes. Of the 218 women incarcerated at Kingston Penitentiary between 1870 and 1895, 156 were convicted of larceny, theft, or burglary. Incidents of violent crime, while higher than in the earlier part of the century, remained low. Even more rare were incidents of "moral crime": three women served time for causing an abortion, two for concealing the birth of a child, one for permitting prostitution of a young girl, and one for child desertion.[76]

Though they were often physically marginalized, the female prisoners were nonetheless deeply integrated with the penitentiary economy due to the domestic labour they provided. Women produced and mended much of the clothing required by penitentiaries and were also relied upon for cleaning all areas of the penitentiary. Considering the small number of women in each penitentiary, the volume of labour they provided was staggering. For example, at Kingston in 1898, twenty-six women produced over 6,000 pieces of clothing and linens, including shirts, towels, handkerchiefs, pillowcases, sheets, socks, and mittens. In addition, the women's department mended 10,425 pairs of socks for the male prison. The same year at Dorchester, the female prisoners performed the equivalent of 52 days of work specific to the maintenance of the female ward. By comparison, they provided 656 days of labour mending apparel for the men's prison and performed 730 days of "washing and housework" for the entire institution. This labour was performed by six women, and the matron noted that due to medical conditions, not all were capable of physical labour.[77] Still, there was little discussion of the moral reform expected of these prisoners, and the positive moral effect attributed to their labour was assumed to be virtually nothing compared to that attributed to the male prisoners' work. For all penitentiaries in this era, this labour was a simple necessity and female prisoners provided a cheap and ready solution. For the most part, these were services without which the institutions could not survive.

RACE

Race was a carefully defined category in the nineteenth-century penitentiary. Noted on registers, in reports about prisoner conduct, and in all other manner of personal records, race also sometimes played a contributing role in particular constructions of criminality. The most obvious targets of differentiated notions of criminality were black prisoners. Although black prisoners were subjected to the same routines and disciplines as all other inmates, their relationship to the penitentiary and daily penal practice was often refracted through racial categories.

Historically, penitentiaries, gaols, and workhouses have been tools of discipline used to maintain racial hierarchies established by systems of slavery. In Québec at the end of the eighteenth century, a number of recently arrived black and Aboriginal, or *panis*, slaves deserted their owners under the pretext that there was no legal slavery in the province.[78] In at least two cases involving black women, slave owners appealed to magistrates for warrants to secure their return. Although it was unclear that such warrants were enforceable, in both cases the women were recaptured and committed to the local gaol. The first, a woman named Jude, obtained a writ of *habeas corpus* and the Court of King's Bench discharged her without costs. The chief justice at the time stated that he would discharge "every Negro, indented Apprentice, and Servant, who should be committed to Gaol under the Magistrates warrants in the like cases."[79] In the second case, a slave named Charlotte belonging to a Montreal merchant deserted and was subsequently incarcerated in the gaol, only to be released after petitioning with *habeas corpus*.[80] The two cases alarmed Montreal merchants, who feared losses to slave owners and their creditors. To clear the legal confusion, a bill was tabled in the House of Assembly of Lower Canada in 1799 that guaranteed slave owners' rights to their property. Furthermore, the bill stipulated that it would be lawful to commit all deserting slaves, apprentices, and servants to the common gaol of the district where they were apprehended until they could be returned to the services of their owners.[81]

After the abolition of slavery in the British Colonies in 1807, Canadian gaols continued to play a role in detaining escaped slaves from US jurisdictions. *Habeas corpus* challenges were often avoided simply by making theft or rape charges against escaped slaves apprehended in British North America. This was the case with Nelson

Hacket, who was pursued by his master from Arkansas and incarcerated in the Sandwich gaol in Chatham after being falsely accused of theft and rape. Hacket faced an insurmountable series of affidavits from legal and government authorities in both Michigan and Arkansas supporting the case of his master, Alfred Wallace. Wallace obtained requisitions from the governors of Arkansas and Michigan supporting his charges against Hacket, who was surrendered to the State of Arkansas to stand trial for grand larceny.[82]

Between 1836 and 1857, Kingston Penitentiary received 250 black convicts. Throughout this period, the shadow of slavery continued to fall on black prisoners. In Kingston's first full year of operation, Chaplain W. M. Herchmer noted that of 148 prisoners, 15 were "coloured people" and "8 are runaway slaves, wofully [sic] ignorant and degraded."[83] Robin Winks notes that before 1850 there was a widespread view in Upper Canada that black convicts made up a disproportionate part of the penitentiary population.[84] Kingston's Protestant chaplain, R. V. Rogers, argued in 1841 that the premise was deeply flawed: "Let our neighbourhood to nearly three million slaves be considered, that the coloured population of Canada is largely composed of runaway slaves, and a reason is at hand for the large number of coloured Convicts, without seeking for one, which white malignity has ever at hand, in the alleged idleness and viciousness of that race." Rogers advanced a more nuanced explanation for the perceived criminality and ignorance of black convicts than his colleagues in the penitentiary. "The previous education of slaves should be considered," he wrote, "or rather the absence of education.—Living as they do on the majority of plantations, in a state of the grossest ignorance and vice, can it be wondered at that some on reaching this land of liberty should commit crimes which render punishment necessary?"[85] This was one view. Winks notes that some held a counter opinion that fugitive slaves were often not punished for crimes out of sympathy for their condition.[86]

Among penitentiary administrators and officials, there was a consensus that blacks exhibited more criminality than whites. Officials produced statistics that purported to prove this. In 1853 the

penitentiary annual report included a table showing "the comparative criminality of different races in Canada." It did this by producing
a ratio of penitentiary convicts to the general population. Of 969,189
Europeans or whites, 233 were committed to the penitentiary, a ratio
of roughly 1 to 4,160. Of 8,000 blacks in Canada, 23 were committed
to Kingston, a ratio of 1 to 348.[87] The meaning was regarded as self
evident. Slavery continued to influence these numbers in the 1850s.
In 1857 Kingston reported 45 black prisoners and 17 mulattoes. The
annual report stated that of these, 20 were born in slavery and 26
were born to slave parents.[88] The direct linkage to slavery affected
more than conviction rates: it played a critical role in the perceived
criminality of black people in Canada. Christopher Adamson argues
that ex-slaves in the American North were seen as a uniquely dangerous class, a construction that was replicated in the South after the
passage of the 13th Amendment in 1865.[89] Under slavery, black
people were punished according to slave codes. After the Civil War,
southern contractual penal servitude replaced slavery as a way to
make this population productive for white landowners.[90] It also
provided an institutional replacement for the control of a population
perceived to be a problem. As fugitive arrivals increased in the
Niagara peninsula after 1850, similar fear and anxiety was prevalent
in Canada.[91]

Within penitentiaries both before and after Confederation,
black prisoners were frequently regarded as objects of fear, mistrust,
and loathing among both staff and convicts. Just as crimes committed
by black people received disproportionate play in the local Canadian
press, the transgressions of black prisoners often occupied a larger
role in the penitentiary record than those of their white counterparts.
This created the impression that black prisoners were more incorrigible, more difficult to control, and more criminally inclined than
white convicts. Warden D. A. Macdonell described William Jones, an
inmate at Kingston, in this way in 1853: "This unfortunate man was
formerly a Convict in the Auburn Penitentiary in the State of New
York, where I find that he sustained various punishments, but being a
very determined character, he succeeded in inducing the authorities to

believe that he was deranged, and was sent to a Lunatic Asylum." Jones eventually escaped from the asylum and entered Canada, where he was convicted and sentenced to life at Kingston Penitentiary. Macdonell reported, "He is a powerful man and very active, but indolent, vicious, and dangerous."[92] This was a commonly held view of black convicts, both in public perception and among penitentiary officials. One Kingston guard told a local newspaper in 1896 that he would "rather mind a dozen white convicts than half-a-dozen negroes. . . . They are treacherous and deceitful, and the guards have to be very shrewd to detect their villainous dispositions."[93]

These negative stereotypes of black prisoners persisted through- out the nineteenth century. Often they were self-fulfilling. Because black convicts were targets of mistrust and animosity, they were involved in more trouble than white convicts, thus cementing their reputation as violent and incorrigible. In some cases, black convicts were driven to protect themselves from attack. In other instances, blacks were involved in so much trouble that prison officials relin- quished them to insane asylums. One such example was John Foy, an inmate at Manitoba Penitentiary who was convicted in the early 1890s of grievous bodily harm (assault). The Protestant chaplain described the fifty-five year old as "grossly ignorant, obstinate and very bad tempered."[94] Much like convicts who were former slaves, officials suggested that Foy's ignorance and illiteracy contributed to his ruth- lessness. Another common characteristic attributed to black convicts was unusual physical strength, a quality that underscored their par- ticular menace. The chaplain's description of inmate Foy reflects that fear: "Being a powerful fellow, it is dangerous to trust him among other convicts and guards, as he is as treacherous as he is violent. It may be useful to transfer him to Kingston where he could be placed under restraint as a lunatic, if necessary." When Foy's sentence was complete, Manitoba Penitentiary detained him for an additional three weeks while attempting to convince the North West Mounted Police to transfer him to Kingston permanently as a lunatic. The police finally took Foy into custody but released him three days later after judging him to be sane.[95]

Finally, black convicts were constructed in ways that conformed to negative notions of criminality because they were at ideological odds with the penitentiary reform project. Adamson argues that in US prisons, the perceived criminality of black people could not be reconciled with American ideologies about reformation because the concept of reformation was tied to the body politic and citizenship. In the antebellum era, this left black people, even in emancipated states, in a precarious position because it was difficult to conceive of a place in society for "reformed" black convicts. While southern slaveholding states considered it "utopian" for Northern prisons to reform black convicts, Adamson suggests that their Yankee counterparts in penal administration struggled with the same ideas, particularly after the influx of emancipated slaves after 1865.[96] Canadian penitentiary officials exhibited similar uneasiness about the future of black prisoners: they could not conceive of them ever joining Canadian society as productive and "reformed" individuals.

FIRST NATIONS CRIMINALITY

The constructions of criminality surrounding black prisoners was turned on its head in the case of First Nations prisoners. In western Canada in the post-Confederation era, the penitentiary increasingly came to represent the punitive arm of Canadian colonial policy in a network that also included the Department of Indian Affairs and the North West Mounted Police (NWMP). While First Nations people were subject to unique constructions of criminality, their position in Canadian society as colonial subjects had a profound effect on how the penitentiary responded to their incarceration. In these constructions of criminality, we see a dramatic contradiction between portrayals in Western society that emphasized the savagery of First Nations people (particularly after the 1885 Northwest Rebellion) and penitentiary responses that were largely paternalistic and condescending.

In the early 1870s, First Nations people in the Canadian North-West Territories faced increasing economic uncertainty. Depleted by decades of epidemic disease and warfare, and the destruction of traditional buffalo-based economies, by 1877 most First Nations people had entered into treaties with the Canadian government.[97] As Cree, Assiniboine, Blood, and Blackfoot tribes settled on reserves in the late 1870s, many bands struggled with the end of their economic independence and autonomy of movement throughout the North-West. Although the buffalo hunt had ceased to be the centre of economic activity by the 1870s, many tribes continued to participate in the related practice of horse stealing, either between tribes or from settlers in Canada or across the American border. While the federal government relied upon the Department of Indian Affairs (DIA) to govern life on reserves, it turned to the NWMP to curtail horse stealing. As Brian Hubner argues, the NWMP and DIA focused on horse stealing not only because it was economically disruptive to new European settlement but also because it represented the incompatibility between traditional First Nations lifestyles and the new economic order.[98] The threat of horse stealing was magnified by the fact that it was carried out by young men, often armed. Indeed, the federal government and the NWMP considered this element of First Nations society a dangerous class and responded to horse stealing with increasing severity. The police were aided in this goal by the opening of Manitoba Penitentiary, which provided the mechanism for much longer sentences than were possible in the early NWMP guard rooms connected to police outposts.

By the early 1870s, First Nations people were already being sentenced to terms in provincial prison. The very first prisoner listed on the Manitoba Penitentiary admittance register was a Dakota man named John Longbones. Longbones was convicted of assault with intention to maim in May 1871 at the General Quarterly Assizes in Red River and sentenced to two years at Lower Fort Garry, which was, at the time, a provincial penitentiary. One of only six prisoners to be incarcerated at Lower Fort Garry before it was designated a federal penitentiary in 1872, Longbones was joined by three Americans, a Métis from Red River, and a Swede convicted of horse stealing. In these early years, it was extremely rare for First Nations people in the

North-West to be convicted of serious crimes. Longbones was one of only three First Nations men, all Dakota from the Red River area, who were sentenced to Manitoba Penitentiary before it moved from Lower Fort Garry to the new facility at Stony Mountain, outside of Winnipeg. The others, Pee-ma-ta-kow and Mc-ha-ha, were both convicted of larceny in September of 1873.[99] While they were at Fort Garry, the Dakota prisoners were visited by John Longbones, who had recently been released. According to Samuel Bedson, the warden at Lower Fort Garry and later at Manitoba Penitentiary, Longbones "exhorted them in a most earnest manner to implicit obedience to the rules, relating his own experience of the advantage so gained, as a case in point."[100] In the early 1880s, the increasing vigilance against horse stealing was made possible by NWMP patrols throughout the North-West and co-operation from the American military in pursuing horse thieves across the border. Starting in 1881, NWMP magistrates and territorial judges began to deliver more serious sentences for horse stealing, sending convicted thieves to Manitoba Penitentiary. The first two such convictions were Ka-ka-wink and Little Fisher, both sentenced to five years at Manitoba. It was Little Fisher's second conviction for horse stealing. His first was in October 1880, when he was punished with six months of hard labour in the NWMP guard room at Fort Walsh.[101] Little Fisher managed to escape the guard room for a time, but he was later recaptured. Possessing impressive determination, he escaped from Manitoba Penitentiary less than two years after his second conviction for horse stealing. He was never recaptured.[102] There were two more individual convictions for horse stealing in 1882. Jingling Bells received a three-year sentence while Na-ke-ew was sentenced to seven years. As the NWMP and the DIA moved to completely end unauthorized First Nations movement across the border, sentences became more severe.

In 1883 the police moved more decisively against cross-border horse stealing. Three Cree men and one Saulteaux man were convicted of bringing stolen property into Canada in May 1883 and received five years each at Manitoba Penitentiary. The following month, the NWMP arrested eleven Cree men for a raid on a Montana rancher. Each was sentenced to two years at Manitoba Penitentiary. NWMP

Commissioner A. E. Irvine reported, "Such punishment has unquestionably been accompanied with most beneficial results, proving as it did, that the Canadian government was determined to use its utmost endeavours towards stamping out pernicious and criminal practices."[103] The convictions for horse stealing resulted in a major influx of prisoners to the newly constructed institution, which housed ninety-nine prisoners by 1883.[104] By 1885 a total of twenty-four First Nations men were imprisoned at Manitoba Penitentiary for horse stealing or bringing stolen horses into Canada. Seven other First Nations individuals were held for other crimes.[105] As Heather Rollason and R. C. Macleod argue, other than those for horse stealing, convictions of First Nations people throughout the North-West were extremely low given that they dramatically outnumbered whites in Manitoba and the North-West Territories.[106] Still, in 1883 the Canadian government was deeply apprehensive of the threatening potential represented by growing First Nations political agitation. In the 1880s, rising political activity among the Plains Cree would confirm the government's worst fears about the criminal threat posed by First Nations autonomy in the North-West.

As early as 1883, the federal government was moving to prevent this possibility by planning to arrest Cree political leaders, including Big Bear, Poundmaker, and Little Pine. Prime Minister John A. Macdonald, also the minister of Indian Affairs, moved to align his department, the NWMP, and local magistrates toward the same goal: the long-term imprisonment of the Cree political leadership.[107] However, in early 1885, the Cree people became embroiled in the spreading violence of the Northwest Rebellion. Big Bear's people were responsible for the massacre of nine white settlers at Frog Lake, and both Poundmaker and Little Pine were drawn into armed conflict with the Canadian militia, which had initially engaged with Louis Riel's Métis forces in Saskatchewan.[108] After a summer of being pursued by the militia, the majority of the exhausted fugitive Cree surrendered or were captured. Eighty-one First Nations men were charged with various crimes, ranging from horse stealing, arson, and murder, to treason-felony.[109] Forty-four men were sentenced to imprisonment at Manitoba Penitentiary, including Poundmaker, One Arrow, and Big

Bear, all convicted of treason-felony for their role in the Rebellion.[110] Thus, the summer of 1885 ended much as Edgar Dewdney, lieutenant-governor of the North-West Territories, and Hayter Reed, then assistant Indian commissioner, had intended: the Cree political movement was decapitated and its leaders incarcerated along with the most "rebellious" and "dangerous" members of the dissident bands.

In the aftermath of the Northwest Rebellion, popular portrayals of First Nations criminality were at their most inflammatory. Anger at the violence committed during the rebellion was immense, and the Canadian press portrayed the rebels in the most inflammatory terms. Editorials stressed the need for vengeance and for subdueing the brutal nature inherent in Native people. Even editorials that criticized the Conservative government's North-West policy resorted to the same themes. The Toronto-based *Globe* condemned the harsh treatment of First Nations people but argued that poor policies had incited the "savage and murderous instincts" of the North-West tribes.[111] In spite of the strength of racialized constructions of criminality involving First Nations people, particularly after 1885, there was also a remarkable dichotomy at work that accented the possibility of change. As Andrea McCalla and Vic Satzewich argue, colonial ideology stressed that the cultural characteristics of First Nations people were never regarded as biologically grounded. In fact, the very basis of the colonial relationship between First Nations people and the Canadian state was premised on their ability to change their fundamental cultural characteristics to become more like Euro-Canadians.[112] This belief permeated colonial relationships between state officials and First Nations people even in situations like the aftermath of the Northwest Rebellion, when individuals were criminalized.

In the late 1870s, Samuel Bedson, warden of Manitoba Penitentiary, developed a philosophy and practice that was uniquely applied to the First Nations prisoners at that institution. Bedson was an atypical warden in the penitentiary service. He had come to Canada at the age of nineteen with the 16th Foot. In 1870 he joined the 2nd Battalion of Rifles and served in the expedition to quell the 1870 Red River Uprising. When the battalion disbanded in 1870, Bedson was chosen as warden of the provincial gaol recently established at Lower Fort Garry. He possessed no penal training. Like D. A. Macdonell at Kingston and Creighton after him, Bedson believed that common sense should guide penal policy, a principle he combined with strict military discipline. He served as warden at Manitoba until his death in 1891 at the age of 49.[113]

Warden Bedson adopted the view that the penitentiary could be used as an instrument of "civilization," and he instituted special education, labour, and religious programs for First Nations prisoners. In 1877 he organized classes for the benefit of Pee-ma-ta-kow, Mc-ha-ha, and Joh-qui-gay-poo. "Most of them at the opening of the school understood English very imperfectly," he reported; "they now can read and write, and their progress is most marked, and much greater than could have been expected. They show great diligence, and seem most anxious to learn."[114] The following year, Bedson declared the program "eminently successful" on the basis of weekly reports submitted to him by the officer in charge of instruction.[115] In the warden's view, the education provided by the penitentiary provided valuable opportunities for the "civilization" of First Nations prisoners. In 1878 he wrote,

> The expiration of the terms of punishment in the case of Indian prisoners is not infrequently looked upon themselves with positive regret. They enter ignorant and superstitious, and easily moulded for good or bad. The routine of prison life, and the opportunities constantly thrust upon them for moral and intellectual improvement, is seldom lost, and they leave, what in their case is virtually an adult reformatory, radically changed for the better, in almost every particular.[116]

As with other prisoners, labour played an important role but assumed colonial overtones in the case of First Nations prisoners. Bedson ensured that they performed labour that would aid them in their new role as agriculturalists. Inspector Moylan commented approvingly in 1887, "The Warden places as many as possible of the Indian prisoners in the workshops, in order that they may learn such trades as will be useful to them on discharge, and especially those for which they show a taste and preference."[117] Father Cloutier, the Catholic chaplain, wrote on the same issues, noting that the Cree prisoners had learned trades and, after being taught the benefits of "manual labour," would "continue to work, and thus help on the civilization of their own people."[118]

Alongside education and labour, religion played an important role in efforts to civilize First Nations prisoners. When the first large groups of horse thieves arrived at Manitoba Penitentiary in 1883, they attracted the special attention of Father Cloutier. After a year of instructing the Cree men, he reported that he was pleased with their progress. "They were eager to learn the principles of a Christian life," he wrote, "and as far as it was possible, I grounded them thoroughly in the lessons I strove to impress on their minds." After the Native prisoners were instructed in the "truths of religion," the archbishop of St. Boniface travelled to the penitentiary to baptize the men. Cloutier reported, "The usual imposing ceremonial made a deep impression on the susceptible minds of the Indians."[119]

Perhaps more important than religious lessons were the messages the chaplain conveyed about the changing relationship between First Nations people and settlers in the North-West. In this respect, Cloutier explained to the Cree horse thieves what the government was trying to accomplish through penitentiary sentences: "They understood that the whites were not their enemies; they understood that in every society there are men who rule, and others who are ruled; that if the law is not to remain a dead letter, it must be upheld; that respect for the law is to their own advantage, and its violation a cause of trouble, and that the welfare of all demands that its violators be punished." The Cree prisoners understood all of this in a general way, noted Cloutier, but he added that their confidence in his lessons about Canadian law was shaken when he tried to make them understand that their imprisonment was "for their own good." Despite their reaction, he truly believed this to be the case, and he echoed the themes of evangelical colonialism in his praise for the good work accomplished at the penitentiary. "I am convinced," he wrote, "that their stay in the institution will have been of real benefit to them." Furthermore, he suggested that upon release, the Cree would carry with them the goodwill instilled in them by their time in the penitentiary: "The Indians are big children, and their sensitive hearts cannot fail to have been touched when they were discharged before the expiration of the full terms of their sentence."[120] Cloutier concluded with an optimistic view of the future:

> They will tell what has been done for them; they will make known the real purpose held in view by those who administer the laws, and they will point out the duties devolving upon those who are subject to those laws. They will help to remove the mistrust existing amongst the Indians towards the officials of the Government, and inspire them with that confidence which is essential to all amicable relations. This will be a great step towards their moral and intellectual improvement.[121]

Though his writing was full of benevolence and sanguine forecasts about the future of the Cree men incarcerated in 1883 and 1884, much of what Cloutier said could be boiled down to a single basic lesson: imprisonment made the horse thieves understand that they had become "the ruled." Still, this was a form of reformation that was inherently more optimistic than could possibly be imagined regarding other groups of racialized prisoners. Depending on the desired outcome of the subject group, race could be remarkably transmutable in how criminality was constructed in the penitentiary. In other categories, such as medical classification, race played a more distinct role. As I discuss below, the racialization of black and First Nations prisoners played an entirely detrimental role in how penitentiaries responded to the deteriorating health of these prisoners.

JUVENILE DELINQUENTS

Some of the most conflicted nineteenth-century constructions of criminality involved juvenile delinquents. When Kingston Penitentiary opened in 1835, among the first prisoners were children as young as eight years old. This was indicative of the lack of social welfare options for children and adolescents charged with criminal offences. It was unlikely that such young offenders would be whipped or banished, and prison often appeared to be the only alternative. Both boys and girls were mixed indiscriminately with the adult convict population and participated in the daily routines of prison life. This included being subjected to the same types of corporal punishment that were given to adult convicts.

The lack of distinction between children and adults gradually changed under the influence of the second wave of penal reform. The Brown Commission condemned the treatment of children at Kingston Penitentiary and recommended the construction of a House of Refuge for young criminals. As with most of his suggestions, Brown was drawing on a changing conception of childhood criminality that was taking root in British and American reform movements. Martin Weiner notes that, as with the mentally ill and "fallen women," the early Victorian period saw new attitudes about the possibilities of reforming young offenders. These were based upon a particular construction of criminality that was distinct from how older deviants were conceptualized since the notion of personal responsibility was far more conflicted where children were concerned. One perspective was that children were not wholly responsible for their guilt in the commission of crime. The more dominant view, however, was that regardless of guilt, children were potentially more socially dangerous than fully formed adults because they acted on impulse and had the potential to develop into truly dangerous individuals if this degeneracy were not checked.[122] As a result of the second perspective, the solutions that reformers proposed for childhood criminality were often no less punitive than those in prison regimes designed for adults. Even in the midst of the rise of the child reformatory movement, the responses to juvenile delinquency remained essentially Lockean. The implication was that these offenders required harsh treatment to stop their slide into absolute criminality.

The solutions proposed by the reform movement mirrored responses to the perceived social crisis surrounding the dangerous classes. In England, this began with voluntary Sunday schools that were designed to teach morality to the children of those classes. The movement became more widespread as the sense of crisis about the poor deepened. Mary Carpenter's "ragged school" movement involved opening voluntary day schools in the poorest neighbourhoods.

But these early endeavours were undertaken without state support because, as Carpenter argued, "it has always been felt that government aid and inspection would be fatal to what must be a heartless labour, if not a labour of love and Christian zeal." Carpenter eventually admitted, however, that these limited efforts were not up to the task of changing "the whole nature of the child."[123] Her solution was to introduce the young offender to a newly moral environment that would restore "the position of childhood." In dedicated reformatory schools, the child would be placed in a family environment that would create the moral influences lacking in the early years of development. "He must be brought to a new sense of dependence by re-awakening in him a new and healthy desire which he cannot himself gratify," wrote Carpenter, "and by finding that there is a power far greater than his own to which he is indebted for the gratification of these desires."[124]

Carpenter constructed classifications for juvenile delinquents that were similar to those that penal reformers created to explain different degrees of criminality. The reformatory school solutions she engineered as a response to juvenile delinquency tell us much about how she viewed childhood criminality. She separated juvenile delinquents into four classes. The first comprised the "hardened young offenders" who were the outlaws of society; the second was composed of the children of habitual criminals, trained in dishonesty; the third encompassed children with no moral influence who were merely susceptible to future crime and lacked the will to choose a moral path; and the fourth was made up of the utterly destitute who were driven to crime by their poverty. All of these categories hinted that juvenile delinquents were in one stage or another of development as members of the dangerous classes. According to Carpenter, each class required "some peculiar and distinct action for its suppression."[125] Thus, Carpenter, who was regarded as one of the "softer" voices on juvenile delinquency, equated youth crime with moral disease that required institutional intervention. In its aims and ideology, her reformatory school network would function as a state moralization project to stop the degeneration of the urban poor. In practice, it created a network of prisons for children.

The drive for separate institutions for children started much earlier in the United States. When Brown suggested that Canada build a House of Refuge for children, he was drawing on American movements under reformers like Charles Eddy. In the 1820s, American reformers constructed Houses of Refuge in New York, Boston, and Philadelphia. While the same reformers inspired Auburn Penitentiary and subsequently Kingston, Canada was slower to adopt reform ideologies that promoted separate institutions for children, largely because the social crisis regarding pauperism and urbanization that characterized New York and Boston in the early nineteenth century was slower to develop in Canadian urban centres. As Anthony Platt argues in *The Child Savers*, it was the demands of a perceived social crisis, and not purely humanitarian responses, that motivated new institutional solutions for children.[126]

By the late 1850s and 1860s, Upper Canada, Lower Canada, and Nova Scotia had opened prisons specifically designed for children and youths. These early institutions, labelled alternately "reformatories" or "industrial schools," were mere prisons for children and young men, and did not address issues of reformation or criminality in their regimes, which were based largely on labour and punishment. A second wave of institutions that opened in the 1880s, including the Victoria Industrial School for Boys in Toronto and the Alexandra Industrial School for Girls, attempted to create more caring and family-like atmospheres for their young inmates. The new institutions were part of a growing progressive agenda with regard to children that included compulsory education, foster care, and parole services.[127] In spite of a growing child-welfare movement that aimed to rescue children from the damaging influences of poverty and criminality, the justice system across the country was inconsistent regarding the treatment of children and youths. Still, by the late 1880s, youth reformatories had reduced the number of children sentenced to penitentiaries in Ontario and Québec: between 1870 and 1900, sixty-three individuals aged sixteen and younger were sentenced to Kingston Penitentiary, but only six of these occurred after 1890.[128] However, in other jurisdictions, young children and teenagers continued to be sentenced to terms in federal penitentiaries in the 1870s and 1880s. Some penitentiary officials suggested that this was the result of decisions made by "benevolent" judges who sentenced children to penitentiaries in the belief that they were more civilized than what one inspector called "the fouler abyss" of local gaols or provincial prisons.[129]

Penitentiaries were certainly more regulated than local gaols or prisons, but they were not safe places for children. The "very special and tender watchfulness" that penitentiary chaplains offered to child convicts was intended to prevent their "moral ruin" through association with hardened criminals.[130] As Robert Mitchell, a surgeon at Dorchester, wrote in 1890, "I can conceive of nothing more likely to complete their moral ruin than to send children of such tender years to associate with a prison which includes among its inmates murderers, thieves, and burglars."[131] In spite of attempts, sometimes only superficial, to separate young convicts from the older prison population, penitentiary officials agreed that the influence of hardened criminals upon youths was impossible to prevent. The notion of moral influence also represented a changing conception of youth criminality, which came to be understood as something distinct from the constructions of criminality commonly associated with adults. Criminality was no longer regarded as an innate characteristic bur rather as a product of circumstances.

By the late nineteenth century, poverty had displaced morality as a dominant theme in the reform discourse about children and crime, with reformers promoting the idea that children could be saved from the clutches of poor parenting and poverty.[132] In 1900 C. E. Cartwright, a Protestant penitentiary chaplain, offered his explanation of the presence of young convicts: "A moiety I believe, have from one cause or another lost their homes at an early age. Many tell such a story as this: 'My mother died when I was five, my father when I was thirteen,

I could not get on with my step-mother and left home then,' or 'I was first arrested for vagrancy when I was ten years old, my step-mother having turned me out.'"[133] There was some recognition, probably more so than with adult convicts, that class was the determining factor in the conviction and imprisonment of youths and children. However, in the eyes of some officials, this did not completely absolve children of the taint of criminality that resulted from their conviction. For example, in 1893 Inspector Moylan linked hardened criminals with a pervasive criminality both inherited from birth and nursed in the commission of childhood crimes. Identifying these young convicts as "sneak thieves and pickpockets," Moylan traced their origins to the British neighbourhoods of Whitechapel, Rotherhithe, and Ratcliff—all notorious East London slums.[134] They were, he wrote, "street Arabs . . . youthful imitators of Fagin and Bill Sykes" who had immigrated to Canada, where they returned to old habits and ended up in reformatories, gaols, and penitentiaries.[135] These constructions played on popular criminal stereotypes that depicted young convicts as ethnic others. In spite of being one of the leading penitentiary reformers in the country, in this instance Moylan resorted to stock descriptions of youth criminality. In these constructions, imprisoned children were relegated permanently to membership in the dangerous classes, the progeny of criminals and the denizens of the proverbial and literal gutter.[136]

Reformers repeatedly expressed conflicted views of youth criminality, particularly when they came face to face with the striking sight of children among the penitentiary population. In 1883 Inspector Moylan wrote on the question of child convicts with considerable disgust:

> If seven years ago, I had not had a like revolting picture presented to me of a certain Gulf province where the shrill falsetto of boys from 8 to 12, mingled with the rough and deep tones of hoary headed men grown old in vice and crime, in giving utterance to obscenity and blasphemy, I might not feel so keenly to write so strongly in condemnation of what I cannot help regard as a revolting anomaly— which is a standing disgrace to Provinces where it suffers to exist.[137]

Moylan was getting at some of the key issues behind the phenomenon of child convicts. New Brunswick—and by extension, Dorchester Penitentiary—incarcerated more children than other jurisdictions because there was no youth reformatory in the province until the late 1890s. In 1884 Moylan noted that Dorchester held twelve children between the ages of nine and sixteen, with sentences ranging from three to six years.[138] In 1890 Dorchester admitted two brothers, aged eight and ten, on a charge of larceny. Upon their arrival, the warden had a suit of clothing made for both and enrolled them in the nearest parish school. "They are fine little boys and doing well," he reported a year into their incarceration. Still, the brothers lived and slept at the penitentiary for two years while serving their sentence. From a complaint issued by Dorchester officials, it was clear that the tragedy, in their eyes, was that no other institution existed for the incarceration of such children, not that they were imprisoned in the first place.[139] This provides a powerful example of the effect of the construction of youth criminality, particularly in individual cases like this where children were already convicted.

Throughout the nineteenth century, constructions of criminality were constantly changing and evolving. In one sense, the penitentiary moved during the Victorian era toward a more individualistic understanding of criminality. Inspired by new reform and evangelical ideologies, reformers and penitentiary officials began to consider each offender on the basis of his or her unique prospects of individual moral reformation. The constructions of criminality in this era were a combination of new and old. Even when criminality was considered an individual attribute, this understanding was always layered with older notions about deviance and with constructions based on class, gender, and race. Most importantly, these constructions did not exist only in the realm of discourse; they played a key role in the development and evolution of penal practice. In the next chapter, I explore some of the manifestations of the complex constructions of criminality. While the idea of criminality affected penal practices and strategies, the remainder of this book is dedicated to how penitentiary life itself affected the subjective views of the prison population.

Prison Life

What gave the penitentiary's keepers and officials their power? Certainly, they possessed physical domination over the prison population: prisoners were restrained, were locked in cells for much of the day, and lived constantly behind walls. But how did keepers compel prisoners to follow the rules of daily life in the penitentiary—to behave in an orderly fashion, to perform their labour, to sit for meals and prayers? In his groundbreaking study of the New Jersey State Prison, sociologist Gersham M. Sykes details the four "defects of total power" inherent to the relationship between prisoners and keepers at that institution. First, although prisoners recognized the legitimacy of penitentiary officials to make rules and give orders, they felt no compulsion to obey such commands: "the prisoner thus accepts the fact of his captivity at one level and rejects it at another."[1] Second, the notion that order could be enforced through violence was only an illusion. Violence was an ineffective means of exercising control or compelling men to perform complex tasks required by the growing industrial demands in the modern penitentiary. Third, the system of rewards was ineffective because penitentiary regimes were so spartan that any privilege to be gained or taken away was insignificant to the prison population.[2] Finally, the penitentiary guard could not sustain the social distance from prisoners that was necessary to maintain absolute power over them: "He cannot withdraw physically in symbolic affirmation of his superior position; . . . and he cannot fall back on a dignity adhering to his office—he is a *hack* or a *screw* in the eyes of those he controls and an unwelcome display of officiousness evokes that great destroyer of unquestioned power, the ribald humor of the dispossessed."[3]

In this chapter, I examine the power relations at the heart of penitentiary life. I look at the rules and regulations as well as the strategies and tactics that characterized the penitentiary in the post-Confederation era, but more importantly, I explore how daily life and the intercourse of power between prisoners and keepers both sustained and subverted domination's development. In the process, we see reform in action and discover the ways in which its principles were constructed as the basis of power in the penitentiary. I look at the structure of penitentiary life and contrast it with examples of resistance and transgression by both prisoners and keepers. This leads not only to a more complex and complete portrait of the penitentiary, but also to an understanding of the myriad ways in which reform was subverted in the lived experience of penitentiary history. In this exploration, I attempt to unearth some of what James C. Scott calls "the hidden transcript" of resistance.[4] However, I try to locate this thread not only in the lives of the prisoners, but also in the experiences of the keepers.

INTO THE PENITENTIARY

Among the significant common experiences in penitentiary life, one that became increasingly standardized in the post-Confederation era was the admission ritual. Thousands of convicts arriving at Kingston Penitentiary experienced the first hours of prison life in much the same way. A great deal of what they encountered was designed to instill important messages about the penitentiary, its power structures, and the new prisoner's place within them. Most offenders came to the penitentiary from local gaols, where they were held while waiting for the quarterly assize and during a short trial before a magistrate. After sentencing, the prisoner departed for the penitentiary in the custody of a sheriff. Most travelled to Kingston by stage or by train. In the early part of the century, it was customary for the sheriff to share a drink with the prisoner just before arriving at the penitentiary. After Confederation, however, prisoners were required to sit silently in handcuffs throughout the journey.

With regard to the "typical" experience, it should be noted that much less is known about the admittance procedure and daily routines of female prisoners. We can be certain that these routines would have differed from what is described below, given the separate confinement of women at Kingston, but the paucity of first-hand records obviously makes it difficult to describe women's experiences behind bars. Thus, although I refer below to specific examples involving women prisoners, the available evidence does not allow definitive conclusions about penal practice with respect to women, and I therefore use the masculine pronoun unless specifically referring to women prisoners.

Arriving at Kingston Penitentiary, the average male prisoner was taken through the main gates at the keeper's lodge and handed over to a steward. Moving into the keeper's hall, the prisoner was searched, relieved of all personal possessions, and then stripped so his clothing could be burned. He was then given a rough haircut and a shave by a convict barber before being bathed. A steward marched the prisoner to the prison storeroom to receive his prison uniform. Meeting the clothing clerk, who was usually a long-serving prisoner, the new inmate quickly realized his position within the convict population. New prisoners and first-time offenders were given the dregs of the penitentiary clothing supply—dirty, used, and shabby clothing and scuffed or broken boots. In this outfit, the "new fish" was easily identified by the other prisoners. "Old hands," or recommitted prisoners, knew enough to stand up to the clothing clerk and demand a newly sewn set of clothing. Even a first-time prisoner could avoid this indignity if he knew enough to have a clergyman or influential citizen write to the warden on his behalf, and the order would be communicated to the clothing supply room.[5]

If a prisoner had no friend to speak on his behalf, much could be accomplished by bribing convict clerks or junior keepers. While prisoners were told upon transfer from provincial or local gaols that money would not be needed and would be taken from them when admitted to the penitentiary, cash was actually a crucial necessity in easing the pains of adopting to penitentiary life. A correspondent writing in *The Labour Union* recounted how a friend thrust a ten-dollar bill into his pocket as he boarded the train from Toronto en route to Kingston Penitentiary as a first-time prisoner:

> God bless him! The officers were lamentably mistaken. Money is the one thing needful there. Never go to the Penitentiary without cash if you can help it. It gets you when there new clothes cut in the latest style, and served with as many different colored threads as you choose. It furnishes you with a patent swing bed, easy chair, carpet slippers for the evening and as many different kinds of boots and shoes as your taste may suggest for working in. It converts your government straw pillow into something nice for your uneasy head. Puts sugar in your coffee, butter on your dry bed, milk in your tea . . . often secures you a "soft job" and procures you a bottle of "booze"— the penitentiary term for spirits—as often as you want it.[6]

This first-time prisoner was shocked to discover that one of the experienced "gaol birds" travelling to Kingston to serve a fourteen-year sentence managed to conceal two hundred dollars in two-dollar bills to help ease his transition back into penitentiary life.[7]

Once dressed, the new prisoner was taken into the heart of the penitentiary to the prisoner cell blocks. At Kingston, men were shown into a cell that measured seven feet long and two and a half feet wide. Cells at the newer institutions were slightly larger.[8] In addition to a bed, which was folded and raised against the wall to allow entry, the cell contained a water jug, a basin, and a night bucket. Two blankets, a sheet, and a rug hung from the wall, and on a shelf beneath the tiny window, the inmate found a Bible and a randomly chosen book from the prison library. If prisoners could read, they would notice a list of detailed penitentiary rules and regulations posted to the wall. The poster listed eighteen "prison offences" and eighteen corresponding "punishments." Starting with admonishment or loss of light for "violation of the rule of silence," the punishments increased in severity for more violent transgressions such as fighting (dark cell for a week), immoral conduct (flogging), and attempted escape (solitary cell, leg irons for a month).[9] If a prisoner arrived in the morning, he was taken to the dining hall to wait for the rest of the working population. When they arrived, he joined them for a soup of beef broth with bread before being swept into the flow of daily labour with the other working inmates.

In the prison yard, the new inmate met with the deputy warden, who questioned him on his mechanical and technical abilities. If he was like the majority of penitentiary inmates, he possessed none and was thus "condemned" to work on the stone pile. For the remainder of the day, he worked his first shift of penitentiary labour—sitting on a low stool, he would break rocks into gravel with an enormous hammer. At 5:30, a bell sounded and he went to supper with the rest of the inmates before returning to his cell for his first night in the penitentiary. At 8:45 a bell sounded again, and the prison lights were turned down for the night. There the prisoner sat or slept in silence until the routine began again the next morning at 5:50. This was the unyielding regimen that he followed every day but Sunday for the remainder of his sentence. The days and weeks after this first day would follow the same dreary and repetitive routine. Table 2 shows the 1886 schedule for Manitoba Penitentiary, but it was remarkably similar for all five federal institutions.

The first hours of a prisoner's time in a federal penitentiary were designed to achieve a symbolic break with his or her criminal past and, importantly, with the criminal subcultures from which authorities assumed prisoners were drawn. This contrasted dramatically with the less formal rhythms of eighteenth century prison regimes that treated inmates more like residents than prisoners. The newly regimented penitentiary included two key elements that submerged the prisoner's

TABLE 2   Daily Schedule of Inmates at Manitoba Penitentiary, 1885

DISTRIBUTION	SUMMER				WINTER			
	From	To	Time.					
	a.m.	a.m.	h.	m.	a.m.	a.m.	h.	m.
Prisoners rise, wash, dress, &c	5:50	6:00		10	6:20	6:30		10
Labor, going & returning included.................	6:00	7:30	1	30	6:30	7:30	1	0
Breakfast	7:30	7:40		10	7:30	7:40		10
In cells..................	7:40	8:30		50	7:40	8:30		50
		p.m.				p.m.		
Labor, going & returning included.................	8:30	12:30	4	0	8:30	12:30	4	0
Dinner...................	12:30	12:45		15	12:30	12:45		15
In cells..................	12:45	1:00		15	12:45	1:00		15
In school	1:00	1:30		30	1:00	1:30		30
Labor, going & returning included	1:30	5:40	4	10	1:30	5:10	3	40
Serving tea, etc., etc	5:40	6:00		20	5:10	5:30		20
Total time			12	10			11	10
Hours appropriated to labor, including muster, going & return			9	50			8	50
Hours appropriated to meals..................				25				25
Hours appropriated to school, &c.				30				30
Hours in cells during day ...			1	05			1	05
Serving tea, etc				20				20
Total time			12	10			11	10

SOURCE: "Warden's Report, Manitoba Penitentiary," *Sessional Papers*, 1886, no. 15, 61.

former identity: the prison uniform and the use of numbers in place of names. The prison uniform was calculated to distance prisoners from their past life, while it also made it easy to recognize inmates and thereby prevent escapes. Canadian penitentiaries featured a variation of prison stripes consisting of a bisected suit of yellow and brown. In the early 1890s, the uniform was altered because reformers argued that the "prison stripes" were a demoralizing and degrading relic of an earlier era. Inspector Moylan wrote,

> If there is one thing more than another, in any system of prison administration, that is calculated to demoralize and stamp out every vestige of manhood and self-respect, it is the zebra and piebald raiment which forms such a cruelly distinctive and prominent feature of some penal institutions. This barbarous relic of a period, when no consideration was extended to the convict, when no interest was felt in his amelioration or well being should, with the "goose step," be incontinently done away with everywhere as out of keeping with our progress and enlightenment and unworthy of a Christian people.[10]

When the minister of Justice announced the change to a new convict uniform in 1890, the praise was overwhelming. Instead of the brown and yellow, the penitentiary system moved to a uniform scheme involving three levels, each corresponding to a classification of convict behaviour. The intended effect was to dress prisoners in uniforms that would give them the appearance of "ordinarily dressed citizens" and help to foster individuality rather than conformity and degradation. Alexander Maconochie had proposed the same reform at Norfolk Island in 1840. But not all wardens agreed with the reform. Warden Bedson at Manitoba Penitentiary argued that the change tended too much toward treating the prisoners like regular citizens and requested permission to dress his prisoners in knickerbockers with coloured stockings for easier detection in the event of escapes.[11]

A similar debate was carried out regarding the use of numbers rather than names to identify prisoners. The rationale behind prisoner numbers was originally to obscure both the identity and the crime of each individual in the institution. This was essentially a less severe method of obscuring identity than the early practice at Pennsylvania Penitentiary, which employed a hood over the head of convicts so they could never be identified in the prison or after release. Not surprisingly, the use of numbers in modern penitentiaries was totally ineffective for the intended purposes. As Moylan noted, "The history of each criminal soon becomes well known to his fellows."[12] In fact, Moylan argued strenuously against the practice of obscuring the identity of convicts, suggesting that it debased and humiliated men to be referred to by anonymous numbers:

> There is a cold cruelty to burying a prisoner's identity, in indicating or addressing him by a number instead of his name, that must constantly humiliate, irritate and wound his feelings and lessen his self-respect. It is one of those relics of the barbarity practiced towards convicts, before Howard and Wilberforce called public attention to the inhuman treatment to which they were subjected. Like the "goose-step" treadmill, shot drill and the like cruelties, the designating of convicts by their "numbers" should become a "memory," though an unpleasant one, "of the past."[13]

Typically, the most vocal proponent of the use of numbers instead of personal names was Samuel Bedson, who emerged at the end of his tenure as something of an anti-reform voice in the penitentiary administration. He was particularly supportive of policies, such as prison uniforms and numbers, that others regarded as degrading to the convict's individuality.[14] The debate, limited as it was in the Canadian context, revealed how the reform movement was gradually exerting influence over penitentiary practices intended to address criminality.

The common elements of the admission ritual, which was bound to hygiene movements of the mid-nineteenth century, eventually included medical inspection. At Kingston Penitentiary, new prisoners were inspected on the morning after admission by the surgeon while he attended to general convict complaints. Some prisoners reported having undergone only a cursory examination, but at certain institutions, it was far more complete. Warden Bedson at Manitoba Penitentiary stated that his medical officer undertook a rigorous inspection of every new inmate, recording all information on a "medical examination sheet," which was used to compare the physical well-being of the same prisoner when he was eventually released.[15] Although the medical inspection was designed to catch contagious or degenerative disease in new prisoners, it was also a method of classifying and identifying new convicts. Tattoos, scars, and deformities were all noted in prison registers. These characteristics were particularly helpful in identifying former prisoners in instances of recidivism or escape. In the years after 1890, most penitentiaries acquired photography equipment to make this task much easier, creating mug shot–style records of every new convict.

THE SILENT WORLD

Life in a modern penitentiary was supposed to be carried out in unbroken silence. Both the separate system and the Auburn system were designed around the idea that prisoners would live from day to day in silent isolation from each other, never speaking or communicating in any way. In reality, penitentiaries were necessarily noisy institutions because their operation included workshops, factories, chapels, hospitals, and dormitories. In the silent system, however, all communication was forbidden under threat of punishment. The first written penitentiary regulations at Kingston demanded unbroken silence and "perfect obedience and submission to the keepers."[16] As noted earlier, the punishment for breaking this rule in the early years at Kingston could be unyielding and brutal.

In the post-Confederation era, Canadian penitentiaries were still organized around the basic principles of the silent system, but the ways in which it was implemented were uneven and conflicted. As late as 1889, the penitentiary regulations stated, "Every officer shall see that the silent system is strictly carried out. He shall not permit one convict to speak to another on any pretence nor to himself on any matter except the work at the moment in hand, and then only in the fewest words and in respectful terms."[17] But several penitentiary officials openly admitted that the rule could not be enforced. In 1878

Inspector Moylan wrote, "It is almost an impossibility to exact a strict observance of the rule of silence where convicts are employed in associated labor during the day. To talk and commune among themselves whenever an opportunity offers, no matter what the penalty, is a temptation which few convicts can resist. It is human and natural."[18] The Roman Catholic chaplain at St. Vincent de Paul in Québec made a similar argument, calling the rule of silence "impossible" and "unnatural." He wrote, "As long as you mix the convicts together, they will converse. To ask an absolute silence and expose them at the same time to the temptation of conversing with each other, or to set them to work side by side, I consider is asking more than we have a right to ask."[19] Such conflicted views help to explain why the rule of silence was enforced so arbitrarily. Conversations at mealtimes were particularly heavily policed. Throughout this era, prisoners sat back to back along just one side of the dining tables so they could not easily converse. But in other situations, during the work day or in the comings and goings of groups of convicts, the rule was certainly relaxed.

Among all wardens in the post-Confederation era, Samuel Bedson at Manitoba was the most rigorous about maintaining silence in the penitentiary. By the late 1870s and early 1880s, breaching the rule of silence was seldom a punishable offence at Kingston, but Manitoba continued to enforce it with rigour. In 1877, shortly after Manitoba Penitentiary opened, Bedson complained in the warden's order book "that a great deal of talking is carried on by the convicts when confined in their respective cells." He cautioned the prisoners that every man in the penitentiary would pay the consequences if the conversations did not stop.[20] Two years later, attempting to identify a prisoner in the west wing who was making noise after lights out, the warden made the same threat. Bedson entered in his order book, "[I am] determined to put a stop to such conduct and in order to reach the individual at fault will punish all in the vicinity of the noises and take the present opportunity of calling upon convicts to protect themselves from being punished by bringing to notice the one at fault."[21] Bedson was so determined to maintain absolute silence on the cell blocks that he devised a system involving signal sticks to prevent any speaking. Each prisoner was given a four-foot wand that was painted white. One end was painted black for signalling non-urgent concerns to the guards while the opposite end, which was red, would signal an urgent situation, all in total silence.[22]

Although it was not always enforced, the rule of silence provided keepers with the mechanism to demand the absolute subservience of the prison population when they so desired. This was a powerful tool, but staff were also aware that their hand could easily be overplayed. Power struggles such as those waged by Bedson were rarely productive, and the more practical wardens studiously avoided showdowns in which they could lose face. Indeed, all of Warden Bedson's efforts amounted to little more than bluster. Prisoners were unlikely to inform on each other or to end their communication. Even with little to lose, prisoners stayed loyal to each other. At British Columbia Penitentiary, the staff interrogated inmates who had been discharged about where conversations were taking place throughout the prison. Nearly every respondent simply said, "I do not know."[23] Throughout the nineteenth century and within different types of disciplinary regime, prisoners found innumerable ways to communicate with each other. In every institution, the prisoners knew of remote locations where they could meet and carry out conversations. In the evenings, they whispered between cells through the ventilators or passed notes up and down the cell blocks using pilfered string and bits of paper.

In spite of the clamour and the concealed conversation, sometimes the penitentiary really did sink into unbearable silence. This was particularly the case in special cell blocks like the Prison of Isolation at Kingston, completed in 1892 and reserved for inmates considered irredeemable, and the women's prison. Louisa Sturdy, a former inmate of the women's prison at Kingston who sold her story to *The Globe*, described a night when she could not sleep: "The solitude seemed to be so dreary that even the footsteps of a rat might have been heard through the corridor." Sturdy listened in the silence and heard the "sweet soprano, tremolo voice" of a young girl singing the lines "Jesus lover of my soul / Let me to Thy bosom fly." She recalled,

How sweet and clear her voice and those words sounded through that silent corridor I shall never be able to tell. No doubt she had learnt it in a Sunday school in her earlier innocent days and had become repentant as she lay sleeplessly on her bed. But this is not all. She had evidently forgotten the other lines of the hymn and there she stopped for a while. But her heart seemed to burst for song, and she struck up again, sweeter than ever,

"Rock of ages . . . For me,
Let me hide myself in thee."[24]

As Louisa Sturdy's account highlights, prison could be a numbing and lonely experience. The constant effort at communication between prisoners speaks not only to conspiracy, as penitentiary officials were apt to see, but also to the desire for human connection. Certainly, penitentiary life offered few other comforts. Illicit communication surely provided some reprieve from the drudgery.

Two small luxuries allowed to prisoners were mail from the outside world and tobacco. Originally, tobacco was introduced to Kingston Penitentiary by contractors in the 1830s and 1840s to secure the loyalty of convicts assigned to the various industries. By the post-Confederation era, tobacco was a standard-issue ration for each inmate, although how it was distributed and in what quantity often varied from one institution to another. Some wardens objected to tobacco entirely, an opinion that was raised repeatedly in the House of Commons when elected members realized that each penitentiary was expending up to five hundred dollars a year in tobacco distribution.[25] Some wardens also campaigned against rampant tobacco use because of its disruptive effect in underground prison economies. In 1900 Kingston surgeon Daniel Phelan wrote, "The nefarious traffic carried on in trading tobacco for other articles among the prisoners, its being offered as a bribe in many instances, and its procurement by those who do not use it, to sell it or trade it to those who do, are some very strong reasons against its use. In many instances the habit of using it has been first acquired in prison."[26] The surgeon also worried that the practice of biting the same plugs of tobacco up and down a cell block was spreading syphilis throughout the prison population. Smoking homemade cigarettes was hardly more sanitary in Phelan's eyes, as it filled the dormitories with a heavy smoke every night.[27] However, like conversation, wardens and keepers were powerless to completely restrict tobacco use, and eliminating it entirely as a matter of discipline would have courted disaster (as we will see below when this measure was taken at St Vincent de Paul in 1897). In most institutions, the officials realized that it was far more effective to use tobacco as an inducement to good behaviour and as a punishment for transgressions. Thus, along with depriving inmates of light or bread and water, one of the most frequent punishments noted on registers in the post-Confederation era was the loss of tobacco.

Mail and personal visitors gave prisoners rare opportunities for connection with the outside world. Both of these privileges were greatly restricted in the pre–Brown Commission era, but under the influence of reform, both became a more regular part of prison life after 1850. Mail was not particularly private because both incoming and outgoing correspondence was read by keepers and heavily censored. In the 1860s, Kingston kept a register of all outgoing mail, tracking who wrote each letter, who it was intended for, and the general subject of correspondence. These subject lines, sometimes recorded verbatim from the text of the letter, provide a glimpse of the alienation of prison life. Many letters written by the prisoners were simple reassurances about the writer's health or adaptation to penitentiary life. One subject line read "Is doing very well and is satisfied. Every one kind to him." Other letters hinted at the pain of being separated from family. The subject of one letter was listed as "Finds the time too long. Do not abandon the children." Often prisoners wrote to family or friends asking for some sort of greater connection or pleading for return correspondence. Many writers requested a "likeness" of family members to keep with them at the penitentiary. The desire for connection is palpable even in the truncated recording of the correspondence register. Several prisoners included "Write often" at the end of a letter. More heartbreaking were letters that asked simply, "Why do you not write?"[28]

That keepers were not all-powerful was underscored by the fact that they too were subject to surveillance and domination while on the job. At each institution, the staff discipline was largely determined by the character of the warden. In Manitoba Penitentiary's early years, Warden Samuel Bedson administered his institution with military precision, subjecting his staff to discipline and surveillance that was hardly less rigorous than what the prisoners experienced. For example, guards were included in Bedson's demand for absolute attention to the rule of silence. In 1879 the warden complained that his staff were conversing with each other too loudly throughout the prison; he ordered them to whisper in a tone low enough that no prisoner could overhear a conversation between two of them.[29] Several years later, he ordered the night shifts to patrol the cell blocks in their stocking feet because the heels of their boots created too much noise.[30] Bedson did not make idle threats against his staff; he enforced staff discipline with a punitive system of fines that kept his inferior officers in a constant state of alertness. Insolence, a missed shift or arriving late, and general misconduct were all punished by surprisingly costly fines. In August 1877 Bedson fined guard Wagner fifteen dollars for "insolence to the chief guard."[31] A turnkey named Davis Little was the target of multiple disciplinary reports: several times in early 1876, he was fined five dollars for lateness or missed shifts, and in late May, he received a fine of thirty dollars for "misconduct."[32] Little was only paid $480.00 per year, and his total fines of at least fifty dollars in 1876 must have seemed onerous.

In 1883 Inspector Moylan lamented that the penitentiary staff itself was a constant hindrance to the progress of penitentiary reform because of both the type of individual that prison work attracted and the often brutal working and living conditions associated with life as a penitentiary guard:

> There never will be any possible improvement in the discipline as long as the *personnel* is not itself improved, and the *personnel*

will never improve as long as the salary remains as it does to-day. Be that as it may, a learned, sober and intelligent man will never consent to come and bury himself, I might say, in a Penitentiary, and pass his time in the midst of criminals—to expose his life and labor incessantly from six o'clock in the morning to six o'clock at night—Sunday not even excepted—for a salary of four hundred and fifty dollars ($450). Some twenty or thirty years ago such a salary was sufficient; but to-day such a thing is unheard of. The necessities of life are far more expensive than they were then; labor is more in demand and the pay is much better.[33]

Moylan's choice of words was appropriate, for taking employment in the penitentiary was indeed similar to being "buried" in the institution. Staff members not only worked in the penitentiary, but they lived there as well, in quarters provided by the institution. Some of the prisons featured staff quarters that were somewhat separate from the actual penitentiary, but other staff quarters were simple apartments in one part of the main penitentiary building. By the 1880s and 1890s, some federal penitentiaries featured small cottages for married staff, and the warden of each institution was provided with a very respectable house connected to the institution. But for the lowest-paid members of the staff, the turnkeys and guards, living conditions were not substantially different from those of the prisoners. In the early 1880s, Moylan admitted that "they live miserably while they are in the service" and that this was largely a function of the extremely low wages that were comparable to the poorest-paid working-class labourers.[34] Table 3 shows the remuneration of officers at Manitoba Penitentiary in 1878; while the staff was small, the salaries were representative of wages for the same positions in penitentiaries throughout the dominion.

INSUBORDINATION AND VIOLENCE

Penitentiary life was a particularly rough culture, but this was often hidden from view and obscured in the official records. Wardens and

TABLE 3   Officers' Salaries, Manitoba Penitentiary, 30 June 1878

RANKS	NAME	AGE	SALARY PER ANNUM
			$ cts
Warden	Samuel L. Bedson	36	1400 00
Surgeon	Roderick Macdonald	26	600 00
Chief Keeper	Edward Armstrong	55	600 00
Accountant and storekeeper .	George Ed. Adshead.	40	540 00
Protestant chaplain.	Samuel P. Matheson	26	200 00
Roman Catholic chaplain . . .	Father Lacombe.	50	200 00
Steward	Davis Little	38	480 00
Guard	Alexander Garvin	39	480 00
Guard	Aeneas D. McDonell	31	480 00
Guard	William Abbott.	26	480 00
Guard	William Mulvaney	28	480 00
Guard	David Taylor	25	480 00
Messenger	Samuel McCormick	25	240 00

SOURCE: "Warden's Annual Report, Manitoba Penitentiary," *Sessional Papers*, 1879, no. 27, 159.

inspectors, the public faces of the penitentiary service, wrote in the language of respectable and gentlemanly bureaucrats. Their vernacular often made the penitentiary appear more civil than it was in daily practice. This was by design, but it also hinted at the fact that, apart from unusual circumstances, the warden had little contact with the penitentiary population in day-to-day life. Although his presence was required at many points throughout the day, he tended to float through the penitentiary like a figurehead and established little real contact with the prisoners under his charge. In fact, junior officers at Manitoba Penitentiary were reminded by the warden that, like the prisoners, they were forbidden to address him directly. All of their questions and concerns were relayed through the deputy warden so that Bedson would be spared any inconvenience.[35]

In the relationship between prisoners and keepers, a far grittier conversation marked the everyday intercourse of penitentiary life. Exchanges between keepers and prisoners were marked with profanity. Some of it was good-natured and ribald. When prisoners spoke to guards like this, it was unlikely to be considered insubordinate. However, in the right context, obscene language was one of the few methods of non-violent resistance that the prisoners could deploy, and guards quickly perceived the difference. It is clear from punishment reports that not every incident of profanity was reported or punished, but certain exchanges clearly raised the ire of guards and were subsequently the subject of disciplinary reports. For example, while performing outdoor labour, George Hewell, a Kingston prisoner (and the subject of a case study in chapter 6), told a guard "to go and fuck [him]self." Hewell was punished for this with bread and water.[36] In another incident that appeared in punishment records, British Columbia prisoner Symon Strater was put in chains for calling a guard, "a God damn brute" and telling him to "go home and kick your wife and children."[37] In most instances, the penitentiary guard could match the prisoner's obscenity. Most exchanges such as these transpired without incident, but the odd prisoner complained about a remark that cut too close. A Manitoba Penitentiary inmate, for instance, complained to the warden that a guard had made an off-colour remark about having sex with the inmate's wife. The warden responded facetiously that it was a "very unlikely remark for one man to make about another."[38]

More effective methods of insubordination involved *doing* something that openly broke the rules for the sake of defiance. Whereas a profane remark could be shrugged off, other acts of insubordination garnered more attention. Refusing to work was the most common method of resistance, and prisoners employed it for a number of reasons. Sometimes they protested poor working conditions or domineering farming or industrial instructors. Private contractors evaded such complaints by dispensing liberal quantities of tobacco, but penitentiary keepers were less inclined to grant this privilege. They could afford to be more stringent because they could also exercise the power to initiate punishment, which contractors could not in the years after 1850. Refusing to work was a dangerous rebellion to which penitentiary officials reacted swiftly. A prisoner's first incident of insubordination of this type resulted in three meals of bread and water, and the punishments grew swiftly more serious after that. The dark cell was threatening enough to keep most prisoners at work, and those who repeated an offence could be flogged on the back or whipped on the hands. As I discuss in the next chapter, a far more effective and less insubordinate way of avoiding labour was to feign sickness, which also entailed a lower risk of punishment.

Occasionally, insubordination flared up as an expression of pure frustration or anger. George Le Londe, a prisoner at Manitoba Penitentiary, erupted in anger after being ordered to clean his untidy cell in March 1889. He swore at the guard and told him to "do it himself." He was dragged to the warden's office, where Bedson told him his remaining remission time would be cancelled. On returning to his cell, Le Londe proceeded to tear his bedding to pieces before moving on to the curtains and rug. He was removed and taken to a bare cell but could not regain his composure. He tore up the oak flooring and threw it, plank by plank, through the bars of his cell. He then spent the week in an isolation cell in darkness.[39] The same year, another prisoner at Manitoba, Richard Phillips, destroyed the walls of his cell in a similar way. The warden reported that he did this in a spirit of "pure wantonness" while refusing to engage in any labour.[40] Such protests were regarded with gravity by penitentiary officials, but they are remarkable for being essentially non-violent expressions of anger and frustration. In fact, violence between prisoners and keepers was extremely rare throughout the nineteenth century, perhaps because the consequences of such attacks were inordinately more severe than for non-violent insubordination and resistance. This is not to say that violence was not an everyday part of penitentiary life, however: incidents of interpersonal violence and assault between prisoners were far more common than those between prisoners and keepers.

Intimidation and bullying, like tobacco, were currencies of power in penitentiary life. Stronger prisoners, those who possessed physical strength or strong social networks within the penitentiary, bullied and exploited the vulnerable. All of this occurred beneath the surface of everyday life, but it was not completely obscured. In some penitentiary records, we can identify bullies and the bullied through disciplinary reports. For example, at British Columbia Penitentiary, an unfortunate prisoner named Charley was the constant target of ridicule and abuse from other prisoners. Probably a First Nations or Chinese man (because he was known only by a first name), Charley was a "waiter" who delivered rations and supplies to prisoners undergoing punishment in the dark cells. In this job, he was a frequent target for the abuse and anger of punished men. In August 1889 he was, on several occasions, doused with the contents of a night bucket by prisoner Ah Pow. Another Chinese prisoner was punished for throwing a cup of coffee in Charley's face as he made his rounds. A prisoner named Thomas Wilson was reported multiple times for fighting but was never regarded as an instigator of these confrontations. Like Charley, he was probably seen by other prisoners as an easy mark and drawn into repeated conflict.[41]

In some instances, long-running feuds between prisoners erupted into sudden violence. In June 1905 a fight broke out at Manitoba Penitentiary between prisoners Biddle and Runwell during Sunday religious services. According to witnesses, some insulting remark passed between the men while they were singing. As Runwell sat back in his pew at the conclusion of the hymn, Biddle kicked him in the back of the head. Runwell turned to deliver a blow and a fight erupted. A nearby friend of Biddle jumped to his defence and joined the melee. All three men spent six months in the Prison of Isolation as a punishment.[42] In other examples, violent confrontations were less spontaneous. In the early 1870s, James McCabe, a prisoner at Kingston, became too close to the penitentiary guard for the liking of the other members of his work detail. He incurred their wrath by urging them to work harder. According to the warden, McCabe was the most useful prisoner in the institution and more knowledgeable about the industries than many of the keepers. The favouritism shown to McCabe by the keepers bred much resentment toward him. The guards learned that a group of prisoners planned to corner McCabe and "lick him" at the soonest opportunity. Anticipating the attack, McCabe carried a long knife with him as protection. All of these details were brought to the attention of Warden Creighton, who wrote this surprising entry in his order book: "These men and one or two others have threatened McCabe's life for no other reason than that he urged them to greater activity when working with him in the stone truck—I have not objected to his defending himself of being murderously attacked."[43] Creighton's trust in McCabe was probably misplaced as he escaped from Kingston Penitentiary in 1881, only to be shot two days later by a constable in Port Hope.[44] The McCabe incident illustrates how dangerous penitentiary life could become for prisoners who ran afoul of particular standards of behaviour that inmates were expected to uphold. In the most extreme circumstances, altercations over these issues led to murder.

One of the most sensational cases involved the murder of Thomas Salter, a St. Vincent de Paul prisoner, in 1881. Salter was the son of a respectable Montreal family who, according to *The Globe,* got into bad company and was sentenced to two years at St. Vincent de Paul for jewel theft.[45] Soon after arriving at the penitentiary, Salter fell in with a group of prisoners plotting an escape, but their plans were discovered. The men apparently blamed Salter for leaking the plot to penitentiary officials and vowed revenge against him. As the inmates marched from dinner on the evening of June 30, prisoner Hugh Hayvern grabbed Salter and plunged a knife deep into his chest. Salter exclaimed, "Oh, my god!" and staggered to the door of the hospital. He was taken by a group of horrified convicts to the nearest bed, where he died less than ten minutes later. Hayvern was tried and convicted for the murder of Thomas Salter and executed six months later.[46]

In addition to violent attack, scattered evidence in penitentiary records show that sexual assault was an ever-present concern. When officials worried about the "corruption" of young prisoners, they were often referencing more than just criminal contamination through contact with hardened offenders. The possibility of sexual assault was a primary motivation in keeping child convicts physically segregated from the adult prisoners. Even older youths of fifteen and sixteen were recognized as being extremely vulnerable to both influence and sexual attack, and were often given special consideration. In 1898, for example, Manitoba Penitentiary received fifteen-year-old Fred Belter, who had been born in Russia and spoke very little English. He was sent to sleep in the hospital rather than a standard cell so that the hospital overseer and the schoolmaster could keep watch over him at all times.[47]

In spite of the extra protection given to young boys, there are clear indications that youths were not kept completely separated from the adults in every institution. This left them vulnerable to contact, which drew them into exploitive relationships, sexual and otherwise, with other inmates. In most cases, the record provides only the barest hint of this subculture. For example, a fight between two convicts at Manitoba Penitentiary in 1905 was explained by the reporting guard: "McInerney seemed jealous of and enraged at Price for some attention shown to a boy convict."[48] Other cases pointed more directly at ongoing sexual contact. At Kingston in 1906, guard Edward Walsh was informed by a prisoner that a young boy named Bruce Mayberry was alone in a cell with another inmate. The informant added "that Mayberry was only a boy and he feared the other fellow would get him into trouble."[49] Walsh rushed to the cell and found Mayberry in a prone position with his pants down. Witnesses later told the keepers that the boy had gone into the cell willingly and was in fact seen climbing from one cell block to another to reach the man. Was this encounter consensual?

Steven Maynard's work on the sexual exploitation of youths at Maple Leaf Gardens in the 1960s reveals the troubling complexities of attempting to attribute motivation to the youthful participants in sexual relationships between men and boys.[50] Maynard tried to interject ambiguity into essentially exploitive relationships. Whether we identify sexual relationships in the penitentiary as "abuse" or mere "illicit sexuality," however, can be settled by attention to what Veronica Strong-Boag calls the contextual importance of violence in such situations.[51] The penitentiary was an environment in which the power imbalance between men and boys often placed young prisoners in an inescapable position that was unlikely to be consensual. But the keepers at Kingston Penitentiary came to a different conclusion on this question. Noting Mayberry's "willingness" to reach the older prisoner, both participants were punished with six months in the isolation cells.[52] Similar to situations when women were assaulted by guards or other prisoners and became pregnant, penitentiary officials were not above blaming youths for their participation in sexual relationships. Children in the penitentiary occupied an impossible position in the power relations between themselves and older, more dominant prisoners.

ESCAPE

One of the enduring realities of penitentiary life was that almost all prisoners were desperate to get away from it. Some took more drastic measures than others, but the widespread desire for escape required officials to be on constant alert. "The thoughts of ninety-nine out of every hundred convicts are constantly bent on escaping," wrote Inspector Moylan.[53] Protecting against escape was often made more difficult by the fact that several of the penitentiaries were surprisingly insecure in design, geographic situation, and management of the prisoners. While Kingston was protected by an impressive boundary wall, Manitoba, British Columbia, and Dorchester did not have this security. When Manitoba Penitentiary opened, it also lacked many other security measures required by a prison. For example, the Department of Public Works originally installed locks that could be opened from the inside. Moreover, within five years of opening, both Manitoba and British Columbia were so overcrowded that some inmates slept on cots in hallways rather than in locked cells.[54] Adding to such insecurities was the fact that all penitentiaries relied upon outdoor labour that often took the prisoners up to two kilometres outside of the boundary walls. This provided a dangerous invitation to escape that some prisoners could not resist.

Between 1867 and 1900, approximately one hundred men escaped from Canadian federal penitentiaries. The exact number is difficult to pin down from penitentiary records because the success of an escape was often relative to whether and how quickly the prisoners were recaptured. Sometimes escapes were noted as "attempted escape," but no uniform system existed for deciding what constituted escapes and attempted escapes. In some instances, prisoners escaped and remained at large for weeks, months, or years before they were found. Once discovered, these individuals were reported as "recommitted" or "recaptured." It is clear that the vast majority of escape attempts were unsuccessful. For example, in 1876 alone, only five of the sixteen attempts at Kingston were successful. In 1885 twenty prisoners attempted escape but only five found freedom.

The most common escape attempt involved running away from outdoor labour details. Some prisoners watched carefully for these opportunities, waiting for short staffing days or diversions in the form of fights and disturbances among other prisoners. In one example, two prisoners at St. Vincent de Paul in 1877 were assigned outdoor labour duties on an extremely foggy day. Working about two kilometres from the prison, Edward McMahan and Levi Joyal escaped by gradually slipping into the fog until they could not be seen.[55] Other impromptu attempts were often less successful. In June 1895 Martin Bogart attempted a casual escape from his work detail on the Kingston harbour pier. Walking to the end of the pier, he stepped off and began strolling away. Guards overtook him immediately.[56] In other instances, prisoners desiring to escape needed only to take advantage of the right opportunity. In 1893 George Gillette noticed an unlocked door as he passed through the cell block at Manitoba Penitentiary. He simply let himself out of the prison and walked to freedom across the open prairie.[57]

Other escape attempts were far more elaborate and involved extensive preparation. For example, in late 1905 the warden at Kingston was notified by a prisoner that James Campbell, a convict in the lunatic asylum, was planning his escape. Campbell's cell was searched immediately and officers discovered that his cell bars had been cut. A container of grease to conceal the cuts was found in his bed. Campbell had been escaping his cell every night with knife blades given to him by the barber, a fellow convict. His plan was to cut through the bars of the outdoor window and use a rope to swing over the outside wall.[58] Other plots involved planning and co-operation among multiple inmates as well as some ongoing deception. In 1871 three inmates, Greenbury Steele, Richard Nelligan, and Benjamin Wilson, colluded to escape from Kingston Penitentiary. Steele and Nelligan feigned sickness to gain admission to the hospital. Wilson was the convict barber and visited the hospital daily, which gave him an opportunity to smuggle a false key and an iron bar into the ward. Finally, Wilson feigned sickness and was admitted to the hospital ward. On the first stormy night after his admission, he opened all three cells. The prisoners then broke through the outside window, stole a boat from the nearby harbour, and, by morning, had escaped across the lake to New York State.[59]

Escape, however, did not necessarily put prisoners out of the penitentiary's reach. Penitentiary budgets provided substantial funds to pursue escaped inmates, expenditures that frequently entailed efforts at extradition from the United States. The most expensive pursuit of escaped prisoners occurred at Manitoba Penitentiary in 1893, when it cost $1,177.88 to recapture prisoners Gillette and Shoults.[60] Sometimes wardens went to extraordinary measures to recapture escaped prisoners. In 1876 Warden Bedson at Manitoba Penitentiary reported on the case of a convict named Daniels, a "native of the country" who slipped away from his work detail. Bedson subsequently learned that Daniels was somewhere on the shore of Lake Winnipeg and made arrangements with some "Indians and traders" to capture him, for which he supplied a set of handcuffs and the promise of a twenty-five dollar reward.[61] If escaped prisoners were recaptured, they generally faced criminal charges at the next available assize. The sentence was usually an additional six months plus the loss of all remission on the original sentence. In some cases, penitentiaries did not prosecute escape attempts but instead simply punished the offender within the institution.[62]

If escaped prisoners put enough distance between themselves and the penitentiary, they could be more assured of remaining at large. This was particularly true if they could avoid subsequent arrest in different jurisdictions. Twenty-three-year-old Leslie Cork escaped from

Kingston Penitentiary in 1890 and made his way to Chicago. Warden
J. M. Sullivan discovered his whereabouts when Cork boldly wrote
a letter to another prisoner at Kingston bragging about his escape.
Sullivan alerted the Chicago police force to be on the lookout for Cork.
He reported to Inspector Moylan, "The effect of showing the other
inmates here how much their chances of successful escape are lessened
would be of great value."[63] But Cork was not recaptured in Chicago.
Kingston Penitentiary officials learned a month later, again through a
letter, that Cork had surfaced in Denver. The warden wrote to the chief
of police in Denver with a detailed description of the prisoner, noting,
"He is a delicate looking fellow with an intelligent face and the appearance of a criminal."[64] Apparently, Cork looked ordinary enough to avoid
detection; he was never recaptured.

Complicated plots to escape usually failed because inmates
informed on each other. In 1883 a prisoner at Manitoba Penitentiary
informed Warden Bedson that inmates on labour detail in the basement were planning an escape. Seeking confirmation, the warden
recruited another inmate whom he trusted to gather information on
the plot. On the day of the outbreak, the warden had the penitentiary
guards replace the bullets in their carbines with blank cartridges. Just
before the time of the anticipated escape, the warden quietly locked
down the prison and awaited the mutiny. As expected, the prisoners
in the basement overpowered their guards, took their weapons, and
headed for the exits. There they faced the entire penitentiary guard
led by the warden, who rushed forward and physically overpowered
the ringleader. The guards then fired their weapons, loaded with blank
cartridges, and the tremendous noise frightened the escaping prisoners into submission. The ringleader later admitted that a number
of prisoners had conceived of the plan at the Winnipeg gaol before
they were transferred to the penitentiary.[65] In a similar situation, the
warden at Kingston was less eager to personally engage in physical
combat to prevent escape. After learning of a plot to mutiny and break
free from the workshops, the warden applied for assistance from the
Department of Militia. Fifty men of "A" Battery were silently marched
into the penitentiary in the middle of the night. The following day, the

soldiers were paraded in the yard, which had an unnerving effect on the prisoners. The escape attempt was abandoned.[66]

In their response to escape, penitentiary officials often resorted to particular constructions of criminality that cast escaping individuals as the most "desperate" of all prisoners. In part, this construction rested on the fact that escape was particularly difficult and many attempts were in fact desperate and irrational. But it also characterized escaping prisoners as particularly dangerous and unpredictable, a description that helped to justify the violence and the frequent use of firearms that accompanied escape attempts in the post-Confederation era. These constructions were similar to those connected to corporal punishment in this era, playing on the "brutality" and "inhumanity" of incorrigible inmates to justify violent responses, as we will see in a later discussion.

Guns were a common feature of penitentiary life. Revolvers were issued to guards and keepers at all institutions, and the boundaries of the penitentiaries were protected by guards armed with rifles and carbines. At Manitoba Penitentiary, Warden Bedson described his state of preparedness for potential escape in his 1875 report: "My turnkeys when in charge of convicts outside the yard are armed with repeating carbines, slung over their shoulder, and a revolver and a pair of handcuffs. . . . I instruct them in rifle and revolver practice, my object in doing so is to accustom them (should it be necessary) in firing at a run-away convict, to maim him and not kill."[67] Given the open spaces that surrounded most penitentiaries, gunfire was the most reliable method of stopping fleeing convicts. In 1871 James McCarron, a prisoner at St. John Penitentiary, crossed the penitentiary fence and started to run. According to the warden, two "'buck shots,' one in the left arm, the other in the right side of the back . . . effectively checked his progress." Warden Quinton noted that McCarron was not seriously injured by receiving these "small missives from the penitentiary guard."[68] In the following decades, however, other institutions employed more powerful weaponry.

Christopher Murray was the first prisoner to be killed while attempting to escape from Kingston Penitentiary. In November 1869

Murray slipped from his cell with another prisoner, making his way to an outside door. A guard called on the men to surrender, and when they continued, he fired on them with his revolver. Another guard finally apprehended Murray, who said, "Do not fire, I have had enough." He then fell and died. As would become customary in such killings, a coroner's jury declared the shooting "justifiable homicide."[69] This incident deeply shook both the convicts and penitentiary staff; it seemed to shatter a calm and place the entire institution on edge. The penitentiary directors ordered that additional patrols be made of all the cell blocks. The night guards were instructed to inspect each cell before the lights went down and to make certain that the "day clothes of every convict are hanging upon the pegs in his cell."[70] The unease throughout the institution worried the penitentiary directors, who felt that it could explode into something more dangerous. As they reported in the aftermath of the shooting, "There exists a very uneasy and dangerous feeling among the convicts—or at any rate among many of them which may gradually subside but which may also exhibit itself in some violent and sudden act of insubordination." The report went on to note that "the Directors have for some time past felt with alarm that the efficient control of the prison has passed from the hands to which the law confides it and that no other hand has taken it."[71]

The "unease" the directors spoke about became a constant state of affairs at Kingston Penitentiary in the years that followed. Guns played no small part in this development. The killing of convicts was deeply upsetting to the rest of the prisoners, and Murray's death in 1869 was not the only incident in the post-Confederation era. Other escaping convicts were gunned down as they fled on foot. In 1877, for example, Thomas Sholvin was killed while escaping from St. John Penitentiary. After he crossed the wall with a twelve-foot plank, the guards fired on him with rifles as he fled toward the woods.[72]

Was the killing of escaping convicts justifiable? Most wardens in the penitentiary service believed that it was. A provision in the 1851 Penitentiary Act stated, "If any officer should in the attempt to prevent the escape of any convict take the life of such convict, such officer will not be held responsible."[73] In fact, efforts to stop escapes by all available means were encouraged: the 1851 legislation stated that a sum of fifty pounds could be levied as a reward for the apprehension of fleeing convicts. In the later nineteenth century, this sum was occasionally paid as a reward to the guard who successfully shot an escaping prisoner. Predictably, Inspector Moylan was the lone voice of doubt about both the legality and morality of taking an inmate's life to prevent escape. In 1883 he wrote that prison officers "are very culpable if through their negligence or carelessness convicts have the chance of running away, and they are still more culpable if they kill or maim the unfortunate being who takes advantage of their dereliction of duty. However jurists may regard the killing of a prisoner, under such circumstances, the interpreters of 'higher law,'—theologians—would define it to be a crime not far removed from murder."[74] Thus, Moylan stressed the responsibility that weighed on penitentiary officials and guards with respect to the lives of prisoners. By the end of the century, the Department of Justice was taking a slightly more cautious approach to the shooting of escaping prisoners. Referencing Joseph Gabbett's 1835 *Treatise on Criminal Law,* the department concluded that a fleeing convict could only be killed in the event that he could not be overtaken by less drastic measures. If that possibility did exist and the convict was still killed, the shooting was to be regarded at least as manslaughter.[75] But no penitentiary officer who fired on an escaping prisoner was ever charged. It was generally accepted that without the threat of firearms, escape attempts would occur far more frequently.

Rumours in penitentiaries could be powerful, affecting both prisoners and keepers alike. In 1883 a rumour swept through St. Vincent de Paul that penitentiary guards did not possess the legal authority to fire their weapons at escaping prisoners. The idea became so entrenched that in the winter of 1883, a number of prisoners planned an escape simply to test whether the guards would fire. Learning of the escape plot five days before it occurred, the guards, keepers, and warden all seemed unsure about using their weapons.[76] When five prisoners finally attempted escape, the guards fired on them, wounding two and killing twenty-three-year-old J. B. Deragon.[77]

Deragon was one of six prisoners to be killed escaping from penitentiaries between 1867 and 1900. James McCabe, who was shot two days after escaping, could be considered the seventh death.[78] At least eight other prisoners were seriously wounded by gunfire during escape attempts in this period. One of the effects of concerns about escape was to entrench firearms in the daily routines of penitentiary practice as a consistent acknowledgement of the threat posed by the penitentiary population. In some cases, the use of firearms resulted in tragedy, as with prisoner George Hewell at Kingston Penitentiary, discussed in detail in the final chapter.

MUTINY AND RIOT

Penitentiary officials worked to prevent escape, but they did not especially fear it. What they feared was the possibility of a convict uprising, a threat that helped to justify drastic disciplinary measures and corporal punishment in the early years of Kingston Penitentiary. In the post-1850 era, though punishment became less severe, officials still felt the dread of a riot. Throughout the century, isolated incidents illustrated the potential for uprising. Of all the inmates at Kingston Penitentiary, perhaps none were more accustomed to resistance and uprising than the members of the Fenian Brotherhood. After unsuccessful raids into New Brunswick and the Niagara Peninsula in April 1866, twenty-five American Fenians were given capital sentences, which were subsequently commuted to life imprisonment.[79] Some of the prisoners were sentenced to provincial prisons, but eventually, all of the Fenian prisoners were moved to Kingston due to fears that members of the brotherhood might cross the border again to attempt a rescue.[80] Penitentiary officials at Kingston regarded the Fenians as some of the most difficult and insubordinate inmates the prison had ever seen.

In October 1868, Fenian Thomas Quinn was working on the stone pile when he put down his tools and refused to continue. When guard Allan Grant ordered him back to work, Quinn replied, "Report me for God's sake, I wish you would! I will withstand any punishment that may be inflicted on me if you report me and thereby prove your loyalty."[81] Grant submitted a disciplinary report and Quinn was brought before Warden Macdonell the next morning to explain himself. Upon hearing the guard read the disciplinary report to the warden, Quinn became enraged and attacked Grant, pummelling him in the face before the guards restrained him. Outbursts of this kind in the presence of senior officers were exceedingly rare. Macdonell was stunned. He sentenced Quinn to five dozen lashes with the cat-o'-nine-tails—an unusually harsh punishment—and sent him to the dungeon in chains.

The events that followed convinced the penitentiary officers that Quinn's attack was part of a plot by the Fenian prisoners to mutiny against the penitentiary. While Quinn was still in the warden's office, the news of his impending punishment spread to the dining hall, where the prisoners were eating breakfast. If there was no preconceived plot, what followed is a testament to the speed of covert communication among the prisoners. As Quinn was being taken past the hall, he whistled loudly, and a group of Fenians sprang to their feet. A guard rose, demanding to know what was happening. Prisoner William Hayden shouted, "I am going to see that that man gets fair play!" From across the hall, John Gallagher cried, "Here is one! Here is one!" Prisoners Michael Purtette and Evan Kennedy were also on their feet, and one of them yelled, "I will not sit down to see my comrade flogged!" Fearing that the Fenians meant to rescue Quinn, the guards drew their service revolvers and threatened to shoot if the men would not return to their seats. "Shoot away and be damned!" Purtette shouted as he slashed at a guard with his table knife. Guards from throughout the prison poured into the dining room, and the Fenians were quickly overpowered and dragged to the punishment cells in the basement.[82]

Warden Macdonell made an example out of what he called "the mutineers." Each of the men was whipped twenty-four times except for Gallagher, who received thirty-six lashes.[83] The outburst and the response by officials hinted at the growing anxiety in the post-Confederation era about the explosive potential of the dangerous elements in the penitentiary population. Although criminality and incorrigibility were sometimes individual constructions, events like the Fenian mutiny supported the persistent fear that the worst qualities of incorrigibility might be writ large across the entire penitentiary population. In these instances, the dangerous classes actually became physically threatening, demonstrating their terrifying potential.

The threat of riot and mutiny prompted specific changes in penal practice. In 1881 Inspector Moylan noted that the dinner hour was inherently threatening, as "no time of the day is more favourable for an outbreak in an institution, when the convicts are massed together in all their full strength." Furthermore, the dining halls furnished prisoners with knives and forks, which, according to Moylan, could be converted into "formidable and effective weapons."[84] In fact, prisoners had always fashioned weapons from all sorts of materials throughout the penitentiary, particularly when they had access to machine and carpentry shops. Knives and "shanks" were common items of contraband discovered in personal and cell searches. In the 1880s, officials fixated on mealtimes as a particular site of potential danger. By 1884 British Columbia and Manitoba had both eliminated communal meals, and the men were fed in individual cells. Going a step further, at the turn of the century, St. Vincent de Paul eliminated cutlery from the penitentiary altogether with the exception of very blunt spoons. After observing the prisoners tearing at their food with their hands and teeth, the surgeon argued that such restrictions only further degraded the prisoners, "placing them on an equal footing to the brute."[85] In spite of the increasing precautions to prevent violent uprisings, such outbursts were actually difficult to predict or prevent. This left penitentiary officials in a constant state of anxiety and preparedness for the worst possible outcome.

ST. VINCENT DE PAUL

It is somewhat surprising that the penitentiary system was not wracked with more examples of prisoners rising up against their keepers. On the one hand, this could be attributed to the draconian discipline that prevailed even after the reforms of the 1850s and 1860s. On the other hand, the same reforms made penitentiary life bearable enough to prevent widespread rebellion among prison populations. Thus, it is remarkable that the scene of the only large-scale penitentiary riots in the post-Confederation era was at St. Vincent de Paul, where the exploitation and indifference of the staff nullified and subverted the path of reform. In the process, the institution became unwieldy and difficult to manage, and the prison population grew increasingly violent and rebellious. The history of riot at St. Vincent de Paul illustrates how mismanagement and exploitation could lead to widespread resistance and violence.

The troubling events at St. Vincent de Paul Penitentiary took place over the course of a decade and were bookended by two riots. Between 1887 and 1897, the regime of Warden Télesphore Ouimet resulted in corruption that overshadowed even the early years of Kingston Penitentiary under Henry Smith. A Royal Commission called to investigate the conditions at St. Vincent de Paul was staffed by James Noxon, O. K. Fraser, and D. A. Lafortune. With eight thousand pages of testimony, the commission detailed the troubled years between 1887 and 1897. Ouimet had an inauspicious beginning in the penitentiary service. He was hired at St. Vincent de Paul as a farming instructor in 1870 but was soon demoted to the position of guard when officials discovered he had no knowledge of farming and was illiterate. Unhappy with the demotion, Ouimet left the prison soon after but returned in 1879, when he was hired as clerk of works. Investigators in the late 1890s were unable to explain how Ouimet obtained this position given his extremely limited abilities. It is clear that he had friends on the inside of the penitentiary service. The commission's report cited "strong influences behind him by which he attained to positions."[86] Ouimet's friends must have been powerful indeed, for his ascent through the penitentiary ranks was startling. In 1881 he was made deputy warden, a position he filled for five years until the first revolt.

Echoing the power struggles among the top penitentiary officials in Kingston's early years, Deputy Warden Ouimet carried out a campaign against St. Vincent de Paul's warden, Godfrey Lavoilette. Ouimet began disregarding orders given by the warden and neglected to submit his disciplinary recommendations through the warden's office. This insubordination split the penitentiary staff: those in a disciplinary role gave their allegiance to Ouimet and the warden became isolated. Much of the staff believed that Ouimet would become the next warden of the penitentiary and were reluctant to cross him. Thus, the keepers adopted an open ambivalence toward Lavoilette's authority. The Royal Commission noted that the effect of this struggle was to completely destabilize security in the penitentiary: "When there is no united action on the part of officers, vigilance and discipline are relaxed. Next, escapes and even mutinies are planned, for convicts quickly perceive the existence of contentions between those placed on guard over them, and are not slow to turn such quarrels to their own account" (49). This dark prediction came to pass in early 1886. With the balance of power at St. Vincent de Paul badly destabilized by the struggle between Lavoilette and Ouimet, a group of prisoners planned a bold escape. The commissioners were distressed to discover evidence that Ouimet played no small role in allowing the revolt to happen. In the days leading up to the "dreaded revolt," Ouimet was absent from his duties without leave. This created a "premonition" throughout the institution that something terrible was about to happen.

On the morning of April 24, while Ouimet was praying in the penitentiary chapel, violence erupted in the stonework department. Eight ringleaders suddenly overpowered their guards, disarmed them, and bound them with cords. The attack was well coordinated: at the same time, the work gangs in the tailor and shoe shops all rose against their keepers. Rushing into the prison yard, the stone shed gang raised a ladder against the southeastern wall and some men began to ascend. Tower guards on either side of the yard fired on the escaping convicts with rifles, and the farm instructor rushed to the opposite side of the wall and fired his rifle. Two of the prisoners were wounded by the first burst of gunfire, and the rest retreated back into the prison yard. There they intercepted Warden Lavoilette, and the prisoners used him as a shield against the gunfire of the tower guards. They demanded that the western gate be opened, but the warden called to the tower guards to fire again on the prisoners. Gunfire erupted from the towers and the warden was shot in the back of the neck. As he staggered away, he was shot twice more with a revolver by one of the prisoners before collapsing. He was then carried into the main building by a group of stunned prisoners. The riot ended. Prisoner Joseph Corriveau lay dead, and the remaining rioters dispersed and returned to their cells with the rest of the prisoners as the muster bell sounded across the empty penitentiary yard.

It took ten years for the truth about the revolt to enter the public record. During the Royal Commission investigation in 1897, it became clear that Ouimet had lured the warden into a deadly situation. In his testimony, Lavoilette stated, "I have reason to be astonished, nor can I even to-day understand why, during the revolt in the yard, and while I was alone facing these insurgent malefactors of whom eight or ten were around me with revolvers; why, I say, a superior officer did not enter the yard at the head of a detachment of ten or twelve guards armed with rifles and revolvers. A considerable number of officers remained inactive in the Keeper's Hall" (Royal Commission, 53). These revelations did not surface in the aftermath of the revolt. Lavoilette was relieved of his position to recover from his gunshot wounds: his jaw had been shattered by the first revolver shot. Ouimet became the acting authority for the rest of 1886, and in 1887 he was made permanent warden of St. Vincent de Paul. The following decade was marked by staggering corruption and exploitation. The 1886 riot and the events of the decade that followed illustrate the delicate balance in the relationships between prisoners and keepers that sustained power relations in a penitentiary at that time. In stark contrast to a restrictive and draconian regime such as Samuel Bedson's at Manitoba, the penitentiary under Ouimet brought prisoners and keepers into a more mutually beneficial and opportunistic relationship. The decade of turbulence illustrated the utter inefficiency of penitentiary governance under the penitentiary inspector's office. Though he was present for yearly visits, Inspector Moylan made no comment throughout the decade on the corruption in Ouimet's administration. It is impossible to know if he was complicit or simply unaware of the extent of the illegal activity at St. Vincent de Paul.

The most serious corruptions under Ouimet's regimes were financial. Under the warden's watch, an underground economy developed throughout the penitentiary in which both prisoners and keepers participated. While a number of officials at St. Vincent de Paul were implicated in financial corruption and mismanagement, the investigating commissioners were most outraged at the extent of convict participation in this economy. A permissive atmosphere allowed certain factions of inmates to completely take control of many areas of the prison economy, both official and underground. Soon after Ouimet took command of the penitentiary, the prisoners employed in the stonework department—the same gang who had initiated the 1886 revolt—turned the department into a capital enterprise for their own profit. The inmates running the scheme obtained "inventory" by creating waste from the raw material provided to the penitentiary. It was penitentiary policy to sell waste stone to outside buyers, but the prisoners controlled these contracts. While dressing a stone, a prisoner would remark, "This will make a good corporation stone," before striking off a corner and spoiling the block for the purposes of construction (Royal Commission, 6). The waste stone was then sold to the highest bidder. Creating waste stone worked to the convicts' advantage as it kept a steady supply of new stone flowing into the penitentiary. The stone was supplied to the penitentiary for various projects, among them the construction of a more secure boundary wall. In 1897 the commissioners were appalled to discover that the penitentiary had paid for $65,000 worth of stone that had not ended up in the penitentiary wall. The prisoners also managed to slow the speed of construction by resorting to a tacit system of "convict rights" by which their work was governed. This was an unspoken agreement between prisoners and keepers that the stonework gang would control the production of their department, deciding which projects they were willing to work on. The penitentiary wall fell into the category of "legitimate" projects, but other requests made of their department were subject to outrageous delays.

The penitentiary administration was complicit in this underground economy. Acting as a banker, the prison accountant accepted cash payments from outside contractors for the stone and held these funds in reserve for the prisoners in the stonework department. The prisoners could then draw on these funds to purchase luxuries or favours from penitentiary staff, and when a member of the department was released from the penitentiary, the accountant would pay out his share in cash (Royal Commission, 6). The stonework department also had direct access to outside suppliers of sundries and groceries—contraband goods that were then trafficked to the rest of the inmates and sold at grossly inflated prices. However, the stoneworkers were not the only such suppliers in the penitentiary. They competed with the prisoners in the pumphouse, who likewise had contact with outside wholesalers and formed a rival trafficking business. The pumphouse group specialized in groceries, supplying butter, ham, eggs, and tobacco to the rest of the institution. Other businesses also flourished within the penitentiary walls. For example, the commissioners discovered a fully functioning printing press operating in the prison's clothing storage room. It was owned by an inmate, who was allowed to accept contracts from outside customers in exchange for providing free printing services to the penitentiary administration (16).

Unsurprisingly, corrupt officers were at the top of this illicit financial network. The prisoners were merely the beneficiaries of a system that funnelled profit and gain into the hands of penitentiary officers. The prison officers regularly sold livestock, milk, vegetables, and other goods to the penitentiary under assumed names or on behalf of relatives and then profited from the inflated prices on these goods. Some prison officers traded tobacco and fruit for clothing produced by the penitentiary tailor shops (17). The stonecutting department ran a steady trade in tombstones and garden monuments, for which they were paid in cash and groceries. The clerk of works took advantage of the stone department by procuring the material to build two houses, paying a total of twelve dollars (18). Warden Ouimet also enriched himself in various ways, the most glaring of which was the sale of three horses to the prison that he had purchased for a very minor sum. In the end, the farmer from whom he was buying the dilapidated animals refused to have any further dealings with the warden (17).

The permissive atmosphere at St. Vincent de Paul also bred distressing exploitation of the prisoners. One of the worst examples concerned the utter disregard for basic prisoner rights with regard to the incoming and outgoing mail. The commissioners reported that "the prison officials responsible for the carrying out of this branch of work have been as callous in their treatment of the unfortunates under their charge as they well could be. During the whole term of office of the present warden and his clerk, the negligence manifested in this connection has been nothing short of criminal" (11). The commissioners discovered a troubling fact that implicated Inspector Moylan in the ruinous administration, or at least pointed to his complicity. When Moylan announced his retirement from the Inspector's Office in 1895, it was reported that Ouimet began systematically burning the records of St. Vincent de Paul Penitentiary. Thousands of documents, registers, and letters were destroyed. What distressed the commissioners the most was testimony suggesting that among these documents were hundreds and possibly thousands of letters to and from prisoners that the penitentiary had amassed over the decade. The commissioners' suspicions seemed confirmed when they inspected the institution and found still thousands more letters in the warden's vault. The vast majority of these were opened. In the clerk's office, the commissioners found a huge collection of Bibles, crucifixes, personal effects, bank notes, and remittances that officials had confiscated from the mail. Among the letters were petitions for clemency addressed to the governor general, the Department of Justice, and various other government officials. In the course of testimony before the commission, it was determined that any prisoner who had complained to the administration about the non-delivery of mail had been brutally punished. When St. Vincent de Paul officials were questioned before the commission about this exploitation, they cited only "carelessness." In their report, the commissioners wrote emotionally about the gravity of the exploitation the prisoners had suffered:

There is nothing perhaps to which the average convict . . . attaches more importance than the correspondence, restricted though it be, which passes between them and the relatives or friends outside. It is the only legitimate mode of communication with the outer world. . . . Apart from the convict himself, only those who stand by and witness the eagerness with which he receives and peruses the messages from his wife, the mother or the child, as the case may be, can fully realize all that such a message means to the unfortunate behind bars, and only the convict can feel the loss which follows the break in the chain of correspondence they strive to maintain. No one should be more impressed with this condition of convict life than those whose duty it is to inspect and deliver all the correspondence coming and going between the prisoners and those with whom they are in communication. (11)

Warden Ouimet was fired in 1897. In his place, Charles Foster, the warden at Dorchester, took temporary control of the penitentiary and attempted to regain control of the institution. Foster's first measure was the total prohibition of all tobacco products from the penitentiary. This disrupted the exchange economy and absolutely enraged the prisoners. One former prisoner interviewed in the press claimed it was "almost impossible for some of the old tobacco-users to do without tobacco. They would rather do without a meal then have it taken from them."[87] The prisoners did not suffer silently. On September 15, the convicts "started in on a preconcerted signal to howl and continued to raise a perfect bedlam until late at night."[88] Fearing a widespread revolt during daily labour, all work was cancelled and the convicts kept in "lockdown," which meant continual confinement in their cells. Thirty-six of the most dangerous prisoners were placed in solitary confinement. The following night, the prisoners continued their "howling" to such an extent that one report stated that the nearby villagers were absolutely panic-stricken by the sound of it. "Mark my word," warned the ex-convict interviewed by *The Globe*, "you will see a hot time at the pen before long."[89]

Convinced that the officials at St. Vincent de Paul faced an overwhelming situation, the Department of Justice ordered a squad of Dominion Police to the penitentiary to prepare for a possible revolt. Some guards, apparently still loyal to the former warden, tipped the prisoners to the awaiting force of Dominion Police, and this ignited new protest. Penitentiary Inspector Stewart acted swiftly, suspending Chief Keeper Thomas McCarthy on suspicion of stoking the protest of the prisoners. On the fourth night of protest, the penitentiary officers turned water hoses on the howling prisoners and, in the days following, regained control of the situation. Eight of the "ringleaders" of the riot were transferred from St. Vincent de Paul to the Prison of Isolation at Kingston, thus removing the most dangerous elements of the prison population. However, the convicts continued their agitation throughout the fall of 1897, allegedly aided by the instigation of three guards remaining loyal to Ouimet. On Christmas Day 1897, the inmates recommenced their howling protest and were locked down again over the Christmas holidays. As a result, the traditional distribution of Christmas delicacies was suspended, causing the outbreak of additional riot and insubordination.[90]

The disturbance was finally subdued when Foster, the acting warden, requested permission from the Justice minister to take "drastic action" and employ corporal punishment. Six of the incorrigible inmates were identified and whipped in front of the entire penitentiary population.[91] This ended the year of riot at St. Vincent de Paul. The fact that it ended with hosing prisoners down like animals and brutalizing them into submission with the whip was a sobering warning of the frightening potential of the penitentiary's dangerous classes.

The exploitation and corruption at St. Vincent de Paul stemmed from the willful pursuit of power by penitentiary staff loyal to Warden Ouimet. It demonstrated the remarkable effect that the corruption of a few individuals could have over the entire institution. In fact, similar scandals surfaced in almost every penitentiary in Canada at some point in the nineteenth century, and they were frequently linked with one or two disruptive penitentiary officials. In the late 1880s, a political scandal erupted over the conduct of James Fitzsimmons, the deputy warden at British Columbia Penitentiary. In 1889 an ex-convict of British Columbia distributed a "fly-sheet" in Washington State containing a list of serious charges against the administration at the penitentiary. It singled out Fitzsimmons specifically. A copy of the sheet was obtained by the *Daily Columbian* and eventually circulated among British Columbian representatives in Ottawa, including Senator Donald McInnes. The Department of Justice investigated but found no evidence of wrongdoing, and the matter was dropped.

In 1893 rumours again surfaced about gross mismanagement at British Columbia and pointed at Fitzsimmons. The Justice Department initiated another investigation, which revealed troubling financial irregularities connected to the deputy warden. Worse, Justice Drake reported to the government that Fitzsimmons had waged a war of attrition against Warden James McBride, attempting for years to undermine his authority and speed his resignation. Fitzsimmons was suspended, but within a year, McBride resigned. In a move that enraged the members of the House of Commons from British Columbia, Fitzsimmons was reinstated. McInnes marshalled the British Columbian representatives to demand a solution, and Fitzsimmons was finally transferred to Manitoba Penitentiary, where he assumed the position of deputy warden. The political masters in Ottawa were most enraged by reports of financial corruption. Lost in this debate was evidence about the exploitation of the prison population under Fitzsimmons's authority.

After the deputy warden's departure from British Columbia Penitentiary, some of the details about his regime were made more public. The prisoners looked upon his departure with absolute relief. Although Justice Drake had interviewed prisoners in the course of his investigation, it was clear that no convict would risk speaking out against the deputy while he still held his position. After his move to Manitoba in 1894, the prisoners talked. In the "Discharged Convict Question and Answer Book," the memory of Fitzsimmons's reign at the penitentiary surfaces repeatedly. The answers of several inmates paint a picture of an exploitative and brutally insensitive disciplinary regime under the former deputy warden. Question three of the standard interview form asked, "Have you ever seen any cruel treatment inflicted upon the prisoners, and what is your opinion generally upon the manner in which convicts are treated?"[92] Prior to June 1894, no prisoner had been willing to answer this question. In all likelihood, Fitzsimmons himself had conducted the interview. After his departure, the prisoners were bolder. "Some are treated well, others are treated like brutes," was one response. Another replied, "Pretty badly treated in the past by guards and officials." Another prisoner singled out the new warden, John Foster, directly: "Appeared in a very humane manner, but previous to your arrival, very brutally." One prisoner even gave a detailed response that implicated Fitzsimmons directly: "Yes. In my opinion No. 399 Cary Jones was hastened into his grave by being compelled to work whilst totally unfit also it was a decided act of cruelty to refrain from taking the leg-irons off No. 403 McCabe until within a few days of his death. These and other cruelties happened prior to June 1894 and under the regime of McBride and Fitzsimmons. Since June 1894 the treatment of the convicts has been humane and proper."[93]

Scandals like the Ouimet or Fitzsimmons affairs both illustrate the distance between the reform vision and the penitentiary system created in Canada in the nineteenth century. Was there a discernible difference between the early corruption at Kingston investigated by Brown and the state of affairs in the 1880s and 1890s? How did incompetent and abusive penitentiary officials persist at their posts for years on end? Was the inspector of penitentiaries too absent or did he possess so little power and influence that corruption existed in spite of him? What is clear is that penitentiaries in Canada near the end of the century had more in common with their early history than officials and reformers were prepared to admit.

In practice, then, the penitentiary was a complex social system over which reform discourses exerted relatively little influence. Day-to-day life within prison walls was a reflection, above all, of the balance of power between keepers and prisoners. Even as reformers attempted to influence the overall structure and terms of the relationship between prison authorities and inmates, it continued to be shaped by the particular patterns of power that lay at the heart of the institution—power that was expressed in ways that were often ambiguous and not necessarily apparent to outsiders and that generally deviated from the reform vision. Reformers were often unable to grasp the degree to which prisoners played an active role in configuring these relations of power. Thus, as I suggest above, the broader trajectory of reform was subverted by individual transgressions and acts of resistance of the sort that marked the daily intercourse of power in penitentiary life.

Medicine

In 1876 Inspector Moylan made a troubling observation about prisoners in federal penitentiaries. "Amongst our prison population," he wrote, "there is a large number of convicts who are absolutely unable, or find it extremely difficult, through mental or physical incapacity, to earn their livelihood, even under favourable circumstances."[1] The inspector noted that without the value extracted from their labour, it was impossible to expect these prisoners to repay the cost of their maintenance to the state. Some of the prisoners were "weak-minded," and some were subject to infirmity that prevented them from all but the lightest work. The inspector concluded that inside or outside a penitentiary, these individuals would always be regarded as a "charge upon the public."[2] While Moylan's concern was articulated largely in economic terms, his observations bring to light one of the central challenges faced by penitentiaries in carrying out reform agendas in everyday practice: How could institutions respond to large numbers of prisoners who could not work?

Non-working prisoners required medical solutions. In the post-Confederation era, penitentiary medical services improved, although they remained very rudimentary in spite of reforms. During this era, medical reforms regarding the mentally ill and the disabled were incorporated into penitentiaries; in the process, the medical categorization of prisoners became far more complex. These reforms included new ways of understanding mental illness and better practical solutions for convicted individuals suffering its effects while incarcerated. However, the experience of some prisoners classified as mentally ill illustrates the troubled translation of medical knowledge into penal practice. While medical professionals could better identify mental illness and intellectual disabilities, penal reforms and changes in penal practice lagged far behind. This left some individuals subject to penitentiary regimes that could not respond to difference in a meaningful way. Often this resulted in sick and disabled prisoners occupying neglected, vulnerable, and marginalized roles within penitentiaries. Moreover, new medical categories and practices were layered upon older moral ideas connected to "lost productivity" that made sick and disabled prisoners the subject of ongoing condemnation.

The ideas about lost productivity were connected to the underlying moral imperative of labour that sustained the penitentiary project. As new medical ideas promoted better understanding of illness and disability, the solutions the medical profession proposed represented a significant obstacle to the moral imperative to reform criminals. Non-working criminals existed in a grey area. Unable to participate in labour, they were subject to the moral condemnation of idleness that labour was intended to address. Thus, some prisoners in the institution existed only in the shadows of labour, marked by their uncertain relationship to the productive core of the penitentiary.

In this chapter, I identify two key groups of "unproductive prisoners": the sick were those individuals with physical ailments or mental illness; the disabled were those with conditions of physical disability or intellectual disability. I explore the evolution of medical responses to both groups in the years after 1850 and argue that nineteenth-century medicine evolved to better explain these conditions through medical discourses that gave rise to a particular set of practices intended to accommodate unproductive prisoners. In examining the intersection of medical reform and penitentiary practice, I attempt to show how medical power evolved and developed in the post-1850 era and what characterized its relationship to other key reform ideas in the penitentiary, particularly those involving labour and productivity. Between 1835 and the post-Confederation era, medical power evolved to become more encompassing. Initially, doctors played a primarily disciplinary role, merely helping to define who was or was not able to participate in penitentiary labour. While this dimension of medical power remained unchanged throughout the century, it expanded to include more complex classification of different types of illness and disability in the later nineteenth century. Medical professionals contributed to understandings of the prison population, productivity, and criminality that often turned on medical categories of illness and disability. Thus, medical discourses played an increasingly central role in the penitentiary reform movement in this era, creating a vocabulary to explain non-workers, women, and non-white prisoners and forming a practical response to their accommodation. But we must begin with an understanding of how medicine intersected with structural categories and constructions of criminality that characterized the penitentiary project.

EARLY MEDICAL PRACTICE

When Kingston Penitentiary opened in 1835, one feature that distinguished it from gaols and workhouses in Upper Canada was the provision for professional medical care. The medical inspection of prisoners was an important component of the new modern institutions like Auburn and Kingston. Gaols and workhouses in this era were cavalier about inmates' health because such institutions did not hold individuals long enough to see the consequences of poor hygiene and deficient medical care. In the penitentiary, medicine assumed new importance as a component of much longer prison sentences. The moral reform of criminals was considered impossible if the institution could not keep them healthy. Furthermore, the rigorous labour regime could not be sustained if prisoners were depleted by poor medical care, deficient diet, and debilitating disease. As Kyle Jolliffe argues,

in the larger sense, the new emphasis on medical care also helped
establish the moral legitimacy of the new institutions. Early reformers
were concerned to demonstrate that the penitentiary was a humane
alternative to brutalizing punishments because of its protection of
inmates' health.[3]

In Kingston's early years, the penitentiary surgeon was expected
to be a constant presence at the penitentiary. It was his duty to
respond to medical complaints each morning. He treated minor concerns such as colds and injuries on an outpatient basis and admitted
those with more serious illnesses and injuries to the penitentiary
hospital. Much like the rest of the early penitentiary, the hospital fell
victim to the chronic delays in penitentiary construction. Although
a dedicated hospital wing was included in the original plans, it was
a low priority for the Building Committee throughout the 1830s
and 1840s. Surgeon James Sampson complained in his 1844 annual
report that he could not treat a sufficient number of prisoners in the
temporary hospital quarters and was forced to discharge convicts to
the confines of their cells.[4] Thus, the number of cases treated in the
hospital was extremely small. Table 4 illustrates the nature of medical concerns treated both in and out of the hospital in the first years
at Kingston Penitentiary. Most involved minor treatment, and the
number of serious cases requiring ongoing care was quite low. In these
early years, the penitentiary surgeon was also on continual watch for
the development of epidemic disease. Outbreaks of fever, cholera, and
smallpox in the Midland district required extra effort on the part of
the surgeon.

The hospital at Kingston was finally finished in early 1852, but
due to overcrowding of female convicts, they were moved into the
newly completed infirmary. Dr. Sampson sarcastically reported to the
government his great satisfaction that the hospital was finished and
expressed his hope that it would one day be used for its intended purpose.[5] These ongoing delays and the willingness to improvise solutions
for medical care illustrated a lack of commitment to the principles of
medical reform on the part of penitentiary administrators. This was a
theme that would be repeated at Kingston throughout the century and

TABLE 4   Ailments Treated at Kingston Penitentiary, 1837

RETURN OF CASES TREATED IN THE HOSPITAL	CASES TREATED OUT OF HOSPITAL	
Fever 7	Rheumatism 71	Sore throat 6
Inflammation of the	Diarrhea 125	Eruptions............. 5
bowels 2	Catarrh 25	Hemorrhoids 6
Inflammation of the	Febrile symptoms...... 22	Ulcer 9
brain 2	Injury of the eyes....... 5	Abscess 8
Lumbago 1	Inflamed eyes. 6	Lumbago 2
Cholera 2	Dysuria 3	Costiveness 8
Hoemoptysis 1	Dysmenorrhea 3	Scorbutic affection 1
Injury of the eye 1	Indigestion 42	Lacerated wounds 7
	Contusions 46	Burns from lime. 4
	Headache............ 49	Itch 3
	Boils. 32	Vaccine inflammation... 2
	Griping 42	Affections of the
	Colic 13	kidneys 2
	Toothache 19	Neuralgia.............
	Sprains 13	Tumor 2
	Ear ache............. 19	Excoriation 1
	Nausea.............. 11	Hernea............... 2
	Giddiness............ 7	Gonorrhea 1
	Muscular pains 36	Carbuncle 1
	Cough 4	Mumps 1
	Asthma 2	Fracture............. 1
		Debility 1

SOURCE: "Surgeon's Report, 1837," *Appendix to the Journal of the House of Assembly of Upper Canada*, 1838, 207–8.

replicated at each institution added to the federal penitentiary system in the post-Confederation era.

Despite the presence of staff doctors, medical care in Canadian penitentiaries remained rudimentary in the years after Confederation. Of the five federal penitentiaries in operation by 1880, only Kingston and St. Vincent de Paul featured separate hospital facilities. British Columbia, Dorchester, and Manitoba had no formal infirmaries; in all three prisons, both minor and serious illnesses and injury were treated in standard punishment cells until very late in the century. Not only was this treatment inconvenient and distasteful to the penitentiary surgeons, but it was a constant danger to the health of prison populations due to the threat of communicable disease.

MEDICAL POWER AND THE LABOUR FORCE

In both *Madness and Civilization* (1967) and *The History of Sexuality* (1976), Michel Foucault writes about the expanding role of medicine in defining relations of production in the industrial era. In the earlier work, Foucault notes that, in dividing the sick from the well, medicine furnished a means by which non-productive individuals could be segregated until they were ready to rejoin the productive world. Underlying this division was an association between physical health, signalled by the ability to perform labour, and moral health. "The prisoner who could and who would work," Foucault wrote, "would be released, not so much because he was again useful to society, but because he had again subscribed to the ethical pact of human existence."[6] A sharp distinction was drawn between productive and unproductive members of society, and Foucault hints at how such categories helped to organize institutional life. In his later work, Foucault investigates medical power (bio-power), examining the specific role that medicine played not merely in segregating the sick but in their potential reformation. Medical power functioned to insert the sick back into productive roles, sustaining their health to ensure their continued participation in the world of production.[7] The history of medical intervention in the lives of the urban poor during the late eighteenth and early nineteenth centuries offers multiple examples of this impulse. Public health initiatives in England stemming from the Poor Law addressed the failing health of the working class. Not only did these initiatives work toward the containment of working-class contagion, but they ensured the vitality of a newly urbanized labour force.[8] As Michael Ignatieff argues, much like penitentiaries, hospital reforms in the late eighteenth century aimed at "saving" the poor played into a new strategy of class control.[9]

Although the primary interest of penitentiary medicine was maintaining the health of the penitentiary labour force, the penitentiary surgeon played a role in the disciplining and policing of the penitentiary labour force from the earliest years. In 1837 the provincial inspector noted, "It will be seen that his office is not merely curative of the health of the prisoners, but it is also necessarily corrective in detecting imposition by feigned sickness, a matter of no small importance as regards both the discipline and pecuniary interest of the establishment."[10] It is significant that discipline and pecuniary interest both tended to coalesce around the issue of regulating the prison labour force. In part, it was this role of policing prisoners and controlling the supply of labour that underpinned the power invested in early penitentiary surgeons. Kingston surgeon James Sampson referred to his task of detecting feigned illness in his 1837 report:

I noticed in my report of last October, the remarkable disposition I had observed amongst Convicts, to feign sickness, or, to complain of very slight ailments. The truth of this observation is also confirmed by experience, and seldom is the Medical Officer's daily visit made, that an example of it does not occur. His attention therefore is as much to be directed to the prevention of fraud as to the treatment of disease. He is regarded by the scheming Convict, as a ready medium through which he can occasionally gain a respite from his labour, and thus elude a material item in the sum of his punishment; and it therefore behooves him to be continually on his guard against this species of fraud.[11]

The ability to detect this type of deception contributed to the standing and power of the penitentiary surgeon in the institution. Sampson noted that not just any practitioner could detect such fraud: it took a professional with long experience in the institution. As an example, he cited a four-day period when he was absent. Upon his return, he found that the sick list had ballooned from eight to thirty-six. When the doctor examined these sick prisoners himself, he determined that twenty-four of the total were fit for labour.[12]

The connection between medicine and discipline was raised in every decade throughout the nineteenth century. Surgeons in the post-Confederation era noted the same ongoing problem with feigning illness. While Kingston's James Sampson viewed the practice with a touch of sympathy for the plight of labouring prisoners, other doctors assumed a harder position. In 1881 Kingston surgeon O. S. Strange wrote: "It is not surprising that the comforts of a fully equipped prison hospital are sought for by others than the really sick. Hard work is not a luxury for those whose previous mode of living has been a constant effort to evade it, and the Surgeon, having to assume the responsibility of deciding in the matter, has not unfrequently had to submit to animadversion."[13] Surgeon Robert Mitchell at Dorchester Penitentiary frequently remarked on the dishonesty of the men requesting his medical assistance to avoid daily labour. In an 1892 annual report, he wrote, "The ills of man are innumerable, and quite enough to occupy our attention; but it is surprising the number of men that labour under supposed infirmities in this prison and are rather indignant when I find myself unable to agree with them as to the seriousness of their complaints."[14] The volume of requests for assistance that Mitchell turned down illustrates the extent of his crusade against feigning. In 1884 he received 837 applications for advice but treated just 225 cases.[15] Three years later, he received a staggering 3,098 applications and offered treatment in just 455 instances, of which only thirteen were deemed serious enough to admit to the penitentiary hospital.[16] Thus, with an inmate population of 150 in 1887, the Dorchester surgeon received, on average, twenty requests per prisoner that year. The disparity between medical assistance requested and offered hints at the persistence shown by prisoners in making medical applications even in the face of unbending authorities. In many cases, doctors offered "just enough" medicine to avoid recording such treatment in their medical records. Robert Mitchell noted in his 1889 report that he avoided medical treatment in the majority of cases by offering the minimal medical intervention; this usually included some liniment for injury or all-purpose cough mixtures for cold and flu.[17]

The most important thing for doctors was to keep prisoners at steady labour. According to the 1868 *Penitentiary Act*, the system of remission was tied to the performance of labour. Prisoners who were ill, whether feigned or not, were ineligible for full remission. Prisoners absented from labour because they were in the hospital or asylum received only half the remission of a working prisoner.[18]

In their encounters with penitentiary doctors, inmates found themselves on the poor end of a power imbalance that was deeply entrenched and difficult to transcend. Prisoners who required assistance appealed directly to the surgeon for inclusion on the "sick list," but they were well aware of the skepticism of penitentiary doctors and were often reluctant to trust the surgeons any more than the disciplinary staff. One former prisoner wrote in a *Globe* story about the intense unease that overtook prisoners as they sat on a wooden bench outside the surgeon's office at Kingston Penitentiary.[19] Another Kingston prisoner, in order to overcome his anxiety, employed the unique strategy of writing to the surgeon to request medical assistance. His note stated,

> Pardon the liberty of my addressing you but your time is so valuable in the morning and my being very nervous cannot explain to you my pain and symptoms properly. The medicine you have kindly prescribed for me of late does not help my sufferings. I am convinced I am suffering from ulcerated stomach, everything I take either eating or in liquid makes me sick and nasty secretion or . . . is passing away from me profusely. I trust my note will not offend, but I do hope that you will change my present medicine and give me something that will meet my present ailment.[20]

Although many penitentiary inmates were not literate enough to express their concerns in this way, the encounter with doctors required careful negotiation, and the anxiety that this clearly caused some inmates hints at the real and perceived power of the penitentiary surgeon.

In spite of advancing medical reform in the years after 1850, the health of penitentiary inmates was generally quite poor. In 1883 Kingston surgeon Michael Lavell reported that many of the men sentenced to the penitentiary were "hopelessly diseased," an assessment that is borne out by the frequency of degenerative illnesses such as cholera and bronchitis recorded on annual sick returns.[21] Given the impoverished material conditions in which the nineteenth-century working class lived, especially its poorest strata, these high levels of disease are hardly surprising. Moreover, penitentiary officials generally expected the prevalence of disease in the criminal class. In a revealing comment comparing the former lives of penitentiary inmates to their experience in prison, Inspector Moylan wrote, "In respect to the condition of their life, their habitation, clothing, and diet are more favourable here than they probably are in a state of freedom."[22] This was a comment on the living conditions of Ontario's industrial poor. However, penitentiary officials linked poor health in the prisons not only with the poor, but more specifically, with the underclass and criminal classes that they already perceived as the primary targets of the penitentiary. This resulted in a discourse connecting disease and illness with compromised morality and degeneracy.

These ideas contributed to medical characterizations of penitentiary inmates, which are illustrated by the broad conclusions that prison medical professionals advanced about their patients. In 1881 Dr. Michael Lavell wrote, "The massing together of men, most of whom are of low moral type, with confirmed filthy habits, and broken down constitutions, inherited and acquired, offer[s] facilities for the encroachment of disease, which demands the most humane and vigilant oversight to avert."[23] In 1900 Kingston surgeon Daniel Phelan reported that a large number of prisoners came to him with broken-down constitutions as a result of "disease, alcoholism, filthy and vicious habits, and exposure to the vicissitudes of criminal life."[24] Phelan explicitly associated poor health with immorality and criminality, but more specifically, he used health to create a demarcation between the working class and the dangerous classes: the following year, he wrote, "Habitual offenders or recidivists, those without any trade or calling, form the largest contingent of those whose health requires attention."[25]

Portrayals of the poor health of inmates were often contrasted with the positive influence of the "penitentiary lifestyle." In his 1874 annual report Kingston surgeon Michael Lavell noted,

> Many of these convicts enter the prison debilitated by dissipation and disease, very soon, however, a marked change is observable, contrasting in an eminent degree their present with their former physical condition, and bearing the best of testimony to the effects of good diet and enforced cleanliness and regularity of living.
>
> I believe that apart from the humane efforts for their personal comfort, the confident feeling that these people have, that their slightest ailments will be attended to promptly, and that in severe disease every provision is made to mitigate their sufferings and promote recovery, have a tendency to maintain a cheerfulness, which contributes largely to the prevention of sickness.[26]

In spite of doctors' insistence that the penitentiary promoted healthful lifestyles, they could not completely ignore the fact that the penitentiary was simply too rigorous for some prisoners to endure. In these cases, doctors frequently referenced "broken down constitutions" when elderly prisoners died while incarcerated.[27] In just one of many examples, the death of a man in his sixties from a bladder infection was attributed to being "a worn out, intemperate debauchee."[28] Such quasi-medical explanations often obscured the fact that penitentiary life was particularly difficult on the elderly. Most elderly prisoners were unable to participate in the daily labour regime, and some were too weak for any form of physical work. In 1887 O. S. Strange reported that a number of Kingston's elderly inmates waited out the working hours in a "dry room" while others were permanently confined to the infirmary. One seventy-four-year-old prisoner at Kingston spent the entire winter of 1886 in the dry room. He was sentenced to ten years, but Strange believed he would not survive half that time.[29] Often doctors argued against the fallacy of incarcerating elderly prisoners only long enough to die in the prison hospital. This argument also stemmed from the fact that the elderly occupied a morally ambiguous position in the institution since they were unable to participate in the reformation offered by penitentiary labour.

Doctors determined a response to the terminally ill on a case-by-case basis. In many instances, doctors and wardens tried to secure pardons for prisoners suffering from the later stages of degenerative diseases, particularly respiratory illnesses such as tuberculosis. In the late 1880s, Dorchester surgeon Robert Mitchell noted that a considerable number of prisoners had been pardoned in hopes of increasing their chances for recovery from the disease.[30] Such pardons were undoubtedly motivated by humanitarian concern, but penitentiary administrators were also charged with reducing the rates of inmate mortality; thus, many terminally ill prisoners were released so they could die outside of the institution. In an 1888 report, the Catholic chaplain at Kingston argued for pardoning these inmates on compassionate grounds:

> Society cannot be injured by their release, and the ends of justice cannot be served by keeping them until they die. No matter what care they receive in the prison hospital (and they are always kindly treated there) the grating sound of the iron doors, and the cheerless cell, and the bare prison walls and all their surroundings, make death more terrible and the consoling truths of religion less sweet, as they fall upon the ears of the dying prisoner. Let a man feel that he is free once more and no longer an outcast from society and he can dispose himself to die with greater resignation to the will of God who calls him hence. Surely Justice, without injury to herself, can afford to be merciful, at the hour of death. I have been led to these remarks by the piteous appeals made to me a few days ago, by a consumptive convict, whose life is fast ebbing away.[31]

While no penitentiary authority disputed these sentiments, pardons were not always possible and sometimes took too long. Wardens did not have the authority to summarily release a prisoner from the institution, even if the inmate was terminally ill, and the granting of pardons from the governor general in Council was a painfully slow political process. Catholic chaplain Denis A. Twomey detailed the tragic consequences of such delays at Kingston Penitentiary. When one prisoner was pardoned and died two days after his release, the chaplain noted, "The life of the [prisoner] would have been prolonged if executive clemency were exercised towards him some months sooner."[32] In a more striking example, eighteen-year-old William Baylis was pardoned from Kingston in July 1888 on the recommendation of the surgeon. He waited three days for his father to escort him home. On the day he arrived, as Baylis was walking toward the warden's office to be released, he collapsed and died.[33]

In many cases, it was the labour regime itself that caused injury or breakdown of prisoners' health. Industrial accidents were common at each institution, frequently claiming digits, eyesight, and even limbs. Eye injuries were especially common wherever stone-work was undertaken. In 1889, for instance, a worker in the Kingston stone shed was struck in the eye by a rock chip, which penetrated the cornea and caused him to lose vision on one side.[34] In addition to accidents causing physical harm, working conditions sometimes led to mental problems. In 1891 Manitoba Penitentiary surgeon W. R. D. Sutherland noted that inmates working in the kitchen were suffering mental breakdowns, and he appealed to the warden to shorten the length of indoor service to allow the prisoners some fresh air.[35] Similar conditions plagued prisoners working in the laundry and tailoring department at St. Vincent de Paul—surgeon L. A. Fortier described his inspection of the workshop:

> Upon entering the tailor's department, a "sui generis," indefinable smell struck me, and then my eyes perceived heaps of dirty stockings and clothes; a cloud of vapour impregnated with unhealthy smell rose up above a large washing machine installed without ceremony alongside a hot air drying apparatus in a hall occupied by about sixty convicts. I asked Dr. Duchesneau to kindly come to the

rescue of a colony of convicts doomed to work in a repulsive and suffocating hall in the name of the grand secular principle: "The action of the atmospheric air on man is of every instant and this gas is the most indispensable agent to life."[36]

In another case, George Garnett, an inmate at Manitoba Penitentiary, suffered from an unlucky assignment to the penitentiary furnace room. He was awakened daily at 3:45 a.m. to begin his work day and remained on duty until 10:00 p.m. Sutherland finally informed Warden Bedson that Garnett was ill with a nervous disposition and was breaking down mentally from lack of sleep.[37]

RACE AND PENITENTIARY MEDICINE

Non-white prisoners were often the subjects of unique medical discourses that stemmed from racist beliefs about their inherent physiological inferiority. In most cases, racial assumptions about this inferiority were supported by health and mortality statistics collected in the penitentiary. In 1858 Kingston surgeon James Sampson noted the shocking mortality rates of black and Aboriginal prisoners over the twenty-five-year history of the institution:

> The mortality among the Protestant Convicts this year, has been very small, being eight only, out of five hundred and thirty-two, less than one per cent. But, as usual, among the Indians, the Negroes, and Negroloids, the mortality has been severe. Out of eight deaths, five were of the latter and one of the former class, while two only were whites. Death has seized one to every eight Indians, one to every twelve Negroes, and one to every two hundred and twenty-five Protestant Convicts.[38]

The most marked examples of racial discourses occurred with First Nations prisoners at Manitoba Penitentiary. Although officials at Manitoba touted the success of their efforts to "civilize" the First

Nations people during their time at the penitentiary, these efforts were obviously undercut by the distressing rates of illness and mortality.

A Blood prisoner named Ka-ka-wink became ill with scrofula soon after arriving at Manitoba Penitentiary to serve a sentence for horse stealing. After spending 309 days in the hospital, he died in early 1882 at the age of nineteen. The same year, Jingling Bells, also imprisoned for horse stealing, died in November.[39] The arrival of larger numbers of First Nations convicts in the following years brought the problem into sharp relief. Beginning with the Cree who arrived in 1883 after being convicted for horse stealing, W. R. D. Sutherland, the penitentiary surgeon, began noting the tendency of First Nations prisoners to become quite weak soon after their sentences began. Some deteriorated faster than others. Cree prisoner The Thigh died in September 1883, just two months after his arrival.[40] Sutherland reported that the men were suffering from "hereditary disease, quite incurable, and clearly aggravated by the confinement of prison life." He stated that he had done everything possible to build the men's strength and combat their deteriorating health. Still, he wrote, "they grew daily worse, until it seemed nothing further which we could do for them here would be of any avail." When Sutherland reported to the Department of Indian Affairs that the fifteen prisoners convicted of horse stealing were in this depleted condition, it helped speed the decision to pardon the men and release them into the custody of the Department of Indian Affairs.[41]

First Nations mortality at Manitoba Penitentiary worsened when the prisoners sentenced after the Northwest Rebellion began to arrive in the summer of 1885. Three of the Cree prisoners died within months of arriving at the penitentiary: Louison McLeod and Leon Francis both succumbed to tuberculosis in March 1886, and Wyinous died of the same disease three months later. Francis was just fifteen years old. A total of six First Nations prisoners from the rebellion died at Manitoba between 1886 and 1890. "During the past year a good many Indians and other convicts were visited by sickness," wrote Father Cloutier in early 1887. "Five times I celebrated the funeral services for some poor unfortunate departed. I visited them often during their illness, and it is my sincere conviction that they received all the care possible. All that was asked for was allowed to them."[42] The previous year, Cloutier had written in his annual report, "I am inclined to think that too long a detention may have caused the sickness which led them to the grave. They were young, healthy, strong; but these advantages were useless preventatives against death. The idea of their detention was for them something very heavy and hard. I often heard them saying: *Wayo otatchi ayayan; Estitotemak ayayayan gakekon*—If I were not here, if I were with my people, I would surely recover."[43] From descriptions of the rebellion prisoners, it is clear that many were already in a depleted state of health when they arrived at the penitentiary. Years of malnutrition on the Canadian plains and a summer of fighting the Canadian militia had left many of the men weak and susceptible to tubercular infection. The poor physical conditions at Manitoba also contributed to the situation: the damp and the cold probably exacerbated existing medical problems in many of the prisoners, who were interned together in common cells without proper ventilation. Their already compromised health would explain the rapid deterioration of some of them. Tuberculosis was a swift killer in the penitentiary, and even though doctors cited "inherited conditions" for the failing health of the rebellion prisoners, they still understood that the men would have a better chance of survival if they were released as quickly as possible.

The number of deaths in the years after 1885 would certainly have been higher if not for pardons secured for several of the men who were critically ill. Chief One Arrow was one of the first rebellion prisoners to be pardoned in early 1886 because officials realized he was terminally ill. The chief made it only as far as St. Boniface, where he died a few days after leaving the penitentiary. The *Saskatchewan Herald* reported that some of the men who were pardoned with One Arrow were so weak that they could not walk: they were taken from the penitentiary in a cart and had to be lifted in and out for the journey.[44] Most of the men were probably sick with tuberculosis. Sometimes the effects of the disease lingered for months or years after release from the penitentiary. Chief Poundmaker left Manitoba Penitentiary at the same time as One Arrow. He had suffered from the effects of tuberculosis in the years prior to the rebellion and died just three months after being pardoned.

Two more cases illustrate the urgency with which penitentiary officials tried to secure pardons for terminally ill First Nations prisoners. In July 1895 Sutherland, a surgeon at Manitoba Penitentiary, wrote to the warden to recommend the release of Wolf Child and Low Man, imprisoned for horse stealing, after less than a year of imprisonment. "I beg to report specially upon the serious condition of convict no. 17 Wolf Child," he wrote. "He is dying of consumption. During the last year he has been constantly under treatment which gave temporary relief. He has now reached the last stage of the disease and cannot live. I would therefore recommend his immediate release." The next day, after removing four scrofulous cysts from Low Man's neck, the surgeon wrote, "I would thoroughly urge his release before the stage is reached which is not far distant. Further confinement is sure to prove fatal to him."[45] Wolf Child and Low Man were both pardoned on 30 July 1895. Wolf Child subsequently died on the Canadian Pacific train outside of Moose Jaw, where the NWMP took charge of his remains, continuing with them on the train for interment on the Blood Reserve.[46]

The comments made by penitentiary officials regarding First Nations health reflected widely held beliefs about the physical inferiority of Aboriginal people. As Maureen Lux argues, government officials were prone to explain higher rates of death among First Nations people in institutional settings by resorting to racial justifications.[47] Transmittable (and preventable) respiratory disease reimagined as racial defect became the standard response to the illness and death of First Nations prisoners. The discourses surrounding the health of Aboriginal people echoed the ideas about social degeneration among other members of the dangerous classes. Anne McClintock explores the discourse of "degeneration" in an imperial context. She argues that social crisis in Britain in the 1870s and 1880s caused a eugenic discourse of degeneration predicated upon the fear of disease and contagion. Ruling elites classified threatening social groups (working-class and racialized people) in biological terms that pathologized their perceived shortcomings and potential to threaten the riches, health, and power of the "imperial race."[48]

These discourses were particularly powerful in the Canadian North-West after the 1870s, when First Nations people struggled with sweeping epidemic disease coupled with the destruction of their traditional economy. Lux argues that bureaucrats, missionaries, and politicians explained the high death rates and continuing poor health in racial terms, inferring that only the fittest should be expected to survive.[49] Penitentiary officials often resorted to similar racial explanations for high rates of illness of black and Chinese prisoners. When British Columbia Penitentiary opened in 1880, the assistant inspector noted that the large number of "Indians" and Chinese among the prison population had the effect of swelling expenditures for the treatment of syphilis and tuberculosis.[50]

Two years later, the surgeon at British Columbia Penitentiary repeated the maxim that First Nations prisoners could not withstand the physical burdens of imprisonment. Reporting on the higher level of hospital committals from the previous year, C. Newland Trew wrote, "This is owing to increased severity of the chronic forms of disease among the Indian convicts—that race, apparently, not able to withstand the depressing effects of confinement so well as the whites or Chinese."[51] In institutional settings, such attitudes proved disastrous for First Nations individuals. Mary-Ellen Kelm explores the health of residential schoolchildren in post-1900 British Columbia and uncovers several similarities to the penitentiary experience. She describes a "scandalous procession" from school to grave that awaited many First Nations children in the early years of the residential school system in British Columbia. They succumbed to the same diseases that claimed penitentiary prisoners—largely respiratory illnesses that were highly transmittable and were preventable with proper nutrition, ventilation, and medical care. The terrible irony, as Kelm aptly describes, was that school officials viewed First Nations children as inherently diseased and susceptible to illness because of what were perceived as unique racial characteristics. In reality, it was exposure to squalid conditions, poor diet, and a harsh work regime that broke the health of residential school children.[52]

The health of First Nations prisoners did not improve in the years following the Northwest Rebellion. Although racial explanations for their poor health prevailed, it is also clear from some penitentiary records that cultural misunderstandings or miscommunication sometimes perpetuated these beliefs and resulted in tragedy for First Nations prisoners. Twenty-six-year-old "Sam," a member of the Nez Perce First Nation, was convicted of murder in 1892 and his sentence was commuted to life at Manitoba Penitentiary. After only a few months in prison, he became unresponsive and unwilling to work. In early March 1893, the surgeon examined him and reported to the warden, "My examination today as well as previous ones made at your request of convict No. 64 Nez Perce Sam leads one to the opinion that this man is intellectually deficient. His unreasonable refusal to leave his cell or do the slightest work throws evidence of a melancholic nature while his periods of brighter intelligence show signs of excitement."[53] The doctor made this diagnosis despite admitting that he could not understand what the patient was saying. He concluded only that he would keep the patient under observation. In late August 1893, Sam was in the hospital again with dropsy and was diagnosed with phthisis two weeks later. He died on October 1.[54]

"Jackson," another Nez Perce, experienced a similar slow deterioration due to tuberculosis. He arrived at Manitoba Penitentiary in July 1886 and by the following January was confined to the hospital. On 1 September 1887, the surgeon noted in the medical casebook that Jackson was "getting more feeble and requires constant attention." By October 1, he was refusing his medicine, and on October 9 he died at 10:30 p.m.[55] That year, Father Cloutier reported again on the failing health of First Nations prisoners. "I have this year again to deplore the poor state of health of a great many Indians," he wrote. "It has happened pretty often that the same men were in the hospital for weeks and for months. If something could be done in their behalf it would be quite an act of charity."[56]

Canadian penitentiaries in the nineteenth century played an important role in shaping the state response to mental illness, particularly in western Canada. Penitentiaries incarcerated several categories of mentally ill individuals in this period, the most common being prisoners who lapsed into mental illness during the course of their sentence. Medical understandings of mental illness in the nineteenth century were often ambiguous. Doctors recognized three primary types of insanity: mania, melancholia, and dementia. Mania exhibited symptoms such as violence, delusions, paranoia, jealousy, excessive drinking, and excessive religious observance. Melancholia was characterized by a depressive tendency and a refusal to eat, work, or participate in daily routines. Dementia was identified by verbal incoherency, paranoia, poor personal cleanliness, and refusal to participate in daily activities. Contributing to the ambiguity of these three categories was the fact that many of these qualities were recognized as both causes and symptoms of the conditions with which they were associated.[57] Penitentiaries also imprisoned individuals who were found "criminally insane" or unfit to stand trial by reason of insanity. In other cases, penitentiaries in Canada were the only institutions that could accept "dangerous insane" individuals who could not be cared for in government asylums.[58] In some jurisdictions, such as Manitoba, the North-West, and British Columbia, any person committed to the care of the state as a result of mental illness was incarcerated in a penitentiary because there were no formal asylum facilities in these regions until the late 1880s.

The mentally ill were always regarded as a problem population in penitentiaries. At Kingston in the 1840s, for example, prisoners who lapsed into mental illness caused great difficulties. The surgeon argued that their "proper moral management" was impossible inside the penitentiary.[59] To relieve the situation, Upper Canada introduced a new penitentiary statute in 1851 that permitted the penitentiary to remove thirteen mentally ill prisoners to the provincial lunatic asylum in Toronto.[60] The Toronto Asylum objected to this arrangement, arguing that it was unequipped to handle the "moral monsters" being transferred from the penitentiary and citing the relative incurability of criminal lunatics compared with regular asylum patients.[61] Joseph Workman, the asylum superintendent, thundered in his 1853 annual report: "An evil of inconceivable magnitude, and distressing results, in the working and present condition of this Institution has been the introduction of Criminal Lunatics from the Provincial Penitentiary and the County Gaol. It is an outrage against public benevolence."[62] After the return of the mentally ill convicts to Kingston Penitentiary in 1855, they were segregated in the west wing of the building. In an arrangement that negated the moral concerns expressed by Workman about combining criminal and non-criminal lunatics, the transfer also included twenty-four regular patients from the provincial asylum to help alleviate overcrowding.[63] Circumstances deteriorated for the entire group of recently transferred patients when they were forced to vacate the west wing and moved to the penitentiary basement in 1856. Although the basement accommodations were intended to be temporary during the erection of a separate penitentiary asylum, construction dragged on for eight years: the Rockwood Criminal Lunatic Asylum was finally opened in 1864. Rockwood operated in this capacity until 1877, when the federal government sold it to the province of Ontario, which was seeking to expand the provincial asylum system. From 1877 onward, all mentally ill prisoners remained at Kingston in a detached wing of the penitentiary. Thereafter, Kingston became the repository for "criminal lunatics" from all over the dominion.[64]

Concerns about mental illness in the penitentiary during this period turned on a medically ambiguous definition of *curability*. Throughout the nineteenth century, approaches to mental illness closely reflected reform views of criminality in that evangelicals and humanists believed both could be "corrected." With this idea at the root of Victorian social reform, asylums assumed the task of attaining the "perfectibility of man" through new psychological medical methods.[65] In the penitentiary, "perfectibility" was never a resounding theme with medical professionals. Rather than an indicator of whether a patient's life could be saved, curability often referred only to the chances of returning the ailing individual from the sick list to the daily routines of prison labour. Penitentiary doctors complained that the number of prisoners confined permanently to infirmaries was turning penitentiaries into "hospitals for incurables."[66] As the population of federal inmates grew toward the end of the nineteenth century, penitentiary doctors and officials struggled with how to respond to increasing numbers of prisoners who were incapacitated. Among those often counted as "incurables" were prisoners suffering from various forms of mental illness. While most doctors would have preferred to offload these prisoners to the care of provincial asylums, the political realities of post-Confederation social policy often made this impossible.

Forced to contend with the care of mentally ill prisoners, penitentiaries in Canada made some efforts to emulate the standards of contemporary asylums. In the mid-nineteenth century, asylum reform was characterized by a movement from "custodial" to "curative" care. Older methods of custodial treatment involved only the most basic medical care, often accompanied by physical restraints or sedative tonics. British asylum reformer James Hack Tuke (great-grandson of philanthropist and asylum reformer William Tuke) visited the Toronto Asylum in 1845 and condemned the outdated medical care and brutal treatment of the inmates under a custodial model. He described "one of the most painful and distressing places I ever visited":

> There were, perhaps, 70 patients, upon whose faces misery, starvation, and suffering were indelibly impressed. The doctor pursues the exploded system of constantly cupping, bleeding, blistering, and purging his patients, giving them the smallest quantity of food and that of the poorest quality. No meat is allowed.
>
> The temples and necks of the patients were nearly all scarred with the marks of former cuppings, or were bandaged from the effects of more recent ones. Many patients were suffering from sore legs, or from blisters on their backs and legs. Everyone looked emaciated and wretched. Strongly-built men were shrunk to skeletons, and poor idiots were lying on their beds motionless, and as if half dead.[67]

The abuse that accompanied custodial treatment was increasingly condemned in favour of a curative program involving "moral therapy." Moral therapy concentrated on the psychological and emotional causes of illness, advocating psychological methods to treat mental medical disorders.[68] This treatment depended on the restful setting of the modern asylum, including plenty of fresh air, sunlight, and exercise. The curative program also assumed a moral dimension that gave meaning to labour as a means of criminal reformation in penitentiaries. Sometimes referred to as "occupational therapy," prescribing work to the mentally ill was intended either to distract them from their delusions or to encourage the growth of mental powers and concentration.[69] As Anne Digby notes, it was the simple process of being employed rather than the quality of the work performed that supposedly offered therapeutic benefits.[70] Although the moral elements of labour were always present in the penitentiary, its practical components often played the greater role in shaping responses to the mentally ill. These practical considerations informed rationales for keeping prisoners engaged in labour. Other elements of moral therapy met with the limitations and restrictions particular to the disciplinary environment.

Some evidence suggests that even transferring prisoners to provincial asylums provided no guarantee that mental illness would be properly treated. In the mid-1850s, Kingston surgeon James Sampson struggled to find adequate care for two mentally ill prisoners but found the provincial asylum in Toronto to be of little assistance. Convicts Therein and Geintner were both convicted murderers whose capital sentences were commuted to life imprisonment for reasons of criminal insanity. Geintner was transferred to the asylum in December 1851 but returned to the penitentiary in mid-1853, when he was reported to be of "sound mind."[71] Sampson, however, could not see any improvement in his case, and Geintner was subsequently confined permanently to his cell to prevent him from doing violence to keepers or other prisoners. Therein's case was even more troubling. While incarcerated in the Three Rivers gaol and suffering a bout of violent delusion, he murdered a fellow prisoner. Once at Kingston Penitentiary, his condition did not improve. Therein undertook a twenty-seven-day hunger strike and was transferred to the provincial asylum. After just forty-four days, the asylum returned him to the penitentiary. Like Geintner, Sampson could see no improvement in Therein upon his return. The most likely explanation for their lack of improvement while at the Toronto Asylum was that the asylum simply refused to treat these men because of their status as convicted murderers.[72]

Although penitentiary reform was closely associated with asylum reform, the conditions in Canadian penitentiary asylums and the methods of treatment for mentally ill prisoners showed little improvement into the late nineteenth century. Daniel Hack Tuke (brother of James) visited the Kingston Criminal Lunatic Asylum in 1877 and described the shocking conditions he witnessed there:

> The patients are treated with almost as much rigour as convicts, though not dressed in prison garb. . . . In the basement are "dungeons," to which patients when they are refractory are consigned as a punishment, although the cells above are in all conscience sufficiently prison-like. The floors of the cells are of stone, and would be felt to be a punishment by any patient in the asylums of Ontario. . . .
> Two men in the cells had once been patients in the asylum. One, with whom we conversed at the iron gate of his dungeon, laboured under a distinct delusion of there being a conspiracy against him. It was certainly not very likely to be dispelled by the dismal stone-floor dungeon in which he was immured, without a seat, unless he chose to use the bucket intended for other purposes, which was the only piece of furniture in the room.[73]

Such conditions had more in common with early pre-reform penitentiaries than with anything required by modern moral treatment. In spite of the construction of a dedicated asylum wing for the criminally insane at Kingston in 1877, the treatment of patients reverted to a neglectful custodial system that reformers thoroughly condemned. In 1890 Inspector Moylan visited the asylum at Kingston and reported on the lack of recreational grounds, fresh air, or opportunity for physical exercise.[74] Featuring similar dimensions to the punishment cells, the rooms in the asylum wing measured a length long enough for a bed and a width of just twenty-eight inches.[75] Dr. O. S. Strange admitted to the inspector that he managed to visit the asylum patients just two or three times a week. When pressed about how he was effecting a "cure" under the restrictive physical conditions in the asylum, Strange responded, "If they require tonics, I give them tonics and different medicines as the case requires. We give them the moral treatment. Talk to them and try to convince them of their delusions."[76] "Tonics" usually referred to the use of sedative medicine, which was administered until a patient was calmed or unconscious. The care at Kingston suggests how easily psychiatric standards could be dismissed or modified to fit the limitations of penal institutions.

Two examples from Manitoba Penitentiary illustrate some parts of the experience of mental illness in a penitentiary in this period. Harry Brown was a thirty-seven-year-old book binder sentenced to fifteen years for stopping mail in 1894. Brown was transferred to Manitoba from British Columbia Penitentiary in April 1895 with thirteen other men to alleviate overcrowding. In June 1895 the Manitoba surgeon treated him for insomnia, which usually involved doses of castor oil. In July the surgeon diagnosed Brown as melancholic.[77] Melancholia was treated similarly to insomnia but was regarded as a mental illness. Brown continued receiving castor oil into 1896 and was also prescribed heavy doses of sedatives. In April 1896 he was listed on the medical register as "well—out of his cell," but he remained under treatment until September of the following year, when he was transferred to the Criminal Insane Asylum at Kingston Penitentiary.[78] This was a final admission of Brown's incurability, at least within the confines of Manitoba Penitentiary.

Frank Jackson was twenty-two when he was sentenced to five years for arson in July 1892. Three years later, he was admitted to the Manitoba Penitentiary hospital with melancholia and treated with "pills" and bromidia. Although he ingested daily quantities of bromidia, in October 1895 he became overly excited and tore his clothing; the next day, he was strapped to his bed. He continued to be treated through the spring of 1896 and in June again became overly excited and had the "lunatic belt" put on him. Jackson was kept in his cell continuously throughout this time: he spent nearly two years in total isolation with no outside stimulation or interaction. He was issued no books from the library and received no visitors. Jackson was finally transferred to local authorities in October 1896, more than eighteen months after he had first exhibited signs of mental disorder.[79]

Between 1870 and 1890, the Criminal Insane Asylum at Kingston received 222 admissions.[80] Thirty-three inmates died while incarcerated, sixty-eight were discharged as "improved," and eighty were "cured." Thirty-three inmates in this period were removed to the provincial lunatic asylum, implying that although these patients' sentences had expired, they were insufficiently well to be safely released from custody. Of the 222 admissions, only 30 percent could be classified as "incurable" since they either died or were transferred to another mental institution. What is suggested here is that medical diagnoses such as "improvement" and "cure" were motivated by their practical outcomes. If a penitentiary inmate was improved or cured by a stay in a criminal lunatic asylum, it would guarantee only a return to the general inmate population and the daily labour of prison life. To this end, penitentiary doctors served conflicting interests of the institution's labour demands and their patients' mental health. The high rate of "success" at Kingston in spite of institutional shortcomings (compared to medical asylums) suggests that doctors effected a "cure" as quickly as possible.

An ongoing component of the "cure" for mental illness was physical labour. Penitentiary doctors enthusiastically subscribed to the occupational elements of moral therapy. In some senses, they believed in its therapeutic benefits, but they were also certainly relieved to find practical solutions preventing the continued confinement of the mentally ill in the same cell or hospital wing without cessation. In 1895 the surgeon at Kingston noted that his hospital ward would be overflowing if all the "weak-minded" convicts were relieved of their daily labour.[81] This labour regime prevailed in most Ontario asylums and, as Geoffrey Reaume suggests, actively promoted the theoretical connection between physical labour and the recovery of the "alienated mind."[82]

Reaume also argues that the interests of economy played a primary role in the constant promotion of labour in these asylums. Penitentiary doctors sometimes advanced similar arguments. At St. Vincent de Paul Penitentiary, Dr. L. A. Fortier defended the use of labour as a form of therapy in penitentiary asylums:

> The fact that an insane convict soon after his arrival at Kingston Asylum is sent to work with a squad of convicts is not proof that the surgeon of a penitentiary was wrong to order the transfer. . . . It is not an argument establishing that the subject is sui mentos compos; far from it; a convict being susceptible to be affected with transient mental insanity, another with intermittent insanity and a third one with permanent mental insanity.
>
> It is elementary [that] in every case of mental insanity the first thing to be done is to isolate the patient from his habitual lodging, to procure him a good change of scenery and to occupy his mind with work, amusements and distractions of all kinds.[83]

Fortier's arguments were aligned with long-standing beliefs in the asylum movement about the importance of patient labour. William Tuke argued that using patients as labourers at the York Retreat was "suitable and proper for them, in order to relieve the languor of idleness and prevent the indulgence of gloomy sensations."[84] It was convenient for medical authorities that labour was not incompatible with the accepted therapeutic response to mental illness; in most cases, penitentiary doctors could offer little else. Under the guise of "moral therapy," labour served mostly practical solutions to the accommodation of the mentally ill. The effect was often that the patient and prisoner experienced confinement in ways that were ultimately very similar. Two factors tended to emphasize this point, the first being gender. Female patients suffering mental illness experienced increased marginality in penitentiaries that were already ill-equipped to handle non-working prisoners. The second factor was the geographic isolation and rudimentary nature of newly built penitentiaries in western Canada.

The first penitentiary facilities in Manitoba were housed at Lower Fort Garry, a former Hudson's Bay Company trading post. Although the site was designated a federal penitentiary in 1874, it also served as the first asylum in Manitoba. Unlike Kingston Penitentiary, the mental patients at Manitoba were not criminal convicts but individuals who were committed by family or friends for "safekeeping" under warrant of the lieutenant governor of Manitoba and the North-West Territories, since the institution served both jurisdictions. The conditions at the early penitentiary did not begin to approximate asylum care or moral treatment. Patients were kept in the centre of the fort in a basic log structure designed only to segregate them from the other prisoners.[85] There was no doctor with psychological expertise on staff, and penitentiary officials exhibited little concern with the possibility of curing anyone. Manitoba Penitentiary was truly the last resort for those patients who could no longer be cared for in the home or the community in this period.

When the mentally ill could not be integrated with the regular workforce, some penitentiaries found unique assignments for such patients. In 1879 Warden Bedson at Manitoba Penitentiary ordered the guard in charge of the mental patients to employ their labour in preparing the prison garden. That same year at Manitoba, two other patients were tasked with supplying the ice house with snow throughout the month of January.[86] Since some of these patients were not criminal convicts, they could be trusted with outdoor labour without the threat of escape. Angus Smith was one such inmate committed to Manitoba Penitentiary as a lunatic in 1878. The warden took advantage of his physical abilities, assigning him a variety of unusual tasks throughout the penitentiary. One job reserved for Smith was attending the fire at the penitentiary lime kiln through the night. The night guards were instructed to visit him at midnight and again at 4:00 a.m. to ensure that he was not asleep and neglecting his "duties." Guards and keepers also sought out Smith to perform extra chores around their domestic quarters. When the warden learned about this, he forbade the staff to employ Smith in this way since it disrupted "the work set out for him."[87] These examples demonstrate the unusual circumstances under which the mentally ill were incarcerated and accommodated to prison life, sometimes in ways that exploited their ability to work. The willingness of penitentiary administrators to press the mentally ill into marginal forms of labour reveals not only the role that work played in medical treatment but the degree to which this ideology contributed to the construction of all penitentiary inmates as workers. The mentally ill were regarded not only through specific pathologies that defined their afflictions but often by categories linked to the foundations of penitentiary labour.

When patients in penitentiaries were too sick for any type of labour, they often experienced remarkable neglect and marginality. Such neglect was experienced more by female mental patients than by any other group. Gender played a key role in the determination of who was committed to penitentiaries as mental patients, particularly in western Canada. That nearly all of the early asylum patients at Manitoba Penitentiary were female makes this plain. Between 1871 and 1885, Manitoba Penitentiary admitted a total of eighteen women as mental patients, five of whom died.[88] Wendy Mitchinson notes that in the nineteenth century, symptoms of mental illness were heavily gender based, which probably accounted for higher committals of women. For example, excitability or overly verbal displays by women could speed the diagnosis of mental illness since such behaviour did not conform to acceptable female behaviour.[89] The gendered division of labour in isolated prairie homes probably caused families to resort to the penitentiary for the care of women who could no longer contribute to the domestic economy. Class also played a role because wealthier families could afford to send mentally ill members to private asylums in Ontario, Québec, or the United States. Thus, in some cases, the penitentiary was largely an institution providing mental health relief to poor and working-class families when formal asylums were not an option. T.J.W. Burgess's turn-of-the-century presidential address to the Royal Society of Canada noted the solution employed by family and friends of the mentally ill: "The Toronto asylum being full, friends in their anxiety to have insane relatives placed in safe-keeping, perhaps also with the object of saving themselves the cost of transport to that institution, soon found a means to evade the law, which but inadequately safeguarded the real purpose of the establishment. The process of evasion was simply to have the poor lunatic committed to jail as dangerous, whether really so or not."[90] When the new penitentiary in Manitoba opened at Stony Mountain in 1877, five female mental patients were transferred from the old prison at Lower Fort Garry. At the new penitentiary, the material conditions of the patients' incarceration deteriorated rapidly. Whereas able-bodied prisoners like Angus Smith were integrated into some form of daily labour, the female patients at Manitoba performed no work. The women's deteriorated condition was the likely reason since female mental patients in other penitentiaries regularly performed basic domestic labour for the institution.[91]

Because male and female prisoners required segregation, the warden and doctor decided that the women should be housed in basement cells next to the penitentiary dungeons. The wretchedness of the basement was remarkable. By 1880 faulty drainage around the penitentiary had caused several inches of waste and fecal matter to accumulate under the flooring, resulting in a wave of typhoid fever that killed three members of the penitentiary staff (but, surprisingly, no prisoners).[92] The unsanitary conditions in the basement were matched by the absolute neglect of the women incarcerated there. One guard reported in 1881 that the women and their bedding had not been washed the entire winter and that the patients received only five minutes of attention each day at meal times. The guard noted that Ellen McLean, who was hired to attend to the women, had been co-opted by the warden's wife to work in her house as a cook and domestic servant; nobody had bothered to hire a replacement.[93]

Eliza Templeton was one Manitoba asylum patient who endured this neglect until the end of her life. She was a forty-six-year-old married mother received at the penitentiary for "safekeeping" in August 1877. Five months after her arrival, she was granted a brief reprieve from the basement cells and released into the custody of friends. (Records are unclear on any further involvement of her family.) A short time later, Templeton was returned to the penitentiary, where her condition deteriorated. Throughout March 1881 she tore at her clothing and blankets, and then began to throw the contents of her night bucket around the cell and corridors.[94] The medical officers could offer no solution to her deterioration. Templeton died in her cell in the basement of Manitoba Penitentiary in July 1882.[95] Although penitentiary officials were not absolutely blind to the neglected state of the female patient, the deputy warden at Manitoba blamed the state of affairs on Ellen McLean rather than the prison administration. He reported, "If the same time was spent on the lunatic women that was spent in looking after the other rooms, the women would be taken care of."[96]

Clearly, gender played a key role in how the mentally ill were cared for in the penitentiary. Basic medical care for women depended upon the labour of poorly paid female matrons. Ellen McLean worked a gruelling schedule as the matron at Manitoba Penitentiary: Bedson noted that she was on duty from 6:00 a.m. until 10:00 p.m. daily, Sunday included, and was charged with cooking, cleaning, and washing for the four female mental patients in the basement.[97] She was paid a salary of $15.00 per month, or $180.00 for the year—$5.00 less per month than the penitentiary messenger, who worked part time, and less than half of the lowest-paid guard, who earned an annual salary of $480.00.[98] McLean was well aware of how inequitable her situation was. In 1880 she personally petitioned the lieutenant governor of Keewatin for compensation for the extra labour she performed at the penitentiary:

> Dear Sir, for the past two years I have had to take charge of the 2 female lunatics from the district of Kee-wa-tin and as you are aware of their very troublesome nature they have much increased my labours, as I am only paid for looking after the insane for Manitoba. I beg to request that you will use your influence in my behalf to get some compensation for my past services and make some arrangements for the future.[99]

Even more important in the care of the mentally ill than the cheap labour provided by women staff members was the free labour gained from inmates. In 1905 the Department of Justice ordered that patients could only be attended to by paid staff. The warden at Manitoba wrote to defend the use of inmate orderlies in the care of the mentally ill. "No guard is fitted for the job and none of them would undertake it," he reported. The warden detailed the extensive duties of the convict nurse to impress upon the penitentiary inspector the importance of this labour:

> In the very case which necessitated the services of convict nurse mentioned in the evidence from which you made the discovery, the bed-pan had to be used as often as 18 times in a single night. And the patient was helpless and delirious. And the bed was soiled from involuntary passages. Such a patient (in all civilized countries) must have constant attention—not by a police officer, but by a nurse; and the time honored custom has been to assign such duties to a fellow convict who may be allowed access to the sick man's cell, but who is supposed to be under the eye of an officer in charge of the ward. Theoretically, such practice is not up to the mark, but practically, it is as near as we can get without extra expense.[100]

At Manitoba Penitentiary in 1905, convict Adelaide Elgin fulfilled the role of nurse during a two-year sentence for larceny. Prior to her conviction, Elgin had been a fixture in the Winnipeg community, providing medical service to the wives of NWMP officers. In the penitentiary, the staff made extensive use of her medical experience. She was entrusted with the full-time care of two mental patients, Josephine Astzman and Maggie Two Flags, for the duration of her sentence. The warden noted that the unpaid services Elgin provided to the penitentiary would have cost the institution hundreds of dollars.[101] Thus, the care of the mentally ill in western Canadian penitentiaries was often improvised and irregular. The inconsistencies highlighted by different responses to gendered mental illness illustrate one more element in the problematic role of the penitentiary as surrogate asylum. They also demonstrate the importance of region in shaping responses to prisoners and patients in the far-flung Canadian system. Geographically isolated prisons simply could not offer specialized care for the mentally ill even if medical experts at the time would have seen this care as preferable.

While particular groups were subject to increased marginalization, the mentally ill were also sometimes the target of overbearing control by penitentiary authorities. In this respect, they were similar to incorrigible offenders whom wardens were often reluctant to release without establishing some form of surveillance in coordination with local police forces. An example is George Dunsterville, who was sentenced to five years at Manitoba Penitentiary for larceny in November 1892.[102] Soon after he arrived, the penitentiary surgeon reported to the warden that Dunsterville was suffering from sub-acute mania. Although he continued to work with the regular convicts, the surgeon strongly recommended his removal to the provincial asylum.[103] Sometime during 1896, Warden William Irvine received communication from a member of Dunsterville's family in Britain informing him that there was money waiting for Dunsterville in England to support him after his release from the penitentiary. Although he was due to be released from the penitentiary the following year, Irvine decided not to inform Dunsterville of the money waiting on his release due to his deteriorated mental condition. "It would be better that nothing be said to Dunsterville about the money," Irvine replied to the family, "until it be definitely decided what is to be done with him. With no resources as he now stands, that fact alone will reconcile him to confinement in an asylum for a time, but once I let him know there is money at his command . . . it [could] do him a great deal of harm."[104] In a subsequent letter, Irvine restated his desire to keep the money for Dunsterville a secret: "I did not tell him of the money lying for him in England as I believe it will be good for him, for a time, to have to rely entirely on himself for support."[105] Irvine's stated concern for Dunsterville's mental condition was thus recast as insistence that the former convict should prove his worth and mental improvement through the fruits of labour in the institution.

The moral imperative functioned even when a convict moved beyond the grasp of institutional confines. Dunsterville was released from the provincial asylum shortly after his committal, and it can be surmised that he subsequently learned of the warden's interference. Perhaps expressing his frustration at the machinations set against him, Dunsterville wrote threatening letters to officials at Manitoba Penitentiary. These letters only confirmed to Irvine that his prognosis on Dunsterville's mental condition was correct. Writing to the inspector of penitentiaries, Irvine included the letters "as a proof that the man is not fit to be at large and that as far as myself and the Surgeon are concerned, we did our duty in having him handed over to the Provincial Authorities as insane."[106] Dunsterville's sentence should have expired sometime in 1896, but the diagnosis of his mental condition made him subject to additional incarceration and control beyond the confines of a traditional penitentiary sentence. When he was finally released from Manitoba Penitentiary, he relocated to Ontario, where he met with more misfortune. In October 1899 he was convicted of arson and sentenced to three years at Kingston Penitentiary.[107] Three weeks after his arrival at Kingston, he was transferred to the insane ward and diagnosed by the surgeon there as "incurable."[108]

SEXUALITY

Among the more unique manifestations of medical power in the penitentiary were doctors' efforts to control and pathologize male sexual activity. The threat of criminal prosecution and disciplinary activity regulated sex between prisoners. Penitentiary surgeons played an important role through the surveillance and restriction of masturbation. In the mid-nineteenth century, masturbation was both pathologized by doctors and condemned in moral terms. Medically, it was believed to contribute to mental and physiological disorders. Robert Darby notes that "a significant stream of medical opinion went further to conclude that almost any seminal emission was damaging, or indeed that sexual excitement could be a symptom of disorder. This amounted to pathologizing of male sexuality itself."[109] In multiple cases, penitentiary surgeons noted that masturbation caused or contributed to mental illness. This medical proscription of male sexuality was heightened by the moral condemnation associated with masturbation. In 1852 penitentiary inspector Wolfred Nelson, who was also a medical doctor, wrote this directive to prison doctors:

> When consulted he should not fail to point out all the circumstances that might militate against the health of his patient, and he should in a most especial manner warn him of the dreadful effects that follow, sooner or later, the baneful and revolting habit of self pollution; a degrading vice that prevails to a frightful extent in all such places of seclusion, a habit that irrecoverably injures the body and stultifies the mind, when persisted in, and is withal the source of the great majority of cases of insanity which are far more frequent in these places than elsewhere.[110]

Given the debilitating effects that surgeons attributed to masturbation, it is unsurprising that they regarded its prevalence as an inherent danger to the health of prisoners. Thus, uncontrolled sexuality was perceived as a real threat to the productivity of the penitentiary labour force. In *The History of Sexuality, Volume 1*, Foucault made this link between the moral imperative of labour and Victorian sexuality: "If sex is so rigorously repressed, this is because it is incompatible with a general and intensive work imperative. . . . At a time when labor capacity was being systematically exploited, how could this capacity be allowed to dissipate itself in pleasurable pursuits, except those— reduced to a minimum—that enabled it to reproduce itself?"[111] The regulation of sexuality by penitentiary medical officials illustrates what Foucault calls scientia sexualis—the power relation created by scientific discourses that determined sexual deviance.[112] In the mid-nineteenth century, this was manifested through the construction of a specific pathology connected to masturbation that doctors called spermatorrhea.

French physician Claude Francois Lallemand wrote an influential treatise on spermatorrhea in the 1840s as part of his three-volume work, *Des pertes séminales involontaires*. He defined spermatorrhea as the excessive discharge of semen resulting from illicit or excessive sexual activity. Much like nineteenth-century understandings of masturbation, the disease was thought to cause male sufferers anxiety, nervousness, lassitude, impotence, and finally death. In his work on Victorian sexuality, Michael Mason describes understandings of spermatorrhea as distressingly contradictory due to its Catch-22 symptomology and solutions. Symptoms included nocturnal emission, premature ejaculation, or impotence.[113] Lallemand argued that masturbation caused the seminal tract to become irritated, causing additional unwanted seminal emission and excitement, leading to even more masturbation. Yet when doctors advised patients to avoid all sexual activity, emissions and unwanted excitement increased, which merely proved evidence of the disease. While Lallemand's ideas were widely accepted in the early Victorian era, by the mid-1870s, many doctors were questioning the logic of classifying both impotence and excessive sexuality under the same pathology. Doctors who continued to subscribe to Lallemand's theory merely argued that spermatorrhea developed in two stages: the first involved overproduction of semen, which caused the acceleration of the disease and led to the second stage, impotence.[114]

All of this ambiguity and contradiction, combined with the social anxiety surrounding male sexuality, fuelled a booming trade in medical quackery. Spermatorrhea commanded the fears and anxieties of middle-class men who sought to shape their sexuality according to strict Victorian moral codes. Some doctors established a swift trade in treating spermatorrhea, targeting bourgeois men who could afford to seek medical advice for their anxieties. Doctors emphasized the consequences of the disease that Victorian men found especially troubling, including not only the physiological outcomes listed above but also threats to normative masculinity: loss of confidence, lack of control over emotion, nervousness, poor concentration, and an inability to work productively.[115] Playing on these anxieties, doctors encouraged their patients to confess their sexual anxieties and sexual habits so that spermatorrhea could be properly diagnosed. The seedier practitioners promoting "cures" for the disease could usually be assured that their patients' shame would prevent them from questioning the diagnosis or the sale of expensive remedies.

The medical treatment for spermatorrhea was first developed by Lallemand in the 1850s. It involved cauterization of the urethra by depositing nitrate of silver at the prostatic portion of the canal. Doctors used an instrument called a bougie: a long thin metal rod with a ball on its end. Coated in the caustic substance, the instrument was passed down through the urethra.[116] The treatment was designed to deaden nerve endings so the patient would become less susceptible to sexual arousal. While most practitioners claimed the procedure was painless, some admitted that the treatment caused violent spasms or that their patients were in visible agony during the application of the bougie. Worse, painful side effects of exposure to the nitrate persisted well after the procedure.[117] By the md-1880s, spermatorrhea was being attacked by more reputable surgeons as a scam perpetuated for profit by quacks and pseudo-doctors. For example, in 1882 the *Canadian Medical and Surgical Journal* reviewed a popular manual on the disease and suggested that true instances of spermatorrhea (defined as the involuntary discharge of seminal fluid) were extraordinarily rare. The review concluded that readers suffering from sexual anxieties would be better served reviewing Sir James Paget's classical essay on sexual hypochondriasis.[118] Respectable surgeons warned that true instances of spermatorrhea had nothing to do with masturbation and that there was no specific pathology associated with an excess of sexual energy.[119]

In spite of the waning medical belief that spermatorrhea was a legitimate affliction, it continued to be treated in Canadian penitentiaries until the turn of the century. The first appearance of spermatorrhea on a penitentiary medical register was in 1853, but it is difficult to know the exact nature of what penitentiary surgeons were observing when they recorded its appearance. It is possible that spermatorrhea was used as a medical euphemism for masturbation, but this seems unlikely given that doctors also listed instances of masturbation on medical registers as an indicator of declining mental health. For example, in five cases of mental illness at Kingston in 1859, the cause was attributed to masturbation.[120] This approach to masturbation persisted throughout the 1860s and 1870s, but during this period, patients were also treated specifically for spermatorrhea. At Manitoba Penitentiary, prisoner Alexander Munro was treated for spermatorrhea in January 1878. The remedy listed in the medical records is strikingly similar to the cure offered by quack doctors: he was cauterized with a silver solution. Two weeks after his first treatment, he was treated again. Subsequent to these treatments, Munro was admitted to the penitentiary hospital to address the side effects of his original treatment, including irritable bladder and a painful rash on his penis.[121]

Treatment for spermatorrhea was relatively isolated in the years after Confederation, but some prisons treated it with increasing frequency in the last decades of the century. Thirty cases were treated at St. Vincent de Paul in 1894, and twenty-five cases the following year.[122] Spermatorrhea was treated twenty-three times at Kingston in 1898, and Dorchester surgeon Robert Mitchell noted thirty cases in 1900.[123] After the turn of the century, incidences of the disease disappeared from medical registers altogether. The strange surge in cases in the last decade of the century raises several questions to which there are no clear answers. Did doctors seek out sufferers of spermatorrhea, or was the condition raised by the prisoners themselves? Given what we know about how penitentiary medicine worked in this era, patients were usually required to make their complaints directly to penitentiary surgeons if they wanted medical assistance. Yet spermatorrhea was also directly associated with masturbation, which was the subject of ongoing surveillance and regulation by penitentiary staff. One explanation for the surge in cases may have been renewed investment in detecting masturbation by either surgeons or keepers during these years. But none of this answers the question of whether each of these cases was treated with a method similar to that used on Alex Munro at Manitoba Penitentiary. The great irony of such a possibility is that in an effort to forestall lost production on the basis of a moral panic, the treatment for spermatorrhea was likely more debilitating than the effects of unregulated prisoner sexuality.

INTELLECTUAL DISABILITY

Although some penitentiary doctors and wardens found workable solutions to employing the mentally ill, often a greater struggle was to respond to cases of intellectual disability. In 1882 Inspector Moylan alerted the minister of Justice to the increasing presence of "imbecilic and idiotic" prisoners in the federal system. As Jessa Chupik and David Wright argue, during this era, there was only a vague notion of the difference between mental illness and intellectual disability.[124] These prisoners were difficult to discipline, and Moylan noted that "they are in constant violation of the rules for which it were a cruelty to punish them."[125] Five years later, after a visit to Kingston, Moylan identified the same problem, reporting that a "certain class of imbeciles" were misfits at the penitentiary, "not crazy enough to confine them in a criminal lunatic asylum; but . . . sufficiently gone to render their treatment in a penal establishment extremely difficult and embarrassing."[126] Moylan referred to a group that included those labelled by doctors as "idiotic," "feebleminded," or "weak-minded." While "feebleminded" and "weak-minded" individuals were difficult to identify, "idiotic" was a more specific designation. David Wright describes the concept of idiocy in the nineteenth century:

> The nineteenth-century term of "idiot" referred to persons who were considered as suffering from mental disability from birth or an early age, or what is now commonly referred to in Britain (though not in North America) as learning disability. It was packed with social, medical, and legal meanings. Commonly the term "idiot" did not stand alone, and was associated with childhood hence "idiotic and imbecile children", reflecting, in part, the life-expectancy at the time for those born with severe mental disabilities.[127]

Comments of penitentiary administrators such as those of Inspector Moylan above illustrate the difficulty of properly classifying the intellectually disabled in this era. Anne Digby argues that penitentiary surgeons contributed to assumptions regarding the criminality of "weak-minded" individuals who faced incarceration. She notes that prisons were the focus of the worst kinds of stereotyping of imbecility due to the perceived social threat in the condition. Thus, the driving force for segregation of these individuals often originated with penitentiary surgeons.[128]

Although the medical classification of intellectual disability in this era was not exact, penitentiary officials seemed to have a clear idea that individuals who fell into these categories did not belong in penitentiaries. Their status was informally determined by whether such intellectual disability prevented participation in the routines of daily labour. Penitentiary labour—which could be heavy, demanding, and often unrelenting—probably taxed the abilities of individuals who, prior to institutionalization, may not have been diagnosed in less structured environments in the home or community. Indeed, Angus McLaren suggests that the spread of compulsory education in the twentieth century precipitated the widespread "discovery" of "feeblemindedness" in modern society.[129] Once these individuals were incarcerated, however, the demands and rigours of penitentiary labour may have helped prison doctors identify and define the characteristics of intellectual disability.

Much like his arguments about the mentally ill, Moylan complained that penitentiaries were becoming convenient repositories for the intellectually disabled. Penitentiary officials blamed magistrates, prosecutors, and municipal and provincial prison authorities for "passing along" these individuals to federal penitentiaries. Moylan argued that the asylum was the only proper place for "such poor creatures" and that an interest in saving money and institutional space caused other medical and legal authorities to allow the intellectually disabled to be sentenced to time in federal penitentiaries.[130] Moylan stressed the problem in his 1882 annual report: "I would most earnestly beg to call your attention to a class of convicts that is becoming more numerous every year, namely the imbecile and idiotic. . . . It is the experience of the Wardens, the Surgeons, and other officers who have to deal with such prisoners that, for the most part, they should have been sent rather to the insane asylum."[131] The continued presence of the intellectually disabled in penitentiaries, like that of the mentally ill, was often premised on class and domestic circumstances that precluded them from finding more appropriate solutions. In the absence of care in the community or the home, these individuals sometimes became pauperized and were often convicted on vagrancy or burglary charges. Even in instances where they had committed no crimes, the intellectually disabled were sometimes criminalized on the authority of local or provincial judges so they could be institutionalized in local gaols or prisons, where they became official wards of the state. When faced with evidence of intellectual disability, some "benevolent" judges even handed out sentences in excess of two years so that such individuals would be sent to federal penitentiaries, which were considered more humane environments than chaotic municipal or provincial prisons.

Penitentiary officials deeply resented this method of handling individuals with intellectual disabilities. In the resulting squabbles among different institutions and legal jurisdictions, disabled individuals were caught in the middle. In one striking example, St. Vincent de Paul Penitentiary received sixteen-year-old Oscar Gagné in 1899, committed by the district magistrate of Trois-Rivières on a four-year sentence for burglary. In his report, under the subtitle "Idiot," Fortier, the penitentiary surgeon, stated, "His arrival was illustrated by the hilarity of the convicts, the surprise of all the officers and the indignity of the Warden. The unhappy sentenced boy is a poor likeness of a human being, unfavoured by nature, delayed in his mental and physical unfolding, and bearing strong marks of cretinism. His sole appearance provokes a feeling of repulsion engaged with compassion."[132] Clearly, doctors understood that individuals like Gagné deserved better than to become the objects of derision and humour. Fortier appealed directly to the federal minister of Justice to intervene in the case. It seemed that no medical or legal authority wanted to assume responsibility for the boy, and the minister replied that he could not secure a pardon from St. Vincent de Paul until an asylum space was found. The situation deteriorated into a bitter squabble among the penitentiary, the district magistrate at Trois-Rivières, and the minister. The warden fumed in his annual report, "His arrival provoked my indignation, because I saw in this event the municipal egotism repulsing in the name of the law, an irresponsible unfortunate."[133] Finally, Gagné was sent back to prison at Trois-Rivières, after which his family secured a spot for him at the Beauport Asylum in Québec.[134] By condemning local authorities who "passed along" intellectually disabled people to federal penitentiaries, wardens were offering a critique of a larger problem in the legal system that paid scant attention to disability among convicted criminals. Pressing cases such as that of Gagné received attention, but the majority of such prisoners were simply lumped among increasing numbers of the "weak-minded" and "feebleminded."

As with other medical diagnoses, the classification of intellectual disability in the penitentiary was linked to the imperative of labour. Digby notes that British workhouses favoured the imbecilic and idiotic because they were usually sufficiently able-bodied to participate in daily labour.[135] This eagerness for able-bodied workers in institutions contrasted with a growing pessimism about the "curative potential" of such inmates. In asylums and prisons, authorities fretted over the inability of medical treatment to effect any change or improvement for years on end. These "incurables" consumed considerable time, manpower, and expense in the institutions charged with their care. Gradually, the idiotic and lunatic patients came to be represented by the "incurable" label, and authorities abandoned the pretense that confinement in the penitentiary could effect improvement or cures. Within Kingston's insane ward, surgeon O. S. Strange noted in 1897 that "most of those here are incurable."[136]

The status of intellectually disabled people in penitentiaries was ambiguous because they could not be adapted to either medical models or the prevailing division of labour. In contrast, the status of the mentally ill was clearer. Some individuals could be cured, and thus returned to productive roles. In cases of intellectual disability, doctors and administrators struggled because these were prisoners who existed outside of this division, both within and outside the penitentiary: they would never be regarded as either productive or curable. Disability historians have noted that classical political economy often constructed the disabled in ways that were inaccurate. For example, Marx wrote about those individuals who succumbed to "their incapacity for adaptation, an incapacity which results from a division of labour."[137] As Paul Abberly argues, viewing disabled people through the lens of political economy in this way is inadequate because it positions them as only the inversion of able-bodied workers. This reproduces the suggestion that in a utopian economic society, the disabled could be "cured." Abberly writes, "Marx's and Engels' description of capitalism captures the way in which capitalism creates both disabled people and a concept of disability as the negative of the normal worker. It is labour power which workers sell to capitalists for a money-wage, and impaired labour-power that characterises and accounts for the specific character of disablement under capitalism."[138] Peter Linebaugh addresses the same issue, emphasizing the ideological fetters of political economy that "chain the understanding of living labour to the wall of capitalist development."[139] The great difficulty faced by disabled people in the nineteenth-century penitentiary illustrates how inadequate prison medicine was at the task of understanding and responding to difference. It also makes clear the purchase of ideas about industrial production over the lives of these individuals, who often had no choice over their internment in these institutions.

One conclusion that can be drawn from the history of medicine in Canadian penitentiaries is that evidence about the material condition of incarceration must be weighed carefully against the influence of penitentiary and asylum reform ideologies in the nineteenth century. In the late nineteenth century, Canadian penitentiaries exhibited deep connections to transnational ideologies about labour, punishment, and medicine. However, several factors also undercut these influences. First, the Canadian penitentiary system was indeed far-flung, with each institution operating in an isolated and autonomous fashion throughout the nineteenth century. Inspection was difficult and intermittent because of the vast distances between each penitentiary in the dominion. Second, the penitentiaries themselves were ill-equipped to carry out the ideological projects promoted by reformers. The ad hoc administration of each institution undercut the cohesion of a federal system and disrupted attempts at standardization or regulation of how medical services were delivered across the country.

It was clear to penitentiary officials and administrators that not everyone in the institution could serve as a worker; some prisoners would never fill this role. Not only did this limitation disrupt the practical demands of labour in the penal system, but it called into question the moral imperatives of the penitentiary project itself. These questions were seldom explicitly stated but are evidenced by the abandonment of unproductive prisoners to the margins of penitentiary life when they could not play an economic role. Questions about the possibilities of their moral redemption remained unanswered. However, as part of a program of penitentiary reform, Canadian institutions began to recognize and organize social and medical responses to prisoners who could not meet the demands of the labour regime. Thus, prison medicine greatly expanded between 1867 and 1900, particularly in the medical response to mental illness. Its function evolved from merely policing and maintaining the penitentiary workforce to creating acceptable care for non-labouring prisoners. But in this response, medicine also continued to play a distinct role in the moral regulation of the penitentiary workforce. This history reveals the enduring effect of moral ideas about work and idleness in penitentiary medical practice. A prisoner's relationship to the labour regime sometimes strongly determined his or her experience of confinement. For the sick, mentally ill, and intellectually disabled, this experience could be one of remarkable neglect. The spectre of these prisoners' incurability, together with their inability to be productive, subjected them to both moral condemnation and marginalization.

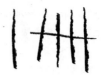

Punishment

In 1870 John Flanigan, the warden at Kingston Penitentiary, addressed changing attitudes about corporal punishment in the penitentiary system.[1] He suggested that the long-standing tradition of whipping as a form of punishment be phased out "in favor of a system of discriminative kindness as opposed to one of indiscriminative repression."[2] Flanigan's view reflected ideas about corporal punishment that dominated reform thinking in the mid-nineteenth century. Sir Walter Crofton distilled these ideas when he argued that the lash must be retained "in order that the necessity might never arise for its exercise."[3] These reform views raise several questions. Given that corporal punishment was never entirely eliminated in the nineteenth century, what sustained it? What were officials responding to when they resorted to violence? Finally, in the transition to "discriminative kindness," how did old attitudes about the necessity for violence affect new practices that were intended to be more humane?

This chapter explores reform ideas about punishment and the practices that penitentiaries deployed in efforts to maintain domination over the "worst" elements of the prison population, the incorrigible offenders. I examine primarily the relationship and tensions between two practices. The first comprised violent punishments that persisted from the penitentiary's earliest days. Why did corporal punishment continue in spite of reform discourses that condemned it as barbaric and ineffective? Looking at instances of corporal punishment in the years after the Brown Commission, I argue that corporal punishment was tied to specific discourses and constructions of criminality. Descriptions of depraved, incorrigible, or unmanageable prisoners emphasized the need for violent responses. These discourses and constructions proved remarkably resilient throughout the nineteenth century in justifying a violent and reactionary response to prisoners who would not bend to the dominations of penitentiary life.

The second practice involved the isolation of incorrigible offenders. Isolation was regarded as more humane and as an attractive alternative to corporal punishment. The increasing reliance on isolation in the last decades of the century made penal practice more compatible with how reformers like Crofton and Maconochie viewed the modern prison. First, it allowed prison authorities a more nuanced and individualized method of punishment. Isolation wings allowed for the observation of the most criminal elements of the prison population, which gave rise to practices consistent with the emerging criminology and ideas that would dominate criminal justice in the twentieth century. Isolation was part of a progression toward a more serious attempt at the reformation of each offender, from which arose twentieth-century innovations like indeterminate sentencing and parole. In practice, however, although the isolation wing constructed at Kingston was less violent than corporal punishment, it was not necessarily more precise in meeting the goals of reformation. Isolation practices continued to be prejudiced by the same constructions of criminality that informed corporal punishment. As a result, newer and more humane methods of punishment were often just as oppressive and damaging to the reform project as the violent practices they replaced.

The punishments at Kingston raise questions about how early reformers in both Canada and the United States viewed corporal punishment.
Did they not condemn such practices as a matter of principle and
see them as antithetical to the reform vision? It is clear that early
reformers in fact held conflicted views on violence and the necessity
of corporal punishment. The ambiguity of these views often helped
to perpetuate violent practices in the often uncertain and experimental first years of the penitentiary. What is also clear is that milder
reform voices, such as those of Charles Duncombe in Upper Canada
and Charles Eddy in New York, were drowned out by political calls for
harsher penitentiary regimes, which were implemented in both locations. The 1849 Brown Commission, however, did change the use of
punishment in Canadian penitentiaries: while prisons in other (primarily American) jurisdictions continued to resort to widespread and
brutal corporal punishment, the violence at Kingston was dramatically
curtailed because of the attention generated by the commission.

The second Brown Commission report provided a blueprint for
reforming the disciplinary regime at Kingston. The commissioners
argued, "It is conceded now, as an admitted principle in prison discipline, that there is no occasion to govern solely by terror, and in the
best regulated institutions the lash is seldom, if ever, resorted to."[4] In
fact, prisons that dispensed with corporal punishment entirely were
rare. In the years before 1850, only very experimental regimes such as
Maconochie's on Norfolk Island abolished corporal punishment, and
these experiments were routinely dismissed as failures. Thus, one of
the central contradictions in the reform movement was that while corporal punishment and violence were abhorred, there was no sustained
movement to eliminate such practices.

The reforms that followed the Brown Commission aimed at
making corporal punishment more rational, not to eliminate it. The
statute that followed the commission's reports made punishment
subject to far greater bureaucratic control and medical and inspectorial
oversight. The 1851 *Penitentiary Act* limited the number of lashes any

one prisoner could receive to seventy-five. No punishments could be awarded until the day after a disciplinary report: this was intended to remove the impulses of anger and emotion. Confinement in a punishment "box" was abolished altogether, as was the corporal punishment of women and children. Even on these issues, though, there was no universal agreement, particularly outside of reform circles. The Tories split on the question while debating the new act. John A. Macdonald argued that corporal punishment must be retained for both sexes in the service of "combating insubordination."[5] There was general agreement on the idea that the deterrent value of corporal punishment was too important to abolish it completely. The Brown Commission report stated that with "proper management," the punishments in the penitentiary would be "few and mild." Corporal punishment would be used only rarely and in special circumstances. The commission detailed the circumstances under which this might happen: "There are, however, a few characters in most prisons whom too much lenity only tends to make refractory, and who are only to be ruled by bodily fear. On such persons and for such offences as seriously involve the discipline of the prison, such as assaults on the officers, it will undoubtedly be a matter of necessity, sometimes, to inflict the severe punishment of the dark cell, or failing that, of the cat."[6] Thus, corporal punishment was retained due to the prevailing construction of the incorrigible offender who made "severe punishment" an absolute necessity.

The 1850s and 1860s saw greatly reduced corporal punishment at Kingston Penitentiary. For example, before the meeting of the Brown Commission imposed a moratorium on corporal punishment in 1847, Kingston recorded 2,133 corporal punishments in that year. Ten years later under Warden D. A. Macdonell, there were just fifty-three.[7] In the post-Confederation era, incidents of corporal punishment continued to fall. The yearly punishment returns demonstrate that the frequency of corporal punishment fell steadily between 1870 and 1900. Prisoners were also whipped less brutally than in the previous era. For example, at Kingston in 1875, eight inmates were punished with the cat-o'-nine-tails, with each one receiving between twenty-four and thirty-six lashes. By the late 1870s, it was more common to inflict punishments of only eight to twelve lashes. At the new penitentiaries in British Columbia and Manitoba, the wardens used corporal punishment even more sparingly. Manitoba adopted the practice of "awarding lashes" but inflicted far fewer when the actual punishment occurred. For example, in 1882 a total of 104 lashes were "awarded" to six different prisoners but only thirty-one were inflicted.

Flogging was used sparingly in the last decades of the nineteenth century. At British Columbia, no prisoners were flogged in 1882 or 1883. When three men were whipped the following year, it was after a daring escape attempt. Kingston flogged no prisoners in 1885 and 1886. St. Vincent de Paul broke the trend in this decade, being the site of the heaviest punishments under the disciplinary regime of the corrupt deputy warden Télesphore Ouimet. For example, in 1884 seven men were flogged at St. Vincent de Paul with a total of 230 lashes, more than five times the combined total of the other institutions. Apart from Ouimet's punitive approach, corporal punishment was becoming an increasingly rare event in Canadian penitentiaries.[8] But the fact that corporal punishment was not eliminated also hints at how entrenched it had become in penitentiary practice.

RATIONALIZING VIOLENCE

In *Men of Blood*, Martin Weiner argues that the nineteenth century exhibited a "civilizing offensive" in which the infliction of physical suffering was increasingly stigmatized throughout the Western world.[9] By the 1860s, a cultural shift had brought about a legal curtailing of the rights of chastisement previously extended to masters, teachers, and even parents. Two areas of European society were most influenced by this shift. First, by the 1860s, corporal punishment in the British Navy had become subject to increased legal regulation. This was supported by a growing public sentiment against the most brutal aspects of military discipline.[10] From military settings, the movement extended to factories, workhouses, and, finally, the domestic realm. The debate also raged within the world of primary education after several high-profile cases where the "correction" of pupils by their schoolmasters resulted in the deaths of punished children. Weiner cites the significance of a manslaughter charge brought against schoolmaster Thomas Hopley in England after beating a pupil to death in 1860. Hopley was not absolved by the fact that he had obtained written permission from the boy's father to administer a "severe beating."[11] Thus, while cultural attitudes about violence were changing in multiple realms, penitentiary reformers argued for the abolition of similar violence in penal institutions. Beginning with the Brown Commission, the cultural shift is evident in Canadian penal administration, but corporal punishment and the infliction of pain also proved curiously resilient to the growing chorus of calls for its abolition.

It was not that penitentiary administrators resisted the calls to end the use of violence. Not infrequently, wardens and keepers spoke in the same voice as reformers in condemning the use of violence in their institutions. However, in many settings, reform discourses simply had the effect of prompting prison authorities to develop new explanations of disciplinary practices that were more sensitive to the growing abhorrence of violence. As penitentiary reformers succeeded in positioning prisons as institutions with a moral mission, prison administrators adjusted their arguments regarding corporal punishment to accord with this shift in cultural attitudes. Whereas early penitentiary administrators presumed the administration of corporal punishment to be their right in the service of order and discipline, by the late 1860s such punishments were rationalized as painful necessities that keepers inflicted with regret. In an 1872 annual report, Kingston Warden John Creighton put forward his views on punishment:

> When men are to be corrected or rebuked, and the proper effect is desired, they must be made to feel that they deserve the punishment, and that it is inflicted more in pity than in anger. Few even of the worst criminals have lost all faith, and hope, and aspiration, and a yearning at times for things more pure and true; and these attributes can be stimulated to increased action. . . . To stir up men's evil feelings, and to excite the lower part of their nature, only makes

them reckless, hardened demons; whilst these same men under different treatment may at least be human.[12]

Reference to the "low nature" of penitentiary inmates hints at the older and pessimistic constructions of criminality built on the savagery of the criminal type. Progressives recoiled from these constructions, arguing that the moral institution must not resort to inciting such passions through violence. In 1880 reformer E. C. Wines argued, "It is possible to subdue a man, to break his spirit, by flogging; it is not possible to improve him morally by such a punishment. In many convicts, punishment by scourging excites undying hate. An indignity has been offered to their manhood, which they can never overlook nor forget."[13] Both arguments suggested that if keepers treated their prisoners like savages, only savagery would result.

As argued earlier, popular constructions of criminality routinely suggested that incorrigibility could not be addressed by moral means. Although the warden warned against the "hardened demons" that violence created, other administrators paradoxically suggested that these individuals already existed and could only be controlled by the use of violence. Thus, many Canadian officials emphasized that corporal punishment must be retained for its deterrent value. A long-standing advocate of corporal punishment, Prime Minister John A. Macdonald argued in the House of Commons in 1869 that only corporal punishment struck fear in the hearts of the criminal class: "Mere imprisonment has little or no terror for a very large body of criminals. They viewed imprisonment as a matter of course as a place of retreat to rest and recruit themselves when weary and worn down with ranging to and fro in search of wicked-ness."[14] In 1875 Warden Creighton wrote, "I only resort to [flogging] in extreme cases, where the convict is violently insubordinate. . . . This punishment cannot safely, be wholly dispensed with. I have found it most efficacious in checking assaults where solitary confinement and low diet had failed."[15] The same year, the penitentiary directors characterized prisoners deserving of corporal punishment as only the "exceptionally evil disposed men" who necessitated "the severe mode of treatment."[16]

The construction of criminality played a role in these justifications. In 1888 Moylan argued that "the deterrent factor should not be overlooked. Its infliction, however, should be restricted to cases where convicts are so degraded and brutalized that the lash alone would compel them to good behaviour. There is a class of men who thought nothing of disgrace, but cared only for the stripes they received."[17] By resorting to the worst constructions of criminality, penitentiary officials absolved themselves of the inhumanity of violent punishments. These rationalizations were common and ranged from alarmist to absurd. For example, in 1877 Moylan wrote, "It can be stated as a fact, that flogging is never inflicted until a verdict of the convicts, generally, if asked, would pronounce the penalty well-merited."[18] Such statements merely emphasize that the debate within the penitentiary system was largely one-sided, carried out between officials who had already achieved consensus on the meaning and importance of corporal punishment to the larger penitentiary project.

The discourse surrounding corporal punishment was characterized by a dichotomy that contrasted penitentiary officials with the brutality of the punished. This humanity/brutality discourse said as much about how officials viewed their role as their understandings of criminality that necessitated violence. It was paramount to the reform view of the penitentiary that responses to brutality and savagery not be perceived as being equally brutal. Because penitentiary officials succeeded in casting corporal punishment as a response to particular criminality, it followed that they needed to portray themselves as paragons of detached rationalism and civility. These were the qualities prized in notions of an idealized Victorian masculinity. The privileging of masculine civility, at least in theory, was advanced repeatedly as one method of justifying the more brutal elements of penitentiary administration. In 1877 Moylan paid tribute to these qualities in his penitentiary wardens. Describing each one as a gentleman, he wrote, "One and all, are guided by the strictest regard to the dictates of justice and humanity, in awarding penalties, especially those of a severe character."[19] Moylan referred to masculinity again in 1882:

If the officers treat the convicts like men, with humanity, kindness and forbearance, thus seeking to give them back their manhood, they will do more towards their reformation, than could be wrought by all the tortures and terrors in vogue a century ago. Brute force alone will not answer, and muscular power is only one of the essentials in a guard or keeper. A good officer must have a clear intellect and a sound judgement to enable him to act quickly, firmly and justly. It is rare such men offer for the Penitentiary service. They usually command more pay at other pursuits.[20]

The qualities that Moylan prized in prison officers, even if highly idealized, hinted at one important dimension that rationalized corporal punishment. It was a duty performed by dispassionate practitioners, void of emotion and informed by the soundest judgement. This was a particular construction of masculinity that created impossibly high standards for the penitentiary staff. Officials within the service subscribed to such notions but often found the men in their employ to be wanting. Warden Bedson at Manitoba Penitentiary made connections between "manliness" and qualities of honour when addressing his staff in 1881. He was disgusted to report that his staff was known to act dishonourably toward each other, informing on the transgressions of other staff members in a "cowardly" manner. He wrote in his order book, "The warden very much fears that some officers of this prison are not as manly and straight forward to each other as he would like."[21] Still, such rationalization provided an answer to the demands of the reform sentiments of the Victorian era. It absolved officials of the uncomfortable realities inherent to corporal punishment and suggested that emotion, anger, and passion played no role.

EMOTION

In spite of reform discourse that suggested otherwise, corporal punishment was an inherently emotional practice that was tied to the power relations at the heart of the penitentiary. It cannot be understood without some consideration of how historical actors responded to its emotional elements. David Garland defines the very essence of punishment as "irrational, unthinking emotion."[22] Friedrich Nietzsche rejected the idea that violence could ever be dispassionate, arguing that punishing another "gratifies the impulse of sadism and cruelty which a will to power over others produces in the human psyche."[23] Nineteenth-century reform discourses and the importance of order and discipline obscured these elements. David Rothman claims, "In the name of authority, wardens had an excuse to mete out the most severe punishments, while still believing that they were doing more than satisfying their own instincts."[24] Was this in fact the case?

Reformers often addressed the emotional nature of corporal punishment, but how can we understand the actual effect of emotion in the practice of punishment? There are hints throughout penitentiary records of the overwhelming emotion attached to the act of whipping a prisoner. For example, a correspondent for *The Globe* witnessed a whipping at a local gaol on Prince Edward Island in 1876. A sheriff and his deputy, described as "kind hearted," were required to deliver a court-sentenced flogging. The deputy was extremely distraught at the duty that lay before him as the prisoner was affixed to the triangle. He made several false starts toward the prisoner with the cats but nearly fainted with each attempt. The reporter decried the sad spectacle of it, remarking with disgust that the prisoner encouraged the deputy to pull himself together and find the nerve to commence with the punishment.[25] Examples like this were cited by reformers as evidence of the generally debasing effect of corporal punishment. As Weiner argues, it was not only the suffering of the prisoner that raised the objection of reformers, but also the "effects on those inflicting and watching the punishment."[26] Z. R. Brockway, superintendent of the Elmira Reformatory in New York, made this point at the Toronto Prison Congress in 1887. On the question of whether the most brutal criminals should be whipped, Brockway responded:

> Not that the man does not deserve to be whipped, but the trouble is
> to get the man to whip him. You brutalize two men, whenever you

inflict that kind of punishment, in prison or out of it. Its tendency is to make a man hard. It takes a pretty hard-hearted man to lay the lash on so as to be worth anything; and if he is a hard-hearted man, the further you remove him from the treatment of the criminal the better. I have seen prison officers who delight in whipping, and I wish the gates could be closed against them.[27]

E. C. Wines made a similar point at the Toronto Congress. He told the delegates about a meeting several years earlier with a penitentiary warden in the United States. After dinner with the penitentiary staff, Wines inquired whether prisoners were ever flogged at the penitentiary, and the warden replied that they were. When pressed, the warden admitted that he relied upon his deputy to inflict the floggings. When Wines asked, "Suppose the deputy should be absent, what would you do in that case?" the warden replied that he would probably wait for the deputy to return before inflicting the punishment. Turning his attention to the deputy, Wines asked, "What do you think is the effect of flogging?" The deputy answered, "I think it is bad on the man that is flogged." Dropping his eyes, he added, "I think it is bad on the man that does the flogging." Then, straightening himself, he looked the warden in the eye and declared, "I think it is bad on the man that stands by and sees it done."[28]

Canadian prison officials often took a harder view of the disciplinary duties of keepers than did reformers like Brockway and Wines. They expressed disgust with any hint of hesitation or uncertainty over corporal punishment. At Manitoba Penitentiary in 1880, Warden Bedson blustered over a flogging that did not meet his standards. He entered in his order book, "The warden was very much displeased with the manner in which the details for inflicting corporal punishment on convict no 48 were carried out today. There being a want of organization and a knowledge of what was expected. A lack of preparation was also very visible. The conduct of guards McDonald and Garden especially the former officer was such as not to deserve credit."[29] Such failings caused disgust because in the eyes of authorities, they hampered the legitimacy of corporal punishment. If the terror of the punishment was diminished, it would also invalidate arguments about its deterrent effect.

Penitentiary reformers were well aware that the volatile elements of corporal punishment could not necessarily be controlled, and this threatened to make the punishment less legitimate. E. C. Wines cited one such example that happened at Kingston Penitentiary in the era when whippings took place in the dining hall before the entire prison population. A "very bad" convict was punished for an offence of unusual gravity with one of the severest flagellations ever given in the prison. Wines described how the event assumed unexpected significance for the prisoners witnessing the punishment:

> As the terrific instrument came down in successive blows, at each stroke tearing and mangling his flesh, he uttered no groan, moved no muscle, gave no token of suffering, but stood calm, erect, and proudly defiant. The prisoners watched the process with breathless interest, and when the last stroke had fallen, an involuntary and audible "bravo!" burst from the vast congregation of felons, in irrepressible admiration of what they looked upon as an instance of heroic fortitude.[30]

Wines relayed the anecdote to warn penitentiary reformers of the potential damage corporal punishment could inflict upon discipline and authority in the penitentiary. Furthermore, it destroyed the work of moral reformation by the bad feelings it created in punished individuals.

The changing attitude toward corporal punishment is what several historians have identified as an evolving "cultural sensibility" about the use of such violence.[31] This sensibility was evident in various public responses to instances of corporal punishment in late nineteenth-century Canada. In 1888 *The Globe* incited a firestorm of criticism and debate after printing this account of a court-ordered whipping inflicted at the Toronto Central Prison on Michael Fenton for an assault on a young girl:

The flogging took place in the corridor in the presence of Warden Massie, prison surgeon Aikins, several pressmen and prison officials. Fenton looked thoroughly vigorous and there was no hesitation in Dr. Aikins' voice when he said, after looking at the semi-nude form strapped firmly to the triangle, that the prisoner was quite able to bear the lashes demanded by law. The Warden read the sentence by virtue of which he acted, and the guard in attendance drew forth from a bag the "cat" with its knotted tails of cordage.

"One," said the Deputy Warden, and with a sharp swish the weapon descended.

"Oh, Lord! Oh Jesus, have mercy!" wailed the prisoner, and some such ejaculation was repeated after each stroke. The effect at the close was very marked, the cat having been laid very largely upon the space between the two shoulders. On only one small space, however, was the skin broken, and that was by the sixth stroke which brought blood to the wound. When Fenton was unstrapped his face showed but little trace of the agony he must have felt, and he entered into conversation with the doctor before being taken back to his cell.[32]

While many letter writers supported the flogging of violent criminals, a greater outcry was raised over the graphic detail in the story. In August 1888 one reader complained, "I think it would be much better for all concerned if such matters were kept out of our public newspapers. . . . I shudder to think that the account of such revolting scenes should be thrust into the hands of my own children and others."[33] Another questioned, "How is it that Canada is the only country in the world with such a law? Are our people worse than other people? . . . We are told that [the lash] is calculated to put an end to crime, then why not use it for all crimes? You say it is not torture. I say it is, and the worst kind of torture, and more, something diabolical."[34]

The Globe defended itself against charges of sensationalism by suggesting that it was printing the story to aid in the deterrent element of the punishment. An editorial argued, "It is a newspaper's duty to see that the flogging be reported simply, truthfully, and in such ways that it will cause shuddering. The shuddering will harm nobody, and may be the salvation of the shudderers."[35] Thinking about the emotion that accompanied these practices helps us to understand corporal punishment when we look more closely at the evidence of how and when it was used. If we looked only at the discourse about criminality, it would suggest that corporal punishment was primarily a response to particular instances of brutality or violent transgression. But the evidence outlined below about when and how corporal punishment was used suggests that this was not always the case.

KEEPING ORDER, MAINTAINING DISCIPLINE

Were prison officials truly responding to "extreme cases," as they claimed, when resorting to corporal punishment? Inspector Moylan reported one such example where corporal punishment was necessary. By the mid-1870s, St. Vincent de Paul had become overcrowded, housing nearly fifty prisoners more than its capacity. According to Warden L. A. Duchesneau, this caused discipline to break down. He met the challenge with what he called "a display of a determined severity and an active and persistent watchfulness."[36] This "display" also involved a dramatic increase in corporal punishments. In 1876, for example, Duchesneau flogged fifteen men with a total of 414 lashes.[37] In spite of the increase, the warden insisted that the corporal punishments had been judicious and only in response to incorrigible behaviour. He reported, "In the inflictions of punishments I have always taken into consideration the character of the delinquent, and I have had recourse to vigorous repressive measures only after having exhausted all indulgent methods. I conceived that in the punishments to be inflicted, one was necessarily obliged to take into consideration the degree of incorrigibility of the convict."[38]

The warden's dilemma was solved in late 1876 when the Department of Justice authorized the transfer of sixty prisoners from St. Vincent de Paul to Kingston Penitentiary. Included in this number were the most refractory and incorrigible inmates, many who had already been flogged for insubordination and had threatened mutiny. Inspector Moylan reported that disciplinary problems followed the transferred prisoners to Kingston. In 1876 he wrote, "They carried with them the like bad disposition to set regulations and discipline at defiance. It consequently became the painful duty of the Warden, Mr. Creighton, to have recourse to the same unpleasant means of persuading the newcomers to conform to the rules which Dr. Duchesneau had employed, and with the same result." Moylan added with apparent satisfaction, "They became convinced that the Warden was master of the situation and they succumbed."[39]

Punishment records from Kingston Penitentiary provide further details about what happened to the transferred "incorrigibles." In late 1876, eight of the prisoners were reported in the south wing for "singing and shouting in a most disgraceful manner." Warden Creighton wrote in the punishment book: "I personally advised these men for their own sakes to keep quiet when they were going into the punishment cells, but latterly they have been setting all authority at defiance and to bring them to a proper sense of their duty as convicts I find it necessary to sentence them to 3 dozen lashes with the cats. To lose all remission they have earned and have their lights for one month."[40] In his annual report, Inspector Moylan later commended Creighton for the measures taken to consolidate his authority, adding, "It is fatal to the privilege and authority of the chief executive officer of a Penitentiary, and therefore to the success of his administration, to manifest any weakness or indecision of character, or to allow convicts to think they have gained the upper hand."[41]

Penitentiary officials described the above events to demonstrate why prison administrators needed the lash. It helped to maintain order and authority. When discipline was threatened by the mutinous and incorrigible, the lash alone could compel a return to obedience. It is unsurprising that such narratives were frequently repeated in annual reports. These justifications, though, often obscured more mundane examples of corporal punishment as a means of maintaining order. In fact, outright mutiny was quite rare at most penitentiaries; petty disobedience was far more common. When corporal punishment was used to respond to these minor infractions, it presented a difficult contradiction to reform discourse and to administrative explanations that the lash was used only in the most extreme circumstances.

Although the frequency and severity of corporal punishment was greatly reduced after 1850, it is significant that no statute or regulation ever stipulated the circumstances under which such punishment could appropriately be applied. As a result, the use of corporal punishment remained a subjective decision exercised by penitentiary wardens. In the majority of instances, corporal punishment was administered in response to relatively minor offences that disturbed the peace and discipline of the institution. The experience of Ah Sing, a prisoner at British Columbia Penitentiary, is one example of how authorities responded to repeated infractions. Sing's disobedience began in July 1886 when he struck another prisoner while on outdoor work detail. Warden McBride admonished him for this. A week later, Sing was admonished again for singing in his cell and disturbing the peace on the cell block. Four weeks later, Sing was reported for disobedience and punished with three days of bread and water with hard bed. Over the next nine months, he was punished multiple times for similar infractions, but none of the minor punishments had any effect on his behaviour. Finally, in June 1887 Sing was reported for using profane language. The warden decided he had been lenient enough and Sing was punished with twenty-four lashes with the cats. To McBride's dismay, the flogging did not improve Sing's behaviour. After subsequent reports of disobedience, Sing was reduced to a permanent low diet and shackled with irons until his sentence expired.[42]

At the end of his eleven-year sentence for larceny and shop breaking, British Columbia prisoner Thomas O'Connor told prison officials he had been punished more than any other man in the penitentiary.[43] Like Ah Sing, O'Connor found it impossible to avoid trouble with the keepers and other inmates. Over the first half of 1888, he was cited in the punishment register twelve times, mostly for minor infractions like talking, idling at his work, and smoking a pipe in his cell. In August 1888 a guard caught O'Connor passing a slip of paper to another prisoner during Sunday religious services, and Warden McBride sentenced him to receive sixty lashes with the cats (the maximum allowable by law after 1875).[44] The whipping had no effect on O'Connor's bad behaviour, but he was not punished a second time. Comparisons with other prisoners in the same penitentiary suggest the subjective nature of punishments for "incorrigibles" like Sing and O'Connor. Prisoner Charles Johnson was cited for multiple disciplinary infractions throughout 1887 at British Columbia Penitentiary, yet he was never whipped. McBride only ordered him shaved and confined to isolation. The same year, John Kelly was cited less than six times, all for minor offences. When he was reported for talking to another convict on their way to the chapel, the warden had him flogged with the cats sixty times and he was thereafter confined in shackles.[45]

The subjective nature of corporal punishment sometimes revealed authorities' discomfort with its role in the penitentiary. However, when faced with individual instances where such punishments were ineffective, wardens seemed to have no ready answer. In the three cases above, corporal punishment was a last resort, but it was seldom regarded as an actual solution. In April 1887 Kingston prisoner James Harris was sent to the isolation wing for refusing to work. Once in isolation, he shouted and pounded on the door of his cell. Warden Creighton wrote in the punishment register, "Previous entries in this book will shew that my patience with this man has been tried to the utmost. He is sentenced to three dozen lashes."[46] The flogging did not improve Harris's behaviour. He continued to work slowly and idle his time. When he was next reported for failing to break the required quantity of stone, Creighton's feelings about Harris had seemingly changed. The warden noted in the punishment register that Harris was "mentally weak" and ordered that he should not be punished. When he was cited again in October, Creighton's only written response was "another idiotic character." In fact, Creighton was alluding to Harris's declining mental health: he was transferred to the Rockwood Asylum when his sentence expired.[47]

As seemed to be the case in multiple instances of corporal punishment in this era, Harris was whipped for actions that could not be considered violent, incorrigible, or malicious. What determined the use of violence in such cases? There are hints in the above cases suggesting that a lack of patience or frustration played a role. These were the exact elements that reformers had tried to eliminate from the practices of punishment. Furthermore, reform discourses repeatedly congratulated prison officials for conquering impulse and emotion. Evidence suggests that these impulses continued to play a role, however, and not only in support of violence. In March 1877 Kingston convict John Kenney struck an inmate orderly and severely cut his face. As he was already serving time in the punishment wing, Warden Creighton sentenced Kenney to two-dozen lashes with the cats. The whipping was to occur on the same day that the inspector visited the penitentiary. With the inspector watching, the guards brought Kenney to the triangle and began to tie his arms and legs. Just before the first blow, Moylan was overcome with emotion and ordered the guards to remove Kenney from the triangle. His punishment was pardoned and the prisoner returned to his cell.[48]

The penitentiary was not the only area of Canadian society where corporal punishment resisted reform impulses for change. Reformatories and schools both struggled with similar issues in their attempts to rationalize disciplinary demands with changing attitudes toward corporal punishment. At the Penetanguishene Reformatory, corporal punishment was a regular occurrence. *The Globe* reported that it was "rarely" resorted to, and only in cases where "it is found absolutely necessary, other methods having failed."[49] In fact, public schools in both Canada and the United States debated the utility of corporal punishment and, in the vast number of cases prior to 1900, concluded that its merits outweighed the costs. In just one example, the Windsor School Board debated the issue of corporal punishment in December 1894. After a lengthy and lively exchange, it was decided that corporal punishment was essential to the maintenance of discipline in Windsor schools.[50]

In some ways, the disciplining of children and youths was similar to that of prisoners. The widespread belief in the efficacy of corporal punishment persisted throughout the nineteenth century in spite of reform discourses that condemned such practices. Indeed, Canadian penitentiaries even continued to use corporal punishment on young prisoners. After the Brown Commission, penitentiary regulations prohibited the flogging of children and youths with the cats, so penitentiary officials simply devised less severe methods of corporal punishment. At Manitoba Penitentiary, prisoners younger than sixteen were lashed on the hands with a leather strap, and at Halifax and Kingston in the early 1870s, keepers used a birch rod or switch. The Kingston punishment return for 1870 noted that the rod was given to two boys.[51] A birch rod was also used against five young inmates at Dorchester in 1885, each receiving ten "cuts."[52] Though the severity was dampened, the intent of these corporal punishments was no different from that of more severe versions.

While attitudes toward flogging changed during the second era of penitentiary reform after 1850, other prison practices based on the infliction of pain were not transformed. In fact, most punishments in the penitentiary involved some degree of pain. Disciplinary practices involving confinement or isolation, particularly in Kingston's earliest years, could still be extremely painful forms of punishment. Only the most shocking examples of these practices, such as the box, were condemned by the Brown Commission. Although reformers were horrified by the box because it was so painful, they did not condemn altogether the infliction of pain through isolation or confinement. In the post-Confederation period, each penitentiary still used various forms of confinement and restraint as punishments, the most common involving shackling or chaining prisoners to an iron ball or cell wall. In 1871 a total of six men were chained at Kingston. Most confinement in chains lasted for days or a few weeks, but prisoners Peter Almond and Philander Allen remained in chains from September to late December.[53] The practice could be dangerous or fatal when taken to extremes. In 1891 at St. Vincent de Paul, convict Ned Haggart died while chained to a wall for two consecutive weeks.[54]

While traditional methods of corporal punishment, including flogging and whipping, held the attention of reformers throughout the nineteenth century, less painful practices like confinement never elicited the same response in spite of the potential abuse of such punishments. Other forms of punishment could also be physically painful, yet these too often eluded the attention of reformers and inspectors. At Manitoba in the 1870s, Warden Bedson instituted the use of the Oregon boot, an iron shackle that locked around a prisoner's ankle and attached to the heel of a boot. It weighed as much as twenty-eight pounds and was worn on only one leg to keep the inmate off-balance. Wearing the boot was said to cause extreme physical pain.[55] Other corporal punishments drew on military traditions to inflict pain. In 1870 Kingston instituted "shot drill practice," a punishment devised by the British army. Philip Priestley's *Victorian Prison Lives* contains a description of the exercise that invokes the imagery of bygone punishments such as the crank and the treadmill: "It consists . . . of stooping down (without bending the knees) and picking up a thirty-two pounder round shot, bringing it slowly up until it is on a level with the chest, then taking two steps to the right and replacing it on the ground again."[56] This exercise would go on for four hours with five minutes rest every hour. Shot drill was used sparingly at Kingston Penitentiary and Manitoba Penitentiary.

In the late 1890s, William Irvine, warden of Manitoba Penitentiary, instituted a new punishment that harkened back to earlier methods of confinement. Irvine reported to Inspector Stewart that he had learned about the success of the punishment at Stillwater Penitentiary and recommended it for Canadian prisons. Used for prisoners who refused to work or were confined to their cell for other disciplinary reasons, it involved handcuffing the prisoner's hands to a cell door so that he would be forced to stand. Irvine wrote, "While undergoing this punishment he is kept in this position during the working hours of the other convicts and is released for the ordinary meals, being again returned to his position until the allotted time has expired. It is not cruel . . . and it prevents a man from lying down and taking it easy, which many convicts would rather do than work."[57] The inspector evidently approved of the punishment as it was still in use at Manitoba a decade later. In 1905 a prisoner was sentenced to seven days on bread and water with his hands cuffed to the cell door as a punishment for "step-dancing in his cell."[58]

More common alternatives to whippings were punishments that isolated offenders from the general prison population. With the decline of flogging as a serious penalty, isolation in the dark cell (not to be confused with regular cells being deprived of electric or gas light) was the next most serious punishment available to officials. There are virtually no descriptions of the dungeons or punishment cells used in Canadian penitentiaries. Officials referred to them only sparingly in their annual reports, and because they did not fall into the realm of violent punishment, reformers were largely unconcerned with isolation as a form of punishment in the late nineteenth century. Not surprisingly, this lack of attention to the use of the dark cells created vast potential for abuse. Isolation was certainly less brutal than corporal punishment, but it was also far from painless.

The experience of Garry Hill, a prisoner at Manitoba Penitentiary, provides some insight into the brutal nature of prolonged isolation. At Manitoba, the penal cells were in a separate structure from the main penitentiary building. Hills spent extended periods of time in an isolation cell in late 1890. In mid-November, hospital overseer David Bourke reported on Hill's condition. When he asked Hill if he had any complaints, the inmate replied that he was suffering from pains in his shoulders and hips because he had been sleeping on the stone floor of the cell. Bourke wrote, "His complaint about the cell being cold is, in my opinion, well founded. There is a large stove in the penal cell building, but on careful examination of the cell with thick stone wall and heavy close-fitting wooden door inside . . . which is constantly kept closed, I was unable to see how he could get any benefit from the stove."[59] Warden Bedson received the report and ordered extra blankets to be sent to Hill's cell. When Bourke visited Hill again two days later, the prisoner complained about a terrible smell in the cell and showed the overseer his badly chafed shoulders and hips. Two days later, Hill complained about pains in the pit of his stomach, which arose after his attempt to get some exercise in the tiny cell. Bourke clearly felt some sympathy with Hill's plight, going to unusual lengths to communicate the prisoner's discomfort to the warden. His final report to Bedson stated only, "Visited No. 39 in penal cell yesterday.

He has no accommodation for washing or bathing."[60] The overseer's record is truncated and it is not clear when Hills was freed from the isolation cell, but the final notation indicates that he was still undergoing punishment on December 4; he served at least sixteen days on a low diet in total darkness.[61] In spite of the notion that punishments involving isolation were more humane, they still tended to brutalize the body. Significantly, punishments involving isolation became the main response to incorrigibility as corporal punishment waned in the decades after Confederation.

THE PRISON OF ISOLATION

In the early 1870s, the penitentiary board of directors raised the possibility of a penal wing, or a Prison of Isolation, at Kingston Penitentiary. This idea was inspired by the Crofton system, which involved a progressive classification of prisoners. Reformers viewed such a classification as the best method of preventing the intercourse of hardened criminals with first-time offenders, a prison reality that was widely regarded as the most damaging prospect to individual reformation. Various schemes were promoted in Canada to approximate some version of the Crofton system. In 1873 the penitentiary directors suggested that each newly received prisoner should be isolated for a short period while internalizing the rules of the penitentiary and the advice of his chaplain.[62] Ten years later, Inspector Moylan continued to promote this idea, suggesting that the period of isolation should last six to eight months for newly received convicts. Furthermore, he suggested that the penitentiaries use some system of classification to segregate the incorrigibles from the rest of the prison population so their influence would not deter the reformation of others.[63]

In 1877 Moylan wrote, "The recommitted convicts are the bane of our Penitentiaries."[64] This idea about hardened or career criminals was an old one. Moylan attacked this issue with surprising enthusiasm and joined it to the emerging liberal reform concern about individualism and classification. "It is of paramount importance," he continued, "in order to prevent the penitentiaries from any longer being nurseries of crime . . . to separate the hardened offenders and habitual wrongdoers from the orderly and well-disposed prisoners."[65] Moylan suggested a very simple solution to what he viewed as the penitentiary's central failure: he argued that the "hard cases" needed to be separate from the rest of the population. This practice, he explained, "not only affords a certain protection to the less depraved against further contamination, and debars the more guilty from spreading their evil taint, but it also offers opportunities to the latter of self-examination and of receiving uninterruptedly moral and religious education."[66]

In his second decade as penitentiary inspector, Moylan focused on better classification of prison populations. He actively promoted the Crofton system, arguing that it would raise the classification of inmates to the level of a criminological science. In this system, reform would be accomplished through detailed and scientific knowledge of each individual prisoner. Thus, the individuality of each inmate would be uncovered, analyzed, and subjected to the discretionary expertise of penitentiary officials. In 1888 Moylan wrote, "In a better system, which raises the Penitentiary question to the rank of a science, each prisoner should be studied individually and treated according to his character and according to the degree of moral idiocy with which he is affected. To treat all criminals in the same manner is as absurd as would be the proposition to cure all the diseases of the body, diversified as they are, by the same medical agents."[67] Although classification seemed like a bold new idea in an emerging modern penology, it was actually a concept dating back to the first penitentiaries. Old ideas about isolation were recast as new reform ideologies about the benefits of individual classification. The principle of pure isolation had been discredited decades before Moylan's tenure, largely due to the overwhelming mental illness that accompanied long-term solitary confinement practices at the penitentiaries in Philadelphia and Pentonville.[68] While more complex methods of classification, such as the Crofton system, invested greater energy into the segregation and evaluation of each inmate, in the Canadian context the most complex elements of these practices were stripped away until all that was left was the impulse to isolate prisoners who could not be managed—the incorrigible offenders. But to what effect? Stripped of its positivist criminological elements, the reforms that came to the Canadian system at the end of the nineteenth century only served the purposes of domination and oppression of the most dangerous (whether real or perceived) members of the prison population.

The move to isolate hard offenders was one part of an expanding movement to judge the criminality of individual offenders. Inspector Moylan increasingly suggested that when the work of the penitentiary was unsuccessful in reforming the offender, such individuals should not be released. In 1889 Moylan began to advocate for a system of indeterminate sentencing that would allow penitentiary officials to judge when a prisoner was sufficiently reformed. He argued, "By sentencing the prisoner without specifying the length of time he is to serve, leaving this to be determined by his keepers, who are the most competent judges, it is fair to assume that the sentence in any given case would be more equitable than if left to be fixed arbitrarily in advance, without knowledge of the prisoner's character and qualities."[69] This was an argument aimed squarely at the same class of prisoners who necessitated the Prison of Isolation. Although the language was steeped in "hope" and "reformation," it was the failure of these objectives that motivated the desire to keep certain prisoners incarcerated indefinitely. Moylan further suggested that the criminal should be regarded as an insane person and should be restrained so long as his liberty would pose a danger to society. The inspector was no doubt buoyed when the National Prison Congress advocated similar ideas, arguing in 1890 that punishment in fixed terms should be abolished. Moylan also pointed to the passage of a habitual criminals act in Ohio that legislated the incarceration of offenders for life after their third conviction. Britain introduced its own habitual criminals act in 1899.

Although he had few compatriots in the Canadian prison reform movement, Moylan's ideas about penology certainly reflected the direction of international reform and even provided early glimpses of twentieth-century criminology. A parallel development in international prison reform complemented this new direction: while habitual criminals legislation gave penitentiaries more power to control hardened and incorrigible offenders, "ticket of leave" legislation created a converse movement to expedite the release of prisoners who showed a better potential for reformation. By the end of the century, prison reformers had embraced the idea that successful rehabilitation required release from prison and integration with the community. By the early 1900s, the Canadian Justice Department had partnered with the Salvation Army to administer an early version of the Canadian Parole Service. Salvation Army workers, along with local police forces, assumed responsibility for the monitoring and assistance of prisoners who were released before the end of their court-ordered sentences.

It is significant that the construction of the Prison of Isolation at Kingston Penitentiary, a response to incorrigibility, was the only large-scale reform in prison practice accomplished during Moylan's long reign as penitentiary inspector. This "reform" succeeded where others failed because it appealed to both reformers and justice officials. To reformers, it was an enlightened step toward a more individualized response to criminality. For penitentiary and justice officials, it offered a practical response to a perceived problem of security and the threat of the incorrigible offender. While other projects, such as a criminal insane asylum at Kingston or improved quarters for women, dragged on for decades, the Prison of Isolation was completed relatively quickly.

While previous generations of reformers identified inhumane treatment or lack of religion and education as the failures of the penitentiary project, Moylan's conclusions suggested a somewhat more cynical application of reform ideology: some men could not be reclaimed and posed a grave threat to the salvation of those who could. This idea obviously appealed to penitentiary wardens, who regarded increased segregation of hardened offenders a practical reform that would serve the security of the institution. The appeal of this idea is evidenced by the fact that it was one of the few large-scale reforms proposed by Moylan to ever gain government assent. Construction on the "penal prison" at Kingston began in 1890. Completed by late 1892, the Prison of Isolation was a separate wing containing 108 cells reserved for the most dangerous, incorrigible, and irredeemable inmates from across the country. Although Moylan had planned for the isolation wing to incarcerate the worst incorrigibles from all five penitentiaries in the dominion, soon after 1895 it became clear that the cost and logistics of transferring prisoners from the Maritimes and western Canada was far too expensive.[70] A year after the isolation wing opened, it was only filled to a third of its capacity.

The opening of the Prison of Isolation left Inspector Moylan feeling cynical. Having pushed for this reform for nearly twenty years, he was dismayed to discover that justice officials were disinterested in advancing the criminological science behind the new isolation wing. Though the structure was completed, Moylan warned, "its usefulness and advantage will altogether depend upon the system of management that followed."[71] The inspector wanted the opportunity to travel to Europe, where he might inspect the best penology methods, particularly as they related to the new segregation techniques. He considered isolation wings in Belgium the best example for the Canadian system to follow. But Moylan's requests for such a tour went unacknowledged by the Department of Justice. The inspector stated in his annual report that the decision was not a surprise to him, given that "nothing has been done in this direction, notwithstanding the fact that no opportunity has ever been granted to the board of directors or the inspector to enlarge their views or increase their knowledge of penology, since the opening of Kingston Penitentiary in 1834." Finally, Moylan reported bitterly that without the benefit of learning how other prisons managed isolation quarters, he had simply drawn up his own code of rules, which was "necessarily defective."[72]

Thus, Moylan succeeded in creating a rudimentary method of classifying prisoners, but in the end, it was aimed entirely at the incorrigibles in the prison and was stripped of all potential reformatory effects. Still, other officials saw only the positives. By 1897 Moylan's replacement, Inspector Douglas Stewart, was praising the "wholesome restraint" the Prison of Isolation exerted over the incorrigibles in the prison population.[73] Ironically, Stewart praised the isolation wing as evidence of the superiority of the Belgian system of classification even though the Canadian version scarcely resembled the progressive classification such a system would entail. Although the Prison of Isolation was steeped in reform ideas, its true purpose was to give keepers and officials at Kingston greater control over what they considered to be the worst elements in the prison population. Thus, it gained both political and administrative support where countless other reform initiatives had failed.

THE DEATH OF GEORGE HEWELL

While the Prison of Isolation was a feather in Moylan's cap, at least one incident left an ugly stain on the isolation wing. George Hewell was regarded as a primary candidate for the Prison of Isolation: by all accounts, he was among the most incorrigible and dangerous offenders at Kingston Penitentiary. Hewell was convicted of rape in October 1887 and sentenced to life imprisonment. His behaviour at Kingston quickly earned him a reputation as an incorrigible. In the first ten years of his sentence, Hewell received nearly two dozen disciplinary reports. Some of these were for minor offences. For example, in August 1895 he told a guard "to go and fuck [him]self" while refusing to work.[74] Hewell cemented his reputation for violence, however, when he hit a prisoner in the head with a hammer in 1888. In 1895 he was punished for attempting to throw another inmate over the balcony of a gallery. These transgressions earned him long stretches in the penitentiary dungeon. In February 1896 Hewell attacked a prisoner and then a guard in the dining hall and was sentenced to six months in the Prison of Isolation. As guards dragged Hewell from the dining hall after this final altercation, the assembled prisoners stood to jeer and hiss at him.[75]

Hewell's experience at Kingston was similar to that of John Foy at British Columbia Penitentiary. Like Foy, Hewell was one of the few black prisoners in a predominantly white institution, and race undoubtedly played a role in both his violent experience at Kingston and the construction of him as an incorrigible. He had an exotic and mysterious background that contributed to his strange reputation. He was said to be a circus performer, possibly an acrobat. Warden John Metcalf described him as "very athletic and tiger like in his movements," noting darkly that Hewell was "supple. Very supple."[76] His physical prowess seemed to hint at the dangerous potential that was confirmed by the multiple violent incidents during Hewell's first years of imprisonment.

After the altercation in the dining hall in early 1896, Hewell served seven months in the Prison of Isolation without incident. He spent his days sewing shirt sleeves, receiving no visitor but the keeper of the Prison of Isolation, the prison doctor, and various guards. The standard term of imprisonment in the isolation wing was six months. If prisoners served this time without disciplinary report, they were usually returned to the general population. By October 1896, Hewell was feeling despondent about the extra month he had been kept in the isolation wing. Some prisoners in the Prison of Isolation reported that the isolation keeper, A.D.O. McDonell, was a domineering and manipulative tyrant. Release from the Prison of Isolation was supposed to be under the authority of the warden, but a negative disciplinary report from the keeper could extend the sentence and even keep prisoners isolated indefinitely. One prisoner remarked that McDonell "wishes to have them think that he has full control."[77] Another former prisoner from the isolation wing revealed more, reporting that McDonell would frequently incite the men to anger and "excite words from us until we get so hot that we could not control ourselves."[78] Apparently, McDonell would goad the isolated prisoners into delaying their chances of returning to the regular prison population.

Hewell's agitation about his delayed release from isolation was made worse by the belief that his medical complaints were being ignored by the keepers, the warden, and the doctor. On the morning of October 8, he rose feeling unwell. He did not dress or take his breakfast, and he complained to the keeper about a terrible pain in his chest. The doctor arrived at 10:00 a.m. and examined Hewell, only to conclude that there was nothing wrong with him. By lunch, Hewell was still undressed and in bed. Guard John Donnelly scolded him, telling him, "Come, come get up and be a man. There is nothing wrong with you."[79] Hewell rose and angrily demanded to see the warden. When he would not calm down, Donnelly wrote this disciplinary report, reading it to Hewell before delivering it to the warden:

> Causing a disturbance in the corridor by loudly demanding to see the keeper at noon, and insolently telling me that he was tired of me; that I was always imposing on him, and that he would not put up with it any longer. He refused to rise from his bed at noon hour and take his rations as usual, feigning sickness, and because I refused to pass his meal into his cell he rose from his bed and became abusive.[80]

Donnelly returned from the warden's office to read Hewell his punishment: "This starts Hewell on a new month and for one week to lose light, and to go one week on low diet."[81] The prospect of another month in the isolation wing completely overwhelmed the prisoner. Several members of the penitentiary staff in the isolation wing tried to calm him, but he was inconsolable and his despair soon turned to anger. William Hughes, the chief keeper, told him, "Hewell you are only making it worse for yourself carrying on this way, the quieter you behave the lighter your sentence will be."[82] As Hewell sobbed uncontrollably, Donnelly decided to write a second disciplinary report and again read it aloud to Hewell.[83] As Donnelly left to deliver the second report to the warden, the other members of the staff tried to calm the prisoner again with no success. He cried out, "You are all trying to kill me. . . . Oh God, send me to hell before you allow me to get out of here alive!"[84]

Upon hearing the report of the burgeoning crisis in the isolation wing, Warden Metcalf ordered Hewell to be removed to the dungeon. Hughes set out for the isolation wing, collecting guards George Sullivan and Alexander Spence along the way. The officers arrived to find that the situation had deteriorated. George Hewell was still in his cell, clutching the massive tailor's shears used for his work. Hughes and Spence entered the cell, ordering Hewell to drop the shears and surrender. When he did not submit, Hughes drew his revolver and fired on Hewell, hitting him between the cheek and the ear. "You have me now," Hewell gasped as he fell forward. "You done this," he said to Hughes before collapsing into the keeper's arms and losing consciousness.[85] He was rushed to the penitentiary hospital, where he died later that evening with the bullet lodged in his brain.

A penitentiary commission under James Noxon and former penitentiary board member E. A. Meredith was called in early 1897 to investigate Hewell's death. Questioning each individual involved in the incident, the commissioners uncovered several unsettling inconsistencies. The first involved Warden Metcalf's order to remove Hewell from his cell. William Hughes testified to the investigating coroner that he had reminded the warden that in his agitated state, Hewell might be expected to defend himself with his tailor's shears. According to Hughes, the warden had replied, "If he attempts to use the scissors, *shoot him.*"[86] Warden Metcalf vigorously denied ever having given the order. Under cross examination, Hughes later changed his story, stating, "I do not think he said that. There was something said in conversation, that I would shoot him if he used the shears."[87] The only other witness to the conversation was the warden's chief clerk, who refused to testify as to what he had heard.[88] Either way, it was clear that Hughes had left the warden's office determined to take Hewell out of his cell. After collecting guards Sullivan and Spence to assist him, Hughes had reportedly said to them, "We are going to have a little fun."[89]

The most troubling discrepancy in testimony before the commissioners revolved around Hewell's behaviour when the officers returned to take him from the cell. Chief keeper Hughes and guard Spence both testified that Hewell had acted aggressively, threatening their lives with the shears. Spence told the commissioners that Hewell "jumped around and was as active as a bird in a cage. . . . He made a spring all at once as though he was going to strike with the shears."[90] Spence stressed in his testimony that the chief keeper had fired only as a last resort to save their lives: "He was going like a streak of lightening. The Chief covered him and then shot him, after Hewell made two or three attempts to strike him. . . . If we had turned our backs and had not shot him he would have run those scissors into me, or some of us. When the Chief went up he made at the Chief. I considered my life in danger. That revolver saved mine and his life."[91] Hughes's version was similar. He testified that he had drawn his revolver on Hewell and warned him to drop the shears and that the prisoner had then lunged at him and tried to grab the revolver. "He had come at me from a crouched position," testified Hughes; "he struck sideways at me and jumped forward and struck at me with the shears."[92]

The version of Spence and Hughes that was entered into the record was contradicted by the keeper of the Prison of Isolation, A. D. O. McDonell, and by deputy warden William Sullivan, both of whom witnessed the shooting. McDonell swore that Hewell had not acted aggressively toward the officers as they entered his cell. He testified, "From where I was the convict seemed to be standing perfectly quiet with the shears lifted."[93] Sullivan testified to the same thing but added that Hewell had flinched when the gun was drawn on him and retreated into the cell with his hands in the air in a defensive position. The commissioners pressed Sullivan on this point:

Q. How far did he back up?
A. He backed up quite a ways.
Q. Did he keep backing up before the Chief as the Chief advanced?
A. Yes, pretty much.
Q. His movements were gradually to retreat into the cell?
A. He showed that he was really afraid.
Q. Did he make any thrusts at either the Chief Keeper or Mr. Spence?
A. No, he still held them up.
Q. Did he actually try to strike them?
A. No, no blow.
Q. You could see the shears were constantly above his head and at no time you saw any movement to strike?
A. No.[94]

The commissioners were clearly troubled by the contradictory testimony and tried to work out why the situation had ended violently.

Meredith questioned Alexander Spence on this point, suggesting that it had been unnecessary to enter the cell at all when the situation might have been diffused by waiting for Hewell to calm down. Meredith asked Spence, "You and the Chief were determined to take him out dead or alive?" Spence replied,

A. My determination was to take that man out.
Q. Dead or alive?
A. If I had my gun I would have shot him.
Q. You might have escaped?
A. But I did not go in with that intention.[95]

The Penitentiary Commission seemed aware that violence was not the only possible outcome to the scenario that unfolded in the Prison of Isolation. When Hugh Hayvern stabbed Thomas Salter at Kingston in 1881, he was thrown into an isolation cell before the guards could take away the murder weapon. Hayvern was in state of extreme agitation, slashing at his own throat and at the guards through the bars of his cell. Rather than draw their revolvers, however, the guards summoned the Protestant chaplain, who quickly donned his Sunday garments before arriving at the cell. According to *The Globe*, "the sight of the clergyman in his robes was too much for the desperate man, and without another word he yielded his knife to the reverend gentleman."[96] The contrast with how Hewell died is striking. While the commission concluded that the shooting of George Hewell was a tragic mistake, it assigned no blame to any member of the penitentiary staff. The report concluded paradoxically, saying that Hewell had "stood on the defence, not attacking" while chief keeper Hughes could not have removed the prisoner "without in self defence using his revolver."[97]

Although the Prison of Isolation might have been regarded as a victory for Moylan's reform movement, the Hewell incident showed that the move to greater isolation of incorrigible offenders both strengthened and diminished the project he had fought toward for twenty years. The original idea suggested by early reformers like

Maconochie and Crofton proposed a better classification of all offenders in the institution so they could be treated humanely and reformed by trained experts. In practice, the Prison of Isolation at Kingston was an abdication of this ideal. While it was justified in the language of reform, it actually represented the opposite impulse as it came to be used for incorrigible offenders. Years before the isolation wing opened, Moylan wrote, "Who is wise enough to say what punishment is enough for a criminal? The prison should be a place for his reformation and for the protection of society from the evil he would do it. If he will not reform, then let him stay there where he cannot injure society."[98] In practice, however, the Prison of Isolation expressed only the oppressive portion of his statement.

In fact, by the late 1890s, the Prison of Isolation was merely a crude instrument among other techniques that addressed individual criminality, including measures that made criminal sentencing and release from prison far more flexible and discretionary. Moylan began advocating for indeterminate sentencing in the late 1880s. He argued repeatedly that only prison authorities could reliably judge the reformation of the criminal and should therefore be counted on to know when it might be safe to release offenders back into society. As he had done so often in the past, Moylan looked to other penal regimes for inspiration and support. He cited an argument in a report by the California Penological Commission from 1887:

> As it is now, a judge passes sentence upon a prisoner, aided by the knowledge he can secure. But it is difficult for him to know much of the prisoner's antecedents, and almost impossible for him to predict with any degree of certainty within what time the evil traits of the prisoner may be removed, or whether he is capable of reformation at all. By sentencing a prisoner without specifying the length of time he is to serve, leaving this to be determined by his keepers, who are the most competent judges, it is fair to assume that the sentence in any given case would be more equitable than if left to be fixed arbitrarily in advance, without knowledge of the prisoner's character and qualities.

> By this system it is proposed to draw a line between those in whom reformation may be effected and those in whom reformation cannot be expected.[99]

Moylan cited multiple other reform authorities who advocated for indeterminate sentencing, but the Department of Justice showed little interest in extending this much authority to prison officials.

Indeed, by the 1890s, Canada still lagged behind reform advances in England and America on ideas that would come to define the "penal welfare" state of the early twentieth century. These new ideas revolved around finding more effective ways to reform first-time criminals and eventually secure their release from the penitentiary under conditions that would reduce recidivism. The fundamental departure on these questions was that a new reform movement outside of penitentiary administration was increasingly vocal. In the 1890s, evangelical charities like the Salvation Army began ministries aimed at recently released prisoners. "Prison gate ministries" run by the Salvation Army sought to uplift released convicts in order to prevent a return to a life of crime. Salvation Army officers literally met released prisoners "at the prison's gate" to offer guidance on the correct moral path in the aftermath of a penitentiary sentence. While penitentiary authorities had long argued that the lot of a released convict was difficult, the efforts of the Salvation Army spoke to a larger shift in ideas about reformation and rehabilitation. Seeking the ongoing moral salvation of released prisoners, the prison gate ministries seemed to reject the idea of reformation at the heart of the penitentiary project, suggesting that reformation came after a prisoner's release and that a moral lifestyle guided by the Salvation Army could produce results the prison could not.

By the late 1890s, this new reform movement had assumed a greater position of power in Canadian justice policy. The new *Ticket of Leave Act* in 1899 provided penitentiaries with the legal mechanism to release individuals without the formal ascent of the Governor General's Office. While this reform might have given penitentiary authorities the power that Moylan had agitated for, responsibility for prisoners released under the new act was given to the Salvation Army, not penitentiary authorities. In 1905 Brigadier W. P. Archibald resigned his commission with the Salvation Army to become Canada's first parole officer. In this new position, Archibald personally oversaw the conditional release of convicts from federal penitentiaries across Canada. He travelled thousands of kilometres between institutions each year to interview prisoners eligible for parole and to meet with recent parolees in the community. This was a new era and it ushered forth a new welfarist model of criminality. Where nineteenth-century reformers had positioned the penitentiary as a moral realm in which criminals were transformed, the new ideology looked beyond penitentiary walls. In his first annual report, Archibald wrote, "We must accept the criminal as he is. . . . He cannot be dismissed as an anthropological monster, he is one of us: he belongs to us; he must be met and treated as part of the social fabric of life. He must be helped over the chasm which he has digged [sic] with his own hands. The voice of God may fall into a faint whisper in the human soul, but it never dies away into utter silence."[100]

Conclusion

What questions should we ask about the history of the modern penitentiary? In my experience, the most common questions arise from an interest in "how bad" the first prisons were or how they compared to today's prisons. The history of the Canadian penitentiary provides ample evidence to satisfy any curiosity about poor living conditions, harsh treatment, or barbarous punishments. But this in itself is mere tourism in a foreign past, and one that is artificially divorced from the present. Responses to "how bad" could also convey the startling similarities between the past and the present. Many of the key elements of prison life and its oppressions have not changed; more importantly, many failures and shortcomings that have marked prisons throughout history have not been resolved. This invites a more challenging question that is often invoked by the same casual observers: What does the penitentiary accomplish?

The questions we ask and the responses we give are often rooted in our perceptions of crime and how we conceive of the role of prisons. They are also related to our belief in the value of punishment. There are those who express a wistful admiration for bygone prison regimes that brutalized the bodies of convicted men and women because they feel that this is what convicted criminals deserve. In a more pointed contemporary example, many do not question the suspension of human rights at Guantanamo Bay in the post–9/11 era; at the very least, some feel comfortable with the idea that such conditions are appropriate. This speaks to a central question: How much suffering should punishment inflict? This was one of the key issues at the heart of the humanitarian reform movement that created the penitentiary two hundred years ago. The question remains unanswered, but some would offer the rejoinder, Is it not just that criminals should suffer for their crimes?

Finally, in spite of differences of opinion, most can agree that the penitentiary is troubled on one level or another. At best, the institution is regarded as deeply problematic, yet in what ways and why this is so are also subject to broad disagreement. Both the Left and the Right cite the marginal effect prisons exert upon the incidence of crime. While liberal democracies constructed a penal welfare system that characterized much of the twentieth century, for the past forty years the conservative impulse has, with particular exceptions animated by specific political economies, been ascendant throughout the Western world. We have witnessed four decades of exponentially growing incarceration rates and prison construction that accompany calls to once and for all "get tough on crime." To what effect? The common answer conservatives offer to the failure of the prison is to build more of them. Through this process, the penitentiary has become so deeply entrenched in the fabric of Western society that to suggest alternatives now appears less rational than blind obeisance to the current trajectory. This state of affairs leads finally to the helpless question, Why doesn't the prison work?

There are no ready answers, in part because the question is based on the idea that the penitentiary can one day deliver on its promise of positive outcomes. This idea persists in spite of two hundred years of evidence to the contrary. How would our understanding differ if we accepted that the penitentiary perpetuates harmful consequences in the form of oppression, domination, or alienation? This book is a revisionist account of the penitentiary that reorients the focus of prison history in this direction. As it developed through the nineteenth century, the modern penitentiary was arguably forged by three key forces: the emergence of industrial capitalism, new ways of understanding the criminal in society, and the power relations unique to the newly conceived penal institutions. In exploring how each concern perpetuated and reproduced oppression throughout the nineteenth century, I have drawn a portrait of an institution that was a persistently destructive force of Canadian modernity. If historians begin new investigations of the penitentiary on these terms, they may provide a foundation for new answers to these questions, which seem to linger without hope of response.

PUNISHMENT OR REFORM?

Throughout the book, I have explored the historical evolution of a striking contradiction. From its earliest days, the modern penitentiary has been at cross purposes with itself: some of the first penitentiary promoters intended the new institution to be an alternative method of punishment—a more humane solution than torture or execution—while other voices suggested that the prison could also address the source of crime by transforming individuals. Could the new institutions simultaneously punish and reform? Prison officials and reformers pushed and pulled toward one objective or another throughout the nineteenth century, but evidence suggests that punishment and reformation were never successfully reconciled with each other. What is the purpose of imprisonment? This question continued to define a philosophical divide throughout the nineteenth century with the effect that various proponents and stakeholders defined success or failure on entirely different terms. How critics defined the failures and shortcomings of the penitentiary was largely dependent on their perspective on the purpose of the institution. Even when they agreed on the problem, reasoning about how the penitentiary should factor in responses to it were widely divergent. For example, in the penitentiary's earliest years, it became obvious that prisons were not curtailing crime in a measurable way. For promoters who sought only a fixed measure of punishment, this was not a serious problem. It appeared logical that more crime demanded more prisons and more definite measures of punishment. In effect, as long as there was an ongoing sense of social crisis, the penitentiary could be called upon to provide an appropriate legal response. The penitentiary became a self-fulfilling and unimpeachable necessity in a society beset by constant social upheaval and change. From this perspective, there was seemingly no retreat from the penitentiary and no apparent alternative.

In contrast, humanitarian reformers decried the notion that the penitentiary served only to punish and promoted the potential of the prison to transform individuals. Born of evangelical impulses, the desire to reform individuals ran counter to a Lockean notion that punishment has inherent social value. For reformers, the importance of the criminal offence receded; rather, prison officials were to examine the offenders' childhoods, social surroundings, and individual moral constitutions for answers to *why* the crime had occurred. Reformers sought better methods of transforming prisoners through more education, better religious outreach, and focused vocational training as opposed to brute physical labour. Punishment was to be replaced by moralization as penitentiaries were transformed into reformatories. Had this agenda been successful, it would have produced a different style of institution, but the moralization project was not realized in the nineteenth century. Not all stakeholders shared the reform vision. Prison officials, in particular, were reluctant to relinquish their powers of physical coercion or lessen the punitive effect of hard labour. Most damaging to the reform agenda was the fact that many officials never accepted the legitimacy of the value of individual reformation. Such doubts were easily supported and reform ideas weakened by the fact that in spite of new measures and programs designed for this purpose, crime rates remained largely unaffected.

Understanding these tensions is essential to the project of demonstrating why the penitentiary developed as it did and examining the source of its ideological contrasts. However, merely charting the course of this debate through history also provides an altogether unsatisfying conclusion, or rather a lack of conclusions. It is insufficient to consider the failures of the penitentiary only relative to how its promoters defined its goals. By this measure, far too much can be forgiven in an assessment of what the modern penitentiary created, its effect upon individuals, and its role in shaping Canadian society. If critics are content only to demand that the penitentiary fulfill its promises, whether these are defined as punishment or reform, then history is merely complicit in a much larger and devastating failure than is often acknowledged.

THE HUMAN COST

An important role for prison history is to redefine the terms of the above debate. This can happen through an approach that reorients our attention to new understandings of how the prison fails and asks who has paid the cost for these failures. Above all else, the penitentiary is an intensely social institution. While many historians have contributed greatly to integrating prisons into the fabric of social history, there is more to be done in recognizing the penitentiary as a social realm itself in which the experience and agency of individuals make history. Prison life is an intensely interpersonal experience based on multiple social relationships between keepers and prisoners. If we see keepers as only representatives of the state, or prisoners as a homogeneous body of "criminals," then much of prison history is lost. We should not forget the importance of locating the agency and experiences of prisoners themselves. While the paucity of sources makes this an ongoing challenge, to abandon hope of recovering this history is to portray the prisoner as a faceless entity. It was this very anonymity that often perpetuated the misery of the penitentiary experience, and it should not be reproduced in historical research. Preventing this requires a willingness to look beyond the walls of the institutions to understand the interests, motivations, and backgrounds of prisoners as historical subjects. Penitentiary history can also encompass families, damaged domestic economies, the lives of the workers and unemployed who would become prisoners, and the struggles of the men and women who were once counted among prison populations. This is an ambitious project, but its outcome would provide a broader and more satisfying understanding of the larger importance of prison history. If prison history is to provide a better understanding of how the penitentiary affected individual lives and ultimately the larger social fabric, these new inquiries will necessarily look deeper.

One important issue arising from a focus on individual lives is the question of suffering. The penitentiary reoriented the social contract by establishing precise punishments to match criminal offences. This was an eminently capitalist idea that demanded time and labour power from the guilty party. However, from its earliest days, this new method of punishment also exacted a measure of physical or psychological suffering. This was an unspoken but generally acknowledged element of early penitentiary life, and humanitarian reformers staked their position on demanding a smaller quotient of suffering. However, even the most humanitarian voices seldom called for penal regimes that were free of the most common miseries. The penitentiary was never inimical to the idea of causing pain. While the reform movement often succeeded in diminishing the most brutal elements of penitentiary life, other indices of suffering remained untouched by reformers, and these too should be the subject of searching questions. If history focuses solely on the trajectory of reform ideas, these questions remain obscured.

Who suffered the most under nineteenth-century prison regimes? This question is not mere morbidity, for once it is probed with a focus on the lives of prisoners, it becomes clear that those subject to the worst suffering due to neglect, abuse, exploitation, and violence could also be counted among the weakest, most vulnerable, or marginal members of nineteenth-century society: women, children, racial and ethnic minorities, and the sick and disabled. They suffered in ways that the reform movement did not or could not address. If prison history is to discover the human cost paid by these prisoners, it must make strenuous efforts to appreciate that those who are the most vulnerable are also the most difficult to see in historical sources.

But they *are* there: in basement cells, in sick beds, and in isolation wards. Some experienced neglect that made the penitentiary a physical nightmare. Others faced too much attention due to their vulnerability to predators, exploitive guards, or the hatred incited by racism. These individuals experienced the penitentiary in different ways than how we might commonly perceive the lot of the "convicted criminal." Thus, when conservatives cite the eminent logic of "a just measure of pain" for every crime, we must forcefully reply with the questions, What additional misery were the just deserts of the prisoners we would count as the most vulnerable? Where is the justice in their suffering?

WHO IS A CRIMINAL?

A second approach to the individuals at the centre of prison history addresses questions about how they are understood in the penitentiary and in larger society. Just as the purpose of the penitentiary becomes naturalized, the prisoner as criminal carries an eminent and seductive logic. Criminality was a construction to which the penitentiary contributed, but without rigorous investigation of this process, such constructions can become invisible to us. This myopia often characterizes contemporary debates about prisons in which inmates occupy the position of the Other. Accepting such social divisions at face value causes gross distortions of how we see the historical effect of the modern penitentiary. Such distortions can also misdirect our focus. For example, much of the mistreatment and abuse that would cause us to recoil in the case of an individual becomes more normalized when it involves an unidentified and threatening body of "criminals." Thus, it is more than mere discursive dalliance to investigate the construction of criminality that takes place in the penitentiary. It is essential to understanding how such a construction creates the divisions that sustain and reproduce its oppression.

If we accept at face value who is regarded as dangerous or unfit for society, we also lose the capacity to criticize the effects of such designations. In the realm of penitentiaries, this shroud creates the potential for abuse and tragedy. It was under the circumstances created by particular constructions of criminality that George Hewell was murdered in an isolation cell at Kingston in 1896. This crime was rendered justifiable not on the basis of exonerating evidence but by who and what the penitentiary portrayed this prisoner to be. Similar examples abound in contemporary society. The death of Robert Dziekański in 2007, in which four armed police officers overpowered and killed an unarmed traveller, invokes the Hewell incident with eerie precision. A second troubling reflection of this dynamic is the death of teenager Ashley Smith in a Canadian correctional facility in 2007. Guards watched passively on video monitors as Smith strangled herself to death in her cell. These fatal acts of excess and negligence by authorities were rendered justifiable by the construction of these individuals as a "safety threat" or "disorderly." Such designations served to nullify both reason and caution with tragic consequences.

While historians have made inroads in understanding how race, class, and gender contributed to constructions of criminality, few have considered the specific role played by the penitentiary in forming these constructions. As the penitentiary became more sophisticated and engaged in early versions of a criminological science, its officers claimed expert knowledge about the criminal individual. Thus, an expert discourse arose within the penitentiary about which prisoners should be regarded as potentially violent or disruptive, which could be saved or reformed, and, as the twentieth century drew nearer, which might conceivably pose a threat to society once they were released. In spite of claims to specialized knowledge that allegedly made it possible to assess these qualities of character, however, the resulting distinctions often reflected, and thus sustained, the same structures of domination that underlay social divisions of race and class throughout Canadian society. Prison history can help us to identify the dynamics at work in the creation and reinforcement of broader social hierarchies, as well as to understand how constructions of criminality, in particular, were legitimated by new claims to professional criminological knowledge. Such an understanding is essential, given that the resulting categories did not exist solely in the realm of discourse and theory. Distinctions among types of prisoners played a significant role in the development of prison policy and therefore had an impact on how particular individuals experienced penitentiary life.

The effects of these constructions were also shaped by another central contradiction in the Canadian penitentiary. As David Garland argues, in spite of Victorian ambitions toward new criminological expertise and reform visions of evangelical reformations, the penitentiary in this era was often physically or materially incapable of delivering on such promises.[1] Nineteenth-century prisons were simply too bureaucratic and rigid to accommodate the individualist ambitions of reformers; they were designed specifically to treat every prisoner exactly alike. This shortcoming and the contradiction with reform ideas was just one of many particularities that characterized the Canadian penitentiary. In many senses, such realities demand that our attention to ideology and discourse be complemented by a renewed attention to economy, politics, and geography.

A POLITICAL ECONOMY OF PUNISHMENT?

Canadian prison history has paid too little attention to the importance of political economy in understandings of the modern penitentiary. It is indisputable that the penitentiary rose in direct relationship to industrial capitalism. This is evident in many different manifestations, from the prison architecture that resembled industrial factories to the sale of prison labour that integrated prisons with capital markets. Most importantly, the first penitentiaries were constructed on a plan that would harness the bonded labour of the unemployed for economic profit. This basic fact has been sorely neglected in spite of the enormous economic, political, and ideological effects it had on the development of penitentiaries in North America. In efforts to explore the ideological transformation from pre-modern to modern times, the basic influence of capital has been obscured to the point of invisibility. This has had a tremendously distorting effect on how the penitentiary is interpreted and perceived in contemporary society. When history views the penitentiary only as the product of humanitarian impulses, it will ask the wrong questions. Historians should more readily recognize that in addition to solving a humanitarian dilemma about the legitimacy of legal punishment, the penitentiary proposed a solution to the problem of labour supply. This was particularly true of the Northern states, which were the first to adopt the penitentiary, but the same pattern was repeated in the South after the Civil War as former Confederate states confronted their own threatening labour force in the form of recently freed slaves. In Upper Canada, the Tory aristocracy followed the American lead, because they were impressed not by the humanitarian depth of feeling their representatives witnessed in the Unites States but by the potential for profit.

As Rebecca McLennan notes, the subsequent failure of contractual penal servitude in almost every modern penitentiary has caused historians to underestimate the importance of the original economic basis of the penitentiary as an influence throughout the nineteenth century. In Canada, this failure was nearly immediate, but the lasting effect of the capitalist ideology touched every element of the evolution of the penitentiary throughout the nineteenth century. If we do not acknowledge the importance of the economics, we are also likely to miss the legacy of capital's early influence upon the penitentiary. In fact, it was folded into the penitentiary project in innumerable ways, affecting policy and ideology in ways that demand our attention. Although reformers did not acknowledge it, the capitalist foundations of the modern prison deeply affected the moral culture underpinning the reformation project, which was established on humanitarian and evangelical pretexts. They also played a deforming effect on constructions of criminality in which the unemployed were associated with the criminal underclass. In the reverse of this construction, the escape from criminality was premised on reintegration with the world of capital through productivity and self-sufficiency. As penitentiary medical records make clear, not all prisoners were up to this challenge. Finally, while few are prepared to admit that the prison sentence is little more than a unit of economic exchange, it is inescapable that the penitentiary evolved from the poorhouse and the debtors' prisons. Early capitalist society found it justifiable to affix an economic cost to criminal transgression, and this legacy has shaped every element of the modern penitentiary.

It is important to recognize the Canadian penitentiary as a central component of both local and national histories. A more fully realized political economy of punishment can help push Canadian prison history in this direction. What becomes almost immediately apparent is the importance of locality and geography. Throughout the nineteenth century, the penitentiary was an intensely local and insular institution. In the pre-Confederation era, this was underscored by the obvious fact that Kingston Penitentiary was the only institution of its kind in Canada. However, even after the creation of a federal penitentiary system in the 1870s, each institution remained largely isolated from the others and from hands-on federal control. By the time five federal institutions were in place in the 1880s, each penitentiary was marked by distinctions that were often more important than the weak glue provided by a federalist system, supposedly cementing in place a national penitentiary order. Moreover, for many decades after Confederation, Kingston continued to be the only federal prison that resembled "the modern penitentiary" as it was conceived in the model American institutions of the Northeast. When it came to the other federal penitentiaries, isolation and localism played a much larger role than justice officials were prepared to admit. This was often manifested in the absolute dismantling of reform ideas due to necessity or expediency. Economically, each penitentiary could not stand on common ground due to the disparate nature of markets in each jurisdiction. While Kingston and St. Vincent de Paul struggled to achieve economic viability in Ontario and Québec, any hope of financial self-sufficiency was nonexistent in western Canada. Seeing this gives a clearer picture of the economic health of each institution, but it also helps to reveal an unacknowledged human element. Imprisonment at Kingston Penitentiary would have been a very different experience than incarceration in Manitoba or British Columbia. Given the isolation, the dearth of available labour, and the often brutal living conditions, one might argue that prisoners in the West paid a higher cost than those inside Kingston's walls. There was nothing particularly modern about this discrepancy. For many decades, the federal penitentiary system laboured under the fallacy that it was maintaining a standard of punishment that was actually impossible. If historians can direct attention to the effects of these disparities, they will dispel the tendency to accept reform ideas at face value. It is a valuable reminder that many of the reform ideals of the modern penitentiary were mere lip service to an unattainable standard.

LOOKING THE PRISON IN THE EYE

In February 1969, Johnny Cash performed at San Quentin Prison outside of San Francisco. Cash's flagging career had been revitalized a year earlier by a live recording made at Folsom Prison, and by the time he appeared at San Quentin with his wife, June Carter Cash, and his touring band, he was the most successful country star in the world. Nearly one thousand prisoners jammed into the San Quentin cafeteria to watch the performance, among them some of the most dangerous criminals in the California penal system. A guard warned Cash, "Don't you dare look these men in the eyes. I'd suggest you and your family look just over their heads at the wall in the back of the room."[2] The fear of unrest during Cash's performance was underscored by a complement of one hundred guards armed with machine guns, some of them patrolling above the crowd on suspended catwalks.

Opening the show to thunderous applause, Cash ran through several of his hits before performing a song called *San Quentin*. He had written it the day before the show after visiting with some of the prisoners. It began,

> San Quentin, you've been living hell to me.
> You've blistered me since 1963
> I've seen 'em come and go and I've seen 'em die
> And long ago I stopped asking why.

The audience seemed shocked after the opening line, and then the men seized on the meaning of the verse and erupted in a startled exclamation. By the end of that verse, the audience realized exactly what Cash was singing about. After the first line of the second verse, "San Quentin, I hate every inch of you," the audience exploded in joyful agreement. The short song ended with the verse:

> San Quentin, may you rot and burn in hell
> May your walls fall and may I live to tell
> May all the world forget you ever stood
> And may all the world regret you did no good.
> San Quentin, I hate every inch of you.

The men roared their approval, crying out, "One more time! One more time!" Cash obliged them and played it again. It is easy to see why the song was the emotional high point of an already highly charged performance. When Johnny Cash called San Quentin the hell hole that it was, it gave the prisoners some form of redemption. Cash was like a missionary from both heaven and hell, connecting with the prisoners in a way that no other performer could have achieved. The redemption Cash offered to the prisoners at San Quentin, bigger than any song, was that he was interested in connecting in such a way in the first place. Cash's multiple visits to prisons throughout the 1960s demonstrated a political will to make a statement about prisons and their forgotten inmates. June Carter Cash recalled, "We had come to see the lost and lonely ones."[3] By playing for them and singing *about* them, Cash gave the prisoners at San Quentin a booming voice that was impossible without him.

The novelty of his interest in prisoners and the success of *Johnny Cash at San Quentin* was in part connected to wider social upheaval and unrest in which prison issues, for a short time, were pushed to the forefront of public consciousness. Cash's first visit to San Quentin in 1958 had been a more cheerful affair. By 1969 the mood surrounding penitentiaries, as with the rest of American society, had darkened considerably. Much of this tension came to a head in the Attica Prison riot in September 1971 in which thirty-nine people were killed. The death of Black Panther George Jackson, author of *Soledad Brother*, in an uprising at San Quentin in 1971 further engaged the American revolutionary left. Jackson's death sparked the rise of prison rights movements, calls for reform, decarceration, and the recognition of incarcerated criminals as political prisoners. Canada did not escape this tumultuous moment. A riot at Kingston Penitentiary in April 1971 lasted four days and left two prisoners dead. In France, Michel Foucault, already a respected chair at the Collège de France in Paris, became more deeply involved in the politics of prison reform. Following an uprising at the central prison in Tours, Foucault created the Groupe d'Information sur les Prisons (or GIP) in December 1971. GIP was interested in giving a voice to prisoners as a method of exposing the brutality of penitentiary systems in France. When Foucault announced the creation of GIP, he stated, "We propose to let people know what prisons are: who goes there, and how and why they go; what happens there; what the existence of prisoners is like, and also the existence of those providing surveillance; what the buildings, food and hygiene are like; how the inside rules, medical supervision and workshops function; how one gets out and what it is like in our society to be someone who does get out."[4] Although the GIP recorded some successes initially, the movement gradually gave way to its own revolutionary Prisoners Action Committee, who resented the involvement of "specialists in analysis" in the prisoners' rights movement. Foucault disbanded the movement and turned his attention to the writing of *Discipline and Punish*.

What can we learn from individuals who took an activist position against the penitentiary? For a brief moment coming out of the 1960s, there was sustained interest in the apparent dysfunction of penitentiaries in Western society. Other academic historians, among them David Rothman and Michael Ignatieff, wrote revisionist histories in the 1970s that detailed the structural and ideological origins of punishment. Even though reaction to the explosive events of the 1960s suggested the possibilities of reform or an alternative, this potential ran headlong into an emerging era in which socially conservative movements came to dominate justice agendas and discussions about crime control. While it appears that the moment to seize upon change has passed, there is still value in the struggle. New research into prison history can successfully assume the task undertaken by Johnny Cash, Michel Foucault, George Jackson, Leonard Peltier, and countless others who questioned the penitentiary in real terms and refused to accept its oppressions as inevitable.

Notes

INTRODUCTION

1   Brown Commission, *Reports of the Commissioners Appointed
    to Enquire into the Conduct, Discipline and Management of the
    Provincial Penitentiary*, 202.
2   Ibid.
3   I refer here to the first wave of "revisionist" prison histories that
    emerged in the fields of British and American history in the
    1970s. They include David Rothman, *The Discovery of the Asylum:
    Social Order and Disorder in the New Republic* and *Conscience
    and Convenience: The Asylum and Its Alternatives in Progressive
    America*, and Michael Ignatieff, *A Just Measure of Pain: The
    Penitentiary in the Industrial Revolution, 1750–1850*.
4   See Douglas Hay et al., eds., *Albion's Fatal Tree: Crime and Society
    in Eighteenth-Century England*.
5   E. P. Thompson, *The Making of the English Working Class*, 8–9.
6   "Reformation" was the standard expression in the nineteenth
    century. In the twentieth century, the more common term was
    "rehabilitation," a word that rarely appeared in reform writing
    prior to 1900.
7   H. Clare Pentland, *Labour and Capital in Canada, 1650–1860*, xlv.
8   Karl Marx, *Economic and Philosophic Manuscripts of 1844*, 120–21
    (italics in original).
9   Among many others, see Stanley B. Ryerson, *Unequal Union:
    Confederation and the Roots of Conflict in the Canadas, 1815–1873*;

Stephan Thernstrom, *Poverty and Progress: Social Mobility in a Nineteenth-Century City*; Louis Chevalier, *Laboring Classes and Dangerous Classes in Paris During the First Half of the Nineteenth Century*; Lydia Morris, *Dangerous Classes: The Underclass and Social Citizenship*; John Welshman, *Underclass: A History of the Excluded, 1880–2000*; and Martina L. Hardwick, "Segregating and Reforming the Marginal: The Institution and Everyday Resistance in Mid-Nineteenth-Century Ontario."

10   Some key examples of penitentiary history that accomplish this are Ivan Jankovic, "Labour Market and Imprisonment"; Dario Melossi and M. Pavarini, *The Prison and the Factory: Origins of the Penitentiary System*; Martin B. Miller, "Sinking Gradually into the Proletariat: The Emergence of the Penitentiary in the United States"; Martin B. Miller, "At Hard Labor: Rediscovering the Nineteenth-Century Prison"; and Rosalind P. Petchesky, "At Hard Labor: Penal Confinement and Production in Nineteenth-Century America."

11   See D. Owen Carrigan, *Crime and Punishment in Canada: A History*; Peter Oliver, *"Terror to Evil-Doers": Prisons and Punishments in Nineteenth-Century Ontario*; Donald J. McMahon, "Law and Public Authority: Sir John Beverley Robinson and the Purposes of the Criminal Law"; J. M. Beattie, *Attitudes Towards Crime and Punishment in Upper Canada, 1830–1850: A Documentary Study*; and Russell Smandych, "Beware of the 'Evil American Monster': Upper Canadian Views on the Need for a Penitentiary, 1830–1834" and "Tory Paternalism and the Politics of Penal Reform in Upper Canada, 1830–1834: A 'Neo-Revisionist' Account of the Kingston Penitentiary."

12   This is an argument first advanced by Pieter Spierenburg, who identified responses to poverty in the early 1500s as the ancestor of modern confinement. Pieter Spierenburg, *The Prison Experience: Disciplinary Institutions and Their Inmates in Early Modern Europe*.

13   Originally published in 1939, Rusche and Kirchheimer's study was reissued in 1968 and exerted considerable influence on certain revisionist interpretations of punishment, among them Jankovic, "Labour Market and Imprisonment," and Melossi and Pavarini, *The Prison and the Factory*.

14   See Gertrude Himmelfarb, *The Idea of Poverty: England in the Early Industrial Age*. See also Martin Weiner, *Reconstructing the Criminal: Culture, Law, and Policy in England, 1830–1914*.

15   Foucault, *Discipline and Punish*; Ignatieff, *A Just Measure of Pain*.

16   See Peter Hennessy, *Canada's Big House: The Dark History of the Kingston Penitentiary*; William Calder, "The Federal Penitentiary System in Canada, 1867–1899: A Social and Institutional History"; and William Norman, "A Chapter of Canadian Penal

History: The Early Years of the Provincial Penitentiary at Kingston and the Commission of Inquiry into Its Management, 1835–1851."

17 See John Alexander Edmison, "Some Aspects of Nineteenth-Century Canadian Prisons"; Beattie, *Attitudes Towards Crime and Punishment*; Oliver, *"Terror to Evil-Doers"*; and Michael Jackson, *Prisoners of Isolation: Solitary Confinement in Canada*.

18 David Garland, *Punishment and Welfare: A History of Penal Strategies*, 14.

19 Among many others, two useful interpretations of Foucault's *Discipline and Punish* are David Garland, *Punishment and Modern Society: A Study in Social Theory*, 131–77, and Adrian Howe, *Punish and Critique: Towards a Feminist Analysis of Penality*, 82–123.

20 Michel Foucault, "The Subject and Power," 326. A distinctly Foucauldian analysis of Canadian penitentiary history can be found in Roger Neufeld, "A World Within Itself: Kingston Penitentiary and Foucauldian Panopticism, 1834–1914."

21 Insights on masculinity are drawn from, among others, R. W. Connell, *Masculinities*; Don Sabo, Terry A. Kupers, and Willie London, eds., *Prison Masculinities*; David Morgan, "Class and Masculinity"; and James W. Messerschmidt, *Masculinity and Crime: Critique and Reconceptualization of Theory*.

22 Foucault, "Interview with Michel Foucault," 294.

23 Peter Linebaugh, *The London Hanged: Crime and Civil Society in the Eighteenth Century*.

24 See also James C. Scott, *Domination and the Arts of Resistance: Hidden Transcripts*.

ONE   LABOUR

1 Edward M. Peters, "Prison Before the Prison: The Ancient and Medieval Worlds," 14–16.

2 Ibid., 16–18.

3 Peters argues that what we know of confinement in this period stems from narratives telling of the liberation of prisoners by Frankish saints such as Gaul, Eparchius, and Eligius. For example, the narrative of St. Eligius notes that when the saint approached a prison in Bourges, the gates opened miraculously, and the prisoner's chains fell off. Ibid., 24.

4 Ibid., 26–28.

5 Pieter Spierenburg, "The Body and the State: Early Modern Europe."

6 Torsten Eriksson, *The Reformers. An Historical Survey of Pioneer Experiments in the Treatment of Criminals*, 9.

7 Max Grünhut, *Penal Reform: A Comparative Study*, 18.

8 Norman Longmate, *The Workhouse*, 25.

9 Michael Ignatieff, *A Just Measure of Pain: The Penitentiary in the Industrial Revolution, 1750–1850*, 47.

10 This idea is explored at length in Douglas Hay et al., eds. *Albion's Fatal Tree: Crime and Society in Eighteenth-Century England.*

11 Randall McGowen, "The Well-Ordered Prison: England, 1780–1865," 76.

12 Ignatieff, *A Just Measure of Pain*, 48.

13 Eriksson, *The Reformers*, 13–15.

14 Quoted in Ignatieff, *A Just Measure of Pain*, 93.

15 McGowen, "The Well-Ordered Prison," 78–79.

16 Cesare Beccaria's notions of crime, and punishment were detailed in a 1764 treatise that was widely celebrated in Europe, England, and America for its rational approach to the law. Cesare Beccaria, *On Crimes and Punishment and Other Writings.*

17 W. David Lewis, *From Newgate to Dannemora: The Rise of the Penitentiary in New York, 1796–1848*, 109.

18 David Rothman, *The Discovery of the Asylum: Social Order and Disorder in the New Republic*, 92.

19 The phrase "contractual penal servitude" is drawn from Rebecca McLennan's interpretation of American penal reform. My analysis is indebted to her characterization of the development of the Auburn system and its development of contract labour. See Rebecca M. McLennan, *The Crisis of Imprisonment: Protest, Politics, and the Making of the American Penal State, 1776–1941*, 53–87.

20 Ibid., 57.

21 Ibid., 63.

22 Ibid., 63–70.

23 Rosalind P. Petchesky, "At Hard Labor: Penal Confinement and Production in Nineteenth-Century America," 589.

24 Ibid., 601.

25 "Report of a Select Committee on the Expediency of Erecting a Penitentiary," *Appendix to the Journal of the House of Assembly of Upper Canada*, 1831, 211–12.

26 See *An Act for Building a Gaol and Court House in Every District Within This Province, and for Altering the Names of Said Districts*, Statutes of the Province of Upper Canada, 1792, c. 8. The statute notes that "such buildings are manifestly necessary for the regular administration of justice, and the due execution of the laws."

27 See Peter Oliver, *"Terror to Evil-Doers": Prisons and Punishments in Nineteenth-Century Ontario*, 7–9.

28 *Act to Declare the Common Gaols to Be Houses of Correction for Certain Purposes*, Statutes of the Province of Upper Canada, 1810, c. 5; Oliver, *"Terror to Evil-Doers,"* 9.

29   This view of the motivation for an early Canadian penitentiary
      is drawn from Tom Brown, "The Origins of the Asylum in Upper
      Canada, 1830–1839," and Russell Smandych, "Beware of the 'Evil
      American Monster': Upper Canadian Views on the Need for a
      Penitentiary, 1830–1834."
30   "Report of a Select Committee," 212.
31   Rothman, *The Discovery of the Asylum*, 81.
32   Canada, *Report of the Commissioners Appointed to Superintend the
      Erection of a Penitentiary in Kingston*, 1.
33   Richard Splane, *Social Welfare in Ontario, 1791–1893: A Study of
      Public Welfare Administration*, 129–30.
34   Lewis, *From Newgate to Dannemora*, 2–5.
35   Georg Rusche and Otto Kirchheimer, *Punishment and Social
      Structure*, 36–42; Jennifer Graber, "'When Friends Had the
      Management It Was Entirely Different': Quakers and Calvinists
      in the Making of New York Prison Discipline"; Mark Colvin,
      *Penitentiaries, Reformatories and Chain Gangs: Social Theory and
      the History of Punishment in Nineteenth-Century America*, 47–71.
36   Colvin, *Penitentiaries, Reformatories and Chain Gangs*, 45.
37   On the early life and reform efforts of Thomas Eddy, see Lewis,
      From Newgate to Dannemora, 29–54, and Raymond A. Mohl,
      "Humanitarianism in the Preindustrial City: The New York
      Society for the Prevention of Pauperism, 1817–1823."
38   Quoted in McLennan, *The Crisis of Imprisonment*, 54.
39   Lewis, *From Newgate to Dannemora*, 79–84.
40   McLennan, *The Crisis of Imprisonment*, 72.
41   Ibid., 78.
42   Ibid., 80.
43   Bryan D. Palmer, "Kingston Mechanics and the Rise of the
      Penitentiary, 1833–36," 10.
44   Ibid., 13.
45   Ibid.
46   On "producer ideology," see Bryan D. Palmer, *A Culture in Conflict:
      Skilled Workers and Industrial Capitalism in Hamilton, Ontario
      1860–1914*, 97–122. See also Daniel T. Rodgers, *The Work Ethic in
      Industrial America*.
47   "Report of the Board of Inspectors of the Provincial Penitentiary
      for 1838," *Appendix to the Journal of the House of Assembly of Upper
      Canada*, 1839, 205.
48   Ibid.
49   Christopher R. Adamson, "Hard Labor: The Form and Function of
      Imprisonment in Nineteenth-Century America," 92.
50   Oliver, *"Terror to Evil-Doers,"* 151.
51   "Annual Report, Provincial Penitentiary," *Journals of the Legislative
      Council of the Province of Canada*, 1841, Appendix No. 14, 337.
52   Ibid.

53   Brown Commission, *Reports of the Commissioners Appointed to Enquire into the Conduct, Discipline and Management of the Provincial Penitentiary*, 157.

54   The convict population increased nearly tenfold in the first fifteen years, from fifty-five convicts when Kingston opened in 1835 to nearly five hundred by 1848.

55   Palmer, "Kingston Mechanics," 17.

56   McLennan, *The Crisis of Imprisonment*, 60.

57   Lewis, *From Newgate to Dannemora*, 63.

58   Colvin, *Penitentiaries, Reformatories and Chain Gangs*, 94.

59   Both quoted in Rothman, *The Discovery of the Asylum*, 101.

60   McLennan, *The Crisis of Imprisonment*, 54.

61   Norman notes that Smith was also the beneficiary of his son's increasing political influence in Kingston politics. Henry Smith Jr. was elected as the member for Frontenac in 1841. See William Norman, "A Chapter of Canadian Penal History: The Early Years of the Provincial Penitentiary at Kingston and the Commission of Inquiry into Its Management, 1835–1851," 5–35, esp. 33; Oliver, *"Terror to Evil-Doers,"* 156–57.

62   Oliver, *"Terror to Evil-Doers,"* 158.

63   Ibid., 163.

64   *The Globe*, 4 November 1846.

65   The other commissioners were politicians Adam Fergusson and Narcisse Amiot; E. Cartwright-Thomas, the sheriff of the Gore district; and journalist William Bristow.

66   Drawn from a description in *The Globe*, 7 January 1871.

67   See Steven Mintz, *Huck's Raft: A History of American Childhood*; Neil Sutherland, *Children in English-Canadian Society: Framing the Twentieth-Century Consensus*; and Hugh Cunningham, *The Children of the Poor: Representations of Childhood Since the Seventeenth Century*.

68   Mintz, *Huck's Raft*, 134–36.

69   Oliver, *"Terror to Evil-Doers,"* 245–46.

70   Oliver notes that in 1856, a typical year, the proceeds from contract labour at Kingston were £10,228 while the total cost of running the penitentiary was £24,773. Ibid., 254.

71   Ibid., 250–55.

72   "Second Annual Report of the Inspector of Penitentiaries of the Dominion of Canada for the Year 1876," *Sessional Papers*, 1877, no. 15, 15.

73   H. Clare Pentland, *Labour and Capital in Canada, 1650–1860*, 19–20.

74   Ibid.

75   "Warden's Annual Report, Dorchester Penitentiary," *Sessional Papers*, 1888, no. 11, 50.

76   "Report of the Inspector of Penitentiaries for the Fiscal Year 1895–96," *Sessional Papers*, 1897, no. 18, 5.

77 Prisoners picked apart oakum, or tarred ships' ropes, by hand to "recycle" the fibers. Victorian prisoners described it as a dirty, distressing, and difficult occupation with no real vocational or economic benefit to the penitentiary. Philip Priestley, *Victorian Prison Lives: English Prison Biography, 1830–1914*, 122.

78 "Fourth Annual Report of the Directors of Penitentiaries of the Dominion of Canada for the Year 1871," *Sessional Papers*, 1872, no. 27, 2.

79 "First Annual Report of the Inspector of Penitentiaries of the Dominion of Canada for the Year 1875," *Sessional Papers*, 1876, no. 14, 9.

80 "Second Annual Report of the Inspector of Penitentiaries," 12.

81 "Fourth Annual Report of the Inspector of Penitentiaries of the Dominion of Canada for the Year 1879," *Sessional Papers*, 1880, no. 17, 7.

82 "Tenth Annual Report of the Inspector of Penitentiaries of theDominion of Canada for the Year Ended 30th June 1885," *Sessional Papers*, 1886, no. 15, xv.

TWO   REFORM

1 *Act for the Better Management of the Provincial Penitentiary* (1851), Provincial Statutes of Canada, 14 and 15 Vict., c. 2, s. xv. Similarly, in the warden's absence, it would be the duty of the deputy warden "frequently to visit the Shops, Yards, Hospital Cells, and other apartments, taking every precaution for the security of the Prison and the Prisoners" (s. xvi), thereby making his presence felt throughout the institution.

2 Ibid., s. ix.

3 Ibid., s. xvii.

4 John Beswarick Thomson, "Wolfred Nelson," *Dictionary of Canadian Biography Online* 1861–1870, vol. 9, 2000, http://bit.ly/cM3ybp.

5 Quoted in Robert Christie, *A History of the Late Province of Lower Canada, Parliamentary and Political from the Commencement to the Close of Its Existence as a Separate Province*, 241.

6 "A General Review of Prison Economics," *Journals of the Legislative Assembly of the Province of Canada* (1852), Appendix H.H, 105.

7 Ibid., 105, 110.

8 Thomson, "Wolfred Nelson."

9 "A General Review of Prison Economics," 107.

10 Joshua Jebb, "The Convict Question in 1856," xxvi.

11 J. K. Johnson, "Donald Aeneas MacDonell," *Dictionary of Canadian Biography Online*, 1871–1880, vol. 10, 2000, http://bit.ly/9MROZR.

12   Peter Oliver, *"Terror to Evil-Doers": Prisons and Punishments in Nineteenth-Century Ontario*, 227.

13   Ibid., 215–16.

14   "Angus MacDonell to the Inspectors of the Provincial Penitentiary," *Appendix to the Eleventh Volume of the Journals of the Legislative Assembly of the Province of Canada*, 1853, 132.

15   "Inspector's Report." *Journals of the Legislative Assembly of the Province of Canada* (1853), Appendix I.I.I., 104.

16   Quoted in ibid, 105.

17   Quoted in ibid, 113.

18   M. F. G. Selby, "Maconochie, Alexander (1787–1860)," in *Oxford Dictionary of National Biography*, online ed., ed. Lawrence Goldman, October 2007, http://www.oxforddnb.com/view/article/37725.

19   Torsten Eriksson, *The Reformers: An Historical Survey of Pioneer Experiments in the Treatment of Criminals*, 86–88. See also Norval Morris, *Maconochie's Gentlemen: The Story of Norfolk Island and the Roots of Modern Prison Reform*. Morris's account is a fictional retelling of the Norfolk Island experiment but contains an accurate historical description of Maconochie and his experiments in the penal colony.

20   Selby, "Maconochie, Alexander."

21   Alexander Maconochie, *Crime and Punishment. The Mark System: Framed to Mix Persuasion with Punishment, and Make Their Effect Improving, yet Their Operation Severe*, 1.

22   Ibid., 24.

23   Quoted in Martin J. Weiner, *Reconstructing the Criminal: Culture, Law, and Policy in England, 1830–1914*, 114–15.

24   Ibid., 41.

25   Lawrence Goldman, "Crofton, Sir Walter Frederick (1815–1897)," *Oxford Dictionary of National Biography*, online ed., ed. Lawrence Goldman, October 2007, http://www.oxforddnb.com/view/article/65325.

26   In 1864 Crofton proudly noted that Maconochie had lived to see his idea put into practice in the Irish system. "Address by the Chairman, Sir Walter Crofton," *Transactions of the National Association for the Promotion of Social Science, New York Meeting 1864* (London, 1865), 228.

27   Oliver, *"Terror to Evil-Doers,"* 285; Richard B. Splane, *Social Welfare in Ontario, 1791–1893: A Study of Public Welfare Administration*, 39.

28   "Memorandum on the Provincial Penitentiary," *Sessional Papers*, 1862, no. 19, 9.

29   The term "reformatory prison discipline" was coined by Mary Carpenter, who discussed the Crofton system in her 1865 book, *Our Convicts*. In 1872 Carpenter wrote *Reformatory Prison Discipline, as Developed by the Rt. Hon. Sir Walter Crofton, in the Irish Convict Prisons*, which was essentially a summary of the system

as described by Crofton in an 1862 meeting of the Social Science Association.

30 "Memorandum on the Provincial Penitentiary," 1862, 9.

31 See E. C. Wines amd Theodore W. Dwight, *Report of the Prisons and Reformatories of the United States and Canada Made to the Legislature of New York, January, 1867.*

32 "Principles of Prison Discipline," in *Transactions of the National Congress on Penitentiary and Reformatory Discipline Held at Cincinnati, Ohio, October 12–18, 1870.*

33 "General Remarks on the Discipline Necessary to Be Carried Out in the Provincial Penitentiary of Canada," *Sessional Papers,* 1864, no. 39, 99.

34 Ibid.

35 Jonathan Swainger, *The Canadian Department of Justice and the Completion of Confederation, 1867–78,* 81.

36 On the early history of Lower Fort Garry as a penal institution, see Philip Goldring, *The Penitentiary Building, Lower Fort Garry.*

37 Donald G. Wetherell, "Rehabilitation Programmes in Canadian Penitentiaries, 1867–1914: A Study of Official Opinion," 2–3.

38 Ibid., 83–84.

39 Peter Oliver, "Meredith, Edmund Allen," *Dictionary of Canadian Biography Online,* 1891–1900, vol. 12, 2000, http://bit.ly/dtoPzt.

40 "Third Annual Report of the Directors of Penitentiaries of Dominion of Canada for the Year 1870," *Sessional Papers,* 1871, no. 60, 1.

41 "Sixth Annual Report of the Directors of Penitentiaries of the Dominion of Canada for the Year 1873," *Sessional Papers,* 1874, no. 42, 3.

42 Quoted in ibid.

43 Quoted in "Seventh Annual Report of the Directors of Penitentiaries of the Dominion of Canada, for the Year 1874," *Sessional Papers,* 1875, no. 87, 6.

44 Estelle B. Freedman, *Their Sisters' Keepers: Women's Prison Reform in America, 1830–1930,* 20–22. See also Nicole Hahn Rafter, *Partial Justice: Women in State Prisons, 1800–1935.*

45 Lucia Zedner, *Women, Crime, and Custody in Victorian England,* 113–20.

46 R. W. Emerson, W. H. Channing, and J. F. Clarke, *Memoirs of Margaret Fuller Ossoli,* vol. 2, 146, 147.

47 See Freedman, *Their Sisters' Keepers,* 30–31.

48 Zedner, *Women, Crime, and Custody,* 119–20.

49 Oliver, *"Terror to Evil-Doers,"* 240.

50 "Annual Report of the Provincial Penitentiary for the Year 1858," 6–7.

51 Peter Oliver, "James George Moylan," *Dictionary of Canadian Biography Online,* 1901–1910, vol. 13, 2000, http://bit.ly/c181za.

52 "First Annual Report of the Inspector of Penitentiaries," 6.

53 "Second Annual Report of the Inspector of Penitentiaries of the Dominion of Canada, for the Year 1876," *Sessional Papers*, 1877, no. 15, 8.

54 "Sixth Annual Report of the Inspector of Penitentiaries of the Dominion of Canada for the Year Ended 30th June 1881," *Sessional Papers*, 1882, no. 12, viii.

55 "Nineteenth Annual Report of the Inspector of Penitentiaries of the Dominion of Canada for the Year Ended 30th June 1894," *Sessional Papers*, 1895, no. 18, xi–xxii.

56 Ibid.

THREE   CRIMINALITY

1 Susanna Moodie, *Life in the Clearings Versus the Bush*, 193.

2 "Second Annual Report of the Inspector of Penitentiaries of the Dominion of Canada, for the Year 1876," *Sessional Papers*, 1877, no. 15, 15.

3 Stephen Pfhol, *Images of Deviance and Social Control: A Sociological History*, 55–58.

4 See David Rothman, *The Discovery of the Asylum: Social Order and Disorder in the New Republic*, 60–64.

5 See Ian Taylor, Paul Walton, and Jock Young, *The New Criminology: For a Social Theory of Deviance*, 10–20.

6 Ibid., 7.

7 Paul Rock, "Caesare Lombroso as a Signal Criminologist," 120.

8 Martin J. Weiner, *Reconstructing the Criminal: Culture, Law, and Policy in England, 1830–1914*, 10.

9 David Garland, *Punishment and Welfare: A History of Penal Strategies*, 14.

10 Max Grünhut, *Penal Reform: A Comparative Study*, 60.

11 Rothman, *The Discovery of the Asylum*, 64, 65.

12 *Kingston Chronicle and Gazette*, 5 September 1835, quoted in J. M. Beattie, *Attitudes Towards Crime and Punishment in Upper Canada, 1830–1850: A Documentary Study*, 38.

13 "Kingston Penitentiary Annual Report," *Appendix to the Eleventh Volume of the Journals of the Legislative Assembly of the Province of Canada*, 1853, Appendix I.I.I., 72.

14 Ibid., 74.

15 "Preliminary Report of the Board of Inspectors of Asylums, Prisons, &c., 1859," *Sessional Papers*, 1860, no. 32, 17.

16 "Provincial Penitentiary," *Appendix to the Thirteenth Volume of the Journals of the Legislative Assembly of the Province of Canada*, 1855, Appendix D.D., 1854.

17 *Canadian Temperance Advocate* 10, no. 21 (1844): 324.

18   "Protestant Chaplain's Report, British Columbia Penitentiary,"
      Sessional Papers, 1887, no. 4, 100.
19   Weiner, *Reconstructing the Criminal*, 10.
20   "Preliminary Report of the Board of Inspectors of Asylums,
      Prisons, &c., 1859," 81.
21   "Report of the Inspector of Penitentiaries for the Fiscal Year
      1895–1896," *Sessional Papers*, 1897, no. 18, 5.
22   "Annual Report of the Provincial Penitentiary for the Year 1858,"
      *Appendix to the Seventeenth Volume of the Journals of the Legislative
      Assembly of the Province of Canada*, 1859, Appendix No. 29.
23   In these totals, I count labourers, carpenters, cigar workers, and
      painters. In later years, the unknown variable is often female
      convicts, who are usually listed without trades, the assumption
      being that they worked only at domestic labour. Even employed
      women, particularly seamstresses or factory workers, in later
      years of the nineteenth century were recorded without trades.
24   "Crime Statistics, Kingston Penitentiary," *Sessional Papers*, 1895,
      no. 18, 81–82.
25   "Report of the Board of Inspectors of the Provincial Penitentiary
      for 1838," *Appendix to the Journal of the House of Assembly of Upper
      Canada*, 1839, 62.
26   Cited in Peter Oliver, *"Terror to Evil-Doers": Prisons and
      Punishment in Nineteenth-Century Ontario*, 228–29.
27   "Report of the Board of Inspectors of the Provincial Penitentiary
      for 1838."
28   W. David Lewis, *From Newgate to Dannemora: The Rise of the
      Penitentiary in New York, 1796–1848*, 113.
29   "Report of the Inspector of Penitentiaries for the Fiscal Year
      1895–1896," *Sessional Papers*, 1897, no. 18, 12.
30   Weiner, *Reconstructing the Criminal*, 148–49.
31   Ibid.
32   "Second Annual Report of the Inspector of Penitentiaries for
      the Year 1876," 13. Moylan's suggestion was to appoint a special
      officer to "make himself thoroughly acquainted with the convicts
      in these institutions" so that he could visit each gaol prior to
      the quarterly assize and identify individuals who were former
      convicts awaiting trial. This way judges could assign harsher
      sentences to recidivists.
33   "Fourteenth Annual Report of the Inspector of Penitentiaries
      of the Dominion of Canada for the Year Ended 30th June 1889,"
      Sessional Papers, 1890, no. 10, xii.
34   "Warden's Report, Dorchester Penitentiary," *Sessional Papers*,
      1897, no. 18, 27.
35   "Third Annual Report of the Directors of Penitentiaries of the
      Dominion of Canada for the Year 1870," *Sessional Papers*, 1871,
      no. 60, 9.

36 "Third Annual Report of the Inspector of Penitentiaries of the Dominion of Canada for the Year 1878," *Sessional Papers,* 1879, no. 27, 6.

37 "Twelfth Annual Report of the Inspector of Penitentiaries of the Dominion of Canada for the Year Ended 30th June 1887," *Sessional Papers,* 1888, no. 11, xiii.

38 Quoted in Louis Chevalier, *Laboring Classes and Dangerous Classes in Paris During the First Half of the Nineteenth Century,* 90.

39 Ibid., 63–140.

40 Ibid., 369.

41 Ibid., 365.

42 John Welshman, *Underclass: A History of the Excluded, 1880–2000,* 5.

43 Gertrude Himmelfarb, *The Idea of Poverty: England in the Early Industrial Age,* 12.

44 Mary Carpenter, *Reformatory Schools for the Children of the Perishing and Dangerous Classes and for Juvenile Offenders,* 3.

45 Ibid., 203.

46 Quoted in Lydia Morris, *Dangerous Classes: The Underclass and Social Citizenship,* 18.

47 Gareth Stedman Jones, *Outcast London: A Study in the Relationship Between Classes in Victorian Society,* 262.

48 *Canadian Temperance Advocate* 14, no. 18 (September 1848): 275.

49 *New York Times,* 17 June 1865.

50 Charles Loring Brace, *The Dangerous Classes of New York and Twenty Years' Work Among Them,* ii.

51 Ibid.

52 Ibid., 29.

53 Jeffrey Adler, "The Dynamite, Wreckage, and Scum in Our Cities: The Social Construction of Deviance in Industrial America."

54 The exact number of deaths is not clear, but 120 is the number suggested in James M. McPherson, *Ordeal by Fire: The Civil War and Reconstruction,* 29.

55 Karl Marx and Friedrich Engels, *Manifesto of the Communist Party,* 20.

56 Charles Booth, ed., *Labour and Life of the People,* vol. 1: *East London,* 37, 38.

57 Ibid., 38.

58 "Annual Report of the Lazaretto, Tracadie, N.B.," *Sessional Papers,* 1885, no. 8, 236.

59 *Canadian Magazine* 1, no. 7 (September 1893): 528.

60 "Statement of Knights of Labor L.A. No. 3,017, Nanaimo, B.C.," *Sessional Papers,* 1885, no. 54a, 155.

61 "Report of the Department of the Interior," *Sessional Papers,* 1882, no. 18, 10.

62 Lucia Zedner, *Women, Crime, and Custody in Victorian England,* 15.

63   Ibid., 16.

64   "Preliminary Report of the Board of Inspectors of Asylums, Prisons &c., 1859," 32.

65   Henry Mayhew and John Binney, *The Criminal Prisons of London and Scenes of Prison Life*, 464.

66   Mary Carpenter, *Our Convicts*, vol. 1 (London: Longman, Green, Longman, Roberts and Green, 1864), 31–32.

67   Mary Carpenter, *Reformatory Prison Discipline, as Developed by the Rt. Hon. Sir Walter Crofton, in the Irish Convict Prisons*, 68.

68   Brown Commission, *Reports of the Commissioners Appointed to Enquire Into the Conduct, Discipline and Management of the Provincial Penitentiary*, 136.

69   On Irvine's case, see Oliver, *"Terror to Evil-Doers,"* 239.

70   Ibid.

71   "Kingston Penitentiary Annual Report," 1852.

72   Kingston Penitentiary, "Prisoners' Record Book," 1843–90, RG13, D-1, vol. 1047, reel T-2044, Library and Archives Canada (hereafter LAC).

73   Moodie, *Life in the Clearings Versus the Bush*, 216.

74   Ibid., 232.

75   "Sixteenth Annual Report of the Inspector of Penitentiaries of the Dominion of Canada for the Year Ended 30th June 1891," *Sessional Papers*, 1892, no. 18, vii.

76   Kingston Penitentiary, "Prisoners' Record Book," 1843–90.

77   "Return of Work Done in Female Prison, Kingston Penitentiary," *Sessional Papers*, 1898, no. 18, 69; "Return of Work Done in Female Prison, Dorchester Penitentiary," *Sessional Papers*, 1898, no. 18, 70.

78   *Panis* (possibly a corruption of "Pawnee") slaves were members of First Nations bands, most commonly ones who had been captured in battle by rival nations. They were sometimes traded or sold to colonial administrators or to white settlers.

79   *Journal of the House of Assembly of Lower Canada from the 28th March to the 3rd June, 1799* (Quebec: John Neilson, 1799), 126.

80   Ibid., 122.

81   Ibid., 128.

82   *Appendix to the Second Volume of the Journals of the Legislative Assembly of the Province of Canada: Session 1842*, Appendix S. This case is similar to the events involving John Anderson, an escaped slave who was captured in Canada in Simcoe County. See Patrick Brode, *The Odyssey of John Anderson*.

83   "Chaplain's Report, 6th October 1837," *Appendix to the Journal of the House of Assembly of Upper Canada*, 1837, 207.

84   Robin Winks, *The Blacks in Canada: A History*, 249.

85   "The Chaplain's Report," *Appendix to the First Volume of the Journals of the Legislative Assembly of Upper Canada*, 1841, Appendix M, 30.

86   Winks, *The Blacks in Canada*, 249–50. Winks also notes that anti-slavery organizations attributed such attitudes and rising prejudice primarily to four main groups: American-born settlers, former West Indies planters, Irish settlers, and the working poor, who competed with blacks for subsistence labour. See also Frank Mackey, *Done with Slavery: The Black Fact in Montreal, 1760–1840*.

87   "Provincial Penitentiary, Annual Report," *Appendix to the Twelfth Volume of the Journals of the Legislative Assembly of the Province of Canada, 1853*, Appendix H.H.

88   "Warden's Report for 1857," *Appendix to the Seventeenth Volume of the Journals of the Legislative Assembly of the Province of Canada, 1858*, no. 11.

89   Christopher R. Adamson, "Punishment After Slavery: Southern State Penal Systems, 1865–1890."

90   Ibid., 556.

91   Winks, *The Blacks in Canada*, 251.

92   "Kingston Penitentiary Annual Report," 1852, 27.

93   *Kingston News*, 9 October 1896.

94   "Eighth Annual Report of the Inspector of Penitentiaries of the Dominion of Canada for the Year Ended 30th June 1883," *Sessional Papers*, 1884, no. 16, xxii.

95   Ibid.

96   Adamson, "Punishment After Slavery," 555–59.

97   The commercialization of the buffalo trade from Red River since the early 1800s had also altered the economy of the Canadian prairies. By mid-century, Cree hunters had begun to notice the increasing scarcity of buffalo, and, by the 1870s, the Cree, Blackfoot, and Blood were aware that buffalo had stopped migrating north of the forty-ninth parallel. The very real prospect of starvation among the Blackfoot and Cree people, in combination with massive population loss from diseases such as smallpox, convinced many First Nations leaders that a crisis existed and that treaties with the government, which promised annuities, agricultural implements and training, and access to health care, would provide future security. The Canadian government, under John A. Macdonald, was eager to secure treaties because the land that would be surrendered in return was essential to its plan to open the West to economic development and white settlement. The first eight numbered treaties were signed between 1871 and 1899 and covered most of western Canada, excluding British Columbia. For an excellent overview, see Sarah Carter, *Aboriginal People and Colonizers of Western Canada to 1900*, and, on the numbered treaties, Jill St. Germain, *Indian Treaty-Making Policy in the United States and Canada, 1867–1877*.

98   Brian Hubner, "Horse Stealing and the Borderline: The NWMP and the Control of Indian Movement," 47. See also Roderick C.

Macleod, "The North-West Mounted Police, 1873–1905: Law Enforcement and the Social Order in the Canadian North-West"; John Milloy, *The Plains Cree: Trade Diplomacy and War, 1790–1870*; and John C. Ewers, *The Horse in Blackfoot Indian Culture*.

99 Stony Mountain Penitentiary, "Inmate Admittance Registers," RG73, C-7, acc. W87–88/365, reel T-11089 (1871–85), LAC.

100 "Warden's Annual Report, Manitoba Penitentiary," *Sessional Papers*, 1878, no. 12, 127.

101 Hubner, "Horse Stealing and the Borderline," 62.

102 Stony Mountain Penitentiary, "Inmate Admittance Registers," 1871–85.

103 "Commissioner's Annual Report, NWMP," *Sessional Papers*, 1884, no. 12, 18–19.

104 "Return Showing Movement of Prisoners in Manitoba Penitentiary, from 1st July, 1882, to 30th June, 1883," *Sessional Papers*, 1884, no. 16, 98.

105 These included two convictions for larceny, shooting with intent to bodily harm, rape, felony, and two convictions for assault. Stony Mountain Penitentiary, "Inmate Admittance Registers," 1871–85.

106 Rod Macleod and Heather Rollason, "Restrain the Lawless Savages: Native Defendants in Criminal Courts in the North West Territories, 1878–1885."

107 J. A. Macdonald to E. Dewdney, 23 February 1885, box 2, file 38, 546–47, Dewdney Papers, Glenbow Archives.

108 See G. F. G. Stanley, *The Birth of Western Canada: A History of the Riel Rebellions*; John L. Tobias, "Canada's Subjugation of the Plains Cree, 1879–1885"; and Blair Stonechild and Bill Waiser, *Loyal till Death: Indians and the North-West Rebellion*.

109 For a more comprehensive account of the rebellion trials of First Nations defendants, see Sandra Estlin Bingaman, "The Trials of Poundmaker and Big Bear, 1885," and Stonechild and Waiser, *Loyal till Death*, chap. 10, "Snaring Rabbits," 214–37.

110 Poundmaker was charged with four counts of treason-felony: the sacking of Battleford on March 20; dictation of a letter to Riel on April 29; the battle of Cut Knife Hill on May 2; and the seizure of a supply train on May 14. Big Bear was also charged with four counts: planning the Frog Lake Massacre on April 2; the sacking of Fort Pitt on April 17; the dictation of a letter on April 21; and the battle at Frenchman's Butte on May 28. One Arrow was charged with treason-felony on the evidence that he was in Riel's camp and thereby breached his treaty allegiance to the government.

111 *The Globe*, 17 November 1885.

112 Andrea McCalla and Vic Satzewich, "Settler Capitalism and the Construction of Immigrants and 'Indians' as Racialized Others," 27.

113   Lee Gibson, "Samuel Lawrence Bedson," *Dictionary of Canadian Biography*, 1891–1900, vol. 12, 2000, http://www.biographi. ca/009004-119.01-e.php?&id_nbr=5956.

114   "Warden's Annual Report, Manitoba Penitentiary," *Sessional Papers*, 1877, no. 15, 180.

115   Ibid., 127.

116   Ibid.

117   "Eleventh Annual Report of the Inspector of Penitentiaries of the Dominion of Canada for the Year Ended 30th June 1886," *Sessional Papers*, 1887, no. 4, xxi.

118   "Report of the Roman Catholic Chaplain, Manitoba Penitentiary," *Sessional Papers*, 1885, no. 15, 80.

119   Ibid., 79.

120   Ibid., 80.

121   Ibid.

122   Weiner, *Reconstructing the Criminal*, 131.

123   Mary Carpenter, *Juvenile Delinquents: Their Condition and Treatment*, 10.

124   Ibid., 298.

125   Ibid., 33.

126   Anthony M. Platt, *The Child Savers: The Invention of Delinquency*, 3–9. See also Robert M. Mennel, *Thorns and Thistles: Juvenile Delinquents in the United States, 1825–1940*.

127   Joan Sangster, *Girl Trouble: Female Delinquency in English Canada*, 105. See also Dorothy E. Chunn, *From Punishment to Doing Good: Family Courts and Socialized Justice in Ontario, 1880–1940*.

128   Kingston Penitentiary, "Prisoners' Record Book," 1843–90.

129   "Eighth Annual Report of the Inspector of Penitentiaries of the Dominion of Canada for the Year Ended 30th June 1883," *Sessional Papers*, 1884, no. 16, 22.

130   "Protestant Chaplain's Report, Dorchester Penitentiary," *Sessional Papers*, 1885, no. 15, 56.

131   "Report of the Surgeon, Dorchester Penitentiary," *Sessional Papers*, 1890, no. 10, 165.

132   As one illustration of this, of the sixty-three young convicts at Kingston Penitentiary, all but eleven were sentenced for some form of property crime: theft, larceny, house and shop breaking, and burglary. Kingston Penitentiary, "Prisoners' Record Book," 1843–90.

133   "Protestant Chaplain's Report, Kingston Penitentiary," *Sessional Papers*, 1900, no. 18, 61.

134   "Seventeenth Annual Report of the Inspector of Penitentiaries," vii.

135   Ibid.

136   This idea of the "street" and children is explored in Timothy J. Gilfoyle, "Street-Rats and Gutter-Snipes: Child Pickpockets and Street Culture in New York City, 1850–1950."

137	"Eighth Annual Report of the Inspector of Penitentiaries," 23.
138	Ibid., 22.
139	"Annual Report of the Warden, Dorchester Penitentiary," *Sessional Papers*, 1892, no. 12, 72.

FOUR   PRISON LIFE

1	Gersham M. Sykes, *The Society of Captives: A Study of a Maximum Security Prison*, 47.
2	Ibid., 30–32.
3	Ibid., 54, 55.
4	James C. Scott, *Weapons of the Weak: Everyday Forms of Peasant Resistance*.
5	*The Globe*, 20 May 1899.
6	*The Labour Union*, 17 March 1883.
7	*The Labour Union*, 24 March 1883.
8	For example, at Dorchester the standard cells were 9 feet 9 inches long and 4 feet 6 inches wide.
9	"Amendments to Rules and Regulations—Re Convicts—Generally," RG73, C-1, vol. 134, file 1-21-1, part 1, Library and Archives Canada [hereafter LAC].
10	"Fourteenth Annual Report of the Inspector of Penitentiaries of the Dominion of Canada for the Year Ended 30th June 1889," *Sessional Papers*, 1890, no. 10, xiii.
11	"Warden's Annual Report, Manitoba Penitentiary," *Sessional Papers*, 1891, no. 12, 96–97.
12	"Third Annual Report of the Inspector of Penitentiaries of the Dominion of Canada for the Year 1878," *Sessional Papers*, 1879, no. 27, 19.
13	"Fifteenth Annual Report of the Inspector of Penitentiaries of the Dominion of Canada for the Year Ended 30th June 1890," *Sessional Papers*, 1891, no. 12, xxii.
14	See William Calder, "The Federal Penitentiary System in Canada, 1867–1899: A Social and Institutional History," 328.
15	"Warden's Annual Report, Manitoba Penitentiary," 103.
16	Section 8 of the "Rules and Regulations of the Penitentiary" stated:

They must not exchange a word with one another, nor shall they make use of any signs, except such as are necessary to explain their wants to the waiters. . . . They must not speak to, or address, their Keepers on any subject but such as relates to their duty or want. . . . They are not on any occasion, nor under any pretense, to speak to any person who does not belong to the Prison, nor receive from any such person any paper, letter, tobacco, or any other articles whatever. . . . They are not to gaze at visitors when passing through the prison, nor sing, dance, whistle, run, jump, nor do anything which may have the slightest tendency to disturb the harmony or to contravene the rules and regulations of the prison.

> *Appendix to the Journals of the House of Assembly of Upper Canada*, Session 1836–37 (Toronto: W. L. Mackenzie, 1837), 20–22.

17 "Penitentiary Regulations, January 1889," *Consolidated Orders in Council of Canada*, c. 60, s. 274.

18 "Third Annual Report of the Inspector of Penitentiaries of the Dominion of Canada for the Year 1878," *Sessional Papers*, 1879, no. 27, 6.

19 Ibid.

20 Stony Mountain Penitentiary, "Warden's Order Books," 8 August 1877, RG73, acc. W87–88/365, vol. 87, file 161, LAC.

21 Stony Mountain Penitentiary, "Warden's Order Books," 27 September 1879, RG73, acc. W87–88/365, vol. 87, file 161, LAC.

22 "Warden's Report, Manitoba Penitentiary," *Sessional Papers*, 1879, no. 27, 149.

23 British Columbia Penitentiary, "Discharged Convict Question and Answer Book," n.d., RG73, C-3, acc. V-1984–85/329, vol. 285, LAC.

24 *The Globe,* 12 November 1878.

25 The issue came up in the House of Commons on several occasions in the 1890s and the use of tobacco was generally defended by the government. See 7 March 1890, *Official report of the debates of the House of Commons of the Dominion of Canada: fourth session, sixth Parliament*, 3639–40; 9 June 1891, *Official report of the debates of the House of Commons of the Dominion of Canada: first session, seventh Parliament*, 919–20; 28 July 1899, *Official report of the debates of the House of Commons of the Dominion of Canada: fourth session, eighth Parliament*, 8769–70.

26 "Surgeon's Report, Kingston Penitentiary," *Sessional Papers*, 1900, no. 18, 38.

27 Ibid.

28 Stony Mountain Penitentiary, "Convict Letter Registers," 31 August 1864 to 12 May 1869, RG73, acc. W87–88/013, book 10, LAC.

29 Stony Mountain Penitentiary, "Warden's Order Books," 5 March 1879, RG73, acc. W87–88/365, vol. 87, file 156, LAC.

30 Stony Mountain Penitentiary, "Warden's Order Books," 20 March 1883, RG73, acc. W87–88/365, vol. 88, file 171, LAC.

31 Stony Mountain Penitentiary, "Warden's Order Books," 29 August 1877, RG73, acc. W87–88/365, vol. 87, file 161, LAC.

32 Stony Mountain Penitentiary, "Warden's Order Books," 26 May 1876, RG73, acc. W87–88/365, vol. 88, file 164, LAC.

33 "Seventh Annual Report of the Inspector of Penitentiaries of the Dominion of Canada for the Year Ended 30th June 1882," *Sessional Papers*, 1883, no. 29, 65.

34 "Eighth Annual Report of the Inspector of Penitentiaries of the Dominion of Canada for the Year Ended 30th June 1883," *Sessional Papers*, 1884, no. 29, 65.

35 Stony Mountain Penitentiary, "Warden's Order Books," 27 June 1881, RG73, acc. W87–88/365, vol. 88, file 168, LAC.

36 "George Hewell Investigation," 18 December 1896, RG73, acc. 1985–86-182, box 108, file 1826, LAC.

37 Kingston Penitentiary, "Register of Offences Committed by Inmates in Prison, 1886–1895," RG73, C-3, acc. V-1984–85/329, vol. 280, LAC.

38 Stony Mountain Penitentiary, "Surgeon's Daily Letters, 1885–1897," 31 May 1891, RG73, acc. 87–88/365, reel T-11089, LAC.

39 "Warden's Letterbooks, Manitoba Penitentiary," 7 March 1898, RG73, reel T-11083, vol. 56, LAC.

40 "Warden's Letterbooks, Manitoba Penitentiary," 17 September 1897, RG73, reel T-11083, vol. 56, LAC.

41 Kingston Penitentiary, "Register of Offences Committed by Inmates in Prison, 1886–1895."

42 Stony Mountain Penitentiary, "Correspondence: Convict Letter Registers," 12 December 1905, 5 June 1905, RG73, acc. 1987–88/013, book 11, LAC.

43 "Punishment Record, Kingston Penitentiary," 9 November 1876, RG73, acc. 87–88/014, reel T-1949, LAC.

44 "Ninth Annual Report of the Inspector of Penitentiaries of the Dominion of Canada for the Year Ended 30th June 1884," *Sessional Papers*, 1885, no. 15, vi.

45 *The Globe*, 1 July 1881.

46 Ibid.

47 "Warden's Letterbooks, Manitoba Penitentiary," 8 June 1898, RG73, reel T-11089, vol. 56, LAC.

48 "Correspondence re: Convicts and Convict Letter Registers," 20 June 1905, RG73, acc. 1987–88/013, book 11, LAC.

49 "Correspondence re: Convicts and Convict Letter Registers," 9 February 1906.

50 Steven Maynard, "The Maple Leaf (Gardens) Forever: Sex, Canadian Historians, and National History."

51 Veronica Strong-Boag, "Contested Space: The Politics of Canadian Memory."

52 "Correspondence re: Convicts and Convict Letter Registers," 9 February 1906.

53 "Seventh Annual Report of the Inspector of Penitentiaries of the Domion of Canada for the Year Ended 30th June 1882," *Sessional Papers*, 1883, no. 29, 27.

54 "Ninth Annual Report of the Inspector of Penitentiaries of the Dominion of Canada for the Year Ended 30th June 1884," *Sessional Papers,* 1885, no. 15, xxviii.

55 "Warden's Annual Report, St. Vincent de Paul Penitentiary," *Sessional Papers,* 1880, no. 17, 43.

56 Warden to J. L. Witting, Court Crown Attorney, Kingston, 10 June 1895, RG73, acc. 1987–88/014, reel T-1959, LAC.

57 "Eighteenth Annual Report of the Inspector of Penitentiaries of the Dominion of Canada for the Year Ended 30th June 1893," *Sessional Papers,* 1894, no. 18, xvi.

58 "Correspondence re: Convicts and Convict Letter Registers," 1 August 1905.

59 Steele and Wilson were both apprehended in Boston on burglary charges and extradited to Canada. Nelligan was never recaptured. "Fourth Annual Report of the Directors of Penitentiaries of the Dominion of Canada for the Year 1871," *Sessional Papers,* 1872, no. 27, 20.

60 "Nineteenth Annual Report of the Inspector of Penitentiaries of the Dominion of Canada for the Year Ended 30th June 1894," *Sessional Papers,* 1895, no. 18, xvi.

61 "Warden's Annual Report, Manitoba Penitentiary," *Sessional Papers,* 1876, no. 14, 139.

62 The 1892 Criminal Code stipulated, "Every one who escapes from custody shall, on being retaken, serve, in the prison to which he was sentenced, the remainder of his term unexpired at the time of his escape, in addition to the punishment which is awarded for such escape; and any imprisonment awarded for such offence may be to the penitentiary or prison from which the escape was made." *Criminal Code of Canada,* 1892, c. 29, s. 169.

63 J. M. Sullivan, Acting Warden, to J. G. Moylan, Inspector of Penitentiaries, 4 November 1890, RG73, acc. 1987–88/014, reel T-1959, LAC.

64 M. Laval, Warden, Kingston Penitentiary, to John F. Farley, Chief of Police, 1 December 1890, RG73, acc. 1987–88/014, reel T-1959, LAC.

65 "Warden's Annual Report, Manitoba Penitentiary," *Sessional Papers,* 1884, no. 16, 95.

66 "Fourteenth Annual Report of the Inspector of Penitentiaries of the Dominion of Canada for the Year Ended 30th June 1889," *Sessional Papers,* 1890, no. 10, xv.

67 "Warden's Report, Manitoba Penitentiary," *Sessional Papers,* 1876, no. 14, 139.

68 "Warden's Report, St. John Penitentiary," *Sessional Papers,* 1872, no. 27, 66.

69 "Warden's Report, Kingston Penitentiary," *Sessional Papers,* 1870, no. 5, 26.

70 "Reports on Attempts to escape made by convict Christopher Murray during which he was mortally wounded." RG13, vol. 21, file 121-136, LAC.

71 Ibid.

72 *The Globe*, 13 October 1877.

73 Quoted in "Amendments to Rules and Regulations—Re Convicts—Generally."

74 "Seventh Annual Report of the Inspector of Penitentiaries," 27.

75 Quoted in "Amendments to Rules and Regulations—Re Convicts—Generally."

76 "J. G. Moylan—Inspector of Penitentiaries—Dorchester—Evidence taken by him on the attempted escape of five convicts from the St. Vincent de Paul Penitentiary on the 29th March last," RG13, series A-2, vol. 58, file 1883-1388, LAC.

77 "Surgeon's Report, St. Vincent de Paul Penitentiary," *Sessional Papers*, 1884, no. 16, 73.

78 "Ninth Annual Report of the Inspector of Penitentiaries," vi.

79 An additional 125 members of the Fenian Brotherhood were sentenced to shorter sentences in the provincial prison at Toronto. See Hereward Senior, *The Last Invasion of Canada: The Fenian Raids, 1866–1870*.

80 Lieutenant-General Sir J. Michel to the Right Hon. Earl of Caernarvon, 4 January 1867, in Great Britain Colonial Office, *Correspondence Respecting the Recent Fenian Aggression upon Canada* (London, 1867).

81 "Fenian File, 16th October 1868," RG13, file 18-68-308, series A-2, vol. 18, LAC.

82 Ibid.

83 Ibid.

84 "Fifth Annual Report of the Inspector of Penitentiaries of the Dominion of Canada for the Year Ended 30th June 1881," *Sessional Papers*, 1882, no. 65, 9.

85 "Report of the Surgeon, St. Vincent de Paul Penitentiary," *Sessional Papers*, 1901, no. 34, 39.

86 Canada, *Report of Commissioners Appointed to Investigate, Inquire into and Report upon the State and Management of the Business of the St. Vincent de Paul Penitentiary*, 55.

87 *The Globe*, 18 September 1897.

88 *The Globe*, 16 September 1897.

89 *The Globe*, 18 September 1897.

90 *The Globe*, 28 December 1897.

91 *The Globe*, 8 January 1898.

92 British Columbia Penitentiary, "Discharged Convict Question and Answer Book."

93 Ibid.

1   "First Annual Report of the Inspector of Penitentiaries of the Dominion of Canada for the Year 1875," *Sessional Papers*, 1876, no. 14, 9.

2   Ibid.

3   Kyle Jolliffe, "An Examination of Medical Services at the Kingston Penitentiary," 14.

4   "Report of the Surgeon," *Journals of the Legislative Assembly of the Province of Canada*, 1845, Appendix M.

5   "Report of the Surgeon," *Journals of the Legislative Assembly of the Province of Canada*, 1853, Appendix I.I.I.

6   Michel Foucault, *Madness and Civilization: A History of Insanity in the Age of Reason*, 59–60.

7   Michel Foucault, *The History of Sexuality*, vol. 1, *An Introduction*, 141.

8   Michel Foucault, "The Birth of Social Medicine," 155.

9   Michael Ignatieff, *A Just Measure of Pain: The Penitentiary in the Industrial Revolution, 1750–1850*, 60.

10   "Report of the Penitentiary Inspectors, First November, 1837," *Appendix to the Journal of the House of Assembly of Upper Canada*, 1838, 186.

11   "Surgeon's Report, First October, 1837," *Appendix to the Journal of the House of Assembly of Upper Canada*, 1838, 206.

12   Ibid.

13   "Surgeon's Annual Report, Kingston Penitentiary," *Sessional Papers*, 1882, no. 12, 17.

14   "Surgeon's Annual Report, Dorchester Penitentiary," *Sessional Papers*, 1892, no. 18, 70.

15   "Surgeon's Annual Report, Dorchester Penitentiary," *Sessional Papers*, 1885, no. 15, 58.

16   "Surgeon's Annual Report, Dorchester Penitentiary," *Sessional Papers*, 1888, no. 11, 62.

17   "Surgeon's Annual Report, Dorchester Penitentiary," *Sessional Papers*, 1889, no. 12, 66.

18   *Penitentiary Act*, 1868, s. 62.

19   *The Globe*, 20 May 1899.

20   Baldwin to Penitentiary Surgeon, 24 April 1890, "Hospital, 1880–1890," RG73, acc. 87–88/013 vol. 186, Library and Archives Canada [hereafter LAC].

21   "Surgeon's Annual Report, Kingston Penitentiary," *Sessional Papers*, 1883, no. 29, 53.

22   "Fifth Annual Report of the Inspector of Penitentiaries of the Dominion of Canada for the Year Ended 30th June 1880," *Sessional Papers*, 1881, no. 65, 8.

23   "Surgeon's Annual Report, Kingston Penitentiary," 1882, 17.

24 "Surgeon's Annual Report, Kingston Penitentiary," *Sessional Papers*, 1900, no. 18, 38.

25 "Surgeon's Annual Report, Kingston Penitentiary," *Sessional Papers*, 1901, no. 34, 32.

26 "Surgeon's Report, Kingston Penitentiary," *Sessional Papers*, 1875, no. 87, 14.

27 "Eighth Annual Report of the Inspector of Penitentiaries," 11.

28 "Annual Return of Deaths in the Hospital, Kingston Penitentiary," *Sessional Papers*, 1894, no. 12, 11.

29 "Surgeon's Annual Report, Kingston Penitentiary," *Sessional Papers*, 1007, no. 4, 22.

30 "Surgeon's Annual Report, Dorchester Penitentiary," 1888, 62.

31 "Thirteenth Annual Report of the Inspector of Penitentiaries of the Dominion of Canada for the Year Ended 30th June 1888," *Sessional Papers*, 1889, no. 12, xix.

32 "Report of the Catholic Chaplain, Kingston Penitentiary," *Sessional Papers*, 1888, no. 11, 21.

33 "Surgeon's Annual Report, Kingston Penitentiary," *Sessional Papers*, 1888, no. 11, 22.

34 "Report of the Surgeon, Kingston Penitentiary," *Sessional Papers*, 1889, no. 12, 11.

35 Stony Mountain Penitentiary, "Medical Case Books," 24 January 1891, box 48, RG73, acc. W87−88/365, LAC.

36 "Surgeon's Report, St. Vincent de Paul Penitentiary," *Sessional Papers*, 1899, no. 18, 30.

37 Stony Mountain Penitentiary, "Medical Case Books," 11 April 1891, box 48.

38 "Surgeon's Report, Kingston Penitentiary," *Appendix to the Sixteenth Volume of the Journals of the Legislative Assembly of the Province of Canada*, 1858, Appendix no. 11, 30.

39 "Surgeon's Report, Manitoba Penitentiary," *Sessional Papers*, 1883, no. 29, 133.

40 Stony Mountain Penitentiary, "Inmate Admittance Registers," RG73, C-7, acc. W87−88/365, reel T-11089 (1871−85), LAC.

41 The correspondence can be found in RG10, vol. 3770, file 33972, reel C-10135, LAC.

42 "Report of the Catholic Chaplain, Manitoba Penitentiary," *Sessional Papers*, 1887, no. 4, 34.

43 "Report of the Catholic Chaplain, Manitoba Penitentiary," *Sessional Papers*, 1886, no. 15, 76.

44 *Saskatchewan Herald*, 17 May 1886.

45 Surgeon to Warden, 22 and 23 July 1895, Stony Mountain Penitentiary, "Letter Book—Surgeon's Daily Letters," RG73, vol. 56, reel T-11089, LAC.

46 "Warden's Annual Report, Manitoba Penitentiary," *Sessional Papers*, 1897, no. 18, 65.

47 See Maureen K. Lux, *Medicine That Walks: Disease, Medicine and Canadian Plains Native People, 1880–1984*.

48 Anne McClintock, *Imperial Leather: Race, Gender and Sexuality in the Colonial Context*, 46–51.

49 Lux, *Medicine That Walks*, 4.

50 "Report of the Assistant Inspector of Penitentiaries," *Sessional Papers*, 1880, no. 17, 79.

51 "Report of the Surgeon, British Columbia Penitentiary," *Sessional Papers*, 1882, no. 12, 93.

52 Mary-Ellen Kelm, *Colonizing Bodies: Aboriginal Healing in British Columbia, 1900–1950*.

53 "Nez Percy Sam," Stony Mountain Penitentiary, "Medical Case Books, Manitoba Penitentiary," 1889–1896, box 48, file 79, RG73, acc. W87–88/365, LAC.

54 Ibid.

55 "Nez Percy Sam," Stony Mountain Penitentiary, "Medical Case Books, Manitoba Penitentiary," 1896–1906, box 48, file 80, RG73, acc. W87–88/364, LAC.

56 "Report of the Roman Catholic Chaplain, Manitoba Penitentiary," *Sessional Papers*, 1888, no. 11, 79.

57 Wendy Mitchinson, "Reasons for Committal to a Mid-Nineteenth-Century Ontario Insane Asylum: The Case of Toronto," 95.

58 Simon N. Verdun-Jones and Russell Smandych, "Catch-22 in the Nineteenth Century: The Evolution of Therapeutic Confinement for the Criminally Insane in Canada, 1840–1900."

59 Quoted in Kyle Jolliffe, "An Examination of Medical Services at the Kingston Penitentiary," 156–60.

60 *Act for the Better Management of the Provincial Penitentiary* (1851), Provincial Statutes of Canada, 14 and 15 Vict., c. 2, s. xlvi.

61 Peter Oliver, *"Terror to Evil-Doers": Prisons and Punishments in Nineteenth-Century Ontario*, 232.

62 Quoted in James E. Moran, *Committed to the State Asylum: Insanity and Society in Nineteenth-Century Quebec and Ontario*, 147.

63 Ibid., 234.

64 T. J. W. Burgess, *Abstract of a Historical Sketch of Canadian Institutions for the Insane*.

65 See Abraham S. Luchins, "The Cult of Curability and the Doctrine of Perfectibility: Social Context of the Nineteenth-Century American Asylum Movement."

66 "Eleventh Annual Report of the Inspector of Penitentiaries of the Dominion of Canada for the Year Ended 30th June 1886," *Sessional Papers*, 1887, no. 4, xii.

67 James Hack Tuke quoted in Daniel Hack Tuke, *The Insane in Canada and the United States*, 215.

68 The treatment was developed independently at the end of the eighteenth century by Phillipe Pinel in Paris, Vincenzo Chiarugi

in Florence, and William Tuke in York. See Anne Digby, *Madness, Morality, and Medicine: A Study of the York Retreat, 1796–1914*, 33–34, and Danielle Terbenche, "'Curative' and 'Custodial': Benefits of Patient Treatment at the Asylum for the Insane, Kingston, 1878–1906."

69 Moran, *Committed to the State Asylum*, 5, 18.

70 Digby, *Madness, Morality, and Medicine*, 42.

71 "The Surgeon's Report, 31st December 1853," *Journals of the Legislative Assembly of Upper Canada*, 1853, Appendix D.D.

72 Ibid.

73 Tuke, *The Insane in the United States and Canada*, 237–38.

74 "Fifteenth Annual Report of the Inspector of Penitentiaries of the Dominion of Canada for the Year Ended 30th June 1890," *Sessional Papers*, 1891, no. 12, xviii.

75 "Nineteenth Annual Report of the Inspector of Penitentiaries of the Dominion of Canada for the Year Ended 30th June 1894," *Sessional Papers*, 1895, no. 18, xvii.

76 "Fifteenth Annual Report of the Inspector of Penitentiaries," xviii. One example of a "tonic" used in Canadian penitentiaries was bromidia, produced by Battle & Co. of St. Louis. Bromidia contained pure chloral hydrate and cannabis, which produced a powerful sedative effect on patients. "Medical Items," *Canadian Medical and Surgical Journal* 13, no. 3 (1884): 192.

77 "Harry Brown," Stony Mountain Penitentiary, "Medical Case Books" 1896–1906, box 47, file 79, RG73, acc. W87–88/365, box 49, LAC.

78 Ibid.

79 Ibid.

80 I consider only this twenty-year period because the register does not contain complete information for admissions after 1890 and into the twentieth century. In short, the discharge data for many of these admissions is obscured because many were incarcerated in the asylum after the end date on the register. See "Register of Inmates at Kingston Criminal Lunatic Asylum," RG73, acc. 87–88/013, vol. 34, 8–40, LAC.

81 "Surgeon's Annual Report, Kingston Penitentiary," *Sessional Papers*, 1895, no. 18, 6.

82 Geoffrey Reaume, "Patients at Work: Insane Asylum Inmates' Labour in Ontario, 1841–1900."

83 "Surgeon's Annual Report, St. Vincent de Paul Penitentiary," 1899, 30–31.

84 Quoted in Digby, *Madness, Morality, and Medicine*, 42.

85 Samuel Bedson to Lt. Gov. Morris, 21 December 1875, Stony Mountain Penitentiary, "Warden's Letterbook," RG73, acc. W87–88/365, reel T-11079, LAC.

86   Stony Mountain Penitentiary, "Warden's Order Books," 27 January 1879, RG73, acc. W87–88/365, vol. 87, box 151, LAC.

87   Stony Mountain Penitentiary, "Warden's Order Books," 9 November 1880, RG73, acc. W87–88/365, vol. 87, box 151, LAC.

88   Stony Mountain Penitentiary, "Inmate Admittance Registers," 1871–85.

89   Wendy Mitchinson, *The Nature of Their Bodies: Women and Their Doctors in Victorian Canada*, 313–14.

90   T.W.J. Burgess, *Presidential Address to the Royal Society of Canada, 1905*, 38–39. See also Mark Finnane, "Asylums, Families and the State," and, for a more recent example that advances similar conclusions but employs a quantitative analysis, James Moran, David Wright, and Matt Savelli, "Families, Madness, and Confinement in Victorian Ontario."

91   In 1883 the warden at Kingston noted that three female mental patients worked with the other women inmates and had been "usefully and profitably employed." "Seventh Annual Report of the Inspector of Penitentiaries of the Dominion of Canada for the Year Ended 30th June 1882," *Sessional Papers*, 1883, no. 29, 18.

92   "Warden's Annual Report, Manitoba Penitentiary," *Sessional Papers*, 1879, no. 27, 15.

93   Stony Mountain Penitentiary, "Warden's Order Books," 18 September 1880, 14 January 1881, and 3 March 1881, RG73, acc. W87–88/365, vol. 87, box 151, LAC.

94   It is interesting that the same behaviour was often identified in cases of non-lunatic convicts in all federal penitentiaries. A convict who behaved in this manner was regarded as "insubordinate." See Stony Mountain Penitentiary, "Warden's Order Books," 11 September 1881, 14 October 1881, 19 March 1882, RG73, acc. W87–88/365, vol. 87, box 151, LAC.

95   Stony Mountain Penitentiary, "Inmate Admittance Registers," 1871–85.

96   Stony Mountain Penitentiary, "Warden's Order Books," 7 September 1881, RG73, acc. W87–88/365, vol. 87, box 157, LAC.

97   S. L. Bedson to J. Couchon, Lieutenant Governor of Keewatin, 28 February 1880, RG13, series A-2, vol. 47, file 1880-1024, LAC.

98   "Manitoba Penitentiary, Return of Officers," *Sessional Papers*, 1880, no. 17, 172.

99   S. L. Bedson to J. Couchon, 28 February 1880.

100   Warden to Inspector of Penitentiaries, 8 February 1906, Stony Mountain Penitentiary, "Correspondence re: Convicts and Convict Letter Registers," RG73, acc. 1987–88/013, book 11, LAC.

101   Warden to Minister of Justice, 21 November 1905, Stony Mountain Penitentiary, "Correspondence re: Convicts and Convict Letter Registers."

102 Stony Mountain Penitentiary, "Inmate Admittance Registers," 1871–85.

103 Surgeon to Warden, 20 January 1896, Stony Mountain Penitentiary, "Surgeon's Daily Records," RG73, W87–88/365, reel T-11089, LAC.

104 Irvine to T. N. Stephens, 9 January 1897, Stony Mountain Penitentiary, "Warden's Daily Letter Book," RG73, W87–88/365, reel T-11089, LAC.

105 Irvine to Miss T. N. Stephens, 29 January 1897, Stony Mountain Penitentiary, "Warden's Daily Letter Book."

106 Irvine to Douglas Stewart, Inspector of Penitentiaries, 21 September 1897, Stony Mountain Penitentiary, "Warden's Daily Letter Book."

107 "Criminal Statistics, Kingston Penitentiary," *Sessional Papers,* 1899, no. 18, 85.

108 "List of Insane Convicts, Kingston Penitentiary," *Sessional Papers,* 1899, no. 18, 123.

109 Robert Darby, "Pathologizing Male Sexuality: Lallemand, Spermatorrhea, and the Rise of Circumcision," 289.

110 "Report of Dr. Wolfred Nelson, One of the Inspectors of the Provincial Penitentiary on the Present State, Discipline, Management and Expenditure of the District and Other Prisons in Canada East," *Appendix to the Eleventh Volume of the Journals of the Legislative Assembly of the Province of Canada,* 1853, Appendix H.H.

111 Foucault, *An Introduction,* 5–6.

112 Ibid., 53.

113 Michael Mason, *The Making of Victorian Sexuality,* 211.

114 Ibid., 213.

115 Ellen Bayuk Rosenman, "Body Doubles: The Spermatorrhea Panic," 375.

116 Ibid., 376.

117 Mason, *The Making of Victorian Sexuality,* 215.

118 "Review: On Spermatorrhea: Its Pathology, Results and Complications."

119 Darby, "Pathologizing Male Sexuality," 289 and 309–10.

120 "Report of the Board of Inspectors of Asylums, Prisons &c. for the Year 1859," *Sessional Papers,* 1860, no. 23, 62.

121 "Alexander Munro," Stony Mountain Penitentiary, "Medical Case Books," 1878–1885, RG73, acc. W87–88/365, vol. 47, box 78, LAC.

122 "List of Sick Treated in Hospital and Cells at St. Vincent de Paul Penitentiary," *Sessional Papers,* 1895, no. 18, 40; "Return of Sick Treated in Hospital and Cells," *Sessional Papers,* 1896, no. 18, 52; "Cases Treated In the Prison," *Sessional Papers,* 1900, no. 18, 48.

123 "Annual Return of Sick Treated in Hospital at Kingston Penitentiary," *Sessional Papers,* 1899, no. 18, 32.

124 Jessa Chupik and David Wright, "Treating the Idiot Child in Early Twentieth-Century Ontario."

125 "Seventh Annual Report of the Inspector of Penitentiaries," 13.

126 "Eleventh Annual Report of the Inspector of Penitentiaries of the Dominion of Canada for the Year Ended 30th June 1886," *Sessional Papers,* 1887, no. 4, xii.

127 David Wright, *Mental Disability in Victorian England: The Earlswood Asylum, 1847–1901,* 5. See also Angus McLaren, "The Creation of a Haven for 'Human Thoroughbreds': The Sterilization of the Feeble-Minded and the Mentally Ill in British Columbia," and Steve Noll, *Feebleminded in Our Midst: Institutions for the Mentally Retarded in the South, 1900–1940.*

128 Anne Digby, "Contexts and Perspectives," 10.

129 Angus McLaren, *Our Own Master Race: Eugenics in Canada, 1885–1945.*

130 "Fourteenth Annual Report of the Inspector of Penitentiaries of the Dominion of Canada for the Year Ended 30th June 1890," *Sessional Papers,* 1891, no. 10, xxii.

131 "Seventh Annual Report of the Inspector of Penitentiaries," 13.

132 "Surgeon's Annual Report, St. Vincent de Paul Penitentiary," *Sessional Papers,* 1900, no. 18, 45.

133 "Warden's Annual Report, St. Vincent de Paul Penitentiary," *Sessional Papers,* 1900, no. 18, 18.

134 "Surgeon's Annual Report, St. Vincent de Paul Penitentiary," *Sessional Papers,* 1901, no. 34, 41.

135 Anne Digby, "Contexts and Perspectives," 4.

136 "Report of the Surgeon, Kingston Penitentiary," *Sessional Papers,* 1897, no. 18, 38.

137 Karl Marx, *Capital: A Critique of Political Economy,* 797.

138 Paul Abberly, "The Limits of Classical Social Theory in the Analysis and Transformation of Disablement," 28–32.

139 Peter Linebaugh, "All the Atlantic Mountains Shook," 96.

SIX   PUNISHMENT

1 Flanigan was actually the deputy warden and served as acting warden for only a few months in 1870 between the death of Warden J. M. Ferres and the appointment of John Creighton.

2 "Report of the Acting Warden of Kingston Penitentiary For the Year Ending 31st December 1870," *Sessional Papers,* 1871, no. 60, 7.

3 Quoted in E. C. Wines, *Report of the International Penitentiary Congress of London Held July 3–13, 1872,* 168.

4 Brown Commission, *Reports of the Commissioners Appointed to Inquire into the Conduct, Discipline and Management of the Provincial Penitentiary* [hereafter Brown Commission], 182.

5   Peter Oliver, *"Terror to Evil-Doers": Prisons and Punishments in Nineteenth-Century Ontario*, 211.

6   Brown Commission, 295.

7   Ibid., 192; "Penitentiary Report for the Year 1856," *Appendix to the Fifteenth Volume of the Journals of the Legislative Assembly of the Province of Canada*, 1857, Appendix No. 7.

8   Numbers are drawn from "Returns of Punishment" from all penitentiaries published in the *Sessional Papers of Canada*, 1870–1900. It must be noted that criminal courts in Canada continued to use whipping as a punishment for particular crimes, most often for sexual assaults. In the post-Confederation years, these punishments were often carried out by prison staff in conjunction with a prison sentence.

9   Martin Weiner, *Men of Blood: Violence, Manliness and Criminal Justice in Victorian England*.

10 Ibid., 64–70.

11 Ibid. See also Jacob Middleton, "Thomas Hopley and Mid-Victorian Attitudes to Corporal Punishment."

12 "Report of the Acting Warden of the Kingston Penitentiary for the Year Ending 31st December 1871," *Sessional Papers*, 1872, no. 27, 17.

13 E. C. Wines, *The State of Prisons and of Child-Saving Institutions in the Civilized World*, 99.

14 21 May 1869, *House of Commons Debates*, (Ottawa, Information Canada, 1975), 427.

15 "Seventh Annual Report of the Directors of Penitentiaries of the Dominion of Canada for the Year 1874," *Sessional Papers*, 1875, no. 87, 11.

16 Ibid.

17 "Twelfth Annual Report of the Inspector of Penitentiaries of the Dominion of Canada for the Year Ended 30th June 1887," *Sessional Papers*, 1888, no. 11, xxi.

18 "Second Annual Report of the Inspector of Penitentiaries of the Dominion of Canada for the Year 1876," *Sessional Papers*, 1877, no. 15, 11.

19 Ibid.

20 "Sixth Annual Report of the Inspector of Penitentiaries of the Dominion of Canada for the Year Ended 30th June 1881," *Sessional Papers*, 1882, no. 12, xviii.

21 Stony Mountain Penitentiary, "Warden's Order Books," 20 December 1881, RG73, W87-88/365, vol. 88, file 169, Library and Archives Canada [hereafter LAC].

22 David Garland, *Punishment and Modern Society: A Study in Social Theory*, 32.

23 Friedrich Nietzsche, *The Birth of Tragedy and the Genealogy of Morals*, 198.

24 David Rothman, *The Discovery of the Asylum: Social Order and Disorder in the New Republic*, 246.

25 *The Globe*, 21 April 1876.

26 Martin Weiner, *Reconstructing the Criminal: Culture, Law, and Policy in England, 1830–1914*, 93.

27 *Proceedings of the Annual Congress of the National Prison Association of the United States, Toronto, September 10–15, 1887*, 214.

28 Ibid., 219.

29 Stony Mountain Penitentiary, "Warden's Order Books," 15 September 1880, RG73, W87–88/365, vol. 88, file 66, LAC.

30 E. C. Wines and Theodore W. Dwight, *Report on the Prisons and Reformatories of the United States and Canada Made to the Legislature of New York, January, 1867*, 166.

31 Stefan Breur, "The Dénouements of Civilisation: Norbert Elias and Modernity," *International Social Science Journal*, no. 128 (1991): 414, quoted in Carolyn Strange, "The Undercurrents of Penal Culture: Punishments of the Body in Mid-Twentieth-Century Canada," 8.

32 *The Globe*, 31 July 1888.

33 *The Globe*, 13 August 1888.

34 Ibid.

35 *The Globe*, 17 August 1888.

36 "Warden's Annual Report, St. Vincent de Paul Penitentiary," *Sessional Papers*, 1877, no. 15, 82.

37 "Outline of Punishments on the Prisoners in the St. Vincent de Paul Penitentiary, During the Year 1876," *Sessional Papers*, 1877, no. 15, 80.

38 "Warden's Annual Report, St. Vincent de Paul Penitentiary," 1877, 82.

39 "Second Annual Report of the Inspector of Penitentiaries," 10.

40 "Kingston Penitentiary Punishment Book," 3 November 1876 to 10 March 1880, RG73, acc. 87–88/014, reel T-1949, LAC.

41 "Second Annual Report of the Inspector of Penitentiaries," 10.

42 Kingston Penitentiary, "Register of Offences Committed by Inmates in Prison, 1886–1895," RG73, C-3, V-1984–85/329, vol. 280, LAC.

43 British Columbia Penitentiary, "Discharged Convict Question and Answer Book," RG73, V-1984–85/329, vol. 285, LAC.

44 "Register of Offences Committed by Inmates in Prison, 1886–1895."

45 Ibid.

46 "Punishment Record, Kingston Penitentiary," 3 November 1876 to 10 March 1880, RG73, acc. 87–88/014, reel T-1949, LAC.

47 Ibid.

48 Ibid.

49 *The Globe*, 3 July 1882.

50 *The Globe*, 15 December 1894.

51 "Summary of Punishments Awarded to Convicts in the Kingston Penitentiary, During the Year 1870," *Sessional Papers*, 1871, no. 34, 21.

52 "Summary of Punishments Awarded to Convicts in the Dorchester Penitentiary, During the Year Ended 30th June 1885," *Sessional Papers*, 1886, no. 15, 55.

53 "Summary of Punishments Awarded to Convicts in the Kingston Penitentiary, During the Year 1871," *Sessional Papers*, 1872, no. 27, 10.

54 *The Globe*, 18 February 1891.

55 The Oregon boot was patented and manufactured by Oregon State Penitentiary starting in 1866 (http://www.oregon.gov/DOC/OPS/PRISON/osp_history3.shtml). It was used as late as 1898 at British Columbia Penitentiary. "Summary of Punishments—British Columbia Penitentiary," *Sessional Papers*, 1899, no. 18, 115.

56 Philip Priestley, *Victorian Prison Lives: English Prison Biography, 1830–1914*, 131.

57 Irvine to Stewart, 7 March 1896, Stony Mountain Penitentiary, "Manitoba Penitentiary—Warden's Letterbook," RG73, acc. 87–88/364, reel T-11089, LAC.

58 "Convict no. 58," June 18, 1905, Stony Mountain Penitentiary, "Defaulter's Books," 1905, Stony Mountain Penitentiary, box 1, file 13, RG73, acc. 87–88/364, LAC.

59 "Report of the Hospital Overseer," 1889–1892, Stony Mountain Penitentiary, "Hospital and Sick Reports," box 4, file 19. RG73, W87–88, LAC.

60 Ibid.

61 Ironically, Hills escaped from Manitoba Penitentiary the following year and remained at large for six years until he was arrested again in Vancouver. He was sentenced to another term at Manitoba after officials recognized his face (in spite of his use of the alias John Edwards). In addition to his sentence for shop breaking, Hills served six months for prison escape (Stony Mountain Penitentiary, "Inmate Admittance Registers," RG73, C-7, acc. W87–88/365, reel T-11089 [1871–85], LAC).

62 "Sixth Annual Report of the Directors of Penitentiaries of the Dominion of Canada for the Year 1874," *Sessional Papers*, 1873, no. 42, 3.

63 "Ninth Annual Report of the Inspector of Penitentiaries," iv.

64 "Second Annual Report of the Inspector of Penitentiaries," 15.

65 "Third Annual Report of the Inspector of Penitentiaries of the Dominion of Canada for the Year 1878," *Sessional Papers*, 1879, no. 27, 7.

66 "Fifth Annual Report of the Inspector of Penitentiaries of the Dominion of Canada for the Year Ended 30th June 1880," *Sessional Papers*, 1881, no. 65, 7.

67   "Thirteenth Annual Report of the Inspector of Penitentiaries of the Dominion of Canada for the Year Ended 30th June 1888," *Sessional Papers*, 1889, no. 12, xiv.

68   Rothman, *The Discovery of the Asylum: Social Order and Disorder in the New Republic*, 88; Michael Ignatieff, *A Just Measure of Pain: The Penitentiary in the Industrial Revolution, 1750–1859*, 139–40.

69   "Thirteenth Annual Report of the Inspector of Penitentiaries of the Dominion of Canada for the Year Ended 30th June 1888," *Sessional Papers*, 1889, no. 12, xv.

70   "Report of the Inspector of Penitentiaries for the Fiscal Year 1895–1896," *Sessional Papers*, 1897, no. 18, 10.

71   "Nineteenth Annual Report of the Inspector of Penitentiaries," xvi.

72   Ibid.

73   "Report of the Inspector of Penitentiaries for the Fiscal Year 1895–96," 10.

74   *Penitentiary Commission Separate Report No. 4*, 18 December 1896, RG73, acc. 1985–86-182, box 108, file 1826, LAC. Note that this file contains records of the investigation into the shooting of convict Hewell. In the notes that follow, the titles in quotations refer to the sworn testimony of specific officers, staff, and prisoners. Some of the pages in the original file are numbered and some are not.

75   "Re: Shooting of Convict Hewell," 18 December 1896, RG73, acc. 1985–86-182, box 108, file 1826, LAC.

76   Ibid.

77   "Shooting of Convict Hewell: Convict Corbett," 18 December 1896, RG73, acc. 1985–86-182, box 108, file 1826, 3, LAC.

78   Ibid.

79   Ibid., 2.

80   Ibid.

81   Ibid.

82   "Shooting of Convict Hewell: Chief Keeper Hughes," 18 December 1896, RG73, acc. 1985–86-182, box 108, file 1826, 2, LAC.

83   "Re: Shooting of Convict Hewell," 4.

84   "Chief Keeper Hughes," 2.

85   "Shooting of Convict Hewell: Guard Spence," 18 December, 1896, RG73, acc. 1985–86-182, box 108, file 1826, 3, LAC.

86   "Coroner's Report—W. S. Hughes—Chief Keeper," RG73, acc. 1985–86-182, box 108, file 1826, 1, LAC.

87   Ibid.

88   "Shooting of Convict Hewell: W. J. McLeod, Warden's Clerk," 18 December 1896, RG73, acc. 1985–86-182, box 108, file 1826, 8, LAC.

89   "Shooting of Convict Hewell: Guard Sullivan," 18 December 1896, RG73, acc. 1985–86-182, box 108, file 1826, 2, LAC.

90   "Shooting of Convict Hewell: Alex Spence," 18 December 1896, RG73, acc. 1985–86-182, box 108, file 1826, n.p., LAC.

91   Ibid.

92   "Chief Keeper Hughes," 12.

93   "Shooting of Convict Hewell: Guard McDonell," 18 December 1896, RG73, acc. 1985–86-182, box 108, file 1826, 9, LAC.

94   "Guard Sullivan," 5.

95   "Alex Spence," 3.

96   *The Globe*, 1 July 1881.

97   "Shooting of Convict Hewell," 6.

98   "'Thirteenth Annual Report of the Inspector of Penitentiaries of the Dominion of Canada for the Year Ended 30th June 1888," *Sessional Papers*, 1889, no. 12, xvii.

99   Ibid.

100 "Dominion Parole Officer's Report," *Sessional Papers*, 1906, no. 34, 12.

CONCLUSION

1   David Garland, *Punishment and Welfare: A History of Penal Strategies*, 14.

2   June Carter Cash, "Johnny Cash at San Quentin," liner notes from *Johnny Cash at San Quentin,* Johnny Cash (1969; reissue, Sony Music Entertainment, 2000), 8.

3   Ibid., 9.

4   Quoted in Eribon Dider, *Michel Foucault,* 225.

Bibliography

ARCHIVAL REPOSITORIES AND COLLECTIONS

Library and Archives Canada
RG10: Indian Affairs
RG13: Department of Justice
RG73: Penitentiaries

Glenbow Museum
Edgar Dewdney Papers

GOVERNMENT DOCUMENTS

Appendix to the Journal of the House of Assembly of Upper Canada, various years
Appendix to the First Volume of the Journals of the Legislative Assembly of Upper Canada (1841)
Appendix to the Second Volume of the Journals of the Legislative Assembly of the Province of Canada (1842)
Appendix to the Eleventh Volume of the Journals of the Legislative Assembly of the Province of Canada (1852)
Appendix to the Twelfth Volume of the Journals of the Legislative Assembly of the Province of Canada (1853)
Appendix to the Thirteenth Volume of the Journals of the Legislative Assembly of the Province of Canada (1855)

*Appendix to the Fifteenth Volume of the Journals of the Legislative Assembly
of the Province of Canada* (1857)
*Appendix to the Sixteenth Volume of the Journals of the Legislative Assembly
of the Province of Canada* (1858)
*Appendix to the Seventeenth Volume of the Journals of the Legislative
Assembly of the Province of Canada* (1859)
House of Commons Debates, various years
*Journal of the House Assembly of Lower-Canada from the 28th March to the
3rd June, 1799*
Journals of the Legislative Assembly of the Province of Canada, various years
Sessional Papers, various years

LEGISLATION

*An Act for Building a Gaol and Court House in Every District Within This
Province, and for Altering the Names of Said Districts,* Statutes of
the Province of Upper Canada, 1792, c. 8
*Act to Declare the Common Gaols to Be Houses of Correction for Certain
Purposes,* Statutes of the Province of Upper Canada, 1810, c. 5
Act for the Better Management of the Provincial Penitentiary, Provincial
Statutes of Canada, 1851, 14 and 15 Vict, c. 2
Criminal Code of Canada, 1892, c. 29
Penitentiary Act, 1868, 31 Vict.
"Penitentiary Regulations, January 1889," *The Consolidated Orders in
Council of Canada,* c. 60

SECONDARY SOURCES

Abberly, Paul "The Limits of Classical Social Theory in the Analysis
and Transformation of Disablement." In *Disability Studies: Past,
Present, and Future,* edited by Len Barton and Mike Oliver, 25–44.
Leeds: Disability Press, 1997.
———. "Hard Labor: The Form and Function of Imprisonment in
Nineteenth-Century America." PhD diss., Princeton University,
1982.
———. "Punishment After Slavery: Southern State Penal Systems,
1865–1890." *Social Problems* 30, no. 5 (1983): 555–69.
Adler, Jeffrey. "The Dynamite, Wreckage, and Scum in Our Cities: The
Social Construction of Deviance in Industrial America." *Justice
Quarterly* 11, no. 1 (1994): 33–50.
Baehre, Rainer. "From Bridewell to Federal Penitentiary: Prisons and
Punishment in Nova Scotia Before 1880." In *Essays in the History
of Canadian Law,* vol. 3, *Nova Scotia,* edited by Philip Girard and
Jim Phillips, 163–99. Toronto: Osgoode Society, 1990.

————. "The Ill-Regulated Mind: A Study of the Making of Psychiatry in Ontario, 1830–1921." PhD diss., York University, 1985.

————. "Pauper Emigration to Upper Canada in the 1830s." *Histoire sociale/Social History* 14, no. 28 (1981): 339–67.

————. "Prison as Factory, Convict as Worker: A Study of the Mid-Victorian St John Penitentiary, 1841–1880." In *Essays in the History of Canadian Law*, vol. 5, *Crime and Criminal Justice*, edited by Jim Phillips, Tina Loo, and Susan Lewthwaite, 439–77. Toronto: Osgoode Society, 1994.

Barton, Len, and Mike Oliver, eds. *Disability Studies: Past, Present, and Future.* Leeds: Disability Press, 1997.

Beattie, J. M. *Attitudes Towards Crime and Punishment in Upper Canada, 1830–1850: A Documentary Study.* Toronto: University of Toronto Centre of Criminology, 1977.

Beccaria, Cesare. *On Crimes and Punishment and Other Writings.* 1764. Reprint, Toronto: University of Toronto Press, 2008.

Berkovits, Joseph A. G. "'Us Poor Devils': Prison Life and Culture in Ontario, 1874–1914." PhD diss., University of Toronto, 2000.

Bingaman, Sandra Estlin. "The Trials of Poundmaker and Big Bear, 1885." *Saskatchewan History* 28, no. 3 (1975): 81–94.

Booth, Charles, ed. *Labour and Life of the People.* Vol. 1: *East London.* London and Edinburgh: Williams and Norgate, 1889.

Brace, Charles Loring. *The Dangerous Classes of New York and Twenty Years Work Among Them.* New York: Wynkoop and Hallenbeck, 1872.

Brode, Patrick. *The Odyssey of John Anderson.* Toronto: University of Toronto Press, 1989.

Brown Commission. *Reports of the Commissioners Appointed to Enquire into the Conduct, Discipline and Management of the Provincial Penitentiary.* Montreal, 1849.

Brown, Tom. "The Origins of the Asylum in Upper Canada, 1830–1839." *Canadian Bulletin of Medical History* 1, no. 1 (1984): 27–58.

Burgess, T.J.W. *Abstract of a Historical Sketch of Canadian Institutions for the Insane.* Montreal: Protestant Hospital for the Insane, 1905.

Calder, William. "The Federal Penitentiary System in Canada, 1867–1899: A Social and Institutional History." PhD diss., University of Toronto, 1979.

Canada. *Report of Commissioners Appointed to Investigate, Inquire into and Report upon the State and Management of the Business of the St. Vincent de Paul Penitentiary.* Ottawa: S. E. Dawson, 1899.

Canada. *Report of the Commissioners Appointed to Superintend the Erection of a Penitentiary in Kingston.* Kingston, 1833.

Carpenter, Mary. *Juvenile Delinquents: Their Condition and Treatment.* 1853. Reprint, Montclair, NJ: Patterson Smith, 1970.

————. *Reformatory Prison Discipline, as Developed by the Rt. Hon. Sir Walter Crofton, in the Irish Convict Prisons.* 1872. Reprint, New Jersey: Patterson Smith, 1967.

———. *Reformatory Schools for the Children of the Perishing and Dangerous Classes and for Juvenile Offenders.* 1851. Reprint, London: Woburn Press, 1968.

Carrigan, D. Owen. *Crime and Punishment in Canada: A History.* Toronto: McClelland and Stewart, 1991.

Carter, Sarah. *Aboriginal People and Colonizers of Western Canada to 1900.* Toronto: University of Toronto Press, 1999.

Chevalier, Louis. *Laboring Classes and Dangerous Classes in Paris During the First Half of the Nineteenth Century.* Translated by Frank Jellinek. 1958. Reprint, New York: Howard Fertig, 1973.

Christie, Robert. *A History of the Late Province of Lower Canada, Parliamentary and Political from the Commencement to the Close of Its Existence as a Separate Province.* Montreal: Richard Worthington, 1866.

Chunn, Dorothy E. *From Punishment to Doing Good: Family Courts and Socialized Justice in Ontario, 1880–1940.* Toronto: University of Toronto Press, 1992.

Chupik, Jessa, and David Wright. "Treating the Idiot Child in Early Twentieth-Century Ontario." *Disability and Society* 21, no. 1 (2006): 77–90.

Colvin, Mark. *Penitentiaries, Reformatories, and Chain Gangs: Social Theory and the History of Punishment in Nineteenth-Century America.* New York: St. Martin's Press, 1997.

Connell, R. W. *Masculinities.* 2nd ed. Berkeley: University of California Press, 2005.

Corrigan, Philip, and Derek Sayer. *The Great Arch: English State Formation as Cultural Revolution.* New York: Basil Blackwell, 1985.

Cunningham, Hugh. *The Children of the Poor: Representations of Childhood Since the Seventeenth Century.* Oxford: Blackwell, 1991.

Darby, Robert. "Pathologizing Male Sexuality: Lallemand, Spermatorrhea, and the Rise of Circumcision." *Journal of the History of Medicine and Allied Sciences* 60, no. 3 (2005): 283–319.

Dider, Eribon. *Michel Foucault.* Translated by Betsy Wing. Cambridge: Harvard University Press, 1992.

Digby, Anne. "Contexts and Perspectives." In Wright and Digby, *From Idiocy to Mental Deficiency,* 1–21.

———. *Madness, Morality and Medicine: A Study of the York Retreat, 1796–1914.* Cambridge: Cambridge University Press, 1985.

Edmison, John Alexander. "Some Aspects of Nineteenth-Century Canadian Prisons." In *Crime and Its Treatment in Canada,* 2nd ed., edited by W. T. McGrath, 347–69. Toronto: Macmillan, 1976.

Emerson, R. W., W. H. Channing, and J. F. Clarke. *Memoirs of Margaret Fuller Ossoli.* Vol. 2. Boston: Phillips, Sampson and Company, 1852.

Eriksson, Torsten. *The Reformers: An Historical Survey of Pioneer Experiments in the Treatment of Criminals.* Translated by Catherine Djurklou. New York: Elsevier, 1976.

Ewers, John C. *The Horse in Blackfoot Indian Culture*. Washington, DC: Smithsonian Institution Press, 1955.

Finnane, Mark. "Asylums, Families and the State." *History Workshop Journal* 20, no. 1 (1985): 134–48.

Five Years Penal Servitude by One Who Has Endured It. 3rd ed. London: Richard Bentley and Son, 1878.

Foucault, Michel. "The Birth of Social Medicine." In Foucault, *Power*, ed. Faubion, 134–56.

———. *The Birth of the Clinic: An Archeology of Medical Perception*. 1965. Reprint, New York: Vintage Books, 1975.

———. *Discipline and Punish: The Birth of the Prison*. Translated by Alan Sheridan. 1975. Reprint, New York: Vintage Books, 1995.

———. *The History of Sexuality*. Vol. 1: *An Introduction*. Translated by Robert Hurley. 1978. Reprint, New York: Random House, 1990.

———. *Madness and Civilization: A History of Insanity in the Age of Reason*. Translated by Richard Howard. London: Tavistock, 1967.

———. *Power*. Edited by James D. Faubion. Translated by Robert Hurley. Vol. 3 of *Essential Works of Michel Foucault, 1954–1984*. New York: New Press, 2001.

———. "The Subject and Power." In Foucault, *Power*, ed. Faubion, 326–48. Orig. pub. *Critical Inquiry* 8, no. 4 (1983): 777–95.

———. "Interview with Michel Foucault." In Foucault, *Power*, ed. Faubion, 230–97. Orig. pub. *Il Contributo* 4, no. 1 (1980): 23–84.

Freedman, Estelle B. *Their Sisters' Keepers: Women's Prison Reform in America, 1830–1930*. 1981. Reprint, Ann Arbor: University of Michigan Press, 1984.

Garland, David. *Punishment and Modern Society: A Study in Social Theory*. Chicago: University of Chicago Press, 1990.

———. *Punishment and Welfare: A History of Penal Strategies*. Brookfield, VT: Gower, 1985.

Gilfoyle, Tomothy J. "Street-Rats and Gutter-Snipes: Child Pickpockets and Street Culture in New York City, 1850–1950." *Journal of Social History* 37, no. 4 (2000): 853–82.

Goldring, Philip. *The Penitentiary Building, Lower Fort Garry*. Unpublished manuscript submitted to the Department of Indian Affairs and Northern Development, 27 July 1970.

Goldsmith, Larry. "'To Profit by His Skill and to Traffic on His Crime': Prison Labor in Early Nineteenth-Century Massachusetts." *Labor History* 40, no. 4 (1999): 439–57.

Graber, Jennifer. "'When Friends Had the Management It Was Entirely Different': Quakers and Calvinists in the Making of New York Prison Discipline." *Quaker History* 97, no. 2 (2008): 19–40.

Grob, Gerald N. *Mental Institutions in America: Social Policy to 1875*. New York: The Free Press, 1973.

Grünhut, Max. *Penal Reform: A Comparative Study*. Oxford: Clarendon Press, 1948.

Hahn Rafter, Nicole. *Creating Born Criminals*. Champaign: University of
Illinois Press, 1997.

———. *Partial Justice: Women in State Prisons, 1800–1935*. Boston:
Northeastern University Press, 1985.

Hardwick, Martina L. "Segregating and Reforming the Marginal: The
Institution and Everyday Resistance in Mid-Nineteenth Century-
Ontario." PhD diss., Queen's University, 1998.

Hay, Douglas. "Property, Authority and the Criminal Law." In Hay et al.,
Albion's Fatal Tree, 17–65.

Hay, Douglas, Peter Linebaugh, John G. Rule, E. P. Thompson, and Cal
Winslow, eds. *Albion's Fatal Tree: Crime and Society in Eighteenth-
Century England*. New York: Pantheon Books, 1975.

Hennessy, Peter. *Canada's Big House: The Dark History of the Kingston
Penitentiary*. Toronto: Dundurn Press, 1999.

Himmelfarb, Gertrude. *The Idea of Poverty: England in the Early Industrial
Age*. New York: Alfred A. Knopf, 1984.

Howe, Adrian. *Punish and Critique: Towards a Feminist Analysis of Penality*.
New York: Routledge, 1994.

Hubner, Brian. "Horse Stealing and the Borderline: The NWMP and the
Control of Indian Movement." In *The Mounted Police in Prairie
Society, 1873–1919*, edited by William M. Baker, 41–53. Regina:
Canadian Plains Research Centre, 1998.

Ignatieff, Michael. *A Just Measure of Pain: The Penitentiary in the Industrial
Revolution, 1750–1850*. New York: Pantheon Books, 1978.

———. "State, Civil Society and Total Institution: A Critique of Recent
Social Histories of Punishment." In Sugarman, *Legality, Ideology
and the State*, 75–96.

Jackson, Michael. *Prisoners of Isolation: Solitary Confinement in Canada*.
Toronto: University of Toronto Press, 1983.

Jankovic, Ivan. "Labour Market and Imprisonment." *Crime and Social
Justice* 8 (Fall/Winter 1977): 17–31.

Jebb, Joshua. "The Convict Question in 1856." In *Reports and Observations
on the Discipline and Management of Convict Prisons*, edited by the
Earl of Chichester, Appendix C. London: Hatchard and Co., 1863.

Jolliffe, Kyle. "An Examination of Medical Services at the Kingston
Penitentiary." Master's thesis, Queen's University, 1983.

———. *Penitentiary Medical Services, 1835–1983*. Ottawa: Solicitor
General Canada, Ministry Secretariat, 1983.

Katz, Michael B., Michael J. Doucet, and Mark J. Stern. *The Social
Organization of Early Industrial Capitalism*. Cambridge: Harvard
University Press, 1982.

Kelm, Mary-Ellen. *Colonizing Bodies: Aboriginal Healing in British
Columbia, 1900–1950*. Vancouver: University of British Coulmbia
Press, 1998.

Kimmel, Michael S., Jeff Hearn, and R. W. Connell, eds. *Handbook of
Studies on Men and Masculinities*. London: Sage, 2005.

Lewis, W. David. *From Newgate to Dannemora: The Rise of the Penitentiary in New York, 1796–1848.* 1965. Reprint, Ithaca, NY: Cornell University Press, 2009.

Linebaugh, Peter. "All the Atlantic Mountain Shook." *Labour/Le Travailleur* 10 (Autumn 1982): 87–121.

———. *The London Hanged: Crime and Civil Society in the Eighteenth Century.* Cambridge: Cambridge University Press, 1991.

Longmate, Norman. *The Workhouse.* Norfolk: Lowe and Brydone, 1974.

Luchins, Abraham S. "The Cult of Curability and the Doctrine of Perfectibility: Social Context of the Nineteenth-Century American Asylum Movement." *History of Psychiatry* 3 (1992): 203–20.

Lux, Maureen K. *Medicine That Walks: Disease, Medicine and Canadian Plains Native People, 1880–1984.* Toronto: University of Toronto Press, 2001.

Mackey, Frank. *Done with Slavery: The Black Fact in Montreal, 1760–1840.* Montreal and Kingston: McGill-Queen's University Press, 2010.

Macleod, Roderick C. "The North-West Mounted Police, 1873–1905: Law Enforcement and the Social Order in the Canadian North-West." PhD diss., Duke University, 1972.

Macleod, Rod, and Heather Rollason. "Restrain the Lawless Savages: Native Defendants in Criminal Courts in the North West Territories, 1878–1885." *Journal of Historical Sociology* 10, no. 2 (1997): 157–83.

Maconochie, Alexander *Crime and Punishment. The Mark System: Framed to Mix Persuasion with Punishment, and Make Their Effect Improving, yet Their Operation Severe.* London: J. Hatchard and Son, 1846.

Marx, Karl. *Capital: A Critique of Political Economy.* vol. 1. Translated by Ben Fowkes. 1876. Reprint, London: Penguin Classics, 1990.

———. *Economic and Philosophic Manuscripts of 1844.* 1927. Reprint, New York: International Publishers, 1964.

Marx, Karl, and Friedrich Engels. *The Communist Manifesto.* 1848. Reprint, New York: International Publishers, 1948.

Mason, Michael. *The Making of Victorian Sexuality.* New York: Oxford University Press, 1994.

Mayhew, Henry, and John Binney. *The Criminal Prisons of London and Scenes of Prison Life.* London: Griffin, Bond, 1862.

Maynard, Steven. "The Maple Leaf (Gardens) Forever: Sex, Canadian Historians, and National History." *Journal of Canadian Studies* 36, no. 2 (2001): 70–105.

McCalla, Andrea, and Vic Satzewich, "Settler Capitalism and the Construction of Immigrants and 'Indians' as Racialized Others." In *Crimes of Colour: Racialization and the Criminal Justice System in Canada,* edited by Wendy Chan and Kiran Mirchandani, 25–44. Peterborough: Broadview Press, 2002.

McClintock, Anne. *Imperial Leather: Race, Gender and Sexuality in the Colonial Context*. New York: Routledge, 1995.

McGowen, Randall. "The Well-Ordered Prison: England, 1780–1865." In Morris and Rothman, *The Oxford History of the Prison*, 71–99.

McLaren, Angus. "The Creation of a Haven for 'Human Thoroughbreds': The Sterilization of the Feeble-Minded and the Mentally Ill in British Columbia." *Canadian Historical Review* 67, no. 2 (1986): 127–50.

———. *Our Own Master Race: Eugenics in Canada, 1885–1945*. Oxford: Oxford University Press, 1990.

McLennan, Rebecca M. *The Crisis of Imprisonment: Protest, Politics, and the Making of the American Penal State, 1776–1941*. New York: Cambridge University Press, 2008.

McMahon, Donald J. "Law and Public Authority: Sir John Beverley Robinson and the Purposes of the Criminal Law." *University of Toronto Faculty of Law Review* 46 (1988): 390–423.

McPherson, James M. *Ordeal by Fire: The Civil War and Reconstruction*. 3rd ed. New York: McGraw-Hill, 2001.

Melossi, Dario, and M. Pavarini. *The Prison and the Factory: Origins of the Penitentiary System*. London: Macmillan, 1980.

Mennel, Robert M. *Thorns and Thistles: Juvenile Delinquents in the United States, 1825–1940*. Hanover, NH: University Press of New England, 1973.

Messerschmidt, James W. *Masculinity and Crime: Critique and Reconceptualization of Theory*. Lanman, MD: Rowman and Littlefield, 1993.

Middleton, Jacob. "Thomas Hopley and mid-Victorian Attitudes to Corporal Punishment." *History of Education* 34, no. 6 (2005): 599–615.

Miller, Martin B. "At Hard Labor: Rediscovering the Nineteenth-Century Prison." *Issues in Criminology* 9 (Spring 1974): 91–114.

———. "Sinking Gradually into the Proletariat: The Emergence of the Penitentiary in the United States." *Crime and Social Justice* 14 (1980): 37–43.'

Milloy, John. *The Plains Cree: Trade Diplomacy and War, 1790–1870*. Winnipeg: University of Manitoba Press, 1988.

Mintz, Steven. *Huck's Raft: A History of American Childhood*. Cambridge: Belknap Press, 2004.

Mitchinson, Wendy. *The Nature of Their Bodies: Women and Their Doctors in Victorian Canada*. Toronto: University of Toronto Press, 1991.

———. "Reasons for Committal to a Mid-Nineteenth-Century Ontario Insane Asylum: The Case of Toronto." In *Essays in the History of Canadian Medicine*, edited by Wendy Mitchinson and Janice Dickin McGinnis, 88–110. Toronto: McClelland and Stewart, 1988.

Mohl, Raymond A. "Humanitarianism in the Preindustrial City: The New York Society for the Prevention of Pauperism, 1817–1823." *Journal of American History* 57, no. 3 (1970): 576–99.

Moodie, Susanna. *Life in the Clearings Versus the Bush.* 1854. Reprint, Toronto: McLelland and Stewart, 1989.

Moran, David. "Class and Masculinity." In Kimmel, Hearn, and Connell, *Handbook of Studies on Man and Masculinities,* 165–177.

Moran, James E. *Committed to the State Asylum: Insanity and Society in Nineteenth-Century Quebec and Ontario.* Montreal and Kingston: McGill-Queen's University Press, 2000.

Moran, James E., and David Wright, eds. *Mental Health and Canadian Society: Historical Perspectives.* Montreal and Kingston: McGill-Queen's University Press, 2006.

Moran, James, David Wright, and Matt Savelli. "Families, Madness, and Confinement in Victorian Ontario." In *Mapping the Margins: The Family and Social Discipline in Canada, 1700–1975,* edited by Nancy Christie and Michael Gauvreau, 277–304. Montreal and Kingston: McGill-Queen's University Press, 2004.

Morgan, David. "Class and Masculinity." In Kimmel, Hearn, and Connell, *Handbook of Studies on Men and Masculinities,* 165–77.

Morris, Lydia. *Dangerous Classes: The Underclass and Social Citizenship.* New York: Routledge, 1994.

Morris, Norval. *Maconochie's Gentlemen: The Story of Norfolk Island and the Roots of Modern Prison Reform.* Oxford: Oxford University Press, 2002.

Morris, Norval, and David Rothman, eds. *The Oxford History of the Prison: The Practice of Punishment in Western Society.* New York: Oxford University Press, 1998.

Neufeld, Roger. "A World Within Itself: Kingston Penitentiary and Foucauldian Panopticism, 1834–1914." Master's thesis, Queen's University, 1993.

Nietzsche, Friedrich. *The Birth of Tragedy and the Genealogy of Morals.* Translated by Francis Golffing. New York: Random House, 1956.

Noll, Steve. *Feebleminded in Our Midst: Institutions for the Mentally Retarded in the South, 1900–1940.* Chapel Hill: University of North Carolina Press, 1995.

Norman, William. "A Chapter of Canadian Penal History: The Early Years of the Provincial Penitentiary at Kingston and the Commission of Inquiry into Its Management, 1835–1851." Master's thesis, Queen's University, 1979.

Oliver, Peter. *"Terror to Evil-Doers": Prisons and Punishment in Nineteenth-Century Ontario.* Toronto: University of Toronto Press, 1998.

Palmer, Bryan D. *A Culture in Conflict: Skilled Workers and Industrial Capitalism in Hamilton, Ontario 1860–1914.* Montreal and Kingston: McGill-Queen's University Press, 1979.

———. *Cultures of Darkness: Night Travels in the Histories of Transgression (from Medieval to Modern)*. New York: Monthly Review Press, 2000.

———. "Kingston Mechanics and the Rise of the Penitentiary, 1833–36." *Histoire sociale/Social History* 13, no. 25 (1980): 7–32.

———. *Working-Class Experience: The Rise and Reconstitution of Canadian Labour, 1800–1980*. Toronto: Butterworth, 1983.

Pentland, H. Clare. *Labour and Capital in Canada, 1650–1860*. 1960. Reprint, Toronto: James Lorimer, 1981.

Petchesky, Rosalind P. "At Hard Labor: Penal Confinement and Production in Nineteenth-Century America." In *Crime and Capitalism: Readings in Marxist Criminology*, edited by David F. Greenberg, 595–612. Philadelphia: Temple University Press, 1983.

Peters, Edward M. "Prison Before the Prison: The Ancient and Medieval Worlds." In Morris and Rothman, *The Oxford History of the Prison*, 3–44.

Pfhol, Stephen. *Images of Deviance and Social Control: A Sociological History*. New York: McGraw-Hall, 1985.

Platt, Anthony M. *The Child Savers: The Invention of Delinquency*. 2nd ed. 1969. Reprint, Chicago: University of Chicago Press, 1977.

Priestley, Philip. *Victorian Prison Lives: English Prison Biography, 1830–1914*. New York: Methuen, 1985.

"Principles of Prison Discipline." In *Transactions of the National Congress on Penitentiary and Reformatory Discipline Held at Cincinnati, Ohio, October 12–18, 1870*, 548–68. New York: Argus, 1871.

Proceedings of the Annual Congress of the National Prison Association of the United States, Toronto, September 10–15, 1887. Chicago: Knight and Leonard, 1889.

Radzinowicz, Leon, and Marvin E. Wolfgang, eds. *Crime and Justice*. 3 vols. New York: Basic Books, 1971.

Reaume, Geoffrey. "Patients at Work: Insane Asylum Inmates' Labour in Ontario, 1841–1900." In Moran and Wright, *Mental Health and Canadian Society*, 69–96.

"Review: On Spermatorrhea: Its Pathology, Results and Complications." *Canadian Medical and Surgical Journal* 10, no. 7 (1882): 413–17.

Rock, Paul. "Caesare Lombroso as a Signal Criminologist." *Criminology and Criminal Justice* 7 (2007): 117–33.

Rodgers, Daniel T. *The Work Ethic in Industrial America*. Chicago: University of Chicago Press, 1979.

Rosenman, Ellen Bayuk. "Body Doubles: The Spermatorrhea Panic." *Journal of the History of Sexuality* 12, no. 3 (2003): 365–99.

Rothman, David. *Conscience and Convenience: The Asylum and Its Alternatives in Progressive America*. Toronto: Little, Brown, 1980.

———. *The Discovery of the Asylum: Social Order and Disorder in the New Republic*. Toronto: Little, Brown, 1971.

Rusche, Georg, and Otto Kirchheimer. *Punishment and Social Structure.* 1939. New Brunswick, NJ: Transaction Publishers, 2003.

Ryerson, Stanley B. *Unequal Union: Confederation and the Roots of Conflict in the Canadas, 1815–1873.* Toronto: Progress Books, 1968.

Sabo, Don, Terry A. Kupers, and Willie London, eds. *Prison Masculinities.* Philadelphia: Temple University Press, 2001.

Sangster, Joan. *Girl Trouble: Female Delinquency in English Canada.* Toronto: Between the Lines, 2002.

Scott, James C. *Domination and the Arts of Resistance: Hidden Transcripts.* New Haven: Yale University Press, 1990.

———. *Weapons of the Weak: Everyday Forms of Peasant Resistance.* New Haven: Yale University Press, 1985.

Senior, Hereward. *The Last Invasion of Canada: The Fenian Raids, 1866–1870.* Toronto: Dundurn Press, 1991.

Sim, Joe. *Medical Power in Prisons: The Prison Medical Service in England, 1774–1989.* Philadelphia: Open University Press, 1990.

Sykes, Gersham M. *The Society of Captives: A Study of a Maximum Security Prison.* Princeton, NJ: Princeton University Press, 1958.

Smandych, Russell. "Beware of the 'Evil American Monster': Upper Canadian Views on the Need for a Penitentiary, 1830–1834." *Canadian Journal of Criminology* 33 (1991): 125–47.

———. "Tory Paternalism and the Politics of Penal Reform in Upper Canada, 1830–1834: A 'Neo-Revisionist' Account of the Kingston Penitentiary." *Criminal Justice History* 12 (1991): 57–83.

Spierenburg, Pieter. "The Body and the State: Early Modern Europe." In Morris and Rothman, *The Oxford History of the Prison,* 44–70.

———. *The Prison Experience: Disciplinary Institutions and Their Inmates in Early Modern Europe.* New Brunswick, NJ: Rutgers University Press, 1991.

Splane, Richard. *Social Welfare in Ontario, 1791–1893: A Study of Public Welfare Administration.* Toronto: University of Toronto Press, 1965.

St. Germain, Jill. *Indian Treaty-Making Policy in the United States and Canada, 1867–1877.* Toronto: University of Toronto Press, 2001.

Stanley, G.F.G. *The Birth of Western Canada.* 1936. Reprint, Toronto: University of Toronto Press, 1960.

Stedman Jones, Gareth. *Outcast London: A Study in the Relationship Between Classes in Victorian Society.* London: Pantheon, 1984.

Stonechild, Blair, and Bill Waiser. *Loyal till Death: Indians and the North-West Rebellion.* Calgary: Fifth House, 1997.

Strange, Carolyn, ed. *Qualities of Mercy: Justice, Punishment, and Discretion.* Vancouver: University of British Columbia Press, 1996.

———. "The Undercurrents of Penal Culture: Punishment of the Body in Mid-Twentieth-Century Canada." *Law and History Review* 19, no. 2 (2001): 343–85.

Strong-Boag, Veronica. "Contested Space: The Politics of Canadian Memory." *Journal of the Canadian Historical Association* 5, no. 1 (1994): 3–17.

Sugarman, David, ed. *Legality, Ideology and the State.* London: Academic Press, 1983.

Sutherland, Neil. *Children in English-Canadian Society: Framing the Twentieth-Century Consensus.* Waterloo, ON: Wilfrid Laurier University Press, 2000.

Swainger, Jonathan. *The Canadian Department of Justice and the Completion of Confederation, 1867–78.* Vancouver: University of British Columbia Press, 2000.

Taylor, Ian, Paul Walton, and Jock Young. *The New Criminology: For a Social Theory of Deviance.* London: Routledge and Kegan Paul, 1973.

Terbenche, Danielle. "'Curative' and 'Custodial': Benefits of Patient Treatment at the Asylum for the Insane, Kingston, 1878–1906." *Canadian Historical Review* 86 (2005): 29–52.

Thernstrom, Stephan. *Poverty and Progress: Social Mobility in a Nineteenth-Century City.* New York: Antheum, 1973.

Thompson, E. P. "The Crime of Anonymity." In Hay et al., *Albion's Fatal Tree,* 255–308.

———. *The Making of the English Working Class.* 1963. New York: Penguin Books 1980.

———. *Whigs and Hunters: The Origin of the Black Act.* New York: Pantheon Books, 1975.

Tobias, John L. "Canada's Subjugation of the Plains Cree, 1879–1885." In *Sweet Promises: A Reader in Indian-White Relations in Canada,* edited by J. R. Miller, 212–40. Toronto: University of Toronto Press, 1991.

Tuke, Daniel Hack. *The Insane in Canada and the United States.* London: Lewis, 1885.

Verdun-Jones, Simon N., and Russell Smandych. "Catch-22 in the Nineteenth Century: The Evolution of Therapeutic Confinement for the Criminally Insane in Canada, 1840–1900." In *Criminal Justice History: An International Annual,* edited by Henry Cohen, 85–108. Westport, CT: Greenwood, 1981.

Weiner, Martin J. *Men of Blood: Violence, Manliness and Criminal Justice in Victorian England.* New York: Cambridge University Press, 2004.

———. *Reconstructing the Criminal: Culture, Law, and Policy in England, 1830–1914.* Cambridge: Cambridge University Press, 1994.

Welshman, John. *Underclass: A History of the Excluded, 1880–2000.* London: Hambledon Continuum, 2006.

Wetherell, Donald G. "Rehabilitation Programmes in Canadian Penitentiaries, 1867–1914: A Study of Official Opinion." PhD diss., Queen's University, 1980.

Wines, E. C. *Report of the International Penitentiary Congress of London Held July 3–13, 1872.* Washington, DC: Government Printing Office, 1873.

————. *The State of Prisons and of Child-Saving Institutions in the Civilized World.* 1880. Reprint, Montclair, NJ: Patterson Smith, 1968.

Wines, E. C., and Theodore W. Dwight. *Report of the Prisons and Reformatories of the United States and Canada Made to the Legislature of New York, January, 1867.* Albany: Van Benthuysen and Sons' Steam Printing House, 1867. Reprint, New York: AMS Press, 1973.

Winks, Robin. *The Blacks in Canada: A History.* 2nd ed. Montreal and Kingston: McGill-Queen's University Press, 1997.

Wright, David. *Mental Disability in Victorian England: The Earlswood Asylum, 1847–1901.* Oxford: Oxford University Press, 2001.

Wright, David, and Anne Digby, eds. *From Idiocy to Mental Deficiency: Historical Perspectives on People with Learning Disabilities.* New York: Routledge, 1996.

Zedner, Lucia. *Women, Crime, and Custody in Victorian England.* Oxford: Clarendon Press, 1991.

Zubrycki, Richard M. *The Establishment of Canada's Penitentiary System: Federal Correctional Policy, 1867–1900.* Toronto: University of Toronto Faculty of Social Work, 1980.

Index

Brace, Charles Loring, 111–12
Bridewells, 8, 22–23, 28
Bristow, William, 62–64
British Columbia Penitentiary: corporal
    punishment, 229, 240–41;
    elimination of communal
    meals, 169; financial corruption
    at, 177–78; First Nations
    prisoners, 198; founding date,
    18; geographic isolation of, 271;
    hospital facilities, 185–86;
    intimidation and bullying at,
    156–57; prisoner exploitation
    and cruelty at, 178–79; prisoner
    insubordination, 155; rule
    of silence at, 149; security
    measures, 160
Brockway, Z. R., 234–35
Brown Commission: investigations into
    abuse at Kingston Penitentiary,
    1–2, 47–57, 116; members,
    46, 282n65; recommendations
    for reforming Kingston
    Penitentiary, 61–70; reforms
    for corporal punishment, 10,
    49, 227–28, 243; separate
    institution for female prisoners,
    87; on treatment of children,
    50, 132
Brown, George, 2, 4; editorial on
    corporal punishment, 45;
    proposals for penitentiary
    reform, 62–69, 71–73; solutions
    for childhood criminality, 132,
    134. See also Brown Commission
Brown, Harry, 205
buffalo trade, 125, 290n97
Burgess, T.J.W., 209–10

California Penological Commission,
    257–58
Campbell, James, 161
Canadian Freeman, 88
Canadian Medical and Surgical Journal
    (1882), 217

Canadian penitentiary board:
    administrative strife, 44; power
    relations, 45–46, 82–83, 85;
    prison reform program, 81, 88–
    89, 246; report on prostitution,
    115; responsibilities of, 79
Canadian penitentiary system: Brown
    Commission influence on,
    61–62; capitalist foundations
    of, 270; creation of, 18, 82–84;
    failures or shortcomings of,
    90–91, 261–62, 269; fallacy
    on standard of punishment,
    272; geographic isolation of
    penitentiaries, 223, 271; medical
    services to prisoners, 224;
    prisoner uniform scheme,
    145–46
Canadian Temperance Advocate, 101, 111
capitalism: Calvinism and, 34; and
    class structure, 7; labour-power
    and, 223. See also industrial
    capitalism
capital punishment, 23, 26, 29
Carpenter, Mary: on dangerous classes,
    110; on female criminals, 115;
    "reformatory prison discipline"
    term usage, 284n29; reformatory
    schools for juvenile delinquents,
    133–34; visit to Kingston
    Penitentiary, 84, 93–94
Carter Cash, June, 272–73
Cartwright, C. E., 135
Cash, Johnny, 272–73, 275
cell blocks, 142–43
chaplaincy, 66, 68, 71–73, 98–101, 135
Charboneau, Peter, 49–50
Charlestown Penitentiary
    (Massachusetts), 64
Cherry Hill Penitentiary (Philadelphia),
    63–64
Chevalier, Louis, 108–9
children: corporal punishment inflicted
    on, 1–2, 49–50, 228, 242–43;
    criminality and juvenile
    delinquency, 101, 131–32,

229, 244; origins in ancient times, 20–21; performed in front of prison population, 177; public responses to, 236–37; in public schools, 229–30, 242; rates and incidences at Kingston Penitentiary, 46–53, 167, 228, 241–43; rationalizations for, 230–33, 242; reform ideas and humane approaches to, 10–11, 225–26, 230; as a response to incorrigibility, 12, 105, 164, 228, 231, 238–41; as a response to mutiny attempts, 168; at St. Vincent de Paul Penitentiary, 229, 238–39, 243; subjective nature of, 240–41; survival or sustainability of, 11–12, 230–31

corruption: at British Columbia Penitentiary, 177–79; of children and youth prisoners, 101, 158; at Kingston Penitentiary, 2, 45–46, 51–53, 56, 179; at St. Vincent de Paul Penitentiary, 170–77, 229

Costen, Thomas, 50

Coverdale, William, 53

Cox, Julia, 52

Cree political leaders, 127

Creighton, John: appointment to Kingston Penitentiary, 83–84, 88; on placing trust in prisoners, 157–58; views on punishment, 230–31, 239, 241

Crime and Punishment (Maconochie), 76–77

criminality: causes of, 97–102; classification levels, 65, 70–71, 94–95, 104; and dangerous classes, 111–13; discourses on corporal punishment and, 226, 232, 238; feminine, 86–87, 114–19; of First Nations people, 15, 124–31; of habitual offenders, 103–7; individuality and, 14–16, 96–98, 168–69, 248–49, 257; intellectual disability and,

220; of juvenile delinquents or youth, 101, 131–37; link between intemperance and, 101; and mental illness, 201; penitentiary's role in creating, 267–69; poor health and, 190; positivist views on, 96–98; poverty and, 108–10; race associations and, 15, 121–24; reformation and, 13–16, 89; social perceptions of, 16; Victorian penal responses to, 98; and working-class associations, 15, 102–3, 108

criminology/criminological science, 96–97, 247, 250, 268

Crofton system, 79, 284n29; classification of prisoners, 90, 246–47, 257; principles of, 80–81, 83

Crofton, Walter, 13, 78–79, 105, 225–26, 284n26. *See also* Crofton system

Cultures of Darkness (Palmer), 17

curability and incurability, 201–2, 206, 214, 222

customary rights, 43

dangerous classes: children as, 110, 133, 136; First Nations people labelled as, 113, 125, 197; potential threat of, 112, 169, 177; reform and solutions for, 111–12; tied to poverty and labouring classes, 103, 108–113, 115, 191

Dangerous Classes of New York (Brace), 111–12

Darby, Robert, 214

death penalty, 23, 26, 29

Department of Indian Affairs, 124–25, 195

Department of Justice, 175, 177–78, 212, 238, 258; creation of national penitentiary system, 82, 89; penitentiary board influence on, 79, 81–82; stance on shooting of prisoners, 166

on power relations, 16–17; on reform of the modern penitentiary, 3

Foy, John, 123, 251

Freeland, John H., 48

Fry, Elizabeth, 4, 30, 85–86

Fuller, Margaret, 85–86

Gabbett, Joseph, 166

Gagné, Oscar, 221–22

Gallagher, John, 168

gaols: in England, 21, 24; in Upper Canada, 29–30, 183, 280n26

Garland, David, 14, 98, 234, 269

gender divisions: in constructions of criminality, 15, 114–16, 268; in medical care, 210–12; in treatment of mental illness, 207, 209–10

Globe, The: articles on corporal punishment, 46, 236–37, 242; on death of George Hewell, 256; on murder of Thomas Salter, 158; on prisoner protest at St. Vincent de Paul Penitentiary, 176; story on prisoner anxieties in requesting medical assistance, 189; story on prisoner loneliness, 149–50; on treatment of First Nations people, 128

Grant, Allan, 167–68

Groupe d'Information sur les Prisons (GIP), 274

Grünhut, Max, 22, 98

Habitual Criminals Act: in England, 105, 248; in Ohio, 248

Hagerman, Christopher, 38

Hay, Douglas, 4

Hayvern, Hugh, 158, 256

Herchmer, W. M., 121

Hewell, George, 155, 167, 251–56, 268

Hill, Gary, 245–46

Himmelfarb, Gertrude, 10, 109

History of Sexuality, The (Foucault), 186, 215

Hooper, Thomas, 50

horse stealing, 125–27, 195, 197

House of Assembly, 29, 37, 45, 120

House of Refuge, 132, 134

Howard, John, 23–26, 34, 65, 85

Hughes, William, 253–56

Hugo, Victor, 108–9

human agency, 4, 17, 265

humanitarian reform movement, 2, 5, 33–35, 262–66, 270

hygiene, 25, 113, 146, 183

identity, 143–47

ideology: bourgeois, 34; capitalist, 270; colonial, 128; of contractual penal servitude, 42; contrasts between reform and punishment, 264–65; labour, 19, 33–36, 38–39, 209; and origins of punishment, 274; producer, 38–39; reform and reformers, 15–16, 249, 259; transnational, 223

"idiocy" concept, 219

idleness, 8–10, 22–23, 33–34, 224

Ignatieff, Michael, 11, 24, 186, 274

incorrigibility: and constructions of criminality, 12, 106, 168–69, 231; degrees of, 13, 238; fear and potential threat of, 169; of habitual offenders, 105–8; isolation and segregation as punishment for, 226, 245–46, 249–57; perception of black prisoners, 122–23; violence and corporal punishment as responses to, 12, 105, 164, 228, 231, 238–41

individual criminality, 14–16, 102, 108, 137; isolation system to address, 246–49, 257; and prisoner identity, 145–46; role in

security measures, 160; sexual assault cases, 158–59; staff discipline and living conditions, 152–54, 233

Marks, Grace, 93, 117–18

mark system, 75, 77, 81

Marx, Karl, 6, 112, 223

masculinity, 15, 232–33

Mason, Michael, 216

masturbation, 214–18

Mayberry, Bruce, 159

Mayhew, Henry, 110, 115

Maynard, Steven, 159

McBride, James, 178–79, 240–41

McCabe, James, 157–58

McCalla, Andrea, 128

McCarron, James, 164

McClintock, Anne, 197

McDermott, James, 117–18

McDonell, A. D. O., 252, 255

McGowen, Randall, 25

McLaren, Angus, 220

McLean, Ellen, 210–11

McLennan, Rebecca M., 36, 44, 270, 280n19

McMahan, Edward, 161

mechanics, 36–39, 42

medical power: and control of male sexuality, 214; Foucault on, 186; of penitentiary surgeons, 183, 186–89

medical practice: admission inspections, 146–47, 183; ailments and diseases, 184–85, 190, 196–98; early care at Kingston Penitentiary, 183–85; health of elderly inmates, 191–92; hospital facilities at federal penitentiaries, 185–86; prisoner requests for treatment, 188; race and disease susceptibility, 194–99; responses to non-labouring prisoners, 224; terminally ill prisoners, 192–93; treatment for spermatorrhea, 215–18. See also mental illness

medical reforms, 181–82

Men of Blood (Weiner), 229

mental illness: attributed to long-term solitary confinement, 247; categories of, 200; and control by penitentiary authorities, 213–14; corporal punishment and, 48–49, 241; curability and incurability of, 201–2; custodial to curative care movement, 202–3; experiences of female patients, 207, 209–11; gender divisions in care of, 211–12, 302n91; intellectual disability and, 219–23; Kingston Penitentiary asylum and treatment for, 201, 204–6, 301n76, 301n80; Manitoba Penitentiary asylum and treatment for, 205–6, 208–14; masturbation as a cause of, 215–18; physical labour as a cure for, 206–8; rates at Cherry Hill Penitentiary, 63–64; transferring of prisoners to provincial asylums, 200–203, 241

Mercer Reformatory (Toronto), 88

Meredith, E. A., 79–83, 254, 256

Metcalf, John, 252–54

middle class, 86, 94, 216

Mitchell, Robert, 135, 188, 192, 218

Mitchinson, Wendy, 209

modern penitentiary: based on the silent system, 147; economic basis of, 270–71; Foucault on, 3; historical effects of, 263, 265, 267; prison labour as the foundation for, 8, 19, 33; reform ideals of, 61, 272; and rise of industrial capitalism, 6, 8, 263, 269

Monastic discipline, 21

Moodie, Susanna, 93–94, 118

moral condition, 3, 100

morality: childhood criminality and, 133–35; of killing an escaping prisoner, 166; of poor and working classes, 109–10 moral reformation: in American penitentiaries, 62–64; based on optimistic views of criminality, 95; and desire for prisoner transformation, 264; and redemption through labour, 9, 59, 77–78, 224; and salvation of released prisoners, 258–59; term usage, 277n6; through religious and secular education, 65–66, 68, 71, 73

moral therapy, 203, 206–7, 300n68

Moylan, James G.: appointment as penitentiary inspector, 89; on child convicts, 136–37; complicity in corruption at St. Vincent de Paul Penitentiary, 175; on corporal punishment, 232, 238–39, 242; on escaping prisoners, 160, 163, 166; on habitual offenders, 105–7, 287n32; on indeterminate sentencing, 248, 257–58; on intellectually disabled prisoners, 219–20; on masculinity, 232–33; as penitentiary board member, 88–89; on prison labour, 58–59, 129; on prison uniforms and identity, 145–46; recount of reformer visits to Kingston Penitentiary, 93–94; reform ideas and failures, 90–91; report on recreational grounds at Kingston Penitentiary, 204; on rule of silence, 148; on segregation and isolation of prisoners, 246–47, 249–50; on threat of prisoner outbreaks, 169; on working/living conditions of penitentiary staff, 152–53

Mulkins, Hannibal, 73, 99–100, 102

Munro, Alexander, 218

Murray, Christopher, 164–65

mutiny: at Kingston Penitentiary, 167–69, 239; at Manitoba Penitentiary, 163

neglect, 116–17, 209–11, 267

Nelson, Wolfred: background, 69–70; directive to prison doctors, 215; as member of penitentiary board, 79; praise for female asylums, 87; prison reform ideas, 70–74

Newgate Prison: London, England, 85; New York City, 33–35

New York City Draft Riots (1863), 112

New York Prison Association, 80–81, 86

New York Times, 111

Nietzsche, Friedrich, 234

North West Mounted Police (NWMP), 113, 123–27, 197, 212

Northwest Rebellion (1885), 124, 127–28, 195, 199

Observations in Visiting, Superintendence and Government of Female Prisoners (Fry), 85

O'Connor, Thomas, 240–41

O'Grady, William, 37

Oliver, Peter, 30, 73, 79, 282n70

One Arrow, Chief, 127, 196–97, 291n110

oppression, 91, 248, 261–63, 267, 275

organized labour, 58–59

Ouimet, Télesphore, 170–77, 179, 229

Our Convicts (Carpenter), 115, 284n29

Paget, James, 217

Palmer, Bryan, 17, 42

pardons, 192–93, 196–97

parole, 134, 226, 249, 259

penal colonies, 23, 75–76

Penetanguishene Reformatory, 101, 242

Penitentiary Act (Act for the Better Management of the Penitentiary): post-Confederation (1868), 82–83, 189; Upper Canada (1851), 66, 68–69, 71, 74, 165, 227

Penitentiary Act (England, 1779), 25

Penitentiary Commission, 254–56, 308n74

completion of, 149, 249–50; death of convict Hewell at, 251–56; reformatory effects of, 246, 256–57; transfer of prisoners to, 177

prison reform. *See* reformers; reform movement

prison rights movements, 274–75

producer ideology, 38–39

prostitution, 115, 119

Punishment and Social Structure (Rusche & Kirchheimer), 9

Punishment and Welfare (Garland), 14

punishment, forms of: cat-o'-nine tails ("the cats"), 47–49, 228, 240–43; Oregon boot, 244, 307n55; shackling or chaining, 243–44; "shot drill practice," 244; "the box," 48, 228, 243; whippings or floggings, 1–2, 43, 47–49, 229, 238, 241–43, 305n8. *See also* corporal punishment; isolation

Quaker reformers, 33–35

Quinn, Fenian Thomas, 167–68

race: constructions of criminality and, 15, 119–20, 131; convict ratios by, 122; health assumptions based on, 194, 198; recorded on prison records, 119. *See also* black people; First Nations people

Rasp House, 24–25

Reaume, Geoffrey, 206–7

recidivists or habitual offenders, 104–8, 191, 258, 287n32; habitual criminals acts, 105, 248

Reed, Hayter, 128

reformatories for children, 101, 110, 133–35

Reformatory Schools (Carpenter), 110

reformers: attitudes on corporal punishment, 10–11, 71, 227, 230, 234–36, 243–44; Brown's recommendations for Kingston Penitentiary, 62–69; concerns with repeat offenders, 105–6; Crofton's penal philosophy and system, 78–81, 90; on distinctions between working classes and dangerous classes, 109–11; failure of ideas, 16; for female prisons, 85–87; humanitarian, 264, 266, 270; and ideological importance of labour, 9, 33–35, 59; influence on prisoner power relations, 179–80; influential figures, 3–4, 13, 78; institutional solutions for children, 132–33; Maconochie's ideas and mark system, 75–78; personal approaches to criminality, 13–14; positivists, 96–98; Quaker influence, 33–35; reports for Canadian penal system, 69–72; responses to youth criminality, 132–37; solutions to social problems, 110; views on isolation, 246, 249

reform movement: based on prisoner transformation, 12–13; in Canadian penitentiary system, 2–3, 61, 88–91, 261–65; charity for released prisoners, 258–59; for childhood criminality, 132–37; class and, 7; and contrasts with punishment, 263–65; and corporal punishment, 12, 29, 227–29; and disparities of the modern penitentiary, 272; in England, 23–26, 78; focus on individuality, 14, 34, 96–98; historical impact of, 3; humanitarian, 2, 5, 33–35, 262–66, 270; and human suffering, 5, 266; ideological developments of, 7–8; international, 89, 248; in Ireland, 78–79; isolation and segregation practices, 249–50;